Canada and
International
Civil Aviation,
1932–1948

CANADA AND INTERNATIONAL CIVIL AVIATION

1932-1948

David MacKenzie

UNIVERSITY OF TORONTO PRESS
Toronto Buffalo London

© University of Toronto Press 1989
Toronto Buffalo London
Printed in Canada
Reprinted in 2018
ISBN 0-8020-5828-0
ISBN 978-1-4875-7713-1 (paper)

Printed on acid-free paper

Canadian Cataloguing in Publication Data

MacKenzie, David Clark, 1953–
Canada and international civil aviation
1932–1948

Bibliography: p.
Includes index.
ISBN 0-8020-5828-0

1. Aeronautics, Commercial – History.
2. Aeronautics, Commercial – Canada – History.
3. Aeronautics, Commercial – Law and legislation.
I. Title.

HE9774.M33 1989   387.7'09   c89-094257-9

Frontispiece: TCA Lockheed 14-H2 Lodestar aircraft over the Rocky Mountains, n.d. (Trans-Canada Air Lines, NA, PA 122575) for Terry

Contents

ACKNOWLEDGMENTS ix

1 'Them Things That Buzzed' 3

2 An Effort in Commonwealth Collaboration 20

3 Atlantic Crossing 56

4 Connecting the Capitals 74

5 Globaloney 94

6 1943: The Shape of Things to Come 118

7 The Road to Chicago 144

8 'Everybody Is against Bad Weather' 172

9 Swallowing the Pure Wine of Bermuda 201

10 ICAO and the Failure of Multilateralism 226

11 Across the Pacific and Beyond 244

APPENDIXES

1 CCAC Resolution, June 1937 255
2 The Six Freedoms 256
3 Summary of Canadian Draft Convention 257
  (January 1944)
4 The Two Freedoms Agreement 261
5 The Five Freedoms Agreement 265

ABBREVIATIONS 271

NOTES 273

SELECTED BIBLIOGRAPHY 297

INDEX 307

Acknowledgments

It is a pleasure to thank all the people who have been so helpful to me during the many months of researching and writing this book. I would like to thank my colleagues and friends who took the time to read and comment on the manuscript: Robert Bothwell, Norman Hillmer, and Trevor Lloyd. Many individuals at the National Archives were very helpful and, in particular, I would like to thank Tim Dubé who, thanks to his knowledge of both the archives and of aviation, saved me many hours of work.

Sir Nicolas Cheetham was kind enough to let me read his diary of the Chicago Civil Aviation Conference and then to give me permission to quote from it. A special thanks to John R. Baldwin who not only participated in the events described in this book but also gave of his time to read the manuscript thoroughly and make numerous helpful suggestions to improve it.

Support for the research involved in this project came in the form of a Social Sciences and Humanities Research Council Postdoctoral Fellowship and a Canada Research Fellowship. At the University of Toronto Press, I was fortunate once again to have Virgil Duff as my editor; and my thanks to Lydia Burton for copy-editing the manuscript. Finally, Teresa Lemieux has supported me in numerous ways, and my debt to her is only partly acknowledged in the dedication of this book.

Parts of chapters 3 and 4 have appeared in slightly revised form in the *British Journal of Canadian Studies* and *Aerospace Historian* respectively, and my thanks to the editors of these journals for permission to reprint this material. Quotations from the Beaverbrook Papers in the House of Lords Record Office are reproduced by permission of the Clerk of the Records and of the Trustees of the Beaverbrook Foundation. Quotations from the Malcolm MacDonald Papers are reproduced by permission of the Archives of the University of Durham. Quotations from the Lord Swinton Papers in the Churchill College Archives are reproduced by permission of the Master, Fellows, and Scholars of Churchill College in the University of Cambridge. Permission to quote from the Hugh Dalton diaries has been given by the British Library of Political and Economic Science. Transcripts/Translations of crown-copyright records in the Public Record Office appear by permission of the Controller of HM Stationery Office.

This book has been published with the help of a grant from the Social Science Federation of Canada, using funds provided by the Social Sciences and Humanities Research Council of Canada.

A Curtiss HS2L flying boat of Canadian Airways Limited, Quebec, ca 1926 (L.M. Pelletier Collection, NA, PA 110778)

Douglas DC-2 aircraft of American Airlines Inc. taking on airmail, St Hubert, Quebec, 1938 (NA, PA 61838)

Officials with Lockheed 12A aircraft CF-CCT of the Department of Transport undertaking 'dawn-to-dusk' trans-Canada flight, St Hubert, Quebec, 30 July 1937: left to right, Don Saunders, Lew Parmenter, F.I. Banghart, W.H. Hobbs, H.J. Symington, C.D. Howe, J.H. Tudhope, C.P. Edwards, J.D. Hunter, J.A. Wilson, G.G. Wakeman, D.R. MacLaren (NA, C-63377)

John R. Baldwin before the 1947 ICAO conference (NFB photo, from Canadian Information Service)

Escott Reid and Lester Pearson, December 1949 (Duncan Cameron Collection, NA, PA 121700)

TCA's first Lockheed 10A aircraft on Vancouver–Seattle service, Vancouver airport, 1937 (Air Canada Collection, NA, PA 125393)

The Chicago conference, November 1944: left to right, C.D. Howe, H.J. Symington, and J.A. Wilson (Leo Rosenthol, NA, PA 139755)

A Canadian Pacific Airlines Douglas DC-4, Vancouver airport, 1953 (NA, C-62416)

Canada and
International Civil
Aviation, 1932–1948

1 'Them Things That Buzzed'

'Transportation is Civilization.' That was the motto of Rudyard Kipling's Aerial Board of Control, 'that semi-elected semi-nominated body of a few score persons of both sexes, [which] controls this planet.' Writing during the first decade of the twentieth century, Kipling populated his futuristic world with flying machines of all descriptions and had it ruled by the ABC. 'Theoretically, we do what we please so long as we do not interfere with the traffic *and all it implies.*'[1] And there was plenty of traffic. On one transatlantic flight alone

we met Hudson Bay furriers out of the Great Preserve, hurrying to make their departure from Bonavista with sable and black fox for the insatiable markets. We over-crossed Keewatin liners, small and cramped; but their captains, who see no land between Trepassy and Blanco, know what gold they bring back from West Africa. Trans-Asiatic Directs, we met, soberly ringing the world round the Fiftieth Meridian at an honest seventy knots; and white-painted Ackroyd & Hunt fruiters out of the south fled beneath us, their ventilated hulls whistling like Chinese kites ... Argentine beef boats we sighted too, of enormous capacity and unlovely outline. They, too, feed the northern health stations in ice-bound ports where submersibles dare not rise.[2]

Kipling was just one of the thousands of men and women around the world whose imaginations were fired by the possibilities of air travel. 'Mankind had always travelled on the face of the earth and water,' one Canadian observer wrote, 'and new inventions for doing so came gradually. Their adoption required little mental readjustment. Human flight, though throughout the ages the dream of the poet and scientist, was something entirely new.'[3] Never before could natural obstacles like mountains, oceans, and deserts be crossed so easily; never again would the political boundaries between nations appear impregnable.

Transportation and civilization, whether for good or evil, did go hand in hand. Air travel, in particular, was well suited as a tool for the spread of civilization, and there was an incalculable element of national prestige accompanying the development of international air services. 'I hate the word "prestige,"' Lt-Colonel Moore-Brabazon stated in the British House of Commons in 1939, 'but I like to bring it in, for the reason that every English aircraft which travels from one side of the world to the other is a little bit of England. England will be judged by that little bit by those for whom that is the only thing they know of England.'[4]

The connection between air travel and national interest was explored by an American author, Oliver Lissitzyn, in his book *International Air Transport and National Policy* (1942). 'Nations live in a competitive world,' he wrote. 'Air transport, owing to its intrinsic qualities – speed and relative independence of natural barriers – lends itself in a peculiar degree to use as a tool or weapon in the international struggle for survival and power. The policies of nations can be understood only in the light of this fact.'[5] The military potential was obvious, but aviation also held vast commercial value: to help open up remote areas, to speed up mail delivery and increase personal contact between government officials and businessmen, to link a mother country with its distant colonies, and to act as a vehicle for international propaganda. Indeed, Lissitzyn argued, the 'very existence of such air transport seems to indicate that the nation is progressive, efficient and highly civilized, and that it is contributing its share to the progress of mankind. The prestige thus conferred has economic and military value.'[6] Thanks to this unique potential to enhance prestige and serve the national interest, virtually all governments have been quick to intervene in the promotion, regulation, and development of air transportation.

In its earliest stages the development of aviation was more the domain of the adventurer and scientist than of the diplomat or general. In the immediate aftermath of the Wright brothers' first successful flight in 1903, flight itself remained the goal; few directed much attention to its potential uses. In Canada, the international dimension of aviation was apparent a full fifty years before the 1909 flight of the

Silver Dart in Baddeck, Nova Scotia. In September 1859, two American pilots took off from St Louis, Missouri, on a cross-country excursion in a balloon named the *Atlantic*. Caught by unfriendly winds, the two unhappy flyers were swept far to the north and landed in the wilds of the Canadian forest, 150 miles north of Ottawa.[7] Over the years others followed the American daredevils in balloon and airplane – usually young men seeking the romance and adventure that flight seemed to offer.

The concept of air travel underwent a fundamental re-evaluation beginning on 2 August 1909, when Louis Blériot became the first man to fly the English Channel. Overnight, the existing concepts of national sovereignty were challenged and new, difficult questions had been posed. Sir Frederick Handley Page, the British aircraft designer and manufacturer, later reflected on this aspect of aviation. 'Systems of land transport operate largely within the boundaries of single countries,' he wrote, but 'when land transport becomes international it is subject to easy control at frontiers. Ships ply across sea frontiers, and control can be exercised without difficulty at foreign ports. But the airplane flies over national boundaries and from one country into the heart of another. Thus the development of the skyways of the world has created a new international problem, that of the freedom of the air.'[8]

The debate over the extent of freedom in the air remained at the heart of international civil aviation until the middle of the twentieth century. Could one nation claim ownership or sovereignty over the airspace above its territory? Could one nation exclude another from flying over its territory? Should the right of transit be freely given to all nations, or should it be negotiated and exchanged on a bilateral or multilateral basis? And how could one nation protect its domestic airways from outside competition without resorting to force? To answer one question was to invite a dozen more.

This study examines the efforts made to establish an international system for the regulation and operation of international air services and the role played by Canadians in its development. It is not a history of a particular airline or aircraft manufacturer, nor is it the story of bush pilots and air force aces – although these are all important factors. It is more a diplomatic and political study that examines international civil aviation as an arm of government policy, as the extension abroad of Canadian national policy. In doing so, it also looks at the relation between the bureaucratic and political levels of government and, in the larger context, at the relations between Canada and its two allies, the United States and Great Britain.

There is a tendency in the few scholarly studies in this field to paint a picture of Canada's role in the development of international civil aviation as a brief wartime phenomenon in which a handful of Canadian diplomats came to play a leading role. This picture reveals only half the truth. The following chapters examine that momentary prominence from a broader perspective, tracing the roots of Canada's wartime activities from the previous decade, and continuing through to 1948, by which time the International Civil Aviation Organization was in full operation and the modern system of international air flight was in place.

Air travel was a relatively new field at that time and, thanks to international competition and technological innovation, it was rapidly evolving. Canada was well placed by geography, industrial capability, and political temperament to play a large role in the development of international civil aviation. Canadian diplomats came to be very well respected in the international arena during this period and they, along with those who shaped Canadian policy at home, made a meaningful contribution to world affairs in the twentieth century. Their story deserves to be told.

I

A beginning was made at answering some of the questions surrounding international civil aviation in the wake of the first cross-channel flight at an international conference called by the French government in 1909. The conference, which opened in Paris in 1910, was directed primarily at technical questions, in an effort to establish standards and regulations for the operation of international air services. Inevitably, however, the more fundamental problems over air transit rights were discussed, but the conference adjourned before any real progress was made.[9] There was a reluctance, especially on the part of the British government, to endorse a policy of complete freedom in the air. Britain already lagged behind the Germans and French in the design and manufacture of aircraft, and for reasons of military security it was considered necessary to limit (or even exclude) the flight of foreign aircraft over British territory.

British fears were confirmed with the outbreak of the First World War, when the Royal Flying Corps found itself dependent on the French government for most of its engines and spare parts. The demands of war, however, gave enormous impetus to the development of an indigenous aircraft industry, and the number of British firms producing aircraft jumped from 48 in 1916 to 122 by the end of the war. 'These pioneers,' one historian has written, 'that in years of peace had patiently built small numbers of machines were inundated with orders; others, such as shopfitters, or furniture makers with experience of woodworking found themselves sucked into the airline industry.'[10]

The advances in aircraft performance and production made during the war were, of course, a military phenomenon. European civil aviation all but disappeared between 1914 and 1918, yet it was inevitable that the wartime experience would affect its development. For one thing, the destructive capabilities of aviation were tragically demonstrated, with the result that security questions would be a major factor in international civil aviation negotiations for a generation to come. For another, by the end of the war there were thousands of pilots and crews available for peace-time work, there were thousands of airplanes suitable for service, and there existed in several nations aircraft industries ready to produce if customers could be found.[11] Perhaps most important, the wartime aviation experience revealed the enormous potential of commercial aviation – how easy it would be to carry passengers, mail, and cargo over those routes (and others) where only military aircraft had flown before.

The British government was aware of the future possibilities of civil aviation and, indeed, began to seriously investigate it with the creation of the Civil Aerial Transport Committee in May 1917. This committee was formed for two reasons: first, to consider the 'steps which should be taken with a view to the development and regulation after the War of aviation for civil and commercial purposes from a domestic, and imperial, and an international standpoint'; and second, to examine the 'extent to which it will be possible to utilize for the above purpose the trained personnel and the aircraft which the conclusion of Peace may leave surplus to the requirements of the Naval and Military Air Services of the United Kingdom and Overseas Dominions.' The committee produced two basic recommendations in its 1918 report: first, that each individual state should maintain complete sovereignty over its airspace and, second, that the development of civil aviation would prove to be vital for economic and strategic reasons and thus would need and deserve government support.[12]

In contrast, Canadian civil aviation remained stalled at the preliminary stages at the outbreak of the war, and little post-war planning was undertaken during the war. The Canadian government had been invited to send a representative to the Civil Aerial Transport Committee, but the offer and the committee were virtually ignored by Sir Robert Borden's government. Nevertheless, a copy of the committee's report and a draft Aerial Navigation Bill were sent to Ottawa along with a suggestion that the Allied governments draw up an international aviation convention.[13]

The Canadian government showed neither boldness nor imagination in the formulation of an aviation policy during the First World War, and for the Canadians who wished to fly, the only avenue was through the Royal Flying Corps (RFC). Indeed, the creation of RFC Canada and the development of Canada as a major air-training centre were undertaken by the British government – almost in spite of the efforts of the Canadian government. And efforts to establish a separate Canadian Air Force were less than totally successful, although they did lead to the creation of two small air forces in 1918: the Royal Canadian Naval Air Service and the Canadian Air Force. Neither survived long after the Armistice.

The verdict of the historians has been harsh: Canadian aviation policy during the war, the official historian of the RCAF wrote, 'was variously negative, indifferent, inconsistent, and puzzling. It was almost always ill-informed.' Even after taking into consideration the wartime burden shouldered by the government, 'there remains a small-mindedness, a species of unimaginative colonialism about its attitude towards aviation, out of keeping with its strong stand over command and control of the Canadian Expeditionary Force and with its political and constitutional thrust for recognition and status within the councils of the British Empire.'[14]

Despite government indifference, however, thousands of young Canadians were drawn to the world of flight and were eager to participate in any way they could. 'It would have been strange if young officers had not been attracted to the military possibilities of the aeroplane,' S.F. Wise wrote. 'In those early days powered flight had an irresistible glamour for the bold and the imaginative. Looking down from their open cockpits at the panoramic world spread out below, it must have seemed that they were the heralds of a new and tremendous dawn. The winds that tore at their goggles, the clouds through which they passed, the sweep and soar and dip of their flight brought a joyous exultation, so that even the mundane requisites of their calling – the exposure to vile weather, the smell of engine oil, the dirty work of maintenance and repair – were romanticized.'[15]

Wartime circumstances also prompted the creation of a domestic aircraft industry. In 1916 Canadian Aeroplanes Ltd was established under the supervision of the Imperial Munitions Board to supply RFC Canada with training aircraft (the Curtiss JN-4). By the end of 1918, almost 2900 JN-4 airplanes had been produced in Canada. In addition, under an American contract some Felixstowe F5 flying boats were also produced by Canadian Aeroplanes Ltd. But once the war ended, Canadian aircraft production, like the two Canadian air forces, all but disappeared. It would be twenty years before any aircraft larger than the F5 was manufactured in Canada.[16]

Whether the Canadian government liked it or not, by 1918 the world had entered the air age. The war had demonstrated not only the dangers but also the potential of international aviation – and the return of peace would be followed closely by a rush to establish international commercial air services around the world. The war had rewritten the ground rules, and it was left to diplomats to deal with the questions surrounding the emergence of international civil aviation in the post-war period.

II

Sir Robert Borden had far more pressing issues on his mind than the development of international civil aviation as he crossed the Atlantic bound for England late in 1918. News of the Armistice reached the prime minister while on board his ship the *Mauritania*, and while he rejoiced over Germany's 'complete surrender,' he remained uneasy. 'Revolt has spread all over Germany,' he confided in his diary. 'The question is whether it will stop there. The world has drifted far from its old anchorage and no man can with certainty prophesy what the outcome will be. I have said that another such war would destroy our civilization. It is a grave question whether this war may not have destroyed much that we regard as necessarily incident thereto.'[17]

Accompanying Borden on the long voyage overseas were Sir George Foster, the ageing minister of trade and commerce, and Arthur Sifton, Borden's minister of public works. Sifton was a lawyer by profession and a former Liberal premier of Alberta who had changed his political stripes in 1917 to join Borden's Union government. One of Borden's valued colleagues, Sifton would for a brief moment have a direct influence over Canadian international civil aviation policy. Of the advisers present, the most important was Loring Christie, the Department of External Affair's legal adviser. Christie and Borden had ventured into the arena of imperial relations before; during the 1917 Imperial Conference the two men had been the driving force behind Resolution IX, which recognized the dominions 'as autonomous nations of an Imperial Commonwealth.'[18]

For the Canadians in the British Empire Delegation (BED) to the Paris Peace Conference the first few months of 1919 were busy ones. Sir Robert was appointed vice-chair of the committee defining the boundary between Greece and Albania. Canadians participated in the creation of the International Labour Organization. Within the delegation itself there was much debate over the future of the ex-German colonies. More important, Canadians gave very serious attention to the Covenant of the League of Nations and especially the proposed Article X, which seemed to commit Canada to future involvement in international squabbles. More work and responsibilities were added in March with the creation of the Aeronautical Commission and the addition of civil aviation to the Peace Conference agenda.

The goal of the Aeronautical Commission was to produce an international convention that would regulate international civil aviation during peace-time. In addition, it was intended that this commission would be preserved as a permanent governing body for international civil aviation. The British and French governments both produced detailed draft conventions for examination and debate; the Americans showed decidedly less enthusiasm, and at first even questioned the need for the commission to meet at that time.[19] No Canadian was appointed to the commission, although one Canadian did participate in the Commercial, Legal and Financial Sub-Committee. For Borden and his colleagues the channel of communication ran through Maj.-Gen. Sir Frederick Sykes, chief of the Air Staff and the British delegate on the commission.

The work of the Aeronautical Commission and the various drafts it produced were discussed within the BED several times over the following weeks. To Arthur Sifton, who took a special interest in the work of the commission, the proposed international convention drafted by the Europeans was seriously flawed. In a memo for the prime minister, Sifton called one draft 'the latest and probably the worst case in which an effort is being made to take advantage of the presence of representatives of different countries here to foist on them an absurd, poorly drawn document, evidently prepared by people without the slightest knowledge of the subject of which they were dealing, aside from the actual flying and that under war conditions when the rights of non-flyers and even states remained in abeyance.' The future commercial development of civil aviation remained shrouded in mystery in 1919 and Sifton readily admitted it. 'The whole subject,' he continued, '... is so utterly unknown, that for anyone to sit down and attempt to draw a treaty for the civilized world is a manifest absurdity, and to attempt without consultation to include a country like Canada where if commercial air traffic is a success it will be of vastly more importance than it is likely to be in any of the countries who are assuming to settle the matter, is a blunder that would generally be called a crime. The only excuse that I have yet heard for the haste is that a factory in Great Britain is very anxious to start work making airships.'[20]

Beyond the general scepticism concerning the ability of the commission to settle largely unknown problems, there were two more specific criticisms of the convention shared by Borden, Sifton, and the other Canadians. The first revolved around status. Early drafts seemed to stipulate the automatic inclusion of the dominions under the jurisdiction of the convention – something Borden would not tolerate in constitutional arrangements, and it was the same story here. By the beginning of May the difficult article had been amended, recognizing Dominion autonomy within the terms of the convention.[21]

The second problem was not so easy to solve. The proposed convention gave wide powers to the commission to deal not only with transit rights but also with technical matters and customs. Moreover, although Canadian autonomy was now recognized in the convention, the Canadian voice in any permanent body would be relatively weak when compared to the American. Thus, it was possible that matters affecting civil aviation in Canada would be decided by Europeans, and also that Canada would be at a disadvantage vis-à-vis the United States, a nation far more powerful and better able to influence the direction of the commission.

Borden voiced his concerns during one meeting of the BED. The prime minister 'pointed out the importance which international flying might assume in the Western hemisphere and the difficulties that would ensue if this traffic were in any way regulated by a Body on which Canada did not have a voice equal to that of the United States. With a boundary line 4,000 miles in length, more thickly inhabited on the United States' side than the Canadian, there were already sufficient difficulties in connection with the Customs and immigration administration; and these would doubtless be accentuated by the development of commercial flying.' As for the technical regulations, Borden argued that he was unable 'to anticipate their effects upon the Canadian position; nor would the Canadian Parliament accept an arrangement which empowered a body of people sitting in Europe to make regulations governing traffic between Canada and the United States.'[22]

Efforts to remove Canadian-American aviation relations from the realm of the convention were made – unsuccessfully – over the following weeks. In the end the Canadians had to be satisfied with an amendment to Article 36 of the convention that could be applied to Canadian-American relations. 'Nothing in the present Convention,' the revised article read, 'shall be construed as preventing the contracting States from concluding, in conformity with its principles, special protocols as between States and State in respect of customs, police, posts and other matters of common interest concerning air navigation.'[23]

By October, agreement was reached in Paris, and the Air Navigation Convention was signed by the major European powers. In April 1920, Canada officially signed the convention and, in June, the attached protocol, which permitted the negotiation of bilateral deals with non-contracting nations. A wise move, as it turned out: although the United States signed both the convention and protocol, the documents were never ratified by the Senate and the Americans never became a party to the international convention.

The convention signed in Paris laid down general principles for the operation of international air services. The first articles recognized that each nation exercised exclusive sovereignty over its territorial airspace. Articles 2 and 3 conceded the right of innocent passage for foreign aircraft, but also gave each state the power to restrict foreign aircraft to certain paths across its territory. These last points were reconfirmed in Article 15, which permitted contracting nations to operate over foreign territory without landing, providing the nation being flown over had given its consent. Other articles dealt with the registration of aircraft, licensing of personnel, and standards of airworthiness. Finally, the convention created a permanent organization, the International Commission for Air Navigation (ICAN), to implement, study, and revise the convention.[24]

For Canadians, signing the international convention brought few immediate consequences. It was largely a European document written to settle European problems and, it was hoped, to bypass future ones. Yet the first Canadian foray into the world of international aviation diplomacy is not without interest. Indeed, many of the concerns voiced by Borden, Sifton, Christie, and the others were repeated by their successors over the following decades. In 1919 the Canadian government was willing to participate in the regulation of civil aviation because it had concluded that some international co-operation was necessary. At the same time, however, Sir Robert and his colleagues exhibited a strong independent streak and resisted the surrender of Canadian autonomy to any larger organization – imperial or international. And there was a hard-headed appreciation of the realities of Canadian-American relations – the realization that getting along with the Americans would be a primary and unique component in the development of Canadian international civil aviation. Here, above all, Canadian independence of action needed to be preserved. The echo of those concerns can still be heard today.

III

Speaking before the Empire Club of Canada on 22 March 1926, Sir Sefton Brancker, the director of civil aviation in the Air Ministry, lamented the conservative attitudes of the British people with respect to aviation. He told his audience of the elderly lady living near an airport in southern England who would peer over her garden wall at the comings and goings of the airplanes. When asked by an aviator if she enjoyed watching the aircraft land and take off she replied with an abrupt 'no.' 'It is like this,' she explained to the puzzled airman, 'ever since I was a little girl when a bumblebee got up my drawers, I have hated them things that buzzed.'[25]

The Canadian government, if not actually demonstrating a hatred of 'them things that buzzed,' exhibited a less-than-enthusiastic attitude towards the development of aviation. Yet, for Brancker and other observers, it seemed that Canada was ideally suited to the development of civil aviation. Aviation furnished the opportunity to bridge the great distances between many Canadian cities; Canada's isolation from the problems of the old world permitted the evolution of a more reasoned aviation policy, with relatively less emphasis directed towards the security and prestige components; and aviation seemed to hold enormous potential for opening up to economic development Canada's northern regions. Canadian industry had shown itself able to produce aircraft, and thousands of Canadians had taken to the air 'as ducks to water' and had distinguished themselves during the First World War.[26]

One problem was to decide where civil aviation belonged: Should it be considered civil or military in nature, or, for that matter, a commercial operation? To help resolve the issue, the Air Board was created in 1919 and given jurisdiction over Canadian civil aviation; its various branches could license pilots and set flight standards, as well as formulate policy. In addition, a set of Air Regulations were produced that reflected Canada's obligations under ICAN and would ensure the development of civil aviation in an orderly fashion. The passage of the National Defence Act created a new Department of National Defence (DND) on 1 January 1923, and the following year the Royal Canadian Air Force (RCAF) was created. With these changes the RCAF was granted jurisdiction over civil aviation and it assumed the responsibility for the government's duties and activities in regard to civil aviation.[27]

The development of civil aviation in Canada in the 1920s differed from the European example, where inter-city services sprang up immediately. In Canada, by contrast, the focus of attention was directed to opening up the isolated and unpopulated north. As one government official put it in 1932, 'we deliberately turned our backs on inter-city services and put the whole of our energies into flying in our northern hinterland. We felt at that time that inter-city services could well wait and that the North country offered a field of development where aircraft could play an immediately useful part.'[28]

The uses of aircraft for surveillance and observation purposes were quickly realized. Forest patrols were undertaken for pulp-and-paper companies; geological surveys and mappings were conducted for governments and private business; and Canadians soon became world leaders in the uses of aerial photography. In addition, aviation also had its uses in the north for policing and fire patrols. Indeed, this same official noted, 'today there exist generally throughout northern Canada efficient commercial air services which have been self-sustaining, have required no subsidy, and which give access to the remotest districts of the country. More has been learned of northern Canada during the past ten years than in the preceding three hundred. The forester, surveyor, geologist, prospector, mining engineer; the clergy, the doctors, the nurses, the police; in fact, all whose activities lie in northern Canada find their task greatly lightened, their range of action multiplied many times and their efficiency increased by the use of aircraft.' Was the policy a sound one? yes, he proudly concluded: 'No country has spent less on civil aviation and no country has had greater returns from the money spent.'[29]

The United Kingdom followed a similar course at the end of the war with respect to government subsidies; forcing British civil aviation, as Winston Churchill put it at the time, to 'fly by itself.' The train network in Great Britain was very good and the weather was very bad – the advantages of civil aviation were less apparent than on the continent. As a result, British civil aviation was quickly outdistanced by European rivals. While private British firms struggled and collapsed, in Holland, Belgium, Denmark, and Sweden national airlines were established and supported with government funds. In France, heavily subsidized airlines inaugurated services to Warsaw to the east and Casablanca to the south. The Germans, meanwhile, were excluded from developing military aviation and concentrated on the civil side: by 1926 several state-supported airlines had been established, operating an extensive domestic network and participating in services to Finland and to places as far away as Moscow. German citizens, moreover, held a controlling interest in Sociedad Colombo-Alemana de Transportes Aéreos, or Scadta, a Columbian-based airline founded in 1919.[30]

Increasingly it became clear that private British companies could not successfully compete with state-owned or state-supported European airlines, and in the early 1920s the United Kingdom government began giving limited subsidies to private companies. In an effort to rationalize the competition for domestic services, the government also took on the responsibility for dividing routes between competitors. Then, after years of stops and starts, investigation and debate, domestic competition and private bankruptcies, in 1924 the British government brought together several private companies to form Imperial Airways. The new airline remained privately owned but was supported by guaranteed government subsidies, and government influence was ensured through the government nominees on the board of directors.[31]

Imperial Airways was designated Britain's 'chosen instrument' and was given the responsibility for operating all international services. At first the new airline followed in the pattern established by the private firms by competing for inter-city services on the continent. By 1926, services were operating to Paris and on to Zurich, to Cologne via Brussels, and to Amsterdam. But these routes never proved to be profitable, and increasingly the focus of attention turned to the development of empire routes. In 1927 Imperial Airways took over the RAF airmail service route between Cairo and Baghdad. Two years later the route was extended at both ends, running from London all the way to Karachi. It would not be long before it was extended to Delhi, and there were hopes of linking up with an Australian airline before the end of the decade.[32]

The succession of imperial conferences in the 1920s offered an ideal platform for the discussion of air services within the Empire/Commonwealth, even though the operation of most services was prevented by the problems of enormous distances, the lack of adequate aircraft, and government indifference. At the 1923 Imperial Conference, for example, two resolutions concerning civil aviation were passed dealing with aerial photography and the exchange of information. In 1926, even though constitutional questions topped the conference agenda, an aviation committee was established to discuss imperial air services and a good deal of attention was paid to Britain's airship program. Prime Minister Mackenzie King, who headed the Canadian delegation, expressed himself willing to expand air services and spoke enthusiastically for imperial co-operation, but so long as the Canadian government ignored the development of inter-city services there were few concrete contributions Canada could make to imperial services, even on a rudimentary level.[33]

The latter half of the decade saw a significant increase of interest in the development of civil aviation in Canada, spurred not by imperial prompting but rather by the rapid spread of civil aviation in the United States. The Americans never ratified the Paris Convention and for the first few years after the Armistice had virtually no legislation governing domestic civil aviation. American civil aviation was put on a more solid footing in 1926 with the passage of the Air Commerce Act, which put aeronautics under one branch of the Department of Commerce and opened the door to formal negotiations with foreign states.[34]

Few nations were more blessed than the United States for the growth of civil aviation: a vast land mass, a common culture and language, a large and growing population, and generally good weather conditions all combined to ensure the rise of a dynamic internal system of airways, airlines, and aircraft manufacturing. By 1924, with the help of government subsidies, the US Post Office had a cross-country mail service in operation. By the end of the decade there were three full national services operated by three private companies: American Airlines, United Airlines, and Trans World Airlines.[35]

A fourth airline – Pan American Airways – rose to prominence under the direciton of its first president, Juan Trippe. Trippe began his first airline early in the 1920s with Navy surplus airplanes; in 1924 he formed Colonial Air Transport Co. and operated a Boston–New York airmail service. Colonial disappeared within three years, but in 1927 Trippe's new company merged with another small airline and adopted its name – Pan American Airways. Beginning with an airmail service between Havana and Key West, Florida, Pan Am expanded rapidly and became the American flagship airline on international routes.[36]

American civil aviation quickly took on an international dimension. Transoceanic flight was still to come, but it was relatively simple for American interests to spread into Latin America. Dealings with the Central and South American nations were formalized with the signing of the Pan American Convention on Commercial Aviation in February 1928. The Havana Convention, as it came to be called, was similar in intent to the Paris Convention and was signed by the United States and more than twenty Latin American states. But it could not prevent the inevitable competition between American and German interests in Latin American civil aviation – a rivalry that would continue until the Second World War.[37]

The rapid expansion of civil aviation in the United States inevitably affected Canada. With the boom in aviation and the construction of airports and ground facilities across the country, American airlines increasingly threatened to spill over into Canada to tap the Canadian market. In 1928, for example, a mail and passenger service was inaugurated between New York and Montreal. The following year a Canadian-American agreement was negotiated setting the standards for airworthiness of aircraft and pilot licensing for transborder flights. The new agreement was structured to conform to ICAN regulations, and it prohibited the carrying of passengers between two points inside the other's territory. Clearly, without Canadian services to meet the American challenge, Canadian civil aviation was likely to develop on a north-south rather than an east-west basis.[38]

The problem, of course, was that Canadian bush operations were carried on by seaplanes, which utilized the vast network of northern lakes and rivers for landing sites. By removing the need for airport construction, costs were kept down, but this system was unacceptable for inter-city use.[39] The only alternative was to use land-planes – but such a transition would necessitate the construction of a nation-wide network of airports, ground facilities, and navigational and meteorological aids. And that would require government intervention and support.

The development of a national airway system was given a big boost by the many flying clubs across Canada that spearheaded the development of local airstrips. In addition, a number of small private aviation companies were established and began operations before the end of the decade. The government also began showing more interest. In 1927, responsibility for civil aviation was removed from the RCAF and, although it remained within the DND, it was reorganized into its own independent branches. In the same year, the Post Office let its first airmail contracts with small regional airlines. The system was enlarged in subsequent years and by 1930 most of eastern and western Canada were covered and both areas were linked up to the larger American airmail system. In summer 1927, transatlantic mail was carried on an experimental air service between Montreal and Rimouski, and one or two days was shaved off delivery time to and from the United Kingdom.[40]

'The transformation of Canada's aviation resources in only a few years was remarkable,' noted the RCAF's official historian. 'The water-borne system of bush flying, which was still opening up the northwest, had been supplemented by a land-based aerial network almost spanning the country. It had not been until 1926, when the possibilities of a new phase of development were first being discussed, that the first cross-country flight by a single aircraft – a seaplane – had taken place. Four years later, on the Prairies alone, fully equipped lighted municipal airports in Winnipeg, Regina, Moose Jaw, Saskatoon, Medicine Hat, Lethbridge, Calgary, and Edmonton joined more than 1300 miles of lighted air routes.'[41]

There were developments on other levels as well. At the 1927 dominion/provincial conference, the government's exclusive authority to legislate in aviation matters was challenged by Quebec. The dispute wound its way through the courts and eventually was referred to the Judicial Committee of the Privy Council. In its 1932 decision, the committee argued that under Section 132 of the British North America Act the responsibility to enact foreign treaties fell to the federal government and that 'it would appear that substantially the whole field of legislation in regard to aerial navigation belongs to the Dominion. There may be a small portion of the field which is not by virtue of specific words in the British North America Act vested in the Dominion; but neither is it vested by specific words in the Provinces. As to that small portion it appears to the Board that it must necessarily belong to the Dominion under its power to make laws for the peace, order and good government of Canada.' Indeed, the committee concluded, civil aviation was a matter of 'national interest and importance,' a subject 'which has attained such dimensions as to affect the body politic of the Dominion.'[42]

Thus, by 1932 the infrastructure of a national airway system had begun to take shape. Dozens of airstrips were either built or under construction, with the requisite ground facilities and navigational aids in place. In addition, the focus of Canadian civil aviation had been enlarged to include inter-city development, thereby enhancing the government's ability to participate in the growth of international civil aviation. Furthermore, by 1932 federal control of aviation – and especially of international civil aviation – was confirmed, at least symbolically, by the courts. A dominant role for the Canadian government was ensured; it remained to be seen what direction future governments would take.

2　An Effort in Commonwealth Collaboration

International civil aviation came of age in the 1930s. 'History will mark the third decade of the twentieth century as a period of amazing progress in transportation,' one Canadian observer wrote at mid decade. 'At its opening a journey round the world by the main centres of commerce and including London, New York, San Francisco, Hongkong [sic], Singapore and Calcutta required about seventy days travel. In 1936 the same journey will be possible in fourteen days and before the close of the decade probably in ten.'[1]

No major power could afford to ignore the development of civil aviation; indeed, most came to believe that, for political, economic, and strategic reasons, the development of international civil aviation required massive state support. By the middle of the 1930s virtually all European nations had organized state-supported national airlines to represent and act on their government's behalf. In 1919 KLM was organized in the Netherlands and it quickly became one of the world's most successful airlines. In 1923 the Belgian government organized Sabena to act as its national carrier. That same year the Soviet government established Dobrolet, which was united with other Soviet airlines in 1932 under the name Aeroflot.

The French and Germans competed with each other in many areas, including civil aviation. In 1926 the government-backed Deutsche Luft Hansa (Deutsche Lufthansa after 1934) was established and within a decade German airlines operated services to Amsterdam, London, Copenhagen, Moscow, and Rome, to name but a few destinations. Through the introduction of seaplanes launched by catapult from shipdecks, Luft Hansa inaugurated an experimental air-steamer service to Brazil.[2] In France, meanwhile, Air France, the government airline, assumed several existing services and inaugurated new ones, extending its reach to French colonial possessions in Asia and Africa.

Like the French, the British government quickly recognized the value of air services in its relationship with its colonial possessions. In the 1930s Imperial Airways continued to concentrate on the development of imperial services over European ones. In 1932 a weekly London–Cape Town service was established; the service to India created in 1929 was expanded and by 1935 it snaked its way over 12,000 miles to Australia. The linking together of the empire sparked the creation of the Empire Air Mail Scheme, a plan to carry all empire first-class letters without surcharge.[3]

Even in the United States, where airlines remained privately owned, the government came to play an influential role. The commercial and strategic value of international aviation was not lost on the American government. In the 1930s Pan Am was singled out in all but name as the American 'chosen instrument' in international aviation and the private airline was given lucrative subsidies and a virtual monopoly on international routes. Furthermore, as the American flag carrier, Pan Am had the resources and influence of the State Department behind it during its negotiations with foreign states. In return, Pan Am operated some services – to a number of Pacific islands, for example – for political and strategic rather than economic reasons.[4]

For most European nations, however, overriding security concerns made it next to impossible to completely separate military from civil aviation. Technological innovation had obvious implications for both, as did the building up of large aircraft-manufacturing industries. The linking by air of states and colonies, improvements in communications, the surveying, exploration, and creation of new routes, the training of pilots and air-crew, and the construction of airports all were perfectly legitimate undertakings in the development of civil aviation. Yet a suspicious neighbour could just as easily see such developments only in terms of their military applications. When the security component of aviation was mixed with the less tangible elements of national interest and prestige, the result was a European network of heavily subsidized and ruthlessly competitive airlines jockeying for position beyond the actual need for passenger and mail services.

Not surprisingly, attempts were made to control the development of European civil aviation through ICAN and the League of Nations. In April 1932, for example, at the League Disarmament Conference, the

French government introduced a proposal to 'internationalize' civil aviation. Walter Riddell, the Canadian delegate at the conference, informed Ottawa that internationalization consisted of a plan to create 'an official international enterprise for the control and administration of civil aviation throughout the world, and, secondly, the handing over of personnel and material to the League in case of war.' It was a European scheme, Riddell continued, and 'as our situation was very different, this method of dealing with the problem was for us quite inapplicable.'[5]

Many Canadians agreed with Riddell's conclusions. With respect to the French proposals, one government official wrote that 'this paper is another melancholy chapter in the general bedevilment of Civil Aviation by military interference.' Yes, he admitted, civil aircraft could be used for military purposes. 'So may fishing boats, trawlers, coasting steamers, motor transport of all kinds, railways and their rolling stock. It is not proposed to internationalize these because of this fear and it is no more necessary to internationalize civil air transport on that account.'[6]

Canadians were less concerned over the security aspects of aviation. Sitting comfortably in North America and sharing a continent with a powerful and friendly neighbour made it easy to dismiss European fears as slightly absurd. But Canadians were far less smug when it came to boasting about their own aviation accomplishments. Canada had no national airline and only a handful of bush operations and private companies scattered across the country. The proposed trans-Canada airway, meanwhile, lived only as a dream in the minds of a few promoters and bureaucrats. International services, except for a few short cross-border flights, were non-existent. In 1932, on the eve of one of the greatest explosions in world-wide air travel, Canadians could only wonder what would become of them.

I

Flying the Atlantic had long been the stuff of dreams and wonder. In the spring of 1919 Alcock and Brown took off from Newfoundland on the first non-stop North America–to–Europe flight. Others followed, and in 1927 Charles Lindbergh captured the world's imagination with his remarkable solo crossing. Transatlantic flying on a commercial basis, however, was still impossible because of the great distances involved. Attempts were made to use zeppelins on a regular basis, but with little success. Surveys and plans were drawn up for island-hopping services that would leap-frog their way to Europe. Proposals for mid-flight refuelling and aircraft catapulting were thoroughly investigated and wild schemes were concocted to anchor 'floating islands' at 500-mile intervals as mid-Atlantic refuelling stops.[7] All these schemes would have to wait for technology to catch up with the imagination.

Pan Am's Juan Trippe was captured by the promise of transatlantic flight. In 1928 he visited London and met with Sir Eric Geddes, the chair of Imperial Airways, for preliminary talks on the possibilities of an Atlantic service. Nothing came of these discussions, but in 1930 Geddes returned Trippe's visit and the two men agreed to co-operate on the transatlantic service and, for the immediate future, to investigate a New York–Bermuda air service. With the entrance of Pan Am and Imperial Airways into the project, observers on both sides of the Atlantic sat up and took notice.

'The past few years have seen the building up of a system of air communications on the different continents,' J.A. Wilson, the controller of civil aviation in the Department of National Defence, wrote to a British friend, 'and with the increase in efficiency of aircraft, men's minds are naturally turning towards international services as the next step.' Indeed, Wilson continued, the 'North Atlantic crossing is by far the most important trade route in the world. It joins the greatest industrial districts of the new and the old world. On it, if anywhere, will be found traffic sufficient in volume and value to justify the addition of an air service to the transportation facilities now serving the needs of its trade and commerce.'[8]

John Armistead Wilson had been at the heart of Canadian civil aviation since the end of the First World War. Born in Scotland, Wilson joined the Department of Naval Services in 1910, and then served as secretary to the Air Board from 1920 to 1922. In 1922 he became controller of civil aviation, a post he held with distinction until 1941. Wilson had long advocated federal support for civil aviation in Canada and he had been one of the architects of Canadian policy in the 1920s.[9]

By 1932 Wilson's horizons had stretched to include transatlantic flight. He was well aware of the obstacles but remained confident that they would be overcome. He was equally convinced that Canada must have a part to play in the development of transatlantic aviation. 'If you have a globe,' Wilson challenged the same British colleague, 'trace out the Great Circle track joining, say Constantinople, with Mexico City, and you will find a most interesting picture. The track passes through the greatest industrial regions in Europe, London, the Midlands, North Ireland, across the Atlantic Ocean, through the straits of Belle Isle and straight up the Gulf of St. Lawrence to Montreal, Buffalo, and into the heart of industrial America, then across the lower Mississippi Valley.'[10]

Wilson found a staunch ally in Maj.-Gen. A.G.L. McNaughton. McNaughton served as chief of the general staff from 1929 to 1935 and in 1930 he accompanied Prime Minister R.B. Bennett to London for the imperial conference. Although primarily involved with defence and constitutional questions, McNaughton participated in the aviation subcommittee (the 'Lighter-than-air Committee' as some called it), which examined the present state of airship development. The British government had invested heavily in two airships – the *R100* and *R101* – and anticipated a future role for dirigibles in transatlantic flight. But after the crash of *R101* in France while the imperial conference was in session, with the death of forty-seven persons (including Sir Sefton Brancker and Lord Thomson, the secretary of state for air), the whole airship program ground to a halt.[11]

Despite the tragedy of *R101* and the scrapping of airship development, McNaughton returned to Canada alive to the possibilities of transatlantic aviation. For years he had supported a role for the RCAF in Canadian civil aviation and had promoted the creation of a trans-Canada air network; after 1930 he was determined to protect Canadian interests in transatlantic flying, too. But what were Canada's interests in transatlantic civil aviation? The government of R.B. Bennett had its hands full dealing with the Great Depression, and civil aviation was an easy target for government cut-backs. Federal money for aviation was slashed, airmail contracts were terminated (driving several small private airline companies to the brink of collapse), and McNaughton's dream of a trans-Canada airway appeared increasingly illusory. It hardly seemed the precipitous moment to embark on a new endeavour in transoceanic aviation.[12]

One of McNaughton's responsibilities was the administration of the relief camps set up by the Department of National Defence and here he found a small silver lining in the presence of thousands of unemployed men across the country. Camps were established because the problem of relief for the unemployed was growing beyond the capacity of local governments to handle and because there was fear of 'red agitators' spreading discontent and revolt among the disaffected and idle men in Canadian cities. Something had to be found for the men in the camps to do – some kind of work that was useful, outside the major urban centres, and not likely to take away someone else's job. The construction of airstrips met all the requirements: a network of airstrips would have immediate benefits for military and civil aviation; there were no private interests involved in airstrip construction; and it was a labour-intensive activity. McNaughton set the relief project in motion and, by 1936, work had begun on the construction of forty-eight airfields.[13]

As work progressed on the trans-Canada network, McNaughton and Wilson began considering the route for future transatlantic services. It is important to remember that in the 1930s the thought of dozens of flights a day criss-crossing the oceans in all different directions was beyond the wildest imaginations. On the contrary, it was generally agreed that only a few services a week would be sufficient to carry all the potential transatlantic traffic. Even as late as 1945 the president of United Airlines declared that only twenty-three airliners would be required to handle all the transatlantic traffic for the next ten years.[14] For this reason, the choice of terminal airport in North America assumed a far greater importance than it would today; indeed, for many Canadians at the time, the competition between cities was reminiscent of the nineteenth-century trade and shipping rivalry between Montreal and New York. Thus, Wilson and McNaughton viewed any collaboration between Pan Am and Imperial Airways with great suspicion.

There were three alternatives for the north Atlantic route (table 1). The first – the Arctic route – consisted of three sections: from a point in central Canada to Baffin Island, from Baffin Island across Greenland to Iceland, and finally, from Iceland to Great Britain. The second – the great circle route – envisioned connections between Montreal and Newfoundland, a long stretch from Newfoundland to Ireland, and from Ireland to London. The third projected route went south from New York City to Bermuda, then on to Europe via the Azores.

The Arctic route had the asset of short distances between stops, including two which were in Canadian territory, but for Wilson and McNaughton the drawbacks of inaccessibility and weather made the

TABLE 1
Comparison of transatlantic airways

	Arctic	Direct	Southern
Distance from London			
Montreal	4357	3330	5767 miles
New York	4687	3660	5437 miles
Number of intermediate bases	8	3	4 (to Lisbon)

SOURCE: J.A. Wilson, 'Trans-Atlantic Flying,' Dhist 76/271

route unacceptable. Skis would be needed on some sections, floats on others, while the 'short duration of daylight during the winter months, critical temperatures, favouring ice formation, blizzards, gales and extreme cold are further handicaps,' Wilson recorded. 'The risk of loss of life through forced landings in these unhospitable [sic] and inaccessible regions is greater than that on the open ocean.'[15]

The southern route had the great asset of more favourable weather conditions, but its appeal was suspect on two accounts. The first was a matter of distance; the complete journey was more than 5000 miles, and the long stretch between Bermuda and the Azores was a full 2195 miles – well beyond the operating range of any aircraft on a viable commercial basis. Technological developments might overcome this obstacle in the not-too-distant future, but for the time being, at least, the southern route was unemployable. The second and probably more important reason for opposing the southern route was that it completely bypassed Canadian territory. McNaughton and Wilson both acknowledged that Canada's only bargaining chip in the development of transatlantic aviation would be its geographical position. Canada would neither produce the aircraft nor provide the bulk of the traffic on any service spanning the Atlantic, but if the air services of the future had to cross Canadian territory or utilize Canadian airports, then Canadians would perforce have some say in their development. Indeed, McNaughton and Wilson hoped to make Montreal 'the real entrepot station of the North American mid Continent instead of, as at present, New York.'[16] Any route that bypassed Canadian soil, therefore, posed a very real threat to these goals.

The two Canadians agreed that the best hope for success lay with the development of the great circle route, or the 'direct route' as Wilson liked to call it. 'The manifest advantages of the direct route via Newfoundland and Ireland are that it coincides with the Great Circle track and that it lies wholly within the Empire. Four British Governments control its approaches – Great Britain and Ireland the eastern terminals and Newfoundland and Canada the western.'¹⁷ There were drawbacks of course, the primary one being the approximately 1900 mile stretch between Newfoundland and Ireland. The weather was also a concern; Newfoundland was well known for its fog and poor visibility, and the prevailing westerly winds over the Atlantic made an already arduous crossing much more difficult.

Wilson remained confident that these obstacles could be overcome within a few years: until then every effort must be made to implement those sections of the direct route that could be operated under present circumstances, including a service from Montreal to the Atlantic coast and Newfoundland. Not only would the delivery of mail from Europe be speeded up, he argued, but a link to St John's 'would go far towards solving the problem of trans-Atlantic flying and would secure for Canada and Newfoundland the western terminals of the greatest trans-oceanic air service in the world. Failure to take advantage of our geographical position on this airway now may jeopardize this.'¹⁸

Canadian interests, then, would best be served through the immediate development of the direct route – beginning with a joint air and steamship service – and the establishment of Montreal as the main western terminal of the transatlantic service. The problem was: how could these interests be secured? McNaughton and Wilson could influence but not make Canadian policy, and without direction from the political level there was little they could do on their own. Worse still, there were no guarantees that the Americans or British would bear Canadian interests in mind when planning their own transatlantic routes.

Recent events only confirmed these fears. In 1930 the French government secured monopoly landing rights in the Azores and held discussions with representatives of Pan Am and Imperial Airways concerning the southern route. Moreover, in the wake of the Canadian government's cancellation of its airmail contracts in the Maritimes, Pan Am inaugurated an airmail service of its own between Boston and Halifax (with a stop at Saint John, NB) and began negotiations with the government of Newfoundland to extend the service to St. John's. Pan Am had every right to do so under the terms of the 1929 agreement, but the impact of the American service was no less real. 'We are entering the next phase of flying,' Wilson warned, 'and unless Canada watches her step we might discover that our American friends are gradually working into a position where they will control the routes to Europe and Asia via Canada to the detriment of Canadian and British interests.'¹⁹

By summer 1932, the officials responsible for civil aviation in Canada believed that some action on Canada's behalf was required. The activity of Pan Am on the Atlantic coast heightened Canadian anxiety for no other reason than that it showed just how precarious Canada's position was. Even the smug assumption that Canada would automatically be involved in the operation of the direct route now seemed to be challenged. G.J. Desbarats, the deputy minister of national defence, explained the situation to O.D. Skelton, the under-secretary of state for external affairs, in a letter dated 15 July 1932. 'Unfortunately,' Desbarats wrote, 'Canada's position in regard to the direct route, which, in our opinion, is much the most advantageous, is not so strong. It would be quite feasible for foreign interests, without consulting either Canada or Great Britain, to develop this route, providing the cooperation of the Governments of Newfoundland and the Irish Free State was assured.' Once aircraft capable of spanning the gap between Newfoundland and Ireland are available, he continued, 'a glance at the map will show that from a point of departure at New York, Boston, Portland or other suitable base on the east coast of Maine nearer the Canadian border, a direct flight might be made to a base in Newfoundland and thence to Ireland.' 'This is the reason,' Desbarats concluded, 'for our anxiety to safeguard Canada's interest by participating in the development of air communications on our Atlantic coast leading to Newfoundland. If this is done it will go far to prevent any such development and should ensure that trans-Atlantic traffic will pass through Canadian channels.'[20] The message was clear. If Canadian fears and concerns over any future transatlantic air service were to be assuaged, it was imperative for Canadians to participate in the process of negotiations.

II

An ideal opportunity to pursue Canadian aviation interests presented itself during the Imperial Economic Conference held in Ottawa in July/August 1932. The conference was staged with a view to establishing some empire trade arrangements that would help pull the participant nations out of the depths of the depression. The main focus of the discussions was on tariffs; the British were willing to bargain with imperial preference, while Prime Minister Bennett strove to 'blast his way' into empire markets without reducing Canadian tariffs.

An Effort in Commonwealth Collaboration

Overall, the conference was very disorganized – the agenda was left unsettled to the last moment, and even then remained vague. Sparks flew between the leading personalitites, prompting Neville Chamberlain's biographer to conclude that the conference 'was not a failure, yet neither was it a success, failing in atmosphere rather than achievement.'[21] Nevertheless, a number of bilateral agreements were reached, lowering tariffs on some British goods in the Canadian market in exchange for imperial preference in the British market on wheat, foodstuffs, and dairy products.

A few months before the conference opened McNaughton secured permission to re-establish the airmail service to the Strait of Belle Isle to meet the Atlantic steamers and fly the mail to Montreal and Ottawa. Having a service in operation during the conference, even if only on a temporary basis, would champion the Canadian case for the direct route far louder than any words could. J.A. Wilson described what the service would entail:

The 'Empress of Britain' crosses from Southampton to Belle Isle in three and a half days and enters the Straits at dawn on the 4th day. It is proposed to transfer 800 lbs of mail from the 'Empress' to a Naval tender in the Straits opposite the entrance to Red Bay, 990 miles from Montreal. The Naval tender will then take the mails to the sheltered waters of Red Bay, where they will be transferred to a Bellanca seaplane, which will fly them to Eskimo point, on the north shore of the Gulf of St. Lawrence, 604 miles below Montreal. There they will be transferred to a Vancouver twin engined flying boat, which will fly them to Rimouski, on the south shore of the St. Lawrence, 330 miles from Montreal. There they will be landed and flown from the airport at Rimouski, adjacent to the wharf, direct to St. Hubert airport, Montreal, and thence to Ottawa by landplane.[22]

The first experimental flight went off without a hitch on 28 June 1932. Leaving nothing to chance, McNaughton drafted letters for the members of the cabinet to send to their British counterparts and arranged to have letters sent via the new temporary service from the king to the governor general. Each letter underlined the importance of the new service. One, for example, proclaimed that it 'should be a brilliant demonstration of the inherent advantages of the Saint Lawrence route as compared with the Services to other Atlantic ports, for by taking mail off fast steamers at Belle Isle and flying it to Montreal and Ottawa – roughly one-third of the shortest sea route to Europe – the superiority of the more southerly routes is considerably impaired.'[23] McNaughton's ship-to-shore service operated successfully for the duration of the Imperial Economic Conference, and with one relatively inexpensive stroke the Canadian position had received considerable favourable publicity.

Soon after the economic conference opened, a four-power Committee on Trans-Atlantic Air Services was created with Hugh Guthrie, the minister of justice, in the chair. The reason Guthrie was selected is uncertain; in any event he appears to have played little part in the work of the committee, leaving that task in the capable hands of General McNaughton. Other Canadians on the committee included P.T. Coolican, the assistant deputy postmaster-general, C.P. Edwards, then the director of radio in the Department of Marine, and Hume Wrong from external affairs. J.A. Wilson also participated as secretary. The United Kingdom was represented by two officials: Sir William Clark, the high commissioner in Ottawa, and Col. F.C. Shelmerdine, the director of civil aviation in the Air Ministry. Ireland nominated one representative – Sean Lemass, the minister for industry and commerce – and Newfoundland sent two: L.E. Emerson, the minister of justice, and H.V. Hutchings, the deputy minister of customs.

Due note was taken of the experimental service then in operation, and it was hoped that the discussions would lead to the establishment of a permanent service. High on the Canadian agenda was the desire to ensure the utilization of the direct route. The British, however, came armed with a long confidential government document entitled 'Inter-Imperial Communications,' which acknowledged the negotiations that had taken place between Pan Am and Imperial Airways concerning the southern route.'[24]

The Committee on Trans-Atlantic Air Services and its smaller subcommittee met several times over the next ten days in an effort to produce a joint report. The minutes of the meetings reveal that relations were cordial and there was widespread agreement on the value of a transatlantic air and steamer service; the only area of disagreement arose over the Canadian desire to enshrine a commitment to the direct route in the committee's final report. On 15 August, for example, Sir William Clark challenged one article in the subcommittee report that stipulated the development of the direct route above all others. Clark proposed adding the phrase 'provided that the prospect of successful operation on that route prove equal to those on other routes,' but the Canadians balked, arguing that it would change the whole meaning of the article.[25]

In the end, compromise prevailed: all four governments agreed to give first priority to the direct route and said they would 'not actively support the development of any other route, or give privileges to any foreign Government or their nationals in respect to the operation of trans-Atlantic air services, or air and steamer services, or the establishment of air bases or air navigation facilities for the purpose of such services, without full and prior consultation with each other.' For their part, the Canadians agreed 'to give early consideration to the re-establishment of the airway and air mail service from Montreal to Moncton, Halifax and Sydney.'[26]

In his report to the Air Ministry, Colonel Shelmerdine expressed some misgivings over the work of the committee. He had found the Canadians – and especially General McNaughton –eager to get a permanent service started as soon as possible, but he was reluctant to give the Canadians a blanket endorsement of the great circle route. Thus, he noted, McNaughton labelled him a 'defeatist' because he would not agree to all the Canadian demands. Shelmerdine theorized on the apparent Canadian obsession with the direct route: 'In considering the Canadian attitude to the whole of this matter,' he wrote, 'it is necessary to realize the feeling which undoubtedly exists in Canada – that we have not shown any desire to co-operate in aviation matters or to keep Canada informed as to negotiations in regard to developments of possible trans-Atlantic air services, but have rather entered into negotiations behind their backs with American interests.'

Shelmerdine went on to reveal ambivalent feelings about the Canadian position – feelings that were shared by others in London. 'The Canadian attitude certainly appears unreasonable,' he recorded, 'but it is necessary to remember their geographical position and the intense desire – frequently reiterated by General McNaughton and others – to prevent American encroachment, which is going to be an exceedingly difficult problem.'[27] British interest in the southern route and Anglo-American relations should not be sacrificed, of course, but Shelmerdine argued that the United Kingdom could not afford to neglect Canada, for fear that American aviation interests would move in and dominate the whole continent.

The aviation talks during the Imperial Economic Conference were the first in a series of international discussions and conferences in which Canadians were involved over the next decade and a half. Rarely again, if ever, would Canadian delegates be quite so successful at so little cost. The Canadians entered the talks in a very weak position, relying solely on Britain's support for some degree of imperial unity, and walked away from the conference table with the promise of future consultation and the commitment they had sought on the direct route, without giving anything substantial in return. There were no guarantees that either the British government or Imperial Airways would live totally within the spirit of the committee report but, for the moment at least, this one significant achievement could be savoured.

III

In the weeks following the Imperial Economic Conference, the RCAF carried out an air survey of the Strait of Belle Isle and the western coast of Newfoundland, and determined that a summer service to the strait could be operated. A preliminary report of the survey was ready by October 1932, but no action was taken for several months; in fact, the Newfoundland government did not receive a copy of the report until the following April. And even then, further surveys were still required.[28]

Such a slow start at fulfilling Canada's commitments disturbed J.A. Wilson, who could not help comparing developments in Canada with those in the rest of the world. The depression seemed to be holding down the development of civil aviation only in Canada. Imperial Airways and Pan Am were enlarging their operations in Africa and South America, he wrote, and 'Germany and France are busy on the South Atlantic crossing. Holland, France and Russia are extending their services from Europe to the Far East. Everywhere the growth of traffic and travel by air is phenomenal.' Everywhere but in Canada, it seemed. And the implications of inaction were clear: 'To adapt a negative policy during this formative period,' he warned, 'is to jeopardize our future position.'[29]

Part of the problem lay in the continuing Canadian suspicion of Imperial Airways and its dealings with Pan Am. O.D. Skelton tried to explain the Canadian concerns to Sir Eric Geddes at an informal meeting in London on 6 April 1933. 'I was not very familiar with the details of the position,' Skelton said, but 'there was a definite feeling in Canada that Imperial Airways had been much more anxious to make arrangements with Pan-American Airways than to work with the Canadian authorities.' Geddes brushed these concerns aside, suggesting that they were merely the result of misunderstandings and not based on reality. Imperial Airways was eager and willing to co-operate with Canada, Geddes concluded; the only problem 'was that he did not know with whom to communicate.'[30]

Good point. When Imperial Airways or Pan Am looked to Canada, there was no one there with whom they could deal with confidence. McNaughton, Wilson, and others had for months been advocating government action on Canada's behalf, but to little effect. 'The need for a strong national aircraft operating company comparable to Imperial or Pan American Airways is very evident,' Wilson growled. 'Experience all over the world shows the necessity for consistent support of such an organization if an efficient air transport system is to be created in Canada.'[31]

There was some hope that Canadian Airways, a private company, would gradually assume the role of national airline. Canadian Airways was the child of James Richardson, a Kingston native who had moved west in 1912 to operate the western half of his family's business. In 1926 he formed Western Canada Airways, which operated in Manitoba and northern Ontario before expanding with an airmail service across the prairies. In 1928 Richardson acquired Pacific Airways (which consisted of one Curtiss HS-2L airplane), and the following year began operating into the Northwest Territories. At the same time, several fledgling eastern airline companies amalgamated into the Aviation Corporation of Canada, a new company of which both Richardson and the Canadian Pacific Railway (CPR) were shareholders. Canadian National Railways (CNR) had also expressed an interest in owning part of an airline, and in 1930 a new company was created through the merger of Western Canada Airways and Aviation Corporation of Canada. James Richardson received the bulk of the shares in Canadian Airways, as the new firm was called, and became its first president. The two railways invested $250,000 each in the venture in return for 10,000 shares, and Sir Henry Thornton and Edward Beatty (the presidents of the CNR and CPR respectively) became vice-presidents.[32]

Canadian Airways was the largest and most stable airline in the country in the early 1930s and, with the active support and participation of the two national railways, its viability seemed assured. In 1931 a service between Victoria and Seattle was inaugurated, using two Boeing c-204 flying boats, adding an international dimension to a network of operations that already spanned most of Canada. In addition, Thornton and Beatty both corresponded with Geddes of Imperial Airways about the possibility of co-operation on a transatlantic service. But like virtually every airline in Canada during the depression, Canadian Airways was hurt by the cut-back in government airmail contracts. In 1931 Canadian Airways lost its Montreal–Toronto contract, and the Toronto–Windsor service was dropped the following year. Also in 1932, the airline's lucrative prairie contract was cancelled. By 1933 Canadian Airways was experiencing heavy losses and, without government support, faced bankruptcy.[33]

The plight of private Canadian airlines was sufficiently serious to attract the attention of the prime minister early in the spring of 1933. Bennett expressed his 'concern' to McNaughton over the telephone and asked the general to investigate the 'difficult situation in which the Airway Companies found themselves' and submit a full report within a month's time. McNaughton lost no time in gathering J.A. Wilson and P.T. Coolican into an informal interdepartmental committee 'to review the whole question.'[34]

McNaughton's report was finished by the end of May and was presented to the prime minister at a meeting on 1 June. McNaughton began with a review of air regulations and the growth of air-navigation facilities across Canada. Turning to the operation of air services, McNaughton left no doubt where he stood. 'Adequate communications and transportation services are the nervous system of world commerce. Just as Canadian steamer, railway, highway, telephone, telegraph and radio services have kept pace with world developments and are necessary to ensure the efficiency of our commerce, so, in the air, we must ensure that as world conditions demand the newest form of travel and transport is made available in Canada.'

Much work had already been done, McNaughton pointed out, especially in the provision of ground facilities, but the key question was yet to be resolved. 'The major problem,' he continued, 'is the system under which the trans-Canada airway and its main connections may best be operated. There are two alternatives, one by state operation, the second by operation under contract with a strong aircraft operating company given such support by the state as may enable it to operate successfully until the traffic returns are sufficient to pay for the cost of operation.'[35] McNaughton's committee favoured the latter alternative – going so far as to draw up a draft agreement between the government, the two railways, and Canadian Airways for the operation of a trans-Canada service.

McNaughton's committee continued to meet on an informal basis over the summer, but the development of the trans-Canada airway stalled. In the meantime, Juan Trippe had sent a survey party to Newfoundland to search for potential air-bases and his representatives initiated negotiations for landing rights with the Newfoundland government. When word of these discussions reached London, a meeting at the Dominions Office was hastily arranged for 9 June. Lt-Col. Georges Vanier, a member of the high-commission staff, represented Canada at the meeting, and the other participants included L.E. Emerson, Sir Edgar Bowring (Newfoundland's high commissioner), Sir Harry Batterbee and R.A. Wiseman of the Dominions Office, and Colonel Shelmerdine.

Emerson announced that his government had entered into negotiations with Pan Am and he gave a description of the concessions that his government planned to offer the American company and Imperial Airways (and, interestingly, a Canadian company, should one be created) for the development of ground facilities and landing rights in Newfoundland. Vanier remained silent but Batterbee and Shelmerdine reacted negatively and 'tried to dissuade Mr. Emerson from granting any rights whatever to Pan American Airways.' When Emerson seemed unmoved, a copy of the agreement reached the previous summer was produced and the clause respecting consultation was read. Incredibly, Emerson claimed never to have seen the text before, even though he had been part of the committee that produced it. When confronted, however, he conceded that no negotiations with the Americans would take place without the Canadians, British, and Irish being consulted.[36]

The upshot of the discussion was an invitation from the Newfoundlanders to send representatives to St John's to participate in the negotiations with Pan Am and Imperial Airways. At first the invitation was to the British only, but Batterbee insisted on the participation of the Canadians. Emerson complained that he had written on two occasions to a Canadian cabinet minister (Hugh Guthrie, as it turned out) with no reply, and the Newfoundlander gave Vanier 'the impression of being decidedly antipathetic to Canada and of resenting any possible intervention or interference from Canadian sources.'[37] Nevertheless, within a few days an invitation had arrived in Ottawa.

J.A. Wilson was appointed Canadian representative to the talks; in advance he set to work on a long memorandum reviewing many of the arguments made over the previous two years. The route across Newfoundland, he argued, was 'so clearly a natural extension of the trans-Canada airway that it should not be controlled by interests which, however friendly at present, might, in future, have a detrimental effect on lines of communication of such importance to the Dominion.'[38] Without either government support or the airplanes to operate the service, however, Wilson had only luck to rely on. As if to underline the point, shortly before his departure Wilson received a letter from George Perley, the acting prime minister, reminding him that on financial matters he was 'not authorized to make any promises.'[39]

Wilson and George Herring, the chief superintendent of the airmail service, left for Newfoundland on the morning of 2 July and arrived in St John's a full three days later (demonstrating the value of an air service to St John's). After a few obligatory introductions and visits, the two Canadians met privately with Emerson, Shelmerdine, and Col. H. Burchall, the assistant general manager of Imperial Airways. Wilson discovered that Imperial Airways and Pan Am had indeed been working closely together and that Imperial Airways planned to parallel any Pan Am transatlantic service. As for the ground services in Newfoundland, Imperial Airways wished to keep them in British hands – but was willing to share control with the Canadian government.

Wilson's luck held out. He fully realized that the British would want a service running to New York, but he told Burchall that 'Canada would not be satisfied with any service which did not come via the St. Lawrence route and Montreal,' even if the final destination were New York. He found Burchall very agreeable and sympathetic to Canadian concerns and secured a promise from Burchall to 'make representations to his company immediately with a view to meeting our desires.'[40]

The Newfoundlanders, meanwhile, found themselves in a rather difficult situation, having made promises to Pan Am that they could not keep. Negotiations continued for several days before a satisfactory

An Effort in Commonwealth Collaboration 37

agreement was created. In the end, Imperial Airways was granted exclusive operating rights in Newfoundland for fifteen years and non-exclusive rights for an additional thirty-five years – rights that included the connections to Canada and the United States. Imperial Airways was also given the right to assign similar privileges to foreign intersts, such as Pan Am. In addition, Pan Am was not to be permitted to own any ground facilities in Newfoundland but could use those provided by Newfoundland, Canada, or Great Britain. As for the Canadians, they were to be granted the same privileges as Imperial Airways if and when the government appointed a company to utilize them.[41]

Wilson returned to Canada very pleased with what had been accomplished in St John's. Skelton found his report 'very satisfactory. Our representatives have evidently scored a very definite success.'[42] Imperial Airways was the obvious victor, having secured exclusive rights for fifteen years, but Wilson was satisfied that Canada's concerns over the proposed route had been met. Perhaps even more significant, with a little bit of effort a Canadian company could participate on an equal basis with Imperial Airways in any future air service to Newfoundland. Still, there were no guarantees.

IV

In October 1934, aircraft from around the world participated in the 11,300-mile MacRobertson Race from Mildenhall, England, to Melbourne, Australia. The winning entry was a British-designed DeHavilland DH.88 Comet, a first-class long-distance airplane. To the victor went honour and fame, but really the more significant achievement in this race was made by the second- and third-place finishers, a Douglas DC-2 and a Boeing 247D respectively. The Comet was a beautifully designed racing aircraft built with speed in mind; the two American entries were built as basic passenger aircraft – and yet had still managed to give the British airplane a run for its money. Informed European observers were astounded: Had the Americans jumped that far ahead in aircraft design and technology?[43]

At almost the exact same time, Pan Am put into service its first Sikorsky S-42 flying boat, which could fly an unheard-of 1000 miles non-stop at a cruising speed of 150 mph, carrying thirty-two passengers. Then, in December 1934, Pan Am introduced the Glen Martin

M-130 flying boat, which could do even more – flying over 2000 miles non-stop with approximately thirty passengers. Neither the S-42 nor the M-130 was streamlined in the modern sense, and their significance has been somewhat obscured by the 'DC revolution,' which has focused attention on obvious design innovations such as stressed skin construction and cantilever wings. Nevertheless, the impact of these two American airplanes was profound.[44]

Pan Am was capable of inaugurating an Atlantic service in 1935 but international politics got in the way. With the French in the Azores and the British in Bermuda and Newfoundland, American transatlantic plans were blocked. The British, in contrast, did not have suitable aircraft, but they did have the bases. Indeed, economic disaster had brought Newfoundland to the verge of collapse, and in 1934 the island nation surrendered its dominion status and fell under the direct control of the Dominions Office in London. The 1933 St John's agreement had secured landing rights in Newfoundland for Imperial Airways for fifteen years; the return to colonial status removed any future possibility of Pan Am or the American government negotiating independently with a Newfoundland government.

At first the British were sceptical of what the Americans had accomplished in aircraft performance. The performance estimates of the S-42 and M-130 were known in Britain as early as 1932, but as often as not they were dismissed as too optimistic. For example, in 1933, Robert Mayo, one of Imperial Airways' engineering consultants, reviewed the estimates of the M-130 and concluded that the airplane would be 'quite incapable of operating on an Atlantic service over the Azores–Bermuda or Iceland–Newfoundland routes.'[45] But it became harder to dismiss the aircraft after November 1934 when Pan Am inaugurated its trans-pacific airmail service. By 1935 the M-130, dubbed the *China Clipper*, was routinely spanning the San Francisco–Honolulu leg – a distance of 2410 miles. That this distance was farther than any hop on the transatlantic route was not lost on British and Canadian observers.

The developments of late 1934 and early 1935 produced a sense of urgency in the minds of the Canadian officials who were responsible for civil aviation. McNaughton's interdepartmental committee had continued to meet since 1933, and the development of the trans-Canada airway carried on at a snail's pace. Beginning in 1935, however, it was possible to forecast the operation of a transatlantic service within a year or two. The Canadian government was still years away from operating such a service, but now that the Americans could, it seemed to highlight the startling inadequacy of Canadian civil aviation policy.

The Canadian government had far more important problems to deal with in 1934-5 than international civil aviation. If anything, aviation appeared as an unnecessary and expensive luxury. As R.B. Bennett later explained to the House of Commons, he had slashed government airmail contracts 'because with the crop failure in western Canada, and with 300,000 of a population receiving some form of relief, there was very little gratification in seeing an aeroplane passing by day after day when the unfortunate owner of the soil could hardly see the aeroplane because his crop had gone up in dust.'[46] It was fine that plans were being made by McNaughton, Wilson, and the others, and that some work was being undertaken by men on relief, but when it came to investing money in an aviation project the answer was no.

Bennett's reluctance to make financial commitments had been made clear to McNaughton's committee a few month's earlier. McNaughton submitted a letter to the prime minister outlining the various expenses required for civil aviation purposes, including the airmail service. Bennett quietly glanced over the figures while the others waited. After a few moments he looked up from the paper and informed his officials 'that Canada could not afford an air mail service when she was practically bankrupt, that at the present time he had the task of raising $500,000,000 and that no expenditures which were not essential could be made.'[47] Despite McNaughton's appeal to the national interest, the most Bennett would promise was to refer the matter to a committee of his colleagues.

By spring 1935, McNaughton's committee had gone as far as it could go without further direction from the political level. It would be best if that part of the transatlantic service between Canada and Newfoundland were operated by a Canadian airline – but there was no hope of this happening. On a more realistic level, the committee recommended that Canada at least offer to provide the ground facilities in Newfoundland. 'It is evident that unless Canada decides to participate actively in the development of the trans-Atlantic air services,' J.A. Wilson argued, 'Imperial Airways and Pan American Airways will carry out their programme without reference to Canadian interests, whereas if we are partners in the development, then, in return for our contribution, we may demand consideration of our interests.'[48] But without government action there was nothing McNaughton's committee could do but sit back and wait.

The British could not afford to wait. The officials in Imperial Airways had repeatedly expressed their desire to parallel any transatlantic service operated by Pan Am. But the development of the S-42 and M-130 had demonstrated, in the words of J.A. Wilson, 'that the Air Ministry's programme for the development of long range flying boats is not very advanced and is much in arrears of the corresponding development in the United States.'[49] Clearly, the inauguration of a British transatlantic service was not on the horizon in 1935, but something had to be done – to stall the Americans if nothing else.

The Air Ministry and Imperial Airways both complained about the lack of government funding for aviation, and the British aircraft industry was on the verge of falling even farther behind the American. The United Kingdom did not have the same internal demand for aircraft as the United States did, and even a campaign to 'buy British' was insufficient to ensure an adequate market for British aircraft. Britain's domestic airline companies were floundering and, until a program of rearmament was instituted by the government, the British aircraft industry could do little more than play catch-up to the Americans. Great Britain remained a world leader in the design and production of smaller, short-distance aircraft, but the production of a British flying boat capable of transatlantic flight was still several years away.[50]

In 1935 the British government established the Interdepartmental Committee on International Air Communications, with representatives from the Air Ministry, the Foreign Office, Treasury, Post Office, Board of Trade, and the Admiralty. Taking its name from Sir Warren Fisher, the permanent secretary in the treasury, who was appointed to the chair, the Fisher committee was established to investigate the state of British civil aviation, with particular reference to the European situation. Imperial Airways had long emphasized empire services at the expense of European ones, and one of the first recommendations of the Fisher committee was to improve British services to the Continent.[51]

British officials were also hard at work with respect to the Atlantic service. In June, Georges Vanier was invited to an informal meeting with Sir Harry Batterbee in the Dominions Office, where he 'gathered that an important inter-departmental meeting had taken place,' at which two recommendations were made. First, it was agreed that an imperial airmail service between London and Montreal should be established as quickly as possible and, second, that an agreement on a transatlantic service should be reached with the Americans, dividing the service fifty-fifty between Imperial Airways and Pan Am.[52]

Meanwhile, the French government had re-entered the picture with an offer to the American government to investigate jointly the technical aspects of a transatlantic service. The French foresaw a three-way partnership with the British and Americans, but the British were rather cool to the proposal, believing that Anglo-American arrangements should be made first. For the Canadians such a development held even greater dangers. If the French were involved it could mean only one thing – the supremacy of the Bermuda–Azores route – and there was nothing that the Canadians could do about it.[53]

Fortunately for the Canadians, they didn't have to. In August a long telegram arrived in Ottawa from J.H. Thomas, the dominions secretary, outlining recent developments in civil aviation, including the French government's overtures. Thomas reviewed the pros and cons of the direct and the southern routes, and concluded that it was 'not possible at present to indicate the precise extent to which one or other of these routes may be used.' Nevertheless, the time had come to examine the whole question of transatlantic aviation –within the empire and with the Americans. Thomas then proposed that representatives from the Air Ministry, the Post Office, and Imperial Airways visit North America to discuss the transatlantic services – first with the Canadians in Ottawa, and then with the Americans in Washington.[54]

The British suggestion was met with mixed reactions in Ottawa. Wilson and McNaughton were delighted with the proposal for a conference – Canadian participation in any negotiations was one of their primary goals. But their joy was mixed with a recognition that Canada had taken no steps towards forming a government policy respecting the transatlantic services. 'Reading between the lines' of the Thomas telegram, Wilson sensed 'misgivings' on the British part concerning the direct route, and he was quick to point out the need for government leadership. All efforts must be undertaken to ensure the use of the direct route, he argued, and Canada must be willing to act now to provide the ground services in Newfoundland and provide any necessary air services to and from the Maritimes that might be needed for the transatlantic service.[55]

At the end of June, McNaughton was transferred to the National Research Council, a move that effectively eliminated him from active participation in aviation affairs. Although he maintained a keen interest in the unfolding of events, it was left to Wilson to flood the government with memos and reports pleading the case for active government involvement. It was a frustrating experience, for the government would not budge. Even the relatively inexpensive project to build and maintain ground services in Newfoundland withered on the vine.[56]

Imperial Airways, by way of contrast, was determined to play a major role in Newfoundland and in the transatlantic service. Late in August, George Woods Humphrey, Imperial Airways' managing director, mentioned to Georges Vanier that Imperial Airways would find dealing with the Canadians so much easier if they would only create a national airline.[57] This was not to suggest that Imperial Airways was willing to divide the transatlantic service with a Canadian company or even permit the Canadians to operate that part of the service, say, between Newfoundland and Canada. 'We on this side,' Woods Humphrey wrote Wilson in September, 'have always assumed that co-operation with the United States is inevitable in regard to the Trans-Atlantic service, and, in fact, puts the British and the United States' services in an impregnable position, but if co-operation is essential, then we believe it to be no less essential that the British service shall go through to the United States' terminus.' And to make it clear what lengths Imperial Airways would go to ensure that the Canadians did not operate that part of the service west of Newfoundland, Woods Humphrey added:

I must say that it seems to me quite impracticable to have our service terminating in Newfoundland, leaving onward carriage both to Canada and the United States to be operated by Canadian services. That would put Imperial Airways in a position of considerable inferiority to Pan American Airways, which, I think, would be most undesirable. In fact, if Canada did not want us to land in Canada at all, I cannot help feeling that it would still be desirable for us to fly from Newfoundland to the United States outside Canadian territorial limits so that we could avoid any claim by the United States that they should be entitled to bring the whole of their mail from the

United States as far as Newfoundland, and that we should only share in its carriage from Newfoundland to the United Kingdom. Moreover, I believe that prestige alone would require that if the American Trans-Atlantic aircraft fly into Newfoundland, Ireland and England, it is essential that United Kingdom aircraft should also fly into the United States.[58]

The Canadian government was in no condition to operate a Canada–Newfoundland service in any event. Bennett's government had ignored civil aviation for years, and the policy of neglect was not about to change. Foreign affairs had a low priority in the government and country at large, and Bennett, who faced an election in October, was not likely to embark on a new lavish spending spree on civil aviation. The outbreak of a crisis in the League of Nations in September between Italy and Ethiopia further deflected attention away from the international dimensions of civil aviation. Bennett had no objections to participating in a conference with the British (providing it was held after the election); otherwise there is little evidence that he gave it any more thought than that.

As it turned out, Bennett had no need to concern himself with the upcoming discussions with the British and the Americans. Early in October the Canadian government requested more information on the proposed conferences and by the time the response arrived from London, Bennett's government had gone down to defeat at the polls. The decision to participate in the discussions, then, was left for the new government under Mackenzie King to make.

Wilson had taken a small measure of comfort from the fact that during the election campaign both King and Bennett had advocated spending more on civil aviation, but King was still an unknown quantity when he returned to power in 1935. As prime minister in the 1920s he had spoken in favour of consultation and discussion in aviation affairs, but in the end had done nothing. As leader of the opposition he opposed Bennett's aviation policy, of course; but, equally, had Bennett embarked on a major spending program on aviation, King likely would have opposed that, too, as an extravagant waste of the taxpayers' money. But King was no fool; if there were benefits to accrue from the process already started by Bennett he was willing to reap the rewards – much as he would do in the case of the Canadian-American trade negotiations that Bennett had initiated.

The change of government in October 1935 unintentionally marked the beginning of a long period of anxiety in international affairs, culminating in the outbreak of war in 1939. The Italian/Ethiopian crisis and the collapse of the League of Nations as a viable organization, followed by a series of tragic yet seemingly inevitable crises, focused Canadian attention on Europe's slow and painful descent into war. For King and his government, delving into international affairs could only stir up domestic tensions needlessly. Although there was no doubt where the country stood on the larger issues of war and peace, during the last four years of peace King managed to shroud his foreign policy in a haze of obfuscation behind the rubric 'Parliament will decide.'

For such reasons it would be a mistake to assume that the return to power of Mackenzie King's Liberals in 1935 presaged a new era in Canadian international civil aviation. Bennett had tried to deal with the depression and the Canadian electorate told him that he had failed; there were no indications that Mackenzie King was any better prepared. Besides, Mackenzie King had made no concrete commitments to enhance civil aviation, nor had he evinced much interest in the upcoming Anglo-American discussions. He did, however, agree that Canadians would at least participate, and on 5 November gave directions to initiate an interdepartmental committee to draw up plans for the Canadian representatives. Then he promptly left the country.

On 8 November King met President Roosevelt at the White House, where they made the final arrangements for the trade agreement, which was officially signed on 15 November. King's diary entry for the 8th was longer than usual, as he filled pages with the details of his talk with the president. The trade negotiations dominated the discussion, not surprisingly, but the two leaders also spoke of other matters, like Roosevelt's plans for the development of Boulder Dam and Mackenzie King's hopes for a treaty to preserve the beauty of Niagara Falls. The upcoming aviation talks, however, do not seem to have been discussed. Indeed, after signing the trade agreement in Washington, Mackenzie King left for a holiday in Georgia and New York City and was out of the country for the whole of the Ottawa discussions. Again, his diary for the next few weeks contains virtually no reference to the aviation discussions. King's primary concern was to rein in Walter Riddell, the head of the Canadian delegation at the League of Nations, who, without government approval, had recommended the inclusion of oil, coal, and steel on the list of sanctions against Italy.

In any event, the interdepartmental committee initiated by the prime minister was brought together under V.I. Smart, the deputy minister in the Department of Railways and Canals. Wilson was a member, of course, as was Loring Christie who had recently returned from private life to the Department of External Affairs. The group was rounded out with P.T. Coolican, the assistant deputy postmaster-general, Clifford Clark from the Department of Finance, and John Patterson and C.P. Edwards from the Department of Marine. The committee met several times over the next ten days and submitted its report on 18 November, four days before the discussions were to begin.

Smart chaired the committee, but the words of the report were unquestionably J.A. Wilson's. For the benefit of the new prime minister and cabinet, Wilson reviewed the case that he and McNaughton had been making to Bennett since 1932. Canada was virtually the only civilized nation that did not subsidize its civil aviation with substantial government funds, the fifteen-page memorandum began, but for reasons of size and location Canadians had the right to expect to play a role in the development of international civil aviation. The upcoming talks furnished an opportunity to ensure a voice for Canada in the establishment of transatlantic services – provided the Canadians played their cards right.

The memo continued with a description of the three possible transatlantic routes (and the explanation of why the direct route was the best choice) and a review of the past efforts of Pan Am and Imperial Airways to come to some equitable arrangement. Finally, a number of recommendations were made: (1) Canada should push for the development of the direct route above all others; (2) Canada should participate in any experimental services on the direct route; (3) an effort should be made to secure an agreement with the other states, recognizing Montreal 'as the cisatlantic collecting and distributing centre'; (4) each country should maintain ownership and control of those facilities in their territory; and (5) Canada should offer to help Newfoundland establish and operate its navigational facilities. The memo ended on a familiar note: 'The United Kingdom has proposed that a Canadian organization (with functions similar to those of Imperial Airways Limited and Pan American Airways) should participate in the proposed transatlantic service, but as no such body exists in Canada, no definite recommendation can now be made; though it is considered that the proposal has merit.'[59]

Had a national airline existed it is quite likely that it would have participated in the discussions and carried out the Canadian end of any arrangements made. The British did see a void on the Canadian side of things, but did not see it as an insurmountable problem. For example, one of the British goals was to bring Canada into the Empire Air Mail Scheme (EAMS) by 1937. The EAMS was conceived by Imperial Airways as a subsidized imperial arrangement to carry all first-class mail within the empire. The mail would be carried by Imperial Airways (and sometimes in conjunction with a local service) and each nation would pay an annual fee in return for a very low standard postage rate and improved delivery times. Some arrangements had already been made, and it was hoped that the introduction of a transatlantic service would prompt the Canadians into participation. No Canadian airline was necessary here – Imperial Airways would see that the mail got through.[60]

What the British really were after for the transatlantic service was a Commonwealth airline dominated by Imperial Airways. In India, Imperial Airways jointly operated Indian Trans-Continental Airways with the Indian government; in Australia, Imperial Airways held a 50 per cent share of Qantas Empire Airlines. In May 1935 Anglo-Irish discussions produced an agreement for a joint company (Ireland 51 per cent, United Kingdom 49 per cent), leading to the creation of Aer Lingus Teoranta in March 1936. On several occasions the idea of a joint company (with the Irish, Canadians, and Newfoundlanders) had been put forward as a possible arrangement for the transatlantic service. But this was not to be an equal partnership; as one British diplomat put it to an Irish colleague, Imperial Airways and the United Kingdom government would not agree 'to any arrangement under which less than 51 per cent of the shares would be held by Imperial Airways.'[61]

In Ireland, civil aviation fell under the jurisdiction of the Department of Industry and Commerce. On 8 November the Irish cabinet established a ministerial committee to study the upcoming talks with the British and the Canadians and to approve the instructions for the Irish representatives. At first it was hoped that the three governments would participate in the joint company on an equal basis, but when it became clear that the British would not allow this to happen, the Irish gave in, insisting only that their share of the company be equal to or larger than the Canadian.[62]

The Ottawa conference on transatlantic air services opened on 22

An Effort in Commonwealth Collaboration   47

November 1935 in a conference room in the Centre Block on Parliament Hill. J.C. Elliott, the postmaster-general, acted as chair long enough to welcome the visitors to Ottawa, and then he left the meeting and was replaced by V.I. Smart. The rest of the Canadian delegation consisted of those officials who were members of the interdepartmental committee: Wilson, Christie, Coolican, Clark, Edwards, and Patterson. Among the British team were a number of familiar faces, including Sir Donald Banks of the British Post Office, Shelmerdine of the Air Ministry, Woods Humphrey representing Imperial Airways, and C.G.L. Syers of the Dominions Office. Thomas Lodge, a British member of the Newfoundland Commission of Government, represented Newfoundland, and J.P. Walshe and John Leydon, secretaries of the departments of External Affairs and Industry and Commerce respectively, were the two Irish delegates.

After a few formalities, Sir Donald Banks opened the conversation with a general description of what the British hopes were for the transatlantic service. One primary goal was to link Canada (and, implicitly, the rest of North America) with the Empire Air Mail Scheme. 'The institution of an air mail service across the Atlantic,' Sir Donald suggested, 'would complete the general scheme for linking up the countries of the Commonwealth by air and should bring advantages of the greatest importance to all the countries concerned.' Plans to include Canada in the EAMS raised the question of the North American terminal for the transatlantic service, because, Banks continued, 'if the traffic was centred at New York, the mail for the western points would tend to flow through the United States lines, whereas, if Montreal were utilized, the mail for western points would flow through Canada, both to western Canada points and to Detroit and Chicago, and from there to the western states.'

Minutes taken during meetings are usually a pretty dry affair, and this conference was no exception. Yet it is easy to speculate on the smiles that must have crossed the faces of Wilson and the Canadian delegates at Banks's words. Making Montreal the North American terminal for the transatlantic service was at the top of the Canadian agenda, and Banks was taking it as a given right off the top. He even added that he 'presumed that the trans-Canada airway would be in operation to handle such traffic.'[63]

The first meeting settled nothing, of course, but it allowed for a preliminary exchange of ideas. In any case, three subcommittees and a secretariat were established to examine specific issues and then report back to the conference as a whole. The first was the Postal Sub-Committee under P.T. Coolican; the second, an Operating and Technical Sub-Committee to examine questions concerning operations and radio and meteorological services, and to decide routes; and third, a General, Finance and Co-ordinating Sub-Committee was created with Smart, Clark, Christie, Banks, Shelmerdine, Leydon, Walshe, and Lodge. The latter committee became the key working group.

In the first meeting of the General, Finance and Co-ordinating Sub-Committee held the following morning, Sir Donald Banks introduced a proposal to establish a joint company to operate the transatlantic service. He divided the development of the service into three stages: (1) survey and exploration, (2) irregular seasonal service, and (3) regular service. During the first two stages, he argued, Canada and Ireland would be expected to provide ground facilities only, leaving the total financial responsibility with the United Kingdom and Imperial Airways. At the end of stage two, the 'services with all the experience and knowledge gained would be handed over to a joint operating company representative of the United Kingdom, the Irish Free State and Canada.'

The Canadians were non-committal at first, reserving the final decision for a later internal meeting. The discussion turned to the financial aspects of the scheme and to the extent of present surveys for the northern and direct routes. There was general agreement on the use of the direct route, with the caution that 'this should not prevent use of alternative routes for purposes of development.'[64] The British had made their case; it now was time for the Canadians to decide what they wanted to do.

The Canadian delegates met privately on 25 November to discuss the British proposals. It made sense to collaborate; Canada could not operate a transatlantic service on its own, while the British scheme would let the Canadians in on the ground floor of development. The proposed service would also give preference to the direct route and go a long way to making Montreal the North American terminal. The decision was relatively easy to make, and on 26 November the Canadians agreed in principle, subject to government approval and provided suitable terms could be worked out.[65]

The remaining days of the conference were spent ironing out the details, and the final report received unanimous approval at the meeting on 2 December. The agreement reached in Ottawa was a watershed in a number of respects. The participants agreed to the creation of a joint transatlantic service in two stages: first, preliminary experimental flights would be undertaken, and second, once two regular flights per week were accomplished for a period of three months, a regular service would be inaugurated. The first stage was to be operated and financed by Imperial Airways, but once the regular service had started, it would be run by a Joint Operating Company (JOC). The direct route would be developed, with all flights making mandatory stops in Ireland and Canada. It should also be mentioned that the services discussed were to be for airmail; passenger services were not specifically excluded: it was just that they did not seem practical at that moment.

The proposed JOC was an interesting arrangement because it would be 'incorporated at the instance of three companies acting in co-operation,' including Imperial Airways, an Irish company, and 'a Company incorporated or to be incorporated in Canada and nominated by the Government there of for the purpose.' The JOC would be controlled jointly by Britain, Canada, and Ireland, with Britain retaining 51 per cent of the capital stock and with Canada and Ireland dividing the rest, 24.5 per cent each. The lion's share of the operating costs was to be borne by the British government as well, with the Canadians agreeing to contribute 20 per cent, up to £75,000. A nine-member board of directors would be created with three appointed by each country, but with the chair and managing director coming from the British appointees. In addition, the participating states agreed to grant the JOC transit and landing rights in their territories and promised to provide the necessary ground services and facilities for the successful operation of the route.[66]

Interestingly, there was no termination date written into the agreement, nor was there any mention of unilateral withdrawal. At the same time, no fixed schedule was drawn up for the incorporation of the JOC or for the completion of stage one and the implementation of a regular service. Granted, no one could be expected to foresee all future difficulties, but in effect the Canadians were agreeing to become junior partners in a permanent arrangement that gave no guarantees of completion. During the indefinite 'preliminary' stage, moreover, Canada had agreed to provide navigational aids and meteorological services to Imperial Airways until the JOC was established. Not surprisingly, within a few years certain aspects of this deal had come back to haunt the Canadian government.

With the completion of the Ottawa conversations on 2 December 1935, the members of the Commonwealth delegations travelled to Washington to continue discussions with their American counterparts. Talks in Washington were planned well in advance, and it was hoped that Pan Am could be brought into some arrangement for the operation of transatlantic services. The American delegation consisted of the members of the US Inter-departmental Committee on Civil International Aviation, including Walton Moore, the assistant secretary of state, and Monroe Johnson, the assistant secretary of commerce. Juan Trippe and Woods Humphrey – 'wedded as tightly as a pair of Siamese twins' – represented their airlines.[67] The Washington half of the transatlantic discussions lasted from 5 to 12 December.

The Canadian and Irish representatives were technically full participants in the discussions but in reality all the negotiating was undertaken between Pan Am and Imperial Airways. The Irish delegation, for example, complained to Dublin of the difficulties it had obtaining documents and information on what was going on behind the scenes. The Irish and the Canadians, it was noted, even when present at the discussions were 'benevolent onlookers only.'[68]

Regardless of the impotence of the Irish and Canadian delegations, the Anglo-American agreement reached in Washington had far-reaching effects on Canada, Ireland, and the operation of the transatlantic air services. No arrangement could be made concerning mail services, but after a week of discussions it was agreed that reciprocal rights would be granted to Pan Am and Imperial Airways to operate two weekly round-trip passenger flights each, using either the southern or the direct route. The reciprocal nature of the agreement ensured that one country could not begin operations across the Atlantic unilaterally: the two services must be inaugurated together. Again it was difficult to be precise, but experimental flights were planned for the following summer, and it was hoped that a regular service would be inaugurated in summer 1937. Provision was also made for Imperial Airways management to be replaced by JOC personnel once the services were established.[69]

The Anglo-American agreement was carried out through a series of permit applications from Imperial Airways and Pan Am to the various governments involved. The agreement also included the terms of the operation permits for the two airlines and it set out routes. The clause respecting the route over Canada stated that the port of call would be designated by the Canadian government, 'such as shall neither reduce the efficiency, regularity and reliability of the service, nor unduly increase the cost, or at Montreal (preference being given to the latter, operating conditions and other factors being equal).'[70]

The press communiqué released by the State Department on 12 December made no reference to the use of Montreal on the transatlantic service.[71] There was no question that Imperial Airways had agreed to use Montreal in the Commonwealth service, but the ambiguous nature of the above clause left in some doubt whether or not the Americans were committed to Montreal. But for the time being at least, the Canadians were pleased with the outcome of the two conferences. The arrangements with Pan Am would have to wait for the issuance of government permits, but on 25 March 1936 the cabinet approved the Ottawa agreement. Two days earlier the Irish government informed London that it had approved it as well. By the summer all four Commonwealth governments had given their approval.[72]

V

The use of Montreal as the Canadian stop in the transatlantic air service seemed a logical and wise decision. The British would designate London, the Americans, New York – and no one would complain. It was only fair that Canada should pick its own site. Besides, from a postal and passenger point of view, it made sense to utilize Montreal. It was the country's largest city and a centre of commerce, and would probably be the hub of the future trans-Canada airway. Yet there were doubts that the Americans could be convinced. During the Washington conference, Wilson reported afterwards, 'it became evident that Pan American Airways had not considered the use of Montreal but had continued to base their plans on the earlier assumption that the route would pass along the Atlantic [coast].' This was a far cry from the St John's conference when Pan Am officials had agreed to the use of Montreal, an irritated Wilson pointed out. But no surveys of the route to Montreal had been undertaken, he continued, and Pan Am 'were not therefore in a position to state definitely that the route via Montreal was acceptable to them. In addition, they expressed doubt whether the United States Government would willingly accept such a diversion on account of possible pressure from the New England States.'[73]

Having made no effective arrangement in Washington regarding port of call, it was inevitable that the two interpretations would clash. The inevitable happened late in August 1936 when a map of the proposed American route fell into Canadian hands. Two routes were drawn in: the first or 'primary route' ran from New York along the eastern seaboard through Shediac, New Brunswick, and then on to Newfoundland; the second or 'British route' ran north from New York to Montreal. Early in September the Canadian Legation in Washington protested to the State Department that the proposed route through Shediac was in direct violation of the Washington agreement.[74]

On 7 October Hume Wrong from the Canadian Legation discussed the problem with Monroe Johnson, who had participated in the Washington discussions the previous December. Johnson told Wrong that 'it would be quite impossible' for the American government to sanction the use of Montreal over the coastal route, and he argued that the Washington agreement did not commit the government to do so. Wrong reported that Johnson

gave as his first reason the greater length of the route via Montreal, but it later became obvious – and in the end he stated frankly – that the real objection was that, if the Montreal route were followed, Montreal would in fact become the terminus of the trans-Atlantic service instead of New York. He said that his Government had throughout proceeded on the assumption that what was under discussion was a service between London and New York, and that it would be politically impossible for the United States to commit itself to a route which would place the real terminus of the service outside the United States. He believed that, with the Canadian base at Montreal, the bulk of the United States traffic would eventually join the service at Montreal, and that the Montreal–New York leg would be a sort of branch line.[75]

There was astonishment on the Canadian side, as well as agreement that the Americans were being unscrupulous. That Canada would designate Montreal was made abundantly clear to the Americans during the Washington talks; to come back now and suggest that that arrangement was made with Pan Am and not the United States government was disingenous at best. Besides, it was not a decision for the Americans to make; the choice of a Canadian site was entirely a domestic matter. The Irish and British agreed and were willing to back the Canadians if they wanted to force the issue.[76] And yet to stand and fight on this one point could jeopardize the whole agreement – something no one wanted to do.

To complicate matters even more, in November 1936 Juan Trippe and John Cooper, Pan Am's vice-president, met with Sir Francis Shelmerdine in London. One of the topics of conversation was the Canadian port of call, and Trippe hinted that Pan Am might be willing to use Montreal regardless of his government's policy. Montreal had commercial potential that made it more attractive to Pan Am than Shediac. The US government, however, would probably never be convinced. But Trippe had a plan. He recommended that the Canadians issue the proposed permit and, in addition, approve the use of an experimental route through Shediac. The American government could not dictate where his airline flew, he argued, and once the permits were exchanged, Pan Am would gradually shift its service on to the Montreal route. This way everyone would be satisfied.[77]

This new proposal had several strong points, but it also was a big gamble for the Canadians. For one thing, Trippe had earlier been an opponent of using Montreal on the Atlantic service.[78] Second, if the Canadians let down their guard on the use of Montreal and Pan Am did not respond as planned, then the Canadian case would be destroyed. In effect Trippe was asking the Canadians to put their faith in his promises and trust that he would come through.

The problem over port of call was thoroughly aired on several occasions over the following weeks and even began turning up in the newspapers. Early in 1937 the *New York Times* ran a story on the Canadian-American dispute in which the Canadians were depicted as holding up the completion of an Anglo-American agreement. Pan Am and Imperial Airways were ready to start services as soon as this mess was cleared up, the *Times* reported (incorrectly): the 'chief bone of contention, it was learned today, is a difference of opinion between the Canadian authorities and the Department of Commerce as to whether New York or Montreal shall be the trans-Atlantic terminal.' What the Canadians and British had in mind, the story continued, was an all-red transatlantic route, in which 'New York would be a branch, extending down from Montreal.'[79] Herbert Marler, the Canadian minister in Washington, was dismayed and called the article 'misleading' because it suggested that the Canadians wanted to make Montreal rather than New York the North American terminus.[80] He evidently had not been reading the memoranda and telegrams of the preceding five years, because this was, in fact, precisely what the Canadians wanted to do.

By the time the *Times* story hit the streets, Ottawa had already made its move. The risk of overturning the whole agreement was too great and something had to be done, if nothing else but to prolong the ambiguity of the choice of port of call. In February 1937, after further discussions with Trippe, the Canadian government went ahead and issued its permit to Pan Am (including the clause giving preference to Montreal), and shortly thereafter gave its permission to Pan Am to use Shediac as an experimental base.[81]

The permanent service was still years away, and by raising no objections to the use of Shediac the log-jam was broken. The Canadians could still claim that Montreal would be used for the permanent service, but in the meantime work could begin on an experimental basis. The Americans did not protest and in April permits were granted to Pan Am and Imperial Airways to begin their operations.[82] The two sides had agreed to disagree on the port of call; the showdown had been postponed indefinitely.

VI

Four members of the Commonwealth gathered together in December 1935 in an effort to collaborate on a project they all agreed was worthwhile. In the process of collaboration their differing motives and goals were exposed. The Newfoundlanders had no choice in the matter and were included because the transatlantic service needed to use Newfoundland land or seaplane bases. The Irish and the Canadians participated in a joint effort because neither could operate a service on its own, while both feared being left behind in the development of international air services if they abstained. The similarities did not stop there. Canada and Ireland were neighbours of larger, more-powerful aviation states, and both sought protection against their encroachments through international collaboration. And both lay directly in the path of the transatlantic route.

The British, meanwhile, were trying to compete with the Americans from a position of technological weakness. The American breakthrough in long-range aircraft was followed swiftly by British efforts to unite the British nations that held the key to the Atlantic crossing. Once the Commonwealth was brought together behind British leadership, a more favourable arrangement could be negotiated with the Americans. It was no coincidence that the Washington talks were immediately preceded by talks in Ottawa. Whereas the Canadians and Irish participated in the joint company because it gave them an entrée into the operation of a transatlantic service, the British sought Commonwealth unity with a view to countering the perceived American challenge on the North Atlantic air route.

One member of the Irish Department of External Affairs gave a perceptive analysis of British thinking in an unsigned memo written just after the Ottawa discussions. 'British prestige,' the memo suggested, 'required that Great Britain should participate in and dominate if possible the trans-atlantic service on the shortest route to America.' There was an element of concern in the memo, as well as bitterness. 'The British by bringing us into their Transatlantic Service are going to secure great advantages at a very small price. Apart from controlling the shortest route to America, they will have excluded the active independent rivalry of Pan-America, whose planes in the early stages at any rate could go from the Irish port to France without crossing British territory and dispense with British traffic. French and German rivals will have been equally effectively excluded from the direct route.'[83]

The 1935 Ottawa and Washington agreements were really only the beginning of a process that would last several years, yet they served to introduce Canadian negotiators to the realities of international civil aviation diplomacy. In another respect the agreements culminated almost four years of international negotiations on a route over which no airplanes were flying. Even in 1936-7 both sides were prevented from the operation of the transatlantic service: the Americans by politics, the British by technology.

Canada's geographical location was the primary reason for Canadian participation in the discussions – a circumstance that became perfectly clear during the quarrel over the Canadian port of call. J.A. Wilson, General McNaughton, and the other officials recognized this fact and tried to secure whatever advantages they could from a rather difficult situation. Without either a national airline or political leadership, however, these men were severely limited in what they could accomplish.

3 Atlantic Crossing

The three years of peace preceding the war, which people had long-feared but which most had come to see as inevitable, were crowded with a series of international crises. From 1937, the threatening clouds of war cast their long shadows over all aspects of European life. Canadians were affected, too. A modest rearmament policy was introduced and defence plans were drawn up by military leaders, while politicians scrambled to distance themselves from any association with conscription.

Canada's ability to conduct its civil aviation policy in the international arena was considerably strengthened in the late 1930s. Within a relatively brief period of time, civil aviation was reorganized as part of a new government department and a national airline had been created. More important, for the first time in its short history, civil aviation was singled out for special attention and received the strong political leadership that it desperately needed. By 1939 the foundation of an independent Canadian international civil aviation policy was in place.

I

'In the opinion of this Department,' Col. L.R. LaFlèche, the deputy minister of national defence wrote to O.D. Skelton, 'any further delay in reaching a decision in regard to airway development will place important Canadian interests in jeopardy. Before Canada can play any helpful part in the "Empire Air Mail Scheme" a decision on our policy is necessary in regard to the completion and operation of the trans-Canada airway and our attitude towards trans-Atlantic air services.'[1] LaFlèche was hardly alone in his opinions. By 1936 Canada had made a commitment to act in the field of international civil aviation and the officials in national defence, external affairs, and the interdepartmental committee were unanimous in their calls for government action on the promised national airline.

The first step taken by the new Liberal government was to transfer jurisdiction over civil aviation from the Department of National Defence (DND) to the newly created Department of Transport. The new department was the product of a merger of the departments of Marine and Railways and Canals with the addition of the civil aviation branch from the DND. The rearrangement was in the works for most of 1936 and officially came into being on 2 November. Within the Department of Transport, the Air Services Branch was subdivided into three parts: the Civil Aviation Division (which had its own internal subdivisions), the Radio Division, and the Meteorological Division. The minister of transport was given wide powers over all facets of aviation, including the determination of air routes. Because these powers extended to the negotiation of international services, the new minister inadvertently became an important actor in the conduct of Canadian external policy.[2]

Prime Minister King's choice for the new post of minister of transport was C.D. Howe, a political rookie who had served as minister of both the departments of Railways and Canals and Marine since the new government came to power in 1935. A native of Waltham, Massachusetts, and an engineering graduate from MIT, Howe came to Canada in 1908. After a few years of teaching at Halifax's Dalhousie University and working for the Board of Grain Commissioners, Howe struck out on his own and became very successful in grain-elevator construction. In 1935 he tried his hand at politics and was elected as a Liberal for Port Arthur, Ontario. A hard-working, self-made man with a businessman's mind, Howe brought the same qualities of energy and determination to his political career that he had displayed as a private citizen. As minister of transport, Howe personally guided the development of civil aviation in Canada and gave it the direction that it had been missing in the past.

Like many other Canadians, Howe had travelled south of the border to take advantage of the US transcontinental airlines to fly to the West Coast. The excitement and potential of air travel he already knew; as minister he recognized the possible danger of Canadian civil aviation being reduced to a feeder service for the larger American lines.[3] For Howe the solution was a national airline capable of meeting this US challenge. He was hardly committed to the concept of government ownership, but Howe was willing to do whatever he felt necessary to protect Canadian interests.

Howe participated in the cabinet committee that was formed to examine civil aviation, and long before he became minister of transport he had assumed the responsibility for developing its policy. As early as March 1936 the channel for the interdepartmental committee's recommendations ran through his office.[4] Howe liked to take a personal interest in his projects, to find out for himself everything there was to know. The creation of a national airline was no exception. As his biographers note: 'He consulted with officials and pilots of British Imperial Airways. He made forays across the border to inspect American air fields, to examine airmail facilities, and to climb aboard the Douglas DC-1's and Ford Trimotors. He asked questions about technology, profits and plans for the future. He basked in the company of the legendary Eddie Rickenbacker, head of Eastern Airlines, and Juan Trippe of Pan American. Clearly these men were already running large, successful North American enterprises. Theirs was the pattern he must bring to Canada.'[5]

The story of the creation of Trans-Canada Airlines (TCA) is well known and documented elsewhere: the attempts at bringing the two railways and Canadian Airways into a partnership; James Richardson's growing disillusionment with Howe's scheme; the withdrawal of the CPR; and finally, the decision to keep the airline in government hands and give the majority of shares to the CNR.[6] TCA was created first and foremost as a national carrier to link the major cities in Canada, but it is important for this study to bear in mind the international dimensions of its origins.

Under the terms of the 1935 agreement, Canada was committed to nominate an airline to fulfil its part of the bargain. There should be no surprise, therefore, that the decisions to approve the agreement and to finish the trans-Canada airway were made during the same cabinet meeting.[7] The difficulty of participating in international arrangements without a national air company had been made clear during the preceding years. Time and again the government was reminded by its officials and by those from other countries of this serious deficiency in Canada's ability to participate on the world stage. The wall that separated domestic and international civil aviation was never very high, and the roots of TCA can be found on both sides.

With respect to government ownership, if TCA was to act as Canada's chosen instrument – and Howe made it clear that it was – it might have to take on other responsibilities and operate some services in the national interest. Some degree of government control was essential, and control was easier to maintain over a public airline than a private one. Mackenzie King agreed, and noted in his diary, in relation to an earlier airline bill, that it 'seemed to me the bill was drafted to put air transportation too completely in the hands of the two railways; that it did not recognize sufficiently the need for Government ownership and control.'[8]

The bill to create TCA was introduced in the House of Commons on 22 March 1937 and received royal assent less than three weeks later on 10 April. 'I think most of us are aware of the necessity for such a service,' Howe explained to the House. 'Canada is perhaps one of the few countries in the world without a national scheduled air service.' There had been great advances in aviation in recent years, he continued, and a national airline 'would prove of immense value for national purposes. Canada is a country of vast distances and sparse population, and the time needed to travel between the west and the east is considerable under present circumstances. If that time could be cut in three or four by a new air service, the people living at the extremes of this country would be able to travel more frequently to the centres of government business, and industry, and the inter-relations of the country would thereby be facilitated.'[9]

The new company was incorporated with an authorized capital of $5,000,000, and the total issue of 50,000 shares was acquired by the CNR. The board of directors consisted of four individuals elected by the shareholders and three appointed by the government. The president of the CNR, J.S. Hungerford, became TCA's first president, while the responsibility for the operations of the new airline fell to vice-president Philip G. Johnson, a former president of United Airlines.[10] The government promised to cover the deficit for the new airline and TCA was given monopoly rights to operate the main transcontinental routes, leaving tributary or feeder services in private hands.

TCA's operations got off with a bang. On 30 July, C.D. Howe and a handful of friends and colleagues participated in a cross-country 'dawn-to-dusk' flight from Montreal to Vancouver. It was a historic flight, the first of its kind in Canada. Howe was criticized by competitors and knowledgeable insiders alike for acting in a foolhardy and dangerous manner, but it was just the kind of stunt that grabbed the headlines and gave the new airline a boost of favourable publicity.[11]

The first regularly scheduled service of Canada's new national airline was, ironically, an international one. In September 1937, TCA took over the Vancouver–Seattle service from Canadian Airways. The airline's operations were gradually expanded with airmail services across the prairies and between Montreal, Ottawa, and Toronto. A full-scale regularly scheduled passenger service between Montreal and Vancouver was inaugurated in April 1939. By February 1940 the service had been extended to Moncton, and, in April 1941, to Halifax. In 1937, TCA flew 122 route miles; by 1939 this number had risen to 3,666. The number of aircraft had jumped too, from five in 1937 to fifteen in 1939. Most of the services used the Lockheed Electra, a ten-passenger aircraft that cruised at approximately 175 mph. Before the war broke out, TCA had begun upgrading to the faster Lockheed 14H.[12]

In TCA, Canada had found its chosen instrument; in C.D. Howe, Canadian civil aviation had found its champion. For Howe and Mackenzie King there was room for only one major airline in Canada – TCA – and in the international field it was essential to establish that Canada's domestic aviation was under exclusive Canadian control. Howe had gained control of his department and put his views into action in the domestic field with the creation and defence of TCA. It was up to Mackenzie King, as prime minister and secretary of state for external affairs, to do the same in the international arena.

II

At almost the same time that C.D. Howe was piloting the TCA bill through the House of Commons, Mackenzie King was crossing the Atlantic bound for England to attend his first imperial conference since 1926. The prime minister and his delegation arrived in London in May 1937 ready to do what they could to preserve the peace and to improve Anglo-American relations, but unwilling to commit Canada to any common imperial foreign policy or, for that matter, to any action at all. On the surface, this position appeared to be at odds with the main purpose behind the conference – Great Britain's desire to enhance imperial co-operation in defence and foreign policy. Mackenzie King's point of view generally is seen to have prevailed; conversely, Neville Chamberlain, who became prime minister during the middle of the conference, is seen to have sacrificed any meaningful agreement in order to preserve a rather ambiguous 'Commonwealth unity,' in an effort to enhance Britain's influence and prestige in Europe.[13] Questions of foreign policy and defence dominated the 1937 Imperial Conference, but other matters were discussed, including civil aviation. One of the less-known forums for debate, for example, was the Committee on Civil Air Communications – established to examine ways of enhancing the development of civil aviation within the Commonwealth.

In advance of the imperial conference the British government prepared three documents on civil aviation, outlining the subjects it wanted to discuss: Commonwealth co-operation, consultation, and aircraft production. International civil aviation developed rapidly during the 1930s, especially in Europe, where exorbitant government subsidies had propped up unprofitable companies and air routes for reasons of prestige rather than need. The French, the Germans, the Dutch, and others had established air services across Europe, Asia, and Africa but, the memo warned, the 'first in the lead of the nations who are striving by lavish expenditure of public funds to achieve world domination in civil air transport' was the United States. 'Pan American Airways, which has secured the virtual monopoly of Government support for overseas operations can be seen extending its tentacles with rapidity over the globe.'[14]

Given this state of affairs, the British government believed that the imperial conference provided an excellent opportunity to consider ways for the empire to work together to meet the foreign challenge. 'Civil aviation,' it was pointed out, 'apart from the services which it directly renders to trade, is invested with a special publicity re-acting upon the whole national commerce ... It is moreover, unnecessary to labour the disadvantages incurred by late comers who are constrained to follow the strategy imposed by their competitors, to force their way into established systems and trade connections, and generally to maintain a disproportionate effort in order to secure a fair share of business.'[15]

The 'answer' to American and European competition, the British government believed, could be 'the establishment of a trunk route right round the world with arterial and subsidiary services radiating in all directions from important points.'[16] Envisaged was a continuous air service from Great Britain to India, via Egypt, then on to Australia and

New Zealand. The stretch from New Zealand to Vancouver would be long and difficult and would necessitate negotiations with the Americans for landing rights on Hawaii, but, nevertheless, should be considered. The route would continue across Canada and pass over Newfoundland and Ireland on its way back to Britain, along the lines set out in the 1935 agreement. Subsidiary lines would feed into the main line – two of the most important being from Egypt to South Africa and across West Africa to South America. Such a world-wide Commonwealth air service would produce immediate and real benefits for trade and security within the Commonwealth and would also enhance the prestige of all its members.

Closely linked to this first British goal was the desire for consultation among the members of the Commonwealth. Tough bargaining on bilateral agreements was inevitable and the empire had many geographical advantages that it could use as bargaining chips. What concerned the British government was the possibility of one part of the empire exchanging with a foreign government reciprocal rights that might exclude or put at a disadvantage another part of the empire. Everyone must be 'continually alive to the interdependence of the interests of the several Members of the Commonwealth and of the possibility that the interests of other Members may be affected by the grant of particular facilities to foreign air lines.' Because of this 'community of interests,' the British recommended that 'whenever a particular application is likely to affect another Member there should be consultation between the respective Governments concerned before facilities for foreign air services are granted.'[17]

The third tenet of the British position in 1937 concerned the production of civil aircraft. Not only was the US octopus spreading its tentacles around the globe, but the Americans had surged far ahead of Britain in aircraft production and design. Moreover, British civil aircraft production, after a decade of hard times, was further eclipsed in the late 1930s by the government's rearmament program, which naturally concentrated on military aircraft. At any rate, the Commonwealth remained an important market for British aircraft and it was hoped that Britain's competitive position could be preserved through an agreement 'in principle' that the 'use of foreign aircraft is disadvantageous to the general interests of the British Commonwealth.'[18]

It remained to be seen whether the other Commonwealth nations could be won over to the British position. Agreement would not be automatic; each country came with its own views and special concerns. The South Africans, for example, were uneasy with the British stance on aircraft production. Australia and New Zealand were naturally very interested in services across the Tasman Sea, and the New Zealanders were concerned that they not be bypassed in any transpacific service. The Australians had already experienced difficulties with the British over setting up the airmail route to Australia, and it was hoped that these problems could be cleared up at the conference. In addition, the Australians desired 'to secure a real measure of local control over services operating within Australia or in near parts in which Australia is particularly interested.'[19]

Canada's civil aviation policy during the conference was rooted in the same ideals as its defence and foreign policy. As Mackenzie King described it a few days into the conference: 'We must distinguish between a Conference and a Council; that we were not a Cabinet to frame policies for the Empire, but a Conference of Ministers to state our own position and see how far our policies could be brought toward some point of agreement.'[20] The other members of the Canadian delegation, including Ernest Lapointe, the minister of justice; C.A. Dunning, the minister of finance; Ian Mackenzie, the minister of national defence; and T.A. Crerar, the minister of mines and resources, supported King in his opposition to a common imperial foreign policy. For example, T.A. Crerar, who was Canada's representative on the Committee on Civil Air Communications, earlier wrote to J.W. Dafoe that Canada should remain aloof from any imperial entanglements: 'The more I see of the whole thing, the more I am certain that our destiny is on the North American continent and that if Europe is going to insist on destroying itself, it is no part of our mission to destroy ourselves in attempting to prevent it in doing so.'[21]

How did these sentiments apply to civil aviation? TCA would have to be defended, of course, and all imperial schemes to submerge the Canadian airline would have to be resisted. On the international routes, however, there was more room for manoeuvring. The need for co-operation was recognized in 1935 and had not changed in 1937; but no blanket endorsement of Commonwelath co-operation should be given. Finally, Canadian services to the United States must be recognized for their unique importance in the Canadian scheme of things.[22]

Mackenzie King had not undergone a conversion to a new position supporting a dynamic aviation policy. Overall, he was considerably less interested in the field of aviation than C.D. Howe was, but their views were complementary. King merely applied the same principles to civil aviation that he brought to everything else. Domestically, he did not want to repeat the mistakes made earlier in the century in Canadian railway policy and, therefore, TCA must be protected from Tories, imperialists, and private interests. Internationally, Canadians must be on guard against foreign entanglements and here, too, TCA must be protected from Tories, imperialists, and private interests.

Once the imperial conference officially opened, a number of committees were established to deal with specific issues that were outside the realm of the more-general questions dealt with in the plenary sessions. The Committee on Civil Air Communications (CCAC) was one such committee, and it was chaired by Sir Archdale Parkhill, the Australian representative. In addition, there were representatives from New Zealand, India, Burma, South Africa, Southern Rhodesia, the United Kingdom, and Canada. The Canadian representatives on the CCAC included Crerar and Dunning, along with Loring Christie and Colonel Smart, who had become deputy minister in the new Department of Transport. The British delegation was led by Lord Swinton, the air minister, and included, among others, Sir Francis Shelmerdine, J.E. Stephenson of the Dominions Office, and J.A.N. Barlow of the treasury.

Lord Swinton was a tough and experienced politician with a thick crust from the British upper class. Over the course of his career he appeared under several names – Sir Philip Lloyd-Greame, Sir Philip Cunliffe-Lister, Viscount Swinton, and, finally, the Earl of Swinton. He served as president of the Board of Trade and as Prime Minister Baldwin's colonial secretary before joining the Air Ministry in 1935. An empire man from the old school, Swinton had as his primary concern as air minister the maintenance of aircraft production on a par with Germany.[23]

The first meeting of the CCAC was held on the afternoon of 28 May 1937. The three British documents had already been distributed to the delegates and Lord Swinton led off with a brief overview of his government's position, noting that 'it would be impossible to exaggerate the importance of an Imperial chain of communications, to secure that personal contact between Governments and between individuals which it was the essential interest of the Commonwealth to maintain.' Swinton continued with a review of earlier Commonwealth negotiations, including the Empire Air Mail Scheme, the 1935 Ottawa agreement, and the Wellington Conference, which looked at schemes for air services crossing the Tasman Sea and Pacific Ocean. The other delegations responded with brief summations of their respective government's plans for the future development of civil aviation. There was widespread sympathy for the general idea of co-operation and consultation within the Commonwealth and, as a result, a subcommittee was created to draft a resolution for the committee based on the general discussion of two of the three British documents.[24]

The third document, dealing with aircraft production, ran into trouble from the very beginning. The Canadian government was not keen on enshrining in a resolution a promise to buy British aircraft because some aircraft had to be imported from the United States, in particular those equipped with pontoons or skis. More important, it seemed absurd to risk antagonizing the Americans by publishing such a resolution, even if it stated the obvious, that Canada would continue to buy British aircraft if possible. But it was the South Africans who were the most strongly opposed. The South Africans already bought many of their aircraft from the United Kingdom, but they also depended on other sources – hence, the proposed resolution 'was a perfectly unnecessary pronouncement, on a matter in which the Union were already co-operating to the maximum, which in the peculiar circumstances of South Africa was calculated to cause political trouble.'[25] Clearly there was little to gain but much to lose in passing the resolution; as a result the whole question of aircraft production was quietly dropped.

The subcommittee established by the CCAC at its 28 May meeting was chaired by Sir Francis Shelmerdine and included Colonel Smart as its Canadian representative. Within 48 hours the subcommittee had drafted a five-paragraph resolution that ran along fairly predictable lines. Briefly, the first two paragraphs called for the greatest possible amount of co-operation between governments, and recommended that the Commonwealth 'should pursue a vigorous policy of expansion of air services within each of its territories, interconnecting all its Members and leading to the establishment of a British route encompassing the Globe.' Paragraph 3, which caused some consternation among the Canadian representatives, read: 'While the importance of unity in organization must be borne in mind, the development of routes must be founded on the principle of partnership which should provide, where desired by Governments, a real measure of local control over services operating within their territories and in adjacent areas in which they are particularly interested.' The final two paragraphs dealt with consultation between governments, and reflected the 'all-for-one' nature of the original British document, the belief that facilities granted by one government to an outsider 'should only be secured by arrangement between the Commonwealth and foreign Governments concerned.'[26]

The subcommittee draft resolution was introduced during the second meeting of the CCAC, on 31 may. A number of minor changes were suggested and accepted, and, after further discussion, the committee endorsed the resolution.[27] That settled the matter, so far as Lord Swinton was concerned; two days later he informed the cabinet that he 'had hardly hoped for so good a result.' The CCAC resolution, he noted, was 'in favour of the Governments of the Empire always playing as a combined team.'[28] But Swinton's buoyancy was short lived. The following day, 3 June, at a meeting of the CCAC subcommittee set up to discuss Pacific services, Crerar informed the other members that his government had now had time to study the resolution and that it wished to reopen the whole question.[29]

There had been Canadian representatives on both the drafting committee and the CCAC when the resolution was adopted – why the about-face now? It is safe to assume that despite its rather innocuous content, the resolution's repeated reference to joint Commonwealth action was enough to ensure Mackenzie King's opposition to it. In any event, the Canadians responded with a hastily written draft resolution of their own. Gone were the references to united action; the Canadian draft argued that 'the most effective method of co-operation can best be settled by the Governments concerned in each particular case as it arises, with due recognition of the special interests of each Member in services in adjacent areas.'[30]

The Canadian difficulties with resolution 1 were discussed at the third meeting of the CCAC, on 4 June. Crerar repeated his government's objections, noting that the resolution 'was too rigid in its terms; that it put forward the proposition of developing all-British routes to the prejudice of others; that it did not take account of the necessity of building up air transport on the same broad and non-exclusive principles as had been employed in the case of shipping, and speaking frankly, that Canada's special geographical relations with the United

States rendered it necessary for them to cultivate friendly relations with that country. If the United States got the impression that there was a scheme for British commercial domination in the air, Canadian relations would be prejudiced in other matters.' Dunning added his voice to the conversation, but the words were Mackenzie King's. Canada, he said, 'would prefer not to lay down principles, but to consider the appropriate action in each individual case.'

Lord Swinton reacted with some surprise and bristled at the words 'British commercial domination in the air.' The draft resolution 'contained no suggestion of world domination,' he snapped, 'although other countries had made no secret of their ambitions in this regard. What was stated was that the British Empire should not come under the domination of other countries, but that Empire services should be in Empire hands and not in those of other people.'[31] Swinton continued with a defence of his policy of co-operation and consultation, but it was clear that he could get nowhere with the Canadians. It was agreed to throw the whole messy affair back to a subcommittee to draft a new version of the resolution.

The reconstituted subcommittee consisted primarily of ministers, and included Swinton, Crerar, H.P. Brown, the Australian director-general of postal services, and Walter Nash, New Zealand's minister of finance. Within 24 hours a watered-down version of the original resolution was ready. References to 'the British Commonwealth' were changed to read 'Members of the British Commonwealth'; calls for a 'British route encompassing the Globe' became 'embracing expansion within each of their territories and interconnection between Members.'[32] Co-operation was to be desired, not dictated.

Despite the softened tone of the resolution, however, the Canadians still had reservations, and, moreover, the Australians were unsatisfied with the changes introduced by the Canadians. These differences surfaced on 9 June, in the meeting of the Principal Delegates held in the Prime Minister's Room in the House of Commons. The Australian concerns centred on the Canadian reservation about paragraph 3, which dealt with local control of domestic services and those in adjacent countries. The Australians attached great importance to this paragraph, especially as it would pertain to their Darwin–Singapore service. Sir Archdale Parkhill argued that the paragraph 'could not harm Canada in any way,' and, because it meant so much to Australia, would the Canadians not withdraw their objections?

Mackenzie King was unmoved. Whereas the Australians felt it to be essential to include a reference to local control, the Canadians believed that the inclusion of any such reference indirectly raised the possibility that there might exist some instance where each government did not have complete domestic sovereignty. To the Canadians, local control was self-evident, and, therefore, it was unnecessary to refer to it. As the paragraph stood it 'would in effect throw a doubt upon Canada's complete control over air services within her own territories, and would thus be inconsistent with the relationship subsisting between Members of the British Commonwealth and with Canadian legislative action.' Perhaps, Mackenzie King suggested, a rewording would make the paragraph acceptable to both Canada and Australia; by replacing the word 'provide' with 'recognize' and omitting 'a real measure of' before the words 'local control,' any question of domestic sovereignty would be removed, and this would satisfy the Canadians. The Australians were agreeable, and paragraph 3 was passed in its amended form.[33]

Turning to paragraphs 4 and 5, Prime Minister Chamberlain asked Mackenzie King if there had been any change in the Canadian position. King responded with an attack on the two paragraphs, arguing that as they now were written they, first, gave the impression that the Commonwealth would act as a unit when negotiating with foreign countries (King obviously had the United States in mind here) and, second, could make it appear on occasion that one member was negotiating on behalf of another to secure reciprocal rights. Both these scenarios were unacceptable to the Canadians, who were adamant in their defence of Canada's right to bargain for itself at all times. When Sir Archdale Parkhill suggested that he could see nothing wrong in bargaining on each other's behalf, King responded sharply that 'it almost seemed as if they had different ideas of the British Commonwealth. If it was to become anything like a political unity, that would be a great change from the present conception of the Commonwelath, to put it mildly.'

Lord Swinton countered by noting that 'there had never been the slightest suggestion of any part of the Empire dictating to any other part.' In addition, he reminded King, this system of consultation worked well in 1935, when Britain, Ireland, Newfoundland, and Canada had agreed to co-operate before opening discussions with the

United States on the transatlantic air service. Swinton 'imagined that Canada would have felt aggrieved if they [the Canadians] had been left out and the air line had gone direct from Newfoundland to New York.' There was strength in unity, while, individually, the Commonwealth nations were less able to withstand foreign competition.

It was not that the Canadians were opposed to co-operation, it was just that they did not want to be committed to it beforehand. As Mackenzie King put it, he 'was in favour of agreement *ad hoc*, not of agreement in advance.'[34] In 1935 it suited the Canadians to co-operate, but surely this was a far cry from passing a resolution that dictated consultation in advance.

At this stage Chamberlain intervened. Thinking that there was still room for agreement, he felt that the best way to handle the situation would be to return the resolution to the CCAC to see if some rewording could satisfy the two sides. Chamberlain was more than willing to compromise on this issue, as on others, believing that the appearance of Commonwealth unity, however fragile, was preferable to public acknowledgment of division.[35] For Chamberlain, any agreement was better than no agreement at all.

Next morning the CCAC was back at it again. Over the night, the Canadians had discussed the situation and Crerar arrived at the meeting with three amendments to paragraphs 4 and 5, which, if accepted, would remove the Canadian reservations. First, the Canadians wanted 'Commonwealth' removed from before the word 'service' in the second clause, thus ensuring that it could not be misinterpreted as advocating a common service. Second, the last phrase of paragraph 4 dealt with reciprocal rights and contained the words 'Commonwealth service,' which would have to be omitted, the new ending to read: 'the reciprocal facilities agreed upon.' Finally, paragraph 5 also touched on the concept of reciprocal rights for other Commonwealth nations, but again reference to a 'Commonwealth air line' was removed and the section was amended to read: 'the concession expressly provides for reciprocal rights as and when desired.'[36]

In effect, this last amendment rendered the paragraph virtually meaningless, but there was little fight left in the other committee members. The amendments were agreed to, the Canadian reservations were withdrawn, and Sir Archdale Parkhill thanked everyone 'for the spirit of co-operation in which agreement had now been secured.'[37] Unanimity had been preserved; the work of the Committee on Civil Air Communications was over.

A survey of the CCAC's report, dated 10 June 1937, gives the reader evidence of the divergence of Canadian and British aviation policies only indirectly, through its impotence (see appendix 1). In an effort to achieve some form of unity, all points of difficulty were either removed or ignored. No agreement was reached on aircraft production or the Pacific or Tasman Sea services, and while everyone agreed that the Commonwealth nations should co-operate and consult with one another, nowhere did it say that they were obligated to do so.

Unfortunately for the Canadians, they were cast in the role of opposition from the very start of the discussions. Unfortunate yes – but also largely their own fault. The British representatives arrived at the first meeting armed with three documents outlining their position and what they hoped to achieve in the committee, and these documents served as the basis of discussion and the raw material on which the committee's resolutions were based. The British set the agenda for the committee, and despite the fact that an Australian was in the chair, Lord Swinton and his colleagues were in control of the proceedings throughout.[38] Conversely, the Canadians had no counter-proposals prepared in advance and thus were forced to react to the British proposals rather than initiating their own.

The Canadian delegation participated in the CCAC and endorsed its final report, but the interests of the participating nations were less than completely homogeneous. The Canadians in particular were reluctant to make the kind of commitment to Commonwealth aviation desired by Great Britain and the other participants. Canadian views were largely the product of an increasing awareness of Canada's unique position in civil aviation matters vis-à-vis the United States; the Canadians were intent on distancing themselves from imperial ties in order to negotiate better with the Americans. From the perspective of a one-to-one relationship with the United States, any obligation to act in concert with the Commonwealth or to negotiate for reciprocal rights became a burden to be avoided. If nothing else, the civil aviation discussions in 1937 gave an indication of the increasing distance between the United Kingdom and Canada in these matters, and, furthermore, they foreshadowed many of the problems that would emerge later, during the crucial Commonwelath negotiations on civil aviation that took place during the Second World War.

III

Work on the transatlantic services continued slowly for most of 1937–8. In June 1937 an air service was inaugurated between Bermuda and Port Washington, on Long Island outside of New York. The anticipated experimental flights on the northern route commenced in July. Meanwhile, the British government began developing two bases in Newfoundland for use in the transatlantic service: a seaplane base at Botwood and an air-base at Gander. In Ireland the Irish government began the construction of airfields at Shannon and Dublin.[39]

To facilitate international co-operation, an ad hoc interdepartmental committee was established in London with British, Irish, and Canadian representatives. Here, disputes arising from the Atlantic service preparations were ironed out, and, in addition, some planning was undertaken for the establishment of the JOC.[40] Inquiries from third countries were channelled through this body. The French government, for example, made several representations to the Canadians and British for permission to establish a transatlantic service. The French still directed most of their attention to the Azores, but hoped to have the option of using the northern route. Permission was granted eventually for an experimental service, but the war intervened before it had begun operations. The German government also showed interest and requested permission for a Lufthansa service to New York and for permission for the zeppelin *Von Hindenburg* to fly over Canadian territory. Again permission was granted on a temporary basis, but no regular service was in operation before the outbreak of war.[41]

In March 1938 an international conference was held in Dublin to look at the technical aspects of the transatlantic services. C.P. Edwards represented Canada and he helped in the organization of radio and meteorological services. Further experimental flights were undertaken that summer by both Imperial Airways and Pan Am, and some revisions to the 1935 Washington agreement were discussed.[42] But a regular service was not in operation until the next year.

Late in 1938 Pan Am received the first of the six Boeing 314s it had ordered in 1936. The Boeing 314 flying boat 'looked like a potbellied flying fish,' as one pair of authors described it, but it could fly the Atlantic with a load of more than two-dozen passengers – far more than any British competitor.[43] An agreement with the French government for an Atlantic air service was negotiated, and in May 1939 a Boeing 314, dubbed the *Yankee Clipper*, took off for Marseilles via the Azores and Lisbon.

Meanwhile, American impatience with the British was growing. Earlier in 1939 Pan Am asked if the reciprocal provision of the agreement with Imperial Airways could be waived in order for a Pan Am service to London to begin. The British had their own suspicions of Pan Am and some officials in the Air Ministry and Foreign Office suspected that the Americans were merely bluffing and, in fact, did not have the necessary aircraft to begin a service at that time.[44] For their part, the British were experiencing severe technical problems, which continued to hamper the inauguration of a service.

In any event, Pan Am finally opened its New York–Southampton service on 28 June 1939. Six weeks later, on 5 August, the British reciprocated with the introduction of transatlantic service to Montreal and New York, using two Short s.30 flying boats, the *Caribou* and *Cabot*. The Short s.30s used refitted Harrow bombers stationed at Shannon and Gander for refuelling in mid flight. The contrast with the American Boeings was dramatic: the use of mid-flight refuelling was, one American author wrote, 'a novel and interesting operation, but also somewhat pathetic. Requiring a minimum of three airplanes, it was a poor substitute for one good airplane which could fly the route without such elaborate support. It had no commercial future. This may be viewed as a desperate effort to put some form of British aviation across the Atlantic before the end of 1939 – a year which belonged to the *Yankee Clipper*.'[45] If nothing else, the inauguration of the two transatlantic air services revealed that on the eve of the Second World War the large gap between Great Britain and the United States in aircraft design and technology remained.

Early transatlantic flight was an adventure at the best of times, but luckily these first flights went off without difficulty. One of the earliest Pan Am passengers was a young Canadian official, Lester Pearson, who was returning to England only a few days before the outbreak of war. In his memoirs he recalled the experience: 'Only once did I doubt my good sense in rushing back by air. We had had to come down at Shediac, New Brunswick, because of engine trouble. When we took off again we ran into a fierce North Atlantic storm. I was in an upper berth in the plane, and feeling very miserable for I was then as prone to air-sickness as to sea-sickness. I looked out of a small oval window into the black night and found that we were flying only a few hundred feet above the wild waves. I hoped the engine had been well and truly repaired and I said to myself, "What the devil are you doing here?"[46]

In total, eight round trips were undertaken by Imperial Airways during the first season (compared to over one hundred by Pan Am on its two services) – not enough to meet the description of a 'regular service' under the terms of the 1935 agreement. The service was stopped for the winter and the lack of aircraft prevented its resumption on any regular basis the following year (the two flying boats, the *Caribou* and *Cabot*, for example, were destroyed during the campaign in Norway).[47] The JOC was not established and, because of the war, the British government felt that its formation should be held in abeyance until a regular service was more practicable. Nevertheless, the British government reaffirmed its desire to maintain the agreement.[48]

With the outbreak of war in September 1939 the development of civilian transatlantic services was put on hold. American neutrality legislation made it more difficult for Pan Am to continue its service to Britain. The German service to South America was suspended in 1939 and Air France followed suit in 1940. The war also marked the end of the era of the flying boat. The advent of the pressurized cabin in aircraft (which permitted comfortable flying at high altitudes) effectively made the low-flying seaplane obsolete. In 1940 Pan Am began the long transition from sea- to land-planes when it put in an order for several Lockheed Constellations. The last flight of the *Bermuda Clipper* landed in New York on Christmas Eve, 1945.[49]

Canadian civil aviation on the eve of war was in a far more stable position than it had been a mere three years earlier. The reorganization of air services in the new Department of Transport and the creation of TCA put in place the machinery through which Canadians could conduct a proper international civil aviation policy. Under the watchful eyes of C.D. Howe and Mackenzie King, Canadian interests had been protected in the international arena while, at home, the new airline had been nursed along through its early growing pains. Still, in 1939, Canadians faced an uncertain future; even the determined watch-dogs of Canadian international civil aviation policy stopped to hold their breaths.

4 Connecting the Capitals

Between 1939 and 1945 international civil aviation rose and fell on the surging tides of war. As nations were overrun by the Axis powers, their domestic airlines either folded or escaped to safety in Allied lands. German and Japanese services, by way of contrast, followed their victorious armies into occupied territories, only to shrink again with the turn of the tide and the liberation of Europe and Asia. Air France collapsed in 1942, although some colonial services were maintained by the Free French. KLM was reduced to colonial services in 1940 and eventually disappeared, only to be resurrected in 1945. Sabena's fleet of aircraft escaped before the Nazi occupation and served the military effort from its new base in London.[1]

In Britain, the outbreak of the war intervened in a long period of reorganization of civil aviation. In 1935-6 a group of small independent domestic airlines came together to form a new company, named British Airways, and negotiated a number of mail contracts and subsidies to operate some of those routes that Imperial Airways had neglected. British Airways thus became a kind of second chosen instrument, which only added to the serious problems that faced Imperial Airways. To sort out the mess, in November 1937 a committee was established under Lord Cadman to investigate Imperial Airways' troubles. In its report, the Cadman committee called for the revamping of the national airline and for a greater government commitment to civil aviation. Woods Humphrey resigned as managing director and Sir John Reith was appointed to the chair of Imperial Airways. Reith then worked for the amalgamation of Imperial Airways with the fledgling British Airways, and his efforts were successful: British Overseas Airway Corporation (BOAC) was created by an act of

Parliament in August 1939. The new company officially began operations on 1 April 1940.[2]

British civil aviation was almost totally mobilized for the war effort. All available aircraft were requisitioned for home defence and military use. BOAC's services to the continent were stopped, naturally, and the routes across the Atlantic and south through Lisbon were restricted to urgent war-related duties. Many of the colonial services were maintained (across Africa, for example) and gradually improved as the fortunes of war turned in the Allies' favour.

American civil aviation also underwent a period of transition shortly before the war. With the creation of the Civil Aeronautics Administration in 1938, the regulation, inspection, and development of aviation were removed from the Aeronautics Branch of the US Department of Commerce. Two years later, in 1940, the Civil Aeronautics Board (CAB) was organized to control air fares, to oversee domestic route scheduling, to act as a watch-dog over mergers, and to prevent collusion between airlines.[3] The CAB threw itself into the raging debate between the supporters of competition on international routes and those who subscribed to the doctrine of the chosen instrument.

In 1940, American Export Airlines applied for a permit to operate a transatlantic service and the CAB granted it (on the Azores–Lisbon route), apparently with the approval of President Roosevelt. The service was effectively blocked by Pan Am, however, which wished to preserve the exclusive international agreements it had negotiated with foreign governments. In the face of the American Export challenge, Juan Trippe mobilized his friends in Congress to veto the new airline's airmail subsidies, without which the operation of a transatlantic service was virtually impossible.[4] This tension between rival groups remained a primary factor in American civil aviation for the duration of the war.

Because of American neutrality, the War Department was restricted in what it could do in foreign states, but this was not the case for Pan Am. In November 1940 Pan Am received a War Department contract to construct seaplane bases and airfields in Latin America and the Caribbean. Several of these bases were constructed on the base sites acquired from the British in the destroyers-for-bases deal of September 1940. An additional contract was negotiated to establish a transatlantic route from South America to Africa for the transfer of men, cargo, and aircraft to North Africa. In all, Pan Am built forty airfields in Latin and

Central America and helped to ferry hundreds of bombers across Africa all the way to Khartoum. It was an ideal arrangement, for Pan Am had only recently begun a conversion to land-planes for which such airfields were needed. Now the US government was going to pay for them.[5] In 1939 Pan Am's route system totalled 62,305 miles; in 1941 it had climbed to 98,582 miles, twice that of BOAC and more than all European services combined.[6]

After Pearl Harbor most American airlines cut back domestic services and undertook war-related work. In June 1942 the US Air Transport Command (USATC) was established and it took over 200 of the estimated 365 civilian transport planes in the United States. Pan Am continued to operate in Latin America, the Pacific, and Atlantic, and other airlines were given the opportunity to operate internationally. Northeast Airlines began flying to Newfoundland, Greenland, and Iceland; Northwest Airlines began flying to Alaska; and Eastern Airlines was granted a service to the Caribbean. American Airlines, already the largest domestic carrier, bought American Export Airlines and assumed its transatlantic service.[7] These airlines acquired a taste for international flying that would remain long after the war had ended.

Almost everyone flew during the war. The many advantages of aviation over surface transportation – speed, safety from enemy submarines, and flexibility in choice of route – were readily apparent. Old fears were overcome and air travel became the standard mode of transportation. In August 1941 Prime Minister King took his very first flight – a transatlantic voyage in a Liberator bomber. In January 1942 Prime Minister Churchill flew to the United States to meet with President Roosevelt. The next year Roosevelt became the first president to cross the ocean during wartime to attend the Casablanca conference. 'Amazing,' he declared after his first transatlantic flight. 'Wednesday in Liberia, Thursday in Brazil. And I don't like flying, not one bit. The more I do of it, the less I like it.'[8]

At the same time, the exigencies of war produced startling advances in the technology of flight. Airplanes could fly faster and farther, and the possibility of flight providing a popular and affordable means of transoceanic transportation was no longer unimaginable. Nowhere was this more clearly demonstrated than in the formation of the Atlantic Ferry Organization (Atfero) in 1940–1. In an effort to link American aircraft production with Britain's wartime needs, Atfero was established to transport the new American airplanes overseas. Thanks to the efforts of Lord Beaverbrook, the British minister of aircraft production, Canadian Pacific Air Services was created to help undertake this huge task. Canadian Pacific was eventually replaced by the RAF and the end result was a multi-staged ferry route with air-bases in Newfoundland, Greenland, and Iceland that aided in the transfer of thousands of fighters and long-range bombers. By the end of the war, transatlantic flight, at least for military purposes, had become commonplace.

Canadian pilots played a significant role in Atfero and its successors Ferry Command and No. 45 RAF Transport Command, and in many ways Canada more than kept pace with the expansion of aviation. Within a few short years the RCAF had grown into one of the world's most powerful air forces. At home, thanks largely to the British Commonwealth Air Training Plan, thousands of young men had been recruited and trained as pilots and flight crews, and airports and ground facilities had been constructed across the country.[9]

By the end of the war, moreover, the Canadian aircraft industry had been resuscitated and expanded. In 1939 the industry employed roughly 4000 men and women and produced approximately 40 aircraft; at its peak during the war it employed 116,000 and annual production rose to 4000 airplanes. A variety of bombers and fighter aircraft were produced by Canadian Vickers Limited, de Havilland Aircraft of Canada, Noorduyn Aviation Limited, and a handful of other companies, although Canadian production was limited to the airframes only – all the engines were imported.[10]

Canadian civil aviation, although submerged in the war effort, by no means disappeared. The airports and facilities being built across the country would produce long-term benefits for domestic aviation. In Newfoundland, meanwhile, the Canadian government assumed the responsibility for Gander airport and undertook the construction of Torbay airport near St John's and of the massive Goose Bay air-base in Labrador. These airports were built for military use, of course, but also with one eye on their post-war importance for civil aviation purposes.

TCA's trans-Canadian network was completed by 1941 and, in May 1942, it was extended to Newfoundland with the inauguration of a regularly scheduled service to St John's. For many politicians and bureaucrats in Ottawa this was only the beginning: the war had broadened their horizons and their plans for TCA. Attention turned to the allied capitals of Washington and London.

I

Canadian-American civil aviation relations during the Second World War were defined by a series of conferences and exchange of notes in 1938, 1939, and 1940. The first conference, held in Washington in January 1938, extended the 1929 agreement and covered general aspects of civil aviation: customs, the carriage of photographic equipment, the issuance of certificates, the observance of air law in the other's territory, etc. A further understanding was reached in August of the following year, through an exchange of notes setting out traffic rights for each country.[11]

The division of specific transborder services was left for a third conference, this time in Ottawa in September 1940. Described by one author as a 'session of horse-trading,'[12] the two nations exchanged rights to operate services into each other's countries. These were monopoly rights; there was agreement on both sides that the anticipated traffic would not be sufficient to justify competing services. The Americans received most of the routes, including Bangor–Moncton, Buffalo–Toronto, Great Falls, Montana–Lethbridge, and from any US point to Windsor. In exchange, Canada received the Toronto–New York service and the right to operate from anywhere in Canada to Detroit. The agreement expired on 31 December 1942 and in February 1943 the Cabinet War Committee extended it until the end of the war.[13]

There were a number of other Canadian-American agreements negotiated primarily for military use – on the Atlantic ferry route, for example. Permits were also granted to the United States for operating on the Northwest Staging Route, a series of airfields and facilities constructed in western Canada between the continental United States and Alaska. Although both routes were utilized exclusively for the war effort, few observers could fail to see their potential as future civilian routes to Asia and Europe.[14]

The other civilian route that attracted a good deal of attention (at least on the Canadian side) during the war was the proposed air service to Washington. With the entrance of the United States into the war in December 1941, the amount of official business between Ottawa and Washington grew enormously. The smoke had hardly cleared from

Pearl Harbor before an Ottawa–Washington air service was mooted by a few Canadian officials (those who had to travel back and forth between Ottawa and Washington were especially keen).[15]

The first suggestions for a Washington service were never acted on, but in 1943, when American Airlines applied for a permit to operate a service to Ottawa, the question was revived. Such a route was not included in the 1940 agreement and would, therefore, have to be negotiated; and for some bureaucrats the Canadian case for its operation was clearly superior to the American. 'It would seem to me off hand to be more equitable that if a commercial service between Ottawa and Washington is established,' one official wrote, 'it should be established by a Canadian rather than a United States airline company since at present Canada is running only one line to the United States whereas the United States is running seven lines to Canada. Moreover, since the United States entered the war we have granted transit air rights over Canada to Alaska and the United Kingdom respectively for Pan American and American Export on the plea of wartime necessity and we have not so far asked for any rights from the United States on the same grounds.'[16]

The main opposition to a Washington service came not from the United States but rather from inside the Canadian government. On one side ranged Leighton McCarthy, the Canadian minister in Washington, Lester Pearson, also stationed in Washington, and a number of officials in the Department of External Affairs who agreed that an air service to Washington would constitute a great saving in time and money. On the other side there was an assortment of officials from TCA and the Department of Transport, including J.A. Wilson and C.P. Edwards, who felt that the potential traffic just did not warrant the effort and cost of a new air service. More important, there was little ministerial support for the service – Howe in particular was lukewarm to the idea.[17]

When it became clear that the Department of Transport and TCA were not keen, the supporters of the service turned to the RCAF to see if a strictly military service could be initiated. The approach to the RCAF was equally unsuccessful, but this did not end the debate. Early in 1944 the Washington legation prepared a lengthy memorandum reviewing the pros and cons of the proposed service and outlining its costs (and savings), hoping to revive the discussion once more.[18] Some interest was generated, and finally, on 7 June 1944, a proposal for an

Ottawa–Washington air service was introduced to the Cabinet War Committee (CWC). Arnold Heeney, the secretary of the CWC, set out what was being proposed: a wartime air service operated by the RCAF for mail and official passengers only. Howe's feelings on the service had not changed significantly and he reminded the other ministers that his department had been approached by a number of American companies to operate the service. In his view the government would be better off letting an American airline operate the route in exchange for a really valuable service – Toronto–Chicago was what he had in mind.[19] There was no debate. As usual, Howe got his way.

Howe's opposition effectively blocked any chance for a Canadian service to Washington until the end of the war, when presumably, the 1940 Canadian-American arrangements would be renegotiated. Nevertheless, the idea did not completely disappear, and memos continued to be written expounding the virtues of an Ottawa–Washington air service. The politicians and the bureaucrats could not come together over the service to Washington; they could agree, however, with respect to the proposed service to the other Allied capital – London.

II

At first the Canadians played within the ground rules set down at Ottawa in 1935, but by 1941–2 this position had become increasingly untenable. The 1935 agreement was suitable as long as Canada had neither the men nor the material and was incapable of running its own transatlantic service, but by 1942 this was no longer true. Moreover, because the Joint Operating Company had never been created, the Canadians received few benefits from the transatlantic service, yet Canada was still obliged to provide ground services for the BOAC and Pan Am routes. More important, international aviation was changing so dramatically because of the war that it was evident that a much wider international agreement would be necessary for the post-war period. These developments were beyond the scope of anything imagined in 1935, and Mackenzie King, Howe, and others in the Canadian government were determined to approach the new world of aviation free of any antiquated or burdensome arrangements. Circumstances had changed significantly, indeed, and increasingly the 1935 agreement looked ineffective and outdated to the Canadian government.

Clearly the Canadian government's shifting perception of Canada's role in international aviation and its commitments under the 1935 agreement were on a collision course, and the first signs of a rupture came in 1941. With the increased size of the Canadian military establishment overseas, the need for Canadian officials and military personnel to cross the Atlantic grew as well. Flying overseas rather than going by sea quickly gained preference because it was safer and much faster. Personal experience convinced C.D. Howe; in December 1940 he spent several hours tossing on the open seas after the ship he was sailing on was torpedoed by enemy submarines.[20]

In contrast, it was a relatively easy task getting overseas by air because there were hundreds of planes being flown over the Atlantic ferry route to Britain. The real crunch came in securing a seat for the return flight. Only Pan Am and BOAC had services, and returning pilots had priority, especially on BOAC aircraft. In London, Canada House was inundated with requests for one of the few available seats from Canadian personnel on urgent business. Likewise, diplomatic mail and other cargo that was required immediately in Canada were forced to suffer long delays or travel the more circuitous and dangerous ocean voyage.

The recipient of most of these requests was Vincent Massey, Canada's high commissioner in the United Kingdom. In Massey's view the long delays in waiting for space on British or American flights had become intolerable. In fact, he reported to Ottawa, things had gotten so bad that 'sea passage with all its attendant delays and difficulties has now become the quicker and more dependable means of communication.' Massey brought this problem to the attention of the Canadian government late in 1941, and on 6 December he offered a solution. Perhaps the time had come, he wrote, for Canada to establish its own transatlantic air service. This way more space could be allocated to Canadian needs, and Canadian personnel would have a reasonable guarantee that overseas appointments could be made and kept with relative security.[21]

Copies of Massey's dispatch were circulated to several Canadian ministers and officials, including Howe, C.P. Edwards, C.G. 'Chubby' Power, the minister of national defence for air, and J.L. Ralston, the minister of national defence. Howe and Edwards agreed with Massey's suggestion, but pointed to a number of problems, the main one being the difficulty in securing the aircraft necessary to operate such a service. TCA had no aircraft to spare and at this time the Canadian aviation industry did not manufacture the appropriate long-range airplanes. In addition, the possibility of procuring these aircraft from the British government was slim; the RCAF was already experiencing difficulties in obtaining sufficient aircraft for its enlarged plans for home defence.[22]

C.G. Power also supported the idea in theory, but believed that the problems facing it were insurmountable. The only suitable aircraft, he noted, were manufactured in the United States, and to acquire them the Canadians would have to go through the Munitions Priority Board in Washington, and it was unlikely that the Americans would release these aircraft. Likewise, the creation of a parallel service would probably be in violation of the 1935 agreement, which stipulated that Canada contribute to a joint service, not establish one on its own. Thus, Power suggested that Canada try to work within the existing system and approach the British government to make available additional space on British flights for Canadian government business.[23]

Massey found the British sympathetic to the Canadian predicament, but, while they were always willing to do what they could, they felt it would be impossible to allocate a specific amount of space on BOAC flights for Canadian needs. The British did promise to take Canadian requirements into consideration, but for Massey this was not sufficient. In April 1942 he reported to Ottawa that 'in view of the urgent demand for speedy transportation for Canadian official personnel and mails, further consideration should be given to proposal previously advanced for an all-Canadian service.'[24]

Massey did not let up. On the contrary, he continued to inform Ottawa of the difficulties in securing space on BOAC flights. Clearly, Massey's concern was deeply rooted, and he saw a larger significance in having an independent air service. In his view, Canada would be much better prepared to face the uncertainties of peace if, when the war ended, the Canadian government already had in place an established route to Britain. Massey was well aware that this was what other countries were doing, and he felt that Canada must do the same. In particular, he was concerned with the creation of US routes across the Canadian north. While these projects were undertaken as part of the war effort, once the war was over, all 'they have to do is to repaint their planes and change the clothes of their crews and they will have

Connecting the Capitals 83

their civil routes in being directly peace is declared.'[25] In many ways, during his years as high commissioner in London, Massey appeared out of step with Ottawa, but not with respect to the transatlantic air service. Perhaps it was because he had to deal with flight requests on a daily basis, but Massey was one of the first and most adamant supporters of an independent Canadian transatlantic air service.

Massey's proposals were brought up before the Cabinet War Committee on 22 May 1942. The prime minister reiterated Massey's charge that the British 'could hold out no hope of improved service,' and King suggested that consideration be given to the creation of an independent service. There was little ministerial opposition or discussion of this matter, but two important decisions were made. First, it was agreed that an interdepartmental committee be established to look into the feasibility of such a project. Second, it was recognized that an independent service might contravene the 1935 agreement, and as a result, it was decided that Canada should withdraw from it.[26]

It was easy enough to establish committees and to discuss the need to end the 1935 agreement, but without the necessary aircraft, little action could be taken. The Americans would be difficult; commercial flights in the United States were being cut back. Why should they give the Canadians aircraft to operate in competition with Pan Am? In any event, there were indications that a more likely source for the aircraft would be the British. Already there had been informal hints that the British might be willing to make available two Liberators for Canadian use in the transatlantic service.[27]

The source of this information was Harold Balfour, the parliamentary under-secretary of state in the Air Ministry. Balfour was in Canada on official business and during the first week of June he met with Howe and H.J. Symington, the president of TCA, to discuss the problems of the transatlantic service. Balfour would most likely not have supported an independent Canadian transatlantic air service, but he was willing to meet the Canadians half-way. He formally offered the Canadians two Liberators for TCA use and a tentative agreement was reached that at first appeared to meet Canadian needs. The planes would remain British property but would bear TCA markings and be operated by TCA crews. One of the main duties of the TCA flights, of course, would be to ferry pilots back to North America. The remaining space would then, ostensibly, be made available for Canadian needs.[28]

This agreement was greeted initially with a good deal of enthusiasm.

Norman Robertson, the under-secretary of state for external affairs, wrote to C.P. Edwards that this action would 'constitute the beginning of an all-Canadian service.'[29] Others, too, saw equally profound implications. J.R. Baldwin, the assistant secretary to the CWC, believed that the agreement would 'demonstrate' TCA's 'ability to operate such a service. In other words,' he continued, 'the present arrangement should prove the opening wedge in establishing a Canadian Transatlantic service.'[30] There appeared to be no doubt in anyone's mind that the ultimate goal was an independent service.

This new arrangement appeared beneficial because it brought TCA into the workings of the transatlantic service without having to wait for the creation of the JOC, but it was not clear that it would solve the problems enumerated by Vincent Massey. Although operated by TCA, these planes were to remain within the existing BOAC organization and space allocation was to rest in the hands of the Air Ministry.[31] As for providing for Canadian needs, the British would promise only 'so far as is practicable, we will endeavour, when prominent Canadian ministers or officials are travelling, to get them onto a Canadian-manned aircraft.'[32]

This was small comfort to dissatisfied Canadians to whom the Howe-Balfour agreement increasingly appeared like a double-edged sword. Granted, it would bring TCA into the operation of a transatlantic service and enhance the company's reputation, but chances were that it would solve only marginally the shortage problem. There were implications for the future to be taken into account as well, and for Vincent Massey, this latter aspect was crucial. He informed Ottawa that this new deal 'would not change the situation,' unless Canada House could allocate the space on the planes. Even then this right would probably not be enough: 'I do not think that the importance of the longer range considerations involved can well be exaggerated and I strongly feel that without establishment of a Canadian service now the relative position of Trans-Canada Airlines would be difficult to maintain in the future.'[33]

In the meantime, the Interdepartmental Committee on International Civil Aviation (ICICA), which included Robertson, Baldwin, Edwards, Symington, J.A. Wilson, and Escott Reid, was created. Several of these individuals had very little previous experience dealing with aviation matters, but, in any event, the ICICA evolved into the key working group (on the official level) for the development of Canadian international civil aviation policy.

J.A. Wilson and C.P. Edwards had been involved in civil aviation matters for many years, and, in contrast to the younger members of the committee, showed less interest in the theoretical side of policy making than in the practical requirements of daily operations. Herbert Symington was quite different. A corporate lawyer whose 'mild, round face and pince-nez belied his strength and astuteness,'[34] Symington joined the board of directors of the CNR in 1936, and the following year was appointed as a CNR director on the TCA board. Symington's abilities were noticed by C.D. Howe and in 1941 he took over as president of TCA. An indefatigable worker, Symington stayed on as president until 1947, and, incredibly, never received any salary for all his years of service.[35]

The other members of the committee represented a younger generation of officials who came to the fore in the public service during the Second World War. At the top of this list was Norman Robertson. Vancouver-born and Oxford-trained, Robertson joined the Department of External Affairs in 1929 and participated in the 1932 Imperial Economic Conference (although not with civil aviation matters). Robertson's 'skills as a negotiator were exemplary,' his biographer wrote; 'his ability to move in step with the political leadership in Ottawa almost uncanny, and he found that he had the fortunate knack of being able to get on with King.'[36] Following the death of O.D. Skelton in 1941, Robertson took over as under-secretary. With the job came direct access to the prime minister and from this moment on virtually all bureaucratic input on civil aviation affairs flowed through Norman Robertson.

Escott Reid was a contemporary of Robertson's. The son of an Anglican clergyman and an Oxford student with moderate left-wing views, Reid served as national secretary for the Canadian Institute of International Affairs for several years in the 1930s, before joining the DEA in 1938. A man of boundless energy and ideas, Reid brought his tremendous enthusiasm and interest for international affairs and international organizations to every task he faced. Without a doubt, the bulk of original ideas on civil aviation to emerge from the ICICA – sometimes brilliant, often impracticable – came from the mind of Escott Reid.[37]

If Reid was a visionary, then John R. Baldwin was a pragmatist. Baldwin was a few years younger than Robertson and Reid, but like his colleagues he won a Rhodes Scholarship to study at Oxford. After teaching history at McMaster University, Baldwin followed Reid as national secretary in the CIIA. In 1941 he joined the DEA and the following year was appointed assistant secretary to the Cabinet War Committee. Through his involvement on a number of economic committees, Baldwin was introduced to Howe and Symington, and with the creation of the ICICA he was appointed its secretary. He had no background in civil aviation other than a few airplane flights, so Symington sent him out to TCA headquarters in Winnipeg to learn the practical side of aviation. 'My vision was international,' he recalled, but 'my approach became rapidly much more pragmatic as I moved into this medium.' Unlike Reid, Baldwin easily adapted to the ways of his mentors – Howe and Symington. 'I have to admit,' he explained, 'that I very rapidly began to adjust my thinking as I became, shall we say, more familiar with *their* outlook, and with the practical problems that were involved.'[38]

The ICICA held its first meetings near the end of June 1942. By 7 July a draft dispatch dealing with the withdrawal of Canada from the 1935 agreement was drawn up and agreed to over the telephone by the ICICA members.[39] Two recommendations were offered. The first suggested that a request be sent to the British government for a guarantee that a specific amount of space be set aside for Canadian needs before an acceptance of the Howe-Balfour agreement was made. This plan was dropped, however, because of the opposition of C.D. Howe, who argued that it was clearly understood during the talks that the power to allocate space would remain where it had always been – with the Air Ministry.[40] Second, the ICICA suggested that the US government be approached informally to supply the two aircraft considered necessary for a weekly service.[41] This idea was rooted in the belief that the only solution to the problem – for now and in the future – was the inauguration of an independent transatlantic air service. What the ICICA had in mind was somewhat similar to the proposal for the service to Washington: a wartime service operated by TCA. Once the war was over, it could be easily converted into a commercial line, but until then it should be for official government business only.

The wheels of change were put in motion over the summer months of 1942, but they were slow in turning. Little action had been taken in the wake of the Howe-Balfour discussions, and in September, Howe and Ralston left for Britain, where it was expected that Howe would discuss matters pertaining to the transatlantic service with his British counterparts. Meanwhile, on 26 September, the Canadian high commissioners in London, St John's, and Dublin were informed of the Canadian government's decision to withdraw from the 1935 agreement.[42] There had arisen a degree of confusion in government circles over the relationship between the plans for an independent service and the 1935 agreement. The ICICA proposed service was for government, not commercial, purposes and was ostensibly to last only for the duration of the war. Was this permissible under the terms of the 1935 agreement? Or did the Canadian government have to terminate the agreement first? At any rate, there were no clear answers to these questions in September 1942, and it was considered wise to keep the two issues separate as much as possible. Consequently, the high commissioners were told to withhold notifying the foreign governments of Canada's anticipated withdrawal from the 1935 agreement until after Howe had completed his trip.[43]

While in London, Howe met with Massey and a number of other officials on 10 October to discuss the question of a transatlantic air service. All agreed that an independent service was 'highly desirable.' What opposition there might be would probably come from the Air Ministry, stemming from its desire 'to keep post-war control of the Atlantic air routes in the hands of the United Kingdom.' This would not pose much of a threat; the real problem was in getting the aircraft. Howe was willing to settle for 'anything that would fly the Atlantic,' but he was less certain of a source. This meeting reconfirmed Howe in his views, and he left promising to inform Sir Archibald Sinclair, the air minister, that the Canadians would be setting up their own transatlantic air service.[44]

The evidence is not completely clear at precisely what point Howe decided that the deal struck with Balfour for the loan of the two British airplanes was no longer sufficient and that an independent air service was necessary. It would be idle to speculate, but the fact that no action had been taken concerning this agreement over the summer must have played a central role in his decision. Furthermore, he was also aware of Massey's disapproval and the growing opposition to the Balfour agreement within the ICICA. It is interesting to note the contrast between the largely indifferent attitude of most of the Canadian cabinet (with the major exception of Howe and King) and the whole-hearted support that officials like Massey, Robertson, Baldwin, and others in the ICICA gave to pursuing an independent course in this matter in particular and in international civil aviation in general.

At any rate, Howe returned to Canada on 21 October and wasted no time in initiating action. The following day he informed the CWC that the British government had failed to meet Canadian requirements, either in space allocation or in turning over aircraft for TCA operation. Because of this intolerable situation, Howe argued, Canada should initiate its own air service and the British, Newfoundland, and Irish governments should be immediately informed of Canada's desire to end the 1935 agreement. To meet the situation, Howe recommended the construction of fifty transport planes and suggested that, for the present, the Americans should be asked to supply three planes to tide the Canadians over until the new planes were ready. The CWC agreed, and the decision to establish an independent transatlantic air service was made.[45]

The high commissioners were informed of the CWC decision and the notices of withdrawal from the 1935 agreement were handed over to the governments in London, St John's, and Dublin.[46] The thrust of the Canadian argument was that because the JOC had not been established, the 1935 agreement had never actually come into effect. Moreover, because the state of transatlantic aviation had changed so significantly in the seven years since 1935 and would likely continue changing over the course of the war, 'the arrangement of that year no longer provides a useful basis for dealing with the post-war situation.'[47]

The Canadian request was received rather coolly in London. For several years, British civil aviation policy had looked to Commonwealth collaboration better to meet the US challenge. The 1935 agreement was central to this way of thinking, and, if nothing else, the Canadian querulousness on the matter served notice that the Canadians questioned the basic tenets of this policy. In retrospect, it clearly foreshadowed the future difficulties over civil aviation that surfaced over the following years between the two countries.

In a letter to Vincent Massey dated 9 December 1942, the dominions secretary, Clement Attlee, noted that the Dominions Office agreed with the Canadian description of the existing state of affairs. Nevertheless, there were 'features in the Agreement' that the British 'certainly wish to preserve.' Attlee added that some parts of the agreement had, in fact, come into effect, and he pointed to the provision of ground facilities by Ireland as an example. Besides, the 'principle of inter-Governmental co-operation in the development of North Atlantic air services' set out in the agreement was worth preserving, at least until a better system was found. Thus, Attlee concluded, the British were convinced that 'the abrogation of this Agreement at the present moment would introduce a note of disunity which would be prejudicial to the whole Trans-Atlantic position.' Some alterations might be prudent after the war, but Attlee hoped that the Canadians would not 'wish to press their suggestion' to abrogate the agreement any further.[48]

This was hardly what the Canadian government wanted to hear, but no response was made until after St. John's and Dublin had been heard from. On 29 December the Canadian high commissioner in Newfoundland received the Newfoundland Commission of Government's response, which largely followed the line set down by the Dominions Office. As for the Irish, John Kearney, the high commissioner in Dublin, reported to Ottawa that he had discussed the matter with J.P. Walshe of the Irish Department of External Affairs. Although Walshe 'seemed perturbed at the prospect of Ireland appearing to take sides with Great Britain against Canada,' it was likely that the Irish would oppose discussing changes to the agreement before the end of the war.[49]

For the Canadians these responses did not seem to introduce any new arguments that previously had not been taken into consideration. Nor did they change any minds on the question of the abrogation of the 1935 agreement. Howe remained convinced that Canada should withdraw and the rest of the CWC could be expected to follow his lead. Responsibility now fell to Norman Robertson, C.P. Edwards, and others in the ICICA to produce an acceptable rebuttal to the Irish and British responses.

At this point, J.E. Read, the legal adviser in the Department of External Affairs, was brought in for his assessment of Canada's position. Early in March 1943, after several weeks of study by himself and K.B. Bingay, Read submitted a memorandum to Robertson, in which he outlined two significant points. First, he argued that even though the JOC had not been incorporated, Canada was committed to the agreement. The arrangement was meant to be permanent and so far as he could tell, 'the governments concerned have done what is required of them by the provisions of the agreement.' For these reasons Canada would not be 'legally justified in terminating it.' Second, having noted this, there was no reason why the Canadians could not establish their own transatlantic air service – at least for the war period – within the framework of the 1935 agreement. His recommendation was that Canada should initiate the service and request the other governments to provide the necessary ground facilities. If they refused, 'the Canadian Government would then be in a strong position to repudiate the whole arrangement.'[50]

Ultimately this is what the Canadians did. It would have been fruitless to continue pressing for the abrogation of the agreement in the face of united opposition from Britain, Ireland, and Newfoundland. More important, the raison d'être behind the termination of the agreement was that the Canadians felt that it blocked the creation of an independent transatlantic service. Now it appeared that that problem could be bypassed simply by ignoring it. Thus, on 5 May, the Canadian high commissioners were instructed to inform the British, Irish, and Newfoundland governments that the Canadian government would 'not press its views in the 1935 agreement' for the present. It was still considered ineffective and outdated, but its amendment would have to wait for intergovernmental discussions at some later date.[51]

Although the Canadian government backtracked on the abrogation of the 1935 agreement, plans for the creation of a transatlantic service continued unabated. The legal division's conclusion that a Canadian service would not be in violation of the 1935 agreement was welcome news, but it served little purpose other than as justification for actions already taken. Regardless of potential British and Irish opposition or the diplomatic niceties of the 1935 agreement, C.D. Howe had been preparing for the inauguration of a Canadian service since the previous fall.

All that remained was to get the planes. Not unexpectedly, overtures to the Americans had 'failed completely' and Howe had to fall back on his own resourcefulness to secure the aircraft for the service.[52] In 1942 the Victory Aircraft Plant had been established at Malton, Ontario, near Toronto, to build York transport planes. The York was similar in design to the Lancaster bomber, and Howe secured a single Lancaster from the British government to be used as a model. Howe was overly optimistic that by the end of the year Canada would have enough York aircraft finished to carry all the official government business across the Atlantic. As for immediate needs, however, Howe kept the British Lancaster and had it remodelled for passenger use.[53] Having such a plane would enable the Canadians to establish a weekly return transatlantic service as soon as the weather cleared in the spring.

The other governments concerned had to be informed, and messages to this effect were sent early in May. It was also necessary to secure their co-operation in the provision of landing rights and ground facilities, and efforts to this end were undertaken immediately. J.A. Wilson and Escott Reid were sent to the United Kingdom to help complete the arrangements. The British government noted with satisfaction the Canadian decision regarding the 1935 agreement, and as for the new air service, there was little that could be done about it. Even if there was, however, there is no evidence of any concentrated opposition to the Canadian move. Meanwhile, the Irish government acknowledged the Canadian move and the Newfoundland government gave the Canadians the right to land, take off, and fly over Newfoundland until six months after the war had ended.[54]

The official announcement was made by C.D. Howe on 16 June, prematurely, as it turned out, after the Montreal *Gazette* printed a full disclosure of the Canadian government's plans.[55] Rising in the House of Commons, Howe gave a brief summary of the workings of the new service and explained the move in terms of wartime need: 'The growing strength of the Canadian armed forces overseas and their increasing activities have made it necessary to establish this quick and effective means of communication with the United Kingdom for men and materials. The need for a speedy and regular troops air mail service is particularly pressing. Over a quarter of a million members of the Canadian armed forces are now in the United Kingdom. During the past year, due to lack of space on aircraft, they have unfortunately not been receiving mail regularly and quickly. It is expected that the initial flight of the new service will occur in July.'[56]

The inaugural flight of the Canadian government transatlantic air service took off on 22 July 1943 and it carried a cargo of four passengers and 10,000 pounds of mail. As agreed, the Canadian service was used for Canadian Armed Service personnel and government business only; there would be no fare-paying passengers or cargo, even though the service would be operated by TCA. It was meant to be a wartime service and the rights granted were to last for the duration of the war plus six months. As for space allocation, eastbound traffic fell under the jurisdiction of the deputy minister of transport, while the returning westward voyage was put in the hands of the high commissioner in

London. Both sides had small committees that were to decide if the passenger requests were sufficiently important to get them a seat.

Despite this rather inauspicious start, the Canadian transatlantic air service grew considerably during the last two years of the war. Howe's forecast of over fifty planes proved somewhat optimistic, but several more Lancasters were acquired and put into service by the end of the war. To no one's surprise, the air service continued operations into the post-war era. Ticket selling began late in 1945, and by 1947 Canada and TCA had a full commercial transatlantic air service.[57]

As for the 1935 agreement, it lingered on in a moribund state until the end of the war. No action was ever taken to establish the Joint Operating Company, and, ironically, in January 1945 the Irish government announced its withdrawal from the agreement. Many of the Irish government's fears of being isolated or bypassed in transatlantic flight were calmed by the Chicago conference of November 1944. With the introduction of two international aviation agreements, the protection offered by the 1935 agreement was no longer as vital as it had been in the past.

Although the 1935 agreement was largely forgotten in the rush of events, the direction set by the Canadian government during the creation of the transatlantic service was not. The ICICA continued to function and it was from here that the blueprint for post-war Canadian aviation policy emerged. In a succession of memoranda and reports, the ICICA continued to advocate the policies asserted in 1942-3 – namely, that Canadian aviation policy be flexible with respect to international co-operation, while at the same time safeguarding Canadian sovereignty in the air from outsiders.

III

Much has been written concerning the considerable power and influence yielded by a small group of talented and dedicated civil servants within the Canadian government during these years, and the creation of the transatlantic air service is a good case in point. It was the officials in the ICICA and Vincent Massey in London who consistently kept the proposed service before the Cabinet War Committee. This was especially true concerning the Howe-Balfour agreement during the summer of 1942. On the ministerial level, only Howe and King showed a strong and continuing interest in having a transatlantic air service, and even Howe recognized the influence of his officials. 'Our Department of External Affairs is more or less dictating the policy on International Aviation here,' Howe wrote, with tongue in cheek, in a letter to Lord Beaverbrook in 1944. 'I am trying to guide the viewpoint here, without too much success, but I expect to have considerable say in any concrete arrangements that maybe evolved. After all, I am the Minister responsible here for the administration of Civil Aviation.'[58]

Regardless of bureaucratic influence, however, the final decision was for King and Howe to make, and when the time came they were not found wanting. The service to Washington was unnecessary and therefore was rejected. The transatlantic service, in contrast, had an important wartime function as well as implications for the future, and Howe and King would not have settled for less.

The Canadian government acted in 1942–3 not only through a concern for the Canadian war effort, but also with a clear recognition of the post-war advantages of having an independent transatlantic air service. The existence of such a service would permit Canadians to bargain from a position of strength at the end of the war and it gave notice to the aviation world that the Canadians could be expected to maintain an independent course in international civil aviation matters. British aviation policy had always pressed for close collaboration within the Commonwealth – usually behind a British lead. Circumstances may have dictated Canadian compliance in 1935, but the events surrounding the creation of an independent service showed just how far the Canadian government had come in a very short period of time. What emerged from these experiences was a unique Canadian aviation policy that neither embraced Commonwealth collaboration nor rejected international co-operation, but rather reflected the significant independent role in international civil aviation that geography, war, and technology had furnished for Canada. To a remarkable degree these realities continued to dominate Canadian thinking in civil aviation into the post-war era.

5 Globaloney

In 1942–3 the improving prospects for peace and victory in war began breathing new life into international civil aviation. The disasters of 1940 had been survived and the advancement of the enemy had been halted. By the end of 1942 the Allies had achieved a victory in North Africa, and early the next spring the Battle of the Atlantic reached its apogee. A corner had been turned in the war and if victory was not yet in sight it was at least possible to contemplate the ending of the war. Once it became possible to think about the coming of peace, thoughts turned to the kind of world that would rise from the ashes of war. For the post-war planners in the United States and Great Britain, the field of international civil aviation deserved special attention, and in 1943 the long debate began.

I

British planning for post-war international civil aviation began early in the war. Civil aviation officially fell under the jurisdiction of the Air Ministry; some attempts had been made in the 1930s to separate them, but even with the creation of the Ministry of War Transport in May 1941, civil aviation stayed with the Air Ministry.[1] Sir Archibald Sinclair, the secretary of state for air (1940–5), was a good friend of Winston Churchill and had followed Sir Herbert Samuel as parliamentary leader of the Liberal party in 1935. As air minister, he acted as a general overseer of civil aviation policy. Under Sinclair there were two parliamentary under-secretaries – Harold Balfour and Lord Sherwood – who spoke for the Air Ministry on civil aviation questions in the House of Commons and Lords respectively. Balfour, who played an important role in the creation of the British Commonwealth Air Training Plan, exhibited a continuing interest in civil aviation during his career. On the official side, Sir Francis Shelmerdine remained as director-general of civil aviation until 1941, when he was replaced by William Hildred (later Sir William). Hildred, who had participated in the creation of RAF Ferry Command and served as Shelmerdine's deputy, remained at the centre of civil aviation affairs for the rest of the war.

Other departments participated in planning for post-war aviation. By its very nature, international civil aviation included making arrangements and negotiating bilateral agreements with other nations – here the Foreign Office had an obvious role to play. Anthony Eden, whose interest in aviation stretched back to his maiden speech in the House of Commons, served as foreign secretary throughout the war, and, as a member of the War Cabinet and close associate of Winston Churchill, his influence on civil aviation affairs was extensive. Under Eden, Richard Law, the youngest son of former prime minister Bonar Law and a Conservative MP since 1931, acted as parliamentary under-secretary from 1941 to 1943.

Much of the daily running of the Foreign Office was left in the hands of a small group of officials, led during the war by Sir Alexander Cadogan, the permanent under-secretary (1938–46). But Cadogan rarely devoted much time or effort to civil aviation matters; the real responsibility lay with Sir Orme Sargent, who was appointed deputy under-secretary in 1939 and followed Cadogan as permanent under-secretary in 1946. Sargent, a 'brilliant and rather passionate character,' was later remembered as 'a tiger when it was a matter of the defence of British interests and the maintenance of British security,'[2] and during the war was arguably the most influential man in the Foreign Office on post-war civil aviation. Mention should also be made of John Le Rougetel (later Sir John and ambassador to Iran and high commissioner to South Africa), who was a strong supporter of the internationalist school.

In addition to the Foreign Office and Air Ministry, the Dominions Office and, to a lesser degree, the Colonial Office also contributed to civil aviation policy, although usually more as interpreters of British policy to the dominions and colonies than as instigators of policy. Clement Attlee, the dominions secretary from February 1942 to September 1943, revealed a keen interest in international aviation and post-war organization in general, and his dual role as deputy prime minister gave him a seat in the War Cabinet that, in turn, enhanced his prestige and influence in civil aviation matters. Lord Cranborne (later the fifth Marquis of Salisbury) was dominions secretary before and after Attlee, and, although not a member of the War Cabinet, he had a close friend in Anthony Eden and over the years exhibited a strong sympathy for Canadian interests.

Three other individuals bear mentioning, although none was a member of the above departments: Sir William Jowitt, Lord Beaverbrook, and Winston Churchill, Churchill's attention was usually focused on other, more important, areas of the war effort, but as prime minister and minister of defence he was inevitably involved in the decision-making process at the highest level. His position, prestige, and ability ensured that his views on civil aviation would receive serious considertion. Lord Beaverbrook, the talented and determined ex-Canadian, championed the imperial cause throughout the war in his capacity as minister of aircraft production and later as Lord Privy Seal. In 1943 he was given the responsibility for the international discussions on post-war civil aviation and from that moment the direction of British civil aviation policy bore his personal stamp. Sir William Jowitt, though less dynamic than Beaverbrook, was an influential figure none the less, through his position as chair of the War Cabinet's Committee on Reconstruction Problems.

In July 1941 a small interdepartmental committee was established to investigate the future of British civil aviation. Shelmerdine was appointed to the chair, and the committee included representatives from the Colonial Office, the Treasury, the India Office, the Post Office, and the office of the minister without portfolio. The committee's terms of reference were straightforward: 'To survey the whole field of Civil Aviation in its international, Imperial and national aspects; and to make recommendations as regards reconstruction, organization and development both during the transitional period from war to peace conditions and thereafter.'[3]

The Shelmerdine committee, as it became known, held its first meeting on 25 July 1941 and met several times over the following months. The committee's report, submitted in January 1942, became an important document. Begun as an examination of ways to prevent a recurrence of past problems, the report resurrected and focused government attention on the concept of the complete internationalization of civil aviation. Internationalization was not a new idea – it had received some consideration before the war – but now its time had come.

The Shelmerdine committee argued that before the war the development of civil aviation was hampered by ruthless international competition, based on 'two principal incentives, national prestige and the war potential which a well-developed civil aviation affords.' The possession of a strong civil aircraft industry, well-trained personnel, and ground organizations had obvious military implications, while the quest for national prestige had led to vast government subsidies on unprofitable routes, primarily for political rather than economic reasons. The report made particular reference to the south transatlantic route (to South America), which three European nations were operating at great expense before the war. Rather than establishing a British service along this route, as some had suggested, the committee members argued that in the post-war period only one service would be needed to carry all the traffic along that route. A return to such conditions as existed before the war would be 'inappropriate' the committee argued, and 'we feel, too, that as a contribution to the planning of a new and better world the opportunity should be taken to free from the present forms of uneconomic misuse a means of transport that has such potentialities for promoting international understanding.'

The recommendation of the Shelmerdine committee reflected the idealism of the Atlantic Charter issued by Roosevelt and Churchill earlier that year off the coast of Newfoundland. Air travel should be 'a service to humanity' and should be 'organized and administered in the spirit of that full international collaboration envisaged in Article V [of the Atlantic Charter]; ... it should engender fear, suspicion and jealousy in none.' These goals would be attained, the report concluded, only through the complete internationalization of civil aviation and the creation of a world organization in which 'all nations would merge their national efforts for the fulfillment of their several and joint needs.' Just what exact shape this organization would take would be up to the various states to decide, but, the committee concluded, the time had come to decide. To wait until after the war would be too late: 'If only because in periods of world crisis the thoughts of nations turn to co-operation, which is little sought in times of peace, the closing stages of the present war will afford an opportunity such as is never likely to recur, unless the whole world is again submerged by war, for bringing civil aviation under complete international control.'

The report recognized that a single world organization could not be created overnight and that in the end it may have to be built piece by piece. If that turned out to be the case, the important thing was to create a nucleus that included the European nations and their dependencies (including the dominions). The other key player, of course, would be the United States. If the Americans proved to be 'antagonistic' to internationalization, the Canadians (and perhaps the Australians and New Zealanders) might follow their lead and go it alone after the war, confining internationalization to the European nations. This eventuality would be less than ideal, but still might be better than no agreement at all.[4]

Sir William Jowitt, who, in addition to being paymaster-general, was the chair of the Committee on Reconstruction Problems, read the Shelmerdine report with great interest. In his view, complete internationalization was the ideal solution, but, like the Shelmerdine committee, he realized that the United States and the Soviet Union had both developed extensive internal services and would likely resist surrendering them to an international authority. Thus, he recommended that the Committee on Reconstruction Problems examine an alternative arrangement – the 'regionalisation of civil aviation' – which, 'while affording many of the benefits of full internationalisation, would recognise the special position of these two countries and possibily others.' What Jowitt had in mind was the creation of a 'third system' comprising Europe (excluding the Soviet Union) and its dependencies that would service the European area and limit the 'dangers to security inherent in civil aviation.' And, presumably, once the pan-European organization was created, it could be linked to the American and Soviet systems.[5]

The chancellor of the exchequer, Sir Kingsley Wood, was less sanguine than were the members of the Shelmerdine committee about the chances of reaching an agreement over internationalization before the end of the war. In a letter to Sir William Jowitt he agreed that without the participation of the Soviet Union and the United States there could be no effective world-wide organization, but noted that perhaps it 'might well be unwise to raise the question of post-war policy ... at least until we are in a position to open our general discussions with the American Government on our post-war financial and economic relations.' Wood remained undecided over the best course of action, but seemed to favour regionalization, at least in the short run: 'If we could build up a single organization in Europe,' he wrote, 'and could simultaneously maintain our hold on the routes which run via Europe to The Empire countries and the Dependencies of our European Allies, we should at least emerge from the war in a stronger position *vis-à-vis* Europe than that which we occupied in 1939, and we should have created a system of civil aviation which, by reason of its very diversity and the extent of the world's surface which it covered, could probably be used as the foundation for a future system of complete international control, if such proved possible.' Granted, a 'common front' in Europe would be difficult and time consuming to establish, but once in place, he concluded, 'we should be in a stronger position to deal with the Americans, and might even force them to put forward counter-proposals of their own which would not be too unreasonable.'[6]

The question that faced the Committee on Reconstruction Problems and, ultimately, the War Cabinet was whether complete internationalization or some form of regionalization should become government policy. Other questions remained concerning the shape of any future organization: How would it be organized and operated? Who would pay for it? Should there also be an internationalization of the aircraft industry? How would air-crews and other personnel be recruited? After some discussion of these questions, the Committee on Reconstruction Problems agreed that a more exact understanding of internationalization was required before an informed decision could be made. Consequently, on 21 July 1942, Lord Finlay – a judge and chair of the Contraband committee – was appointed to investigate 'how best the internationalisation of civil aviation can be brought about after the war; and to prepare for this purpose alternative schemes.'[7]

Lord Finlay was on his own in this task; secrecy demanded that he consult no one outside of the government. He did, however, receive assistance from various government departments and officials, and in particular Shelmerdine and Sargent. His 'Report on the Internationalisation of Civil Aviation' (or the Finlay Report) was submitted as a War Cabinet Paper on 17 December 1942.

Finlay began his report with a description of what he called 'The Ideal Scheme' – the complete internationalization of all the world's air services. He recognized that this scheme might either be unattainable or might have to be done in stages, and, consequently, the timing of the negotiations would be a crucial factor in determining ultimate success. In words echoing the Shelmerdine report he noted that

> conditions will prevail at the peace settlement which may not recur for a long period. Internationalisation requires of States that they should renounce certain of their sovereign rights and abandon certain important national functions. These things are so difficult to achieve as to discourage attempts in normal times, but when the social and political structure has been shaken loose by a world-war a brief opportunity occurs in which to rebuild in an atmosphere of idealism. If that opportunity is not grasped it may not recur for many years. It would be unwise, therefore, to hope that what we have been unable to achieve in such favourable conditions would be attainable later when vested interests had recovered their power and national rivalries had reasserted themselves.

In his 'Outline of a Draft Convention to Internationalise all Air Services,' which formed a major part of his report, Finlay proposed the creation of 'a single international organisation to perform all air services,' under the jurisdiction of a supreme authority for Civil Aviation. The authority would consist of an assembly of all contracting nations (which would not include the Axis nations at first) and a smaller air board of control appointed by the assembly to act in an executive fashion. Finlay's draft convention recognized that while every country had 'complete exclusive sovereignty over the air space above its territory,' each member of the assembly would agree to 'give unrestricted passage over and the right of landing within its territory to the air services approved by the Board.' Each member would also provide meteorological services and ground facilities in its territory, while at the same time prohibiting the operation of any non-approved services. Other details were also considered by Finlay, such as the legal aspects of the authority, the treatment of ex-enemy states, and the settlement of disputes between member nations.

Turning to more fundamental issues, Finlay touched on what would likely prove to be the most controversial aspect of his scheme – the proposal to integrate all air services into one organization. In such a scenario, he wrote, 'all national air transportation systems that existed before the war, many of which exist today, would be abolished.' The problem here, as Shelmerdine and others had pointed out, would come from the Soviets, 'whose domestic air lines form an integral part of the administrative machinery of the State,' and the Americans, 'whose internal air network operated by private companies is extensive and highly developed.' Confronting these two countries with the idea of total integration might well lead them to reject internationalization out of hand.

To counter this possibility, Finlay offered an alternative proposal – a slightly revised version of the Ideal Scheme – that permitted the maintenance of domestic services under national control, reserving internationalization to truly 'international' services. Not surprisingly, this raised more questions: Could one country consider an air service to a colony or possession an internal service? Would inter-Commonwealth services, for example, fall into this category? Finlay believed this way of thinking should be resisted, but clearly questions like these would be raised.

Three other alternatives also received brief attention in Finlay's report: a pan-European system, a collection of several regional systems, and the internationalization of only a selected number of important air routes. These schemes, however, were 'open to such serious objections as to rule them out as schemes which His Majesty's Government might put forward as alternatives.' In the end, Finlay recommended complete internationalization, including internal services, and he concluded his report with a warning of the dangers to British aviation 'if the system which I recommend should not be adopted.'[8] Beware of the Americans, he declared. 'I have drawn attention in my Report to the special position of Pan-American Airways,' he wrote to Sir William Jowitt,

and it may be a vital point. It is easy to see that in unscrupulous hands aviation could become a very powerful weapon whereby a particular Government, either openly or under cover of Big Business, could successfully conduct a policy of peaceful penetration in those regions of the world where the local governments are too weak, too poor, or too inefficient to supply for themselves the air services which the stronger nation would be only too ready to provide. In fact it may be argued that, as far as civil aviation is concerned, the choice before the world lies between Americanisation and internationalisation. If this is correct, it is difficult to doubt that it is under the latter system that British interest will best be served.[9]

Finlay's warning was not lost on the Foreign Office. At the same time that he was putting the final touches on his report, the Foreign Office was preparing its own memorandum on the post-war prospects for British civil aviation. This memo, dated 15 December 1942, was submitted to the War Cabinet attached to the Finlay report. The Foreign Office was primarily concerned with the United States and, more specifically, with Pan Am. While Britain had been forced by the exigencies of war to curtail its services, Pan Am had continued to expand. Moreover, the USATC had developed several new strategic air routes in Africa, the Middle East, across the Pacific, and elsewhere (including over British territory). These routes were created solely for military purposes but easily could be converted to civilian use once the war was over. Finally, the US aircraft industry was in a strong position, and when the war ended British airlines would probably have to rely on American imports for their civil aircraft.

The Foreign Office memo took a hard-headed look at Britain's possible situation at the end of the war compared to that of the United States, and its findings were not promising. It would be difficult, if not impossible, to remove the Americans from those lines that they had already established. Even if that could be done, Britain would not be capable of carrying the traffic on those services for some years to come. 'What we should aim at,' the Foreign Office suggested, 'is to maintain the existing arrangements on a temporary or emergency basis until we ourselves are in a position to take advantage not only of the facilities which British-controlled territory provides, but also of those which we might expect eventually to extract by bargaining with the Americans for the more permanent mutual allocation of landing rights.' Finally, 'we shall not ... get the Americans out, and we had therefore better keep arrangements fluid until we are ready to get in with them wherever possible.'

Britain's real handicap vis-à-vis the United States lay in its lack of civil aircraft. The situation was increasingly perilous, and unless 'immediate steps are taken to adopt suitable designs and lay plans for their production ... no amount of haggling and negotiation by the Foreign Office and the Air Ministry will prevent the Americans grabbing the air traffic of the world.' British policy should not be to make futile attempts to exclude the Americans from present routes, the Foreign Office argued, but rather should be to compete with them on an equal basis. For this to happen, Britain would need civil aircraft: 'Policy is one thing, but no policy is any good without the means to carry it out.'[10]

The Shelmerdine and Finlay reports were not released to the public; indeed, circulation of these and other documents was limited to a relatively few persons in government circles. Nevertheless, public interest in post-war aviation was steadily rising in Britain. As the threat of enemy invasion diminished, it became possible to look ahead to the future and to make plans for the kind of world that would emerge after the war. Clearly aviation would play a central role in that new world; one had only to look around at the devastation that aircraft had unleashed on the cities of Britain and Europe as evidence enough of the need for international controls – if only to prevent that kind of thing from happening again. It is interesting that from the very beginning the future of civil aviation was seen as an integral part of the whole question of post-war international security, and proposals for co-operation in civil aviation were often couched in terms similar to those used in describing the need for other international organizations.

Public discussion in the late 1930s over the fate of Imperial Airways and the subsequent formation of British Overseas Airways Corporation (BOAC) in 1940 garnered widespread attention in Britain. As the war progressed, public concern over BOAC and its future competitive position remained, but increasingly the focus of attention shifted to the more general question of civil aviation and the need for some form of international regulation.

The day after Christmas 1942, for example, the Royal Institute of International Affairs published a bulletin on international air transport that raised many of the same questions found in the official government reports. Pre-war competition and petty nationalism had to be eliminated from international aviation, and in their place a new spirit of co-operation must be established if peace and security were to prevail.[11]

Other non-governmental bodies were also becoming involved. Vincent Massey reported to Ottawa from London that the Federation of British Industries had formed an air-transport committee, as had the Association of British Chambers of Commerce and the London Chamber of Commerce. Early in 1943, the General Council of British Shipping published a bulletin entitled 'Air and Sea Transport,' in which it was argued that although the usefulness of aircraft would never surpass the ship, the two should be 'regarded as complementary rather than competitive.'[12] In magazines and newspapers, articles dealing with post-war aviation began appearing regularly. Ideas and phrases such as 'internationalisation,' 'freedom of the air,' and the 'closed sky' were becoming commonplace and no longer accompanied by definitions.[13]

Between December 1942 and March 1943 no fewer than four editorials in the *Times* were devoted to civil aviation. The newspaper's editorial policy shared in the general consensus that the pre-war closed-sky system of air traffic was unprofitable and far too competitive, and should be replaced. In its place, the *Times* proposed international regulation and general freedom of the air. 'The freedom of the skies, like other freedoms,' the *Times* noted on 9 February 1943, 'can be attained not through the abandonment of all regulation but only through careful planning and organisation on a world-wide scale. Here, as elsewhere, international cooperation will be achieved only by deliberately building up an effective machinery of international control. It will not be furthered by a struggle for power in which the strongest emerges as the master: that is Hitler's way, not the way of the United Nations.'[14]

Questions were also being raised in the House of Commons. Robert Perkins, the Conservative back-bencher who had played an important role in focusing public attention on the internal difficulties of Imperial Airways in the late 1930s, continued to act as the 'gadfly in the side of the Air Ministry' during the war.[15] Rising in the House on 17 December 1942, Perkins attacked the government for ignoring the very serious problems concerning civil aviation: Pan American Airways were busy 'stretching their tentacles all over the world,' while the British government took no action and appeared to have no sensible long-term policy. The British had surrendered the Pacific to the Americans and had let them into Africa on military grounds, which, in Perkins's mind, was 'exactly the same, except that the men who are running the line, instead of wearing bowler hats and umbrellas, are now wearing tin hats and gas masks. It is merely a change of uniform.' To make matters worse, the Americans were stockpiling modern transport planes, while BOAC languished with a 'mixed assortment' of airplanes: 'old crocks, five, six, seven years old, many of them ripe for the scrap-heap,' a number of modern airplanes imported from the United States, and 'R.A.F. throw-outs, crumbs from the rich man's table.'

Perkins's solution was to separate civil aviation policy from the Air Ministry to enable it to receive the attention it deserved. He also demanded the creation of a committee to study the problem and to report to the House in three months. Finally, he told the House that it was imperative to make a start in designing new airplanes for the future; otherwise, 'other people will control our trade routes; they will get our trade; the pound sterling will not buy an ounce of confetti; the Beveridge Report will become an interesting relic of the past, and we shall dwindle until we become a second-class Power. Never were the stakes so high as they are now, and never was there such a grand opportunity as we have now.'

Other MPs followed Perkins, and most shared his sentiments. Sir Lindsay Everard reiterated the call to separate civil aviation from the Air Ministry, arguing that it was 'no good trying to run a first-class Empire with third-class aviation.' Later in the debate, similar concerns were echoed by Frederick Montague, who went on to issue an appeal for internationalization, stating that 'the air is not a personal thing, is not a private commercial thing, is not even a national thing, but is a medium which encompasses the whole world.'

Harold Balfour spoke on behalf of the government in an effort to reassure the House that the government was doing all that it could with respect to civil aviation. He acknowledged that Britain had fallen behind the United States in aircraft production and in the establishment of new services, but this was because Britain had directed all its energies towards the war effort. Surely the government could not be faulted on that account. Looking to the future, he told the House that the government was determined to secure a prominent role for the British Commonwealth in the future of civil aviation and would ensure the existence of a stable British aircraft industry. As for American encroachments on British routes and over British territory, Balfour said that 'we have agreed on the highest level with the Americans that as regards routes they are now running for military purposes on lines which may have commercial values "all bets are off" at the end of the war.' In conclusion, Balfour reminded the House that 'post-war civil aviation is but one piece in the jigsaw of the building-up of the post-war world ...,' but, he added, 'I am authorized to say that the Government are now actively considering what these bold measures should be and what form they should take. If decisions can be properly taken now, we shall certainly take them. If further examination is required, this shall be arranged for in the best form to reach a speedy conclusion. In either case the House will be fully informed as soon as we are in a position to do so.'[16]

Balfour's rather vague statement was restricted to a degree by government security requirements, but it also reflected the still-uncertain nature of Britain's international civil aviation policy. Nevertheless, mounting public concern did not go unnoticed in government circles; indeed, the various departments kept a fairly close watch on developments in the media. The Foreign Office, for example, filled numerous files with magazine articles, press clippings, and speeches from Britain and abroad dealing with the whole spectrum of aviation issues.[17]

On the issues that confronted the British governemnt at this time there was ground for agreement as well as room for significant differences. For example, there appeared to be a consensus in the media, in both Houses of Parliament, and in government circles on the need to maintain the British aircraft industry. Britain had been a leader in aircraft design in the past and the aircraft industry had grown significantly during the war. To lose this prominent industry and the thousands of jobs that went with it to American competitors after the war would be unacceptable. A start had been made to prevent such an occurrence: in 1942 a joint committee was created by the Air Ministry and the minister of aircraft production to investigate the design and production of civil aircraft and to make recommendations to the government on the kinds of aircraft that should be developed in the future. Lord Brabazon, the former minister of transport and of aircraft production, was appointed to the chair. The report of the Brabazon committee was submitted on 9 February 1943; it advised that immediate steps be taken towards the designing of new aircraft. Among others, the report recommended the design of a multi-engine landplane for use in the transatlantic air service and on the empire trunk routes, and for medium- and small-size twin-engine aircraft for internal and European services. The report had little immediate effect; less than a month later, the government announced that some initial steps would be taken in the design of new aircraft, but only as the men and material could be spared from the war effort.[18]

A second area of general agreement within the government could be found in the opposition to the concept of freedom of the air. This idea, if put into effect, would lead to a return to the cut-throat competition of the pre-war period and, some believed, would result in anarchy in the air. Without effective restrictions imposed through a system of internationalization, the United States, and in particular Pan American

Airways, would be in a position to dominate post-war aviation. 'At present,' Sir Orme Sargent wrote, 'the only thing standing between the P.A.A. [Pan American Airways] and this monopoly is the power of the individual State to refuse to foreign aircraft the right to fly over and land on its territory.' National sovereignty was one of the few bargaining chips that remained for dealing with the Americans; to give it up under a policy of 'freedom of the air' would put Britain and the other nations of the world 'at the mercy of the P.A.A., who, thanks to greater efficiency and wealth and the vastly larger number of machines at its disposal, would be able to develop services wherever it wanted to without fear of effective competition.' Sargent was able to reconcile the apparent discrepancy between his support of internationalization on the one hand and the preservation of national sovereignty on the other: 'Under any world-wide system of internationalisation the principle of national sovereignty over the air need not be abolished,' he wrote, 'the right would merely be transferred to, and exercised in the common interest by, the International Aviation Authority.'[19]

Differences of opinion arose between those who supported various kinds of internationalization. For example, Oliver Stanley, the colonial secretary, proposed internationalization of the 'main trunk route' around the world leaving the 'local and feeder services' in national hands.[20] Another proposal came from L.S. Amery, the secretary of state for India. In a letter to Anthony Eden, Amery suggested that air traffic within the empire should be considered as internal and hence reserved for empire carriers. The Americans would likely treat their traffic to Hawaii and Alaska as internal – why could the United Kingdom not do the same? Eden made no reply, writing 'I don't think we need answer. A.E.' on the original letter.[21] Limited schemes such as these found few supporters in the government. Philip Noel Baker, who supported internationalization, was one oponent of Amery-like empire schemes. 'I think geography really precludes the attempt to make the British Empire work as a "separate entity,"' he wrote to Sir William Jowitt, 'quite apart from the great political and economic difficulties we should certainly have with more than one of the Dominions.'[22]

The wheels of government continued to turn, however slowly, in 1943. At a meeting of the Committee on Reconstruction Problems on 7 January, a ministerial subcommittee was established to deal specifically with civil aviation. Officially called the Committee on Reconstruction Problems, Sub-Committee on Civil Aviation, this new group took the name of its chair – Sir William Jowitt – and included Sir Kingsley Wood, Sir Archibald Sinclair, Sir Stafford Cripps (who had been appointed minister of aircraft production the previous November), Richard Law, and Lord Leathers, the minister of war transport.

A few weeks later, at the Jowitt committee's first meeting on 26 January, a second committee was created: the Official Committee on Post-War Civil Aviation. This new interdepartmental group consisted of appointed officials only and it was responsible to the Jowitt committee. Its chair was Sir Alan Barlow, who was part of the British delegation during the 1937 Imperial Conference and had been serving as joint second secretary in the treasury since 1938. The Barlow committee also included William Hildred, John Le Rougetel, and Sir John Stephenson from the Dominions Office. There were several other officials as well, from the Colonial Office, the India Office, and the offices of the ministers of transport, aircraft production, and the minister without portfolio. The meetings were also attended by Sir Francis Shelmerdine, but he had no official status.

The Barlow committee was charged with the task of working out 'the essential details' of four different kinds of internationalization: '1) Full internationalisation. 2) A system comprising Europe and the European Dependencies. 3) A European system as outlined in the second alternative, coupled with a scheme whereby the British Empire (and possibly also the Dutch and French Empires) could co-operate as separate entities in close liaison with the European system. 4) International Regulation.'[23] The Barlow committee met for the first time on 17 February and held several meetings over subsequent weeks before submitting its report to the Jowitt committee in March 1943.

Cracks began to appear in the Jowitt and Barlow committees, primarily between the supporters of full internationalization and those who tended towards a regional arrangement, either pan-European or imperial. The strongest support for internationalization came from the Foreign Office. Sir Orme Sargent was particularly concerned over the discussion of European regionalization within the Jowitt committee and, when Le Rougetel reported that the Barlow committee was flirting with a pan-European scheme, he reacted strongly. Sargent later argued that the regionalization of Europe and its dependencies would be interpreted by the United States 'as meaning that we were planning to keep P.A.A. and American industry out of as large a part of the world as possible. The result, to my mind, on Anglo-American relations would be quite disastrous.' Hence, Le Rougetel was instructed to do what he could to prevent the Barlow committee from endorsing a scheme for European regionalization.[24]

The divisions within the Barlow committee were reflected in its report, submitted on 22 March 1943. The report began with a brief description of each of the proposed alternatives: international regulation, in which the various national air services would maintain their separate identities but would be regulated by an international agency comparable to the American Civil Aeronautics Board; full internationalization, under which the control and operation of the world's air services would be under a single international authority; internationalization with domestic services reserved for national operators; a closed imperial system; and a European system (which might or might not include dependencies and could also make reservations for domestic services). Under the latter alternative the following caveat was included: 'The Foreign Office feel that any scheme of internationalisation which did not include the United States, if put forward as a British proposal, would be certain to be interpreted in America as a direct challenge and a repudiation of His Majesty's Government's declared intention to consider civil aviation and other post-war questions in a spirit of friendship and collaboration. Fierce resentment might thus be engendered and competition of the most pernicious kind might follow, as a result of which all prospect of setting up an international order of any kind would be frustrated.'

The Barlow report searched for common ground, notwithstanding the Foreign Office caveat. Although not asked to rank the various alternatives, the committee members felt 'bound to place it on record that, in our view, any of the systems with which we have dealt would probably be preferable to the system of cut-throat competition which prevailed before the war.' If this pre-war competition developed, Britain would 'inevitably have to operate under very severe handicaps – in particular, the necessity of attempting to compete with the United States in the provision of services on a lavish and world-wide scale – and we should be compelled heavily to subsidise our own services in the interests of national prestige.' Assuming that 'every effort will be made to avoid a relapse into the pre-war chaos,' the report concluded that 'full internationalisation without reservation of internal services ..., if it could be made to work, would offer the most radical and satisfactory solution of the problem.' Yet, the committee warned, because of its radical nature, full internationalization may well be rejected by the world community; if this happened, the committee recommended support for a European (with dependencies) scheme, 'subject always to the reservations made by the Foreign Office.'[25] Even with the Foreign Office reservations, however, Sir Orme Sargent found the report 'an unsatisfactory document.' The Barlow committee 'merely looked upon internationalisation as a means of excluding an area of the world's surface from American competition in order to make it a preserve for the British aviation industry and British technical personnel.' With this view in mind, the committee report was 'unfairly weighted in order to make out a case for the internationalisation of Europe, and all the difficulties in the way of universal internationalisation are magnified and stressed for this purpose.'[26]

Nevertheless, by March 1943 the preliminary framework of Britain's civil aviation policy had been put in place. No final cabinet decision had been made concerning internationalization, but its future was not bright, given the likely attitude of the Americans. On other issues, however, there was an emerging consensus: the British aircraft industry should be preserved and expanded with government support; there should be some international regulaton of aviation for reasons of military security and in order to prevent the return to the uneconomical competition of the 1930s' and, most significantly, there was a determination to keep the United States from securing the dominant role in post-war civil aviation through the implementation of an unregulated free-air policy.

These views were put to the House of Commons by Sir Archibald Sinclair on 11 March 1943. 'In the view of His Majesty's Government,' Sinclair informed the House, 'some form of international collaboration will be essential if the air is to be developed in the interests of mankind as a whole, trade served, international understanding fostered, and some measure of international security gained.' Some preliminary steps had been made but before any policy was firmly established, it was essential to begin discussions with the other allied nations in an effort to reach some international understanding. 'For though air transport is a young industry and its potentialities have everywhere fired the imagination,' Sinclair concluded, 'its organisation in the post-war world cannot be considered in isolation but must be so framed as to be consistent, in spirit and in truth, with the principles which should govern the international economic policy of the United Nations after the war.'²⁷

II

The British ambassador in Washington kept a close watch on the discussion of post-war civil aviation in the United States, and he did not always like what he saw. Early in February 1943, Lord Halifax reported to London that American aviation interests – including men such as Juan Trippe – had 'been taking the line that after the war America must be second to none in the air.' Unfortunately, he added, the United Kingdom was perceived as the most serious potential competitor and, consequently, suspicions over Britain's post-war intentions were on the rise. According to Halifax, American concern had two major thrusts: 'The first is that we propose in the post-war period to deny to American aviation the chance to use bases in British territory. The second is that we are using or proposing to use American transport planes, obtained under Lend-lease for war purposes in commercial competition with American air lines.'²⁸

American industry had far surpassed the rest of the world in the production of long-range transport planes and it was clear that this advantage would be maintained for some years after the war was over. But what good were all these planes if the United States was blocked from international routes by far-flung empires that were determined to champion the cause of national sovereignty over the air at the expense of the United States? Thus, Britain's 'trump card' – its widespread possessions – was increasingly perceived, in some American eyes at least, as the primary obstacle to the expansion of American aviation. This in turn raised British fears that the United States would link its lend-lease aid (or provision of transport aircraft) to some kind of reciprocal agreement in which the United States would receive commercial privileges at selected air-bases located on British territories.²⁹

There were genuine reasons for concern. More than any other single development, with perhaps the exception of the war itself, air-flight had ended American isolation forever. One author in *Fortune* wrote early in 1943 that the air was 'a blue-water ocean to which every nation potentially has access for trade and high strategy in all directions. Under its intoxicating implications the ancient ideas of a world divided by land and sea seem to be as outmoded as the Chinese Wall.'³⁰ Others pointed out that the old perception of global geography had been turned on its head; transpolar flight, for example, now exposed the Midwest to attack and at the same time opened it to new markets and gave it access to new trade.[31]

Indeed, aviation would play a major role in defence and in the development of trade in the post-war world, and the United States must bear its share of the responsibility – but what shape should American policy take? To some the answer was clear. Representative Clare Booth Luce outlined her position during her first speech in Congress in February 1943: 'We want to fly everywhere,' she said, 'Period.' As for this talk at home and abroad about internationalization, she described it with one word – 'Globaloney.' Others agreed: 'We have no commercial bases except in the Pacific and the Caribbean,' *Fortune* reported. 'Our problem, therefore, is not to restore the *status quo ante* but to break out.' The United States now had the advantage; other countries had lost their air services, while the USATC had blossomed into one of the largest air transport systems. The US aircraft industry had developed into the strongest in the world, and many communities across the country now depended on the jobs it provided for their survival. Thousands of American airmen were becoming familiar with the international air routes, and the ATC had constructed airports all around the world. 'Shall we withdraw?' the *Fortune* columnist asked rhetorically, 'or shall we insist upon our right as a great power to fly anywhere? And whose air is it, anyway?'[32]

An aggressive and competitive free-air policy based on American productive strength and unique position of influence found many supporters in government and in the press, but it was by no means universally accepted. Public debate elicited a variety of viewpoints, including those much more sympathetic to the idea of internationalization. For example, Harold Stassen, the Republican governor of Minnesota, wrote in the *Saturday Evening Post* on 22 May 1943 that one of the functions of a United Nations government would have to be the 'administration of the key international airports and airways of the world.' It was essential that the future world government be ready to deal with the problems of international aviation – the need for regulations, meteorological and radio services, air traffic control, ground maintenance, etc. 'if we fail to develop administration on a world level,' he argued, 'we shall not only stifle growth but give rein, through nonregulation, to new dangers. International barrier-raising, cutthroat competition and power politics could be the quick cause of another world war. The catch phrase "international freedom of the air" is not the answer. It would lead to anarchy of the air and the basic violation of domestic sovereignty.'[33]

Vice President Henry Wallace was enthralled by aviation and had flown to China wearing two wrist-watches – 'one to tell the time where he was, the other to tell the time back home.'[34] Like Stassen, Wallace was sympathetic to some degree of international control of aviation and, like many of his British colleagues, he wrapped his views on civil aviation together with his hopes for post-war international security. In addition to the creation of an international peace force, he envisaged the establishment of a United Nations investment corporation under which 'the establishment of a network of globe-girdling airways ought to be the very first order of business. The airways I visualize would have as their primary justification the safe-guarding of world peace. They would be operated by the air arm of the United Nations peace force.'[35]

It was with these individuals and other 'New Deal officials' that the British might find allies. Whether this group could exert much influence or effectively limit the power of others, such as Pan Am, remained to be seen. There was considerable opposition to Wallace's views and the idea of internationalization. For example, one official in the Department of Commerce dismissed the Foreign Office proposals as being 'relatively untrammelled by practical considerations.'[36]

On the governmental level, the direction of us civil aviation policy was divided among several departments. In the days following Pearl Harbor, us military aviation was given priority over civil aviation and a director of civil aviation was appointed in the War Department. Subsequently, civil aviation – both domestic and international – was cut back and the secretary of war was 'authorized and directed to take possession and assure control of any civil aviation system, or systems, or any part thereof, to the extent necessary for the successful prosecution of the war.'[37]

The new director of civil aviation and the War Department were concerned primarily with civil aviation as it affected the prosecution of the war effort. Planning for post-war aviation, however, was left in the hands of the CAB, the State Department, Congress, and, ultimately, the president. The CAB was responsible for the regulation of civil aviation and for the allocation of new routes. The war curtailed civil flying and few new domestic routes were established, but in 1943 the CAB initiated a study of post-war civil aviation. In a December 1942 speech, Welch Pogue, the CAB chair, reaffirmed the board's general support for 'regulated competition' and gave a good indication of the direction in which the CAB was moving. The pre-war system based on the closed sky and bilateral agreements between countries placed too many restrictions on the development of international aviation. 'Aviation can be a compelling force in stabilizing the political relationships of the world,' he noted, and the 'present fight for freedom will be lost to no small degree if we miss the opportunity to accelerate this force by making the great international highways open to all nations.'[38]

The responsibility for aviation in the State Department fell to Adolf A. Berle, the assistant secretary of state. Berle, 'a curious little fellow with lots of brain but no personality,'[39] was an ex-Columbia University professor and member of the New Deal 'Brains Trust,' who had become a close adviser to President Roosevelt. Berle personified 'American New Deal internationalism, that ambivalent mixture of idealism and imperialism,' as John Holmes put it.[40] At different times he could exhibit traits of arrogance, impatience, and ruthlessness, which did not endear him to many foreign colleagues, especially in Great Britain. He was a continentalist with a disdain for the British Empire, especially when imperial concerns clashed with the expansion of American interests.

In January 1943, Berle was given responsibility to establish an interdepartmental committee to examine the questions surrounding post-war civil aviation. The Advisory Committee on Aviation was chaired by Berle and consisted of representatives from the various departments that played a role in determining civil aviation policy: Robert Lovett, the assistant secretary of war; Artemus Gates, the assistant secretary of the navy; Wayne Taylor, the under-secretary of commerce; and Welch Pogue of the CAB.

On 15 February 1943, only a few weeks after the formation of the committee, Berle appeared before the House of Representatives Committee on Foreign Affairs, ostensibly to answer questions on the use of lend-lease funds for the construction of airports in foreign territories. Berle was clearly aware of the strong feeling across the country and in the House that the United States should come out of the war with some commercial rights at the air-bases it had built and paid for during the war. He was not optimistic, however, that special rights could or should be negotiated. It would make the United States look like it was trying to gain an advantage over its allies by insisting on post-war rights before taking the necessary steps to defeat the common enemy. Berle did not believe that you could 'bargain for your own safety,' as he put it. He had 'some difficulty in comprehending' how the United States could 'impose conditions which say that you cannot attack or fight an enemy unless you also do thus and so on the side. Wars are not made that way, and they certainly are not won that way. You go after the enemy where you can, and you keep right on going until you have him knocked out. The advantages that you get are the results of the general settlement which you make at the end.' Besides, he told the House committee, it was too late to back out of agreements already made, and, moreover, the air-bases were constructed for military, not economic, purposes; there was no guarantee that they would be of any major commercial value after the war. America's real advantage, Berle suggested, would be found in aircraft production, which would give an important edge to American aviation interests for some years to come.

In Berle's view it was pointless to negotiate 'airfield by airfield'; the best solution would be more general negotiations with the allied nations for the exchange of post-war commercial rights. 'Plainly,' he said, 'it cannot be expected that our planes shall be accorded rights of landing, service, and commercial access in foreign countries if we adopt the policy of denying access to the planes of those countries reaching our shores.' To rush into it 'in the spirit of narrow nationalism' would be to court disaster, he continued; it 'has got to be a fair and equitable basis between nations that recognize that all of them have interests and rights and try to work them out on a decent basis.'[41] Berle was pressed by the House Committee to be more explicit concerning the State Department's aviation policy, but he declined, claiming that it would be unwise to lay out the American position before negotiations had begun.

Berle was more specific in his committee's first report sent to Cordell Hull on 30 April 1943. The Advisory Committee examined the question of Pan Am's monopoly in international aviation and whether or not this should be permitted to continue in the post-war period. 'Due note was taken of the fact that this is going to be a hot political issue,' the committee noted, 'because of the strength of the lobbies of the various contending parties.' Nevertheless, the majority of the committee members agreed that 'American foreign aviation is too large a proposition for any single company; and that the monopoly principle used by other countries has in general produced inefficient service.' In its place the committee suggested that a number of airlines, including Pan Am, be allowed to participate by 'granting to each a particular zone in which it might be dominant.'[42]

Regarding international arrangements, the committee believed that 'the best interests of the United States are served by the widest generalization of air navigation rights.' To this end, a general multilateral agreement should be negotiated – one that would protect the right of innocent passage for all participating nations and in which the entry of American airlines into foreign territory would be exchanged for foreign entry into American territory. It was hoped that all nations would participate eventually, but the 'heart of a general aviation agreement would have to rest on agreement between the United States and the British Empire and Commonwealth of Nations; it may fairly be assumed that once this agreement is reached, practically all countries in the world (with the possible exception of Russia) would accede.'[43]

The negotiation of the broadest possible bilateral or multilateral agreement, with international regulation limited to rate-setting and technical matters, was the course set by Berle in 1943 and followed for as long as he was in the forefront of American aviation policy. The CAB was guaranteed a role in the development of international services because it had the sole power to issue operation permits. The State Department, meanwhile, was flexing its muscles as the vehicle of American foreign policy. No longer would individual private companies bargain for landing rights with foreign governments; the channel of negotiations now would flow through the State Department and the CAB directly to the president.

Berle, Pogue, and their committee were not without rivals. The Senate Commerce Committee established a subcommittee, chaired by Sen. Champ Clark of Missouri, to deal with civil aviation matters, and this committee advocated caution with respect to international aviation, arguing that it was essential to settle on a domestic policy first. Another group, the War Investigating Committee, chaired by the other senator from Missouri, Harry S. Truman, initiated an investigation into the contracts negotiated for the construction of airports in foreign countries. Never far from the surface there lurked the fear that the United States would receive a raw deal at the end of the war.

The internal struggle between the State Department and the CAB on the one hand, and Pan Am and its influential friends in Congress on the other, continued through 1943. Pan Am had lobbied successfully to prevent encroachment on its international routes in the past and it maintained its support for a chosen instrument (i.e., Pan Am) policy. During the summer, meanwhile, the CAB released its survey of American civil aviation and shortly thereafter a joint declaration from sixteen airline companies (Pan Am, United, and American Export Airlines did not participate) was published, calling for private ownership and free competition on international air routes. Without doubt, these airlines argued, 'in air transportation where boundaries become meaningless, there can be no rational basis for permitting air transportation within the country to develop and expand on a competitive basis, while that outside the country is left to the withering influence of monopoly.'[44]

Air Commodore D.C. Blackford, the air attaché at the British Embassy, reported to London in July on the developing situation. 'The general conclusion,' he wrote, 'seems to be that behind the scenes at the present time there is considerable study and perplexity as to the policy to be pursued. It is realized that American claims to special consideration in view of her wartime expenditure of money and labour are on shaky foundations, and there is nervousness that, if this bluff is called, America may not come too well out of a straightforward agreement.'[45] In any event, in both the United States and Great Britain there was a growing realization that the problems of international civil aviation could not be resolved in isolation; the two sides would have to talk.

6

1943: The Shape of Things to Come

Flying westbound across the Atlantic in an RAF Dakota, Harold Balfour, who was no stranger to Canada, recorded how he 'flew at 10,000 feet under a cloudless sky with not a bump in the air. There was no night; only a half twilight. Far away on the horizon the Northern Lights of the Arctic lit up the sky with glorious colours.' As the Dakota approached Labrador, he continued, 'we watched a scattered army of great white icebergs drifting in deep blue sea. The two engines purred away. We were suspended in perfection.'

Once in Ottawa, however, Balfour returned with a jolt to the imperfections of wartime Canada. Meeting his old friend Col. George Drew, the Conservative premier of Ontario, Balfour learned of the colonel's difficulties in securing a seat on a plane flying to Britain. Old animosities die hard, and Balfour later noted that Prime Minister King was 'moving Heaven and Earth' to prevent Drew from making this trip. Drew was keen on visiting the Ontario regiments stationed overseas and, without thinking of any possible political ramifications, Balfour offered Drew a seat in his Dakota. The return flight went off without a hitch, except that at one stopover Drew accidentally fell into a river and was forced to carry on pantless, with only a rug wrapped around his legs for protection from the cold.

Had Mackenzie King known of Drew's accident, he might have drawn some satisfaction from his rival's misfortune; as it was, he was angered by Balfour's actions, which he considered to be an interference in Canada's domestic affairs. An angry telegram of complaint was rushed off to Lord Cranborne, the dominions secretary, but it was all in vain. Showing Balfour the telegram, Cranborne said: 'How silly can a man be?'[1] For Mackenzie King, however, this was not the first time that aviation and politics were mixed up together, nor would it be the last.

I

'The nervous reaction of Canadians to American and British talk about postwar control of the international air,' one American author wrote in 1943, 'suggests the mischief latent in this problem, even for good neighbors.' Behind the public indifference, he added, the Canadians 'turned suspicious and alert.' The war had sparked a 'tremendous expansion in Canada's postwar air potential,' and an accident of geography had put the Dominion squarely in the path of several strategic air routes of the future. The Canadians would be a force to be reckoned with, he suggested, yet there was still a suspicion north of the border that Canada would be left out while Great Britain and the United States negotiated on post-war aviation arrangements.[2]

The Canadians who might have read this article had reason to agree with its conclusions. Canada *was* strategically located – that was beyond question. Canada also had emerged as one of the world's strongest air powers – in real terms as well as potential. Yet there were nagging doubts. The entrance of the United States into the war in December 1941 had effectively eliminated any need for Canada to act as a mediator between Great Britain and the United States; now the two major powers could deal with each other directly. Canada's role was inevitably diminished. As Hume Wrong noted, now that the British and the Americans were partners, 'we become only a junior member of the partnership.'[3]

The events of 1942 seemed to bear out this statement. The creation of combined boards to help co-ordinate the American and British war efforts appeared to ignore the significant contribution made by Canada to the Allied cause; only after months of wrangling did the Canadians achieve limited representation on a number of these boards. At the same time, preliminary plans were being made for the creation of the United Nations Relief and Rehabilitation Administration (UNRRA) and, at first, it looked like the Canadian claim for representation, however reasonable, would again be bypassed. A compromise was eventually negotiated in which Canada was granted influential positions on a number of UNRRA committees, but not the official status of full membership.[4]

In an effort to do what they could to win the war, Canadians had shown themselves willing to make enormous sacrifices – in terms of men and matériel as well as status and prestige. But, as recent studies of Canadian foreign relations during the Second World War have pointed out, Canadians were determined to play a prominent role when it came to planning for post-war international organizations. Mackenzie King's statement of the 'functional principle' in the House of Commons on 9 July 1943 advocated that representation on international bodies 'should neither be restricted to the largest states nor necessarily extended to all states. Representation should be determined on a functional basis which will admit to full membership those countries, large and small, which have the greatest contribution to make to the particular object in question.'[5] Canadians had paid the price through their deeds; now it was time to be accorded responsibility equivalent to their contribution.

Nowhere did the functional principle seem more applicable than in the field of international civil aviation.[6] The success of the British Commonwealth Air Training Plan gave an indication of Canada's potential as an aviation power. The creation of Atfero and the Northwest Staging Route spoke loudly to Canadians that their country would be in the path of post-war air routes. 'Canada is sitting on the crossroads of world aviation,' wrote Leslie Roberts in Maclean's. 'This is all the more obvious when we begin to think of the transpolar routes of the day after tomorrow, when Canada will become the hub for spokes reaching out from America to China, India, Russia and to almost anywhere in the world.'[7]

Many others agreed. 'The plane's conquest of time and space,' one author wrote, 'is giving new meaning to global geography and is radically changing the pattern of international relations.' It was time for a revolution in our perception of Canada's place in the world; time to move our 'Mercator minds' to a new polar perspective. 'We know that the world is round,' he continued, 'yet almost every one of us pictures it as a rectangle ... Most maps cut off the northern 1,000 miles of the world and we never miss them.'[8] All this had now changed. Not only did Canada have the pilots and the skilled workers, it also had the airports, weather facilities, and the industrial base, all of which left the country 'in a strong position to go horse trading with the boys when the question of global aviation comes up for settlement.[9]

Along with new opportunities came new dangers. If Canada was to be the hub of post-war civil aviation, it would also be a buffer between the superpowers and the potential battlefield of future wars. Civil aviation could never be divorced from military aviation – this was a fact of life. Thus, when Canadians examined their country's future role in international aviation they saw not only great possibilities but also security implications and the need for some form of international control.

Geography and science were dragging Canadians into the air age whether they liked it or not. It remained to be seen what they would make of the opportunity. A public opinion poll in summer 1943 revealed that 81 per cent of Canadians wanted the post-war airlines in Canada to be owned and operated either by the government (50 per cent) or by both the government and private business (31 per cent). More interesting was that, in a similar poll, 61 per cent of Canadians were in favour of the establishment of some kind of authority to regulate the international airlines after the war, while only 26 per cent believed there should be free competition in the air.[10]

For some, like George Drew, it was a question of either standing with the empire or being drawn into the American orbit. 'That is our choice,' he wrote, 'to become the centre of a great world girdling British commercial system or to sink back into the unimportant role of a satellite nation using aircraft, instruments and supplies made in the United States.'[11] There was no doubt where Drew stood, but others were not so sure. The efforts of Mackenzie King and C.D. Howe from 1936 onwards pointed in another direction, away from imperial ties and towards establishing a more independent Canadian stance. Now that Canada had emerged as a world-class air power, it was even less likely that the government would submerge Canada's role in any larger unit – British or American.

The focus of study for post-war international civil aviation was centred, quite naturally, in the Interdepartmental Committee on International Civil Aviation, created in May 1942. For the first few months of its existence, the ICICA dealt with immediate problems, such as the transatlantic air service, but by the end of the year some steps had been taken towards the formation of a post-war policy. The number of actual meetings of the committee decreased, while the real burden for the initial investigations fell on the shoulders of three men: Norman Robertson, Escott Reid, and John Baldwin.

From the very beginning these three men exhibited a strong

internationalist streak. In a draft memorandum, dated 20 December 1942, J.R. Baldwin pointed out several reasons why the Canadian government should support some degree of internationalization, despite Canada's economic strength and strategic location. First, if a very competitive system emerged at the end of the war, Canada would be at a disadvantage vis-à-vis the United States and Great Britain. As he put it, 'even though Canada may be able to operate as efficiently as other nations she will not be in a position to subsidize her own international air traffic as heavily as other wealthier governments.' Second, he pointed out that strategic advantage was a fleeting thing – technological advances would eventually diminish the need to use Canada as a stepping-stone. Baldwin's third point took a different approach. There was 'every reason to believe,' he wrote, 'that at the conclusion of the war suggestions for international regulation of aviation will be put forward, possibly by the great powers themselves. It would strengthen Canada's position if the Canadian government prepares and advances proposals along this line, instead of waiting to be presented with ready made plans at the end of the war. Canada as the initiator of action would then be given every consideration on subsequent negotiations.'[12] In Baldwin's mind there were very real reasons to support a scheme for internationalization; taking positive action now might be the best way to secure it.

Escott Reid produced a second draft of this memo a few days later, adding his own comments. Reid agreed with Baldwin's view that Canada's strategic location would decrease in importance relative to the development of the intercontinental air liner, and he firmly dismissed the idea of negotiating forced stops for airlines flying over Canadian territory. If such a policy were adopted on a wide scale and airlines were forced to stop in each country flown over, then international aviation would grind to a halt. Internationalization, in contrast, might provide the solution. Like Baldwin, Reid argued that in the face of deteriorating territorial advantage coupled with the possibility of cut-throat competition from stronger nations, internationalization would provide a suitable atmosphere in which Canadians would be able to develop and control their own air services.

Reid and Baldwin began working on an interim report on post-war aviation that included some preliminary ideas on the workings of internationalization and the shape of the proposed international air authority. No one on the Canadian side was privy to the secret discussions taking place at that moment in Great Britain, but many of the same concerns, ideas, and proposals were present in these early memos on both sides of the ocean. For example, Reid wrote that internationalization would 'contribute greatly to the effectiveness of a new world order,' and he couched his reasoning in terms that easily could have originated in Whitehall: 'Without the internationalization of civil aviation nations with large civil aviation companies accustomed to fly international routes will have a striking power greatly in excess of that possessed by nations with smaller civil aviation companies or with companies unaccustomed to flying strategic international routes. Moreover national civil aviation companies provide a training ground and a reservoir for military air personnel and thus increase the military potential of the country concerned.'

Reid gave his international authority the name 'World Airways,' but in many other respects it resembled what was being proposed elsewhere, including on such issues as the reservation of internal services, the allocation of routes, and the right to fix rates. He also realized that internationalization would have its enemies and might never be fully implemented. Nevertheless, he argued cogently, it would still be in Canada's national interest to push for as much international control as possible. Even without achieving full internationalization, an authority 'might be set up without power to operate air lines but with regulatory powers over all international civil aviation – a sort of international Civil Aeronautics Authority.'[13]

Reid and Baldwin continued to revise their views in the early months of 1943 with a view to presenting to the ICICA a solid memorandum to be discussed and ultimately submitted for consideration by the Cabinet War Committee. At the same time, Norman Robertson contacted Vincent Massey in London for any information he could give on developments in Britain. Robertson was increasingly concerned over what he learned of British and American civil aviation policy, and in his mind the apparent division between them made it imperative for Canada to be prepared with its own policy to better meet the foreign challenge. He told Massey that he could not pass along an official government policy because there wasn't one: 'Our actions up to the present can be interpreted as being based solely on an attempt to leave the issues open until after the war in order that we may then adopt whatever policy seems at the time to be in the best interests of Canada.'

Robertson could, however, give 'an authoritative unofficial statement on the subject' to Massey. He enclosed a copy of a CIIA paper written for the Institute of Pacific Relations Conference held in December 1942 and told Massey that the sections dealing with international co-operation and routes were 'of particular interest.' This paper, Robertson continued, reflected one school of thought in Canada, namely that 'Canada is in a strong geographical position so far as bargaining over international routes is concerned, that TCA can run international air lines, including intercontinental airlines, as efficiently and cheaply as any country and more efficiently and cheaply than most – including the United Kingdom in this latter category – and that, therefore, Canadian policy should be directed to the establishment of strong TCA air routes across the north Atlantic and the north Pacific, between Canada and the United States, and probably between Canada and the British West Indies.'

Robertson was not at all convinced that such an independent policy would be the most appropriate. He agreed with what Baldwin and Reid had already pointed out – that although Canada lay in the middle of the future great circle routes, technological developments would ultimately enable American, British, and Soviet aircraft to fly over Canadian territory without stopping. Taking action to prevent this possibility by negotiating forced stops at Canadian airports in return for the right to traverse Canadian air space would 'exacerbate international relations' needlessly. Robertson went on to make the case for internationalization. It was possible, he argued,

that the real long-run Canadian interest may require us to support or, if necessary, to initiate plans for the effective internationalization of civil aviation instead of trying to exploit our possibly transitory geographical advantages. We might find it easier to work out a scheme of international operation within which our own local system would work than to stand up successfully to competing United States, Russian, and British efforts to expand their national air services over intercontinental routes, for while Canada might be able to operate as efficiently and cheaply as these and other nations, Canada would not be in a position to subsidize Canadian intercontinental airlines as heavily as could wealthier nations.[14]

Views such as these were very much a part of the numerous draft memos on post-war policy prepared for the Cabinet War Committee over the winter and spring of 1943. The CWC had dealt with civil aviation topics primarily in connection with the establishment of the transatlantic air service, but some preliminary discussions on post-war policy began during these months. Not surprisingly, the prime movers in the CWC, now as in the past, were C.D. Howe and Mackenzie King.

Howe's feelings on TCA were well known, and his experiences during the negotiation of the transatlantic service served only to reinforce his view that Canada and TCA should pursue an independent course after the war. 'Through our geographical position, if for no other reason,' he wrote Robertson on 8 February, 'Canada will have an important place in post-war civil aviation, provided we are able to work out our own situation apart from that of the United Kingdom.'[15] Mackenzie King held similar beliefs and, like Howe, saw Canada's strategic geographic location as an advantage not to be given away.

Canada would have its place in the post-war aviation world, and it was left to Mackenzie King to make this clear to the people of Canada. On 2 April the prime minister rose in the House of Commons to issue a statement on government civil aviation policy. King began with a review of the 'remarkable expansion' that had taken place in Canadian aviation during the war and how geography had ensured an important place for Canada after the war. He reconfirmed the government's commitment to TCA as Canada's 'chosen instrument,' noting that TCA would continue to operate the main domestic lines and would have exclusive rights on the international services. With respect to the international routes of the future, the government intended 'to press vigorously for a place in international air transportation consistent with Canada's geographical position and progress in aviation. All concessions and privileges that have been granted by Canada to other countries as part of the war effort will terminate at the end of the war or almost immediately thereafter.'

The prime minister pointed out that Canadian policy for the immediate future would be to make temporary arrangements, in an effort to maintain government flexibility when the time came to negotiate international agreements. Yet, within this loose framework there was a determination to co-operate and negotiate with the other countries of the world. 'The Canadian government,' he concluded, 'strongly favours a policy of international collaboration and co-operation in air transport and is prepared to support in international negotiations whatever international air transport policy can be demonstrated as being best calculated to serve not only the immediate national interests of Canada but also our overriding interest in the establishment of an international order which will prevent the outbreak of another world war.'[16]

Mackenzie King alluded to the need for international negotiations, but when questioned by the opposition, he made no reference to the fact that some unofficial discussions had already been held. In Washington, Lester Pearson met with Adolf Berle on 16 February, the day after the latter's appearance before the House Foreign Affairs Committee. The two men agreed that full-scale international negotiations would be premature at that point, but agreed that it was important for Canada and the United States to co-operate closely. Berle emphasized the important position of Canada and hoped that the two countries would negotiate a workable agreement. Pearson could not agree more and he gave his opinion that Canada and the United States should hold talks with each other before Washington began discussing civil aviation with London.[17]

Not every American official was filled with goodwill for Canada, however. Welch Pogue wrote to Berle about the Canadians and he was not so sure that it would be a good idea to negotiate with them first. They could turn around and make arrangements with the British and be difficult about American transatlantic services over their territory. He reminded Berle that 'Newfoundland is not Canada' and that although it would be inconvenient, it was not absolutely necessary to fly over Canadian soil to get to the United Kingdom.[18]

In any event, Pearson had touched on what was becoming an important issue for the Canadians, namely, the desire to negotiate one-on-one with the Americans and not as part of a Commonwealth delegation. For Pearson, Canada's aviation relations with the United States were far too important to be left in the hands of others. Indeed, Canada's relationship with the United States was more important than that with most Commonwealth nations.

In London, views on Commonwealth collaboration were quite different. On 18 February, Clement Attlee wrote to Sir Archibald Sinclair that civil aviation matters were 'clearly worrying the House and public opinion in this country and the question is becoming active in the U.S.A. as evidenced by the activities of Mrs. Clair Luce and others.' As dominions secretary, Attlee had been approached for information and informal discussions by several high commissioners, but as of yet, 'at the request of the Air Ministry, I have told them that we are not ready for this.' Talks would have to be held with the Americans and the Soviets eventually, he reminded Sinclair, but beforehand 'it is essential that we should consult the Dominions and be able to carry them with us.'[19]

In his reply, Sinclair recommended 'off the record' talks with the dominion high commissioners rather than official negotiations at this stage.[20] To this end, Attlee arranged a meeting for 25 February between representatives from Canada, Australia, New Zealand, South Africa, India, Southern Rhodesia, and the members of the Jowitt committee. Vincent Massey was away from London at the time and Canada was represented by Frederic Hudd, the deputy high commissioner. Internationalization was the topic of conversation and while none of the dominion representatives could give official statements, there seemed to be general agreement that some form of internationalization would be worthwhile and that efforts should be made not to alienate the United States. It was equally clear, however, that the British representatives hoped for a united Commonwealth policy to emerge. No steps would be taken vis-à-vis the Americans behind the backs of the dominions, Anthony Eden promised, and while Britain did not have a firm policy at that moment, Sinclair suggested that 'the first step was to obtain agreement on the policy which the Dominion and United Kingdom Governments would pursue for the post-war organisation of air transport throughout the world.'[21]

A second meeting was held near the end of March, after the submission of the Barlow report. The conversation ran along familiar lines, again dealing with internationalization. Massey was in attendance at this meeting, and, while the talk was very general and no commitments were sought or made, he and the other high commissioners were inevitably drawn into Commonwealth policy making and exposed to the divisions that had emerged within the Jowitt committee. For Massey it was not a question of picking sides; his mere presence gave credence to Commonwealth collaboration, despite Ottawa's plans to take a more independent stand. This was just the kind of thing that Howe and King abhorred, but Massey did not seem to mind. In his diary he wrote: 'Nine ministers present who for the most part held divergent views on the problem. They range all the way from the toughness of Kingsley Wood and Amery to the moderation of Cripps. The one thing on which we all agreed was that the Americans should be approached first and asked whether they would accept a system of complete internationalism. This committee is a good example of real consultation between the U.K. and the Dominions. We are not being informed at an early date as to what British policy is, we are asked to help to make it.'[22]

Events moved quickly over the following weeks. Copies of the Shelmerdine, Finlay, and Barlow reports were distributed and transmitted to Ottawa by Massey. Study began immediately in the ICICA and some initial work was done on revising Finlay's draft convention. Massey's reports were followed by official requests from the Dominions Office for dominion opinion concerning the proposal to approach the Americans with a scheme for the full internationalization of air transport. The responses from the various dominions were not overly positive: while most governments, including Canada, Australia, and New Zealand, favoured a degree of internationalization, it was felt that the Americans should not be approached with a concrete plan for them either to accept or reject. A final settlement would have to be negotiated over a period of time.[23]

The British government responded by doing what it had promised to do – invite the dominion governments to London to discuss international civil aviation before opening informal talks with the Americans. Because the dominions had expressed a variety of opinions, it was important to attempt 'to reach some general conclusions as to the scheme of post-war air transport which would be generally acceptable to and best serve the interests of the members of the British Commonwealth.'[24] Because the Americans had intimated that they might be ready to talk, the British hoped that a Commonwealth meeting could be arranged for the middle of June.

Almost without realizing it, the Canadians were embroiled in a sticky misunderstanding. Canadian policy had never favoured preliminary Commonwealth talks; unfortunately, as Massey pointed out, the 'United Kingdom Government has however assumed for some months that Canada is prepared to take part in prior Commonwealth discussions on air transport.'[25] Canadian representatives had participated in the informal meetings in February and March and had agreed to the conclusions that just such an event should take place. British ministers had repeatedly stressed the importance of Commonwealth collaboration; their government had introduced a proposal for full internationalization that was opposed by several dominions; it seemed natural and right that the members of the Commonwealth should meet to discuss what steps should be taken next.

The Canadian government was caught off guard. The ICICA had not yet submitted its interim report and Mackenzie King's 2 April statement stood as the sole statement of Canadian policy. There was a strong resistance to preliminary Commonwealth talks, however. First, Howe, King, and many officials believed that Canada's post-war position would be so strong that, in dealings with the United States in particular, Canada would be better able to pursue its policy alone, rather than as part of a Commonwealth team. Second, from a tactical point of view, it was argued that any hint of an empire policy would be badly received by the US government and public, making any chance of a future agreement less likely. In Canadian eyes, therefore, it was important that the United States be involved in any discussions from the very start. Still, there is no evidence that any measures were taken by the Canadians to check the unfolding of these events before a problem developed. Late in May, some efforts were made by Massey and Escott Reid (who was in Britain making final preparations for the inauguration of the transatlantic air service), but to no avail.[26]

The British proposal was discussed in the Cabinet War Committee on 2 June, and opinion against prior Commonwealth talks remained strong. The feelings of the CWC were expressed in the Canadian response, dated 6 June: 'Having in mind that our connections in the civil aviation field with the United States are as close and numerous as our connections with any of the Commonwealth countries, we see obvious objections to a course of preliminary consultation in London which might be construed as an attempt to formulate a concerted Commonwealth policy before we had had an opportunity of exchanging views direct with the United States.'[27] The Canadian government tried to sooth the bad news with a counter-proposal: Why not hold the preliminary conversations in Ottawa instead of London, and invite American representatives to participate from the very start?

Before responding to the Canadian suggestion, the British government called together another meeting of the dominion high commissioners with the members of the Jowitt committee. Massey attempted to explain the Canadian position to the others, but he was badly outnumbered. Several UK ministers voiced their opinions on the need for Commonwealth consultations before meeting the Americans. These sentiments were shared by W.J. Jordan, the high commissioner for New Zealand, Colonel Reitz from South Africa, and the two Australian representatives, S.M. Bruce and H.V. Evatt. Indeed, the minutes of the meeting show that Massey was alone in opposing the proposed Commonwealth talks.

Early in the meeting, Anthony Eden set a new wave in motion. He informed the others that after talks with the Soviet ambassador, he felt obligated to invite the Soviets to the Ottawa discussions. This suited him fine, but if the Soviets attended the meetings he expected that the Americans would also want the Chinese to be involved. Thus, a Commonwealth plus United States meeting was becoming a truly international gathering. The possibility of a large conference heightened the desire of others to have prior discussions alone, and Sir Stafford Cripps then suggested that preliminary Commonwealth meetings be held in Ottawa before the opening of the proposed conference. H.V. Evatt, the Australian minister for external affairs, went so far as to oppose a conference in Ottawa 'without previous agreement on principles between the members of the Commonwealth.'[28]

The Canadians were being outflanked. The original intention of the Ottawa talks was to prevent the creation or appearance of a Commonwealth bloc before opening talks with the Americans; there had been little desire for a conference on the scale now being discussed. To make matters worse, because of the size of this proposed conference, Britain and the other members of the Commonwealth were insisting on prior Commonwealth discussions in Ottawa before the talks began – precisely what the Canadians had hoped to prevent in the first place. Ottawa's response was predictable; while welcoming the views of Britain on international civil aviation, the Canadians argued that it was not necessary to hold preliminary Commonwealth talks in Ottawa in the days before the international conference.[29]

At this stage both sides pulled back to reconsider their positions. On 17 June the ICICA submitted its Interim Report to the CWC, setting out the alternatives for Canada in the future of international civil aviation. The different schemes were discussed – ranging from the closed sky to regionalization to complete internationalization – although the general thrust of the report suggested that at the present stage it did 'not appear necessary or desirable for Canada (or indeed any nation) to lay down its policy in too precise terms since too early a crystallization of national policies will make it more difficult for the nations to reach agreement.'[30] On the question of preliminary Commonwealth talks, however, the Canadians remained firm. 'If we give in on this question,' Escott Reid wrote, 'where we should have peculiar knowledge and peculiar interest we must face the fact that we shall have committed ourselves to prior Commonwealth discussions on every issue of the postwar settlement.'[31] The Cabinet War Committee agreed; on 2 July the Canadian position that the United States not be excluded from any initial talks was reconfirmed.[32]

A second matter dealt with was the proposed Ottawa conference, the original intention of which was to hold talks in Ottawa as a way of bypassing preliminary Commonwealth talks in London. This scheme failed and what were intended to be informal discussions on the official level only suddenly blossomed into an international conference of ministers – a turn of events the Canadians were unprepared for and did not want. As a result, the CWC decided to cancel the Ottawa talks; Massey informed Attlee of the decision on 12 July.[33]

In London, other factors were at play. In some quarters the recalcitrant Canadians were blamed for holding up the commencement of civil aviation talks; in others there was more sympathy. John LeRougetel, for one, did not see Mackenzie King as 'a snake in the grass.' The Canadian just did not want the Commonwealth lining up against the United States at the start –and neither did the Foreign Office.[34]

Late in June several ministers, including Sir William Jowitt, L.S. Amery, and Harold Balfour, presented memos to the War Cabinet, each arguing their own vision for development of international civil aviation. Perhaps the most important, however, was submitted by Winston Churchill. Churchill was less troubled by the lack of dominion support than he was in getting along with the United States. The Americans were the real focus of his concern: they had the industrial strength and the determination to use it; they held the key to the post-war world. In Churchill's view, it was essential not to let idealism cloud the issues or obscure Britain's genuine interests. With respect to internationalization he wrote: 'If by this is meant a kind of Volapuk Esperanto cosmopolitan organisation managed and staffed by committees of all peoples great and small, with pilots of every country from Peru to China (especially China), flying every kind of machine in every direction, many people will feel that this is at present an unattainable ideal.' More important, at least for Churchill, was the fact that these proposals 'are clearly unacceptable to the United States, the Dominions and probably Russia.' Churchill argued for agreement 'upon some less high-spirited line of approach to guide us in the forthcoming international discussions.'[35]

Churchill was not the first to make such a suggestion, although his views undoubtedly carried more weight. Every report from the United States repeated the American commitment to the private ownership of airlines, the negotiation of bilateral or multilateral agreements, and the desire to attain as much freedom of the air as possible. Surely, one Foreign Office official argued, the best way to handle the Americans was not to confront them with a scheme favouring internationalization only to fall back 'by merely indicating those parts of the earth's surface in which we feel compelled to assert our national sovereignty, thus assuming the role of dog in the manger, which at a later stage in the discussions we should, almost certainly, be compelled to abandon. Were we foolish enough to take such a line at the start – and those who advocate it are not lacking – we should merely embitter the atmosphere, fling the u.s. Government into the arms of the American commercial interests and alienate the Dominions.'[36] Increasingly it was argued that the best approach would be to try to build upon what the Americans offered rather than staking out a position diametrically opposed. Accepting the freedom of the air as a basis for discussion, the British negotiators might be able to persuade their American counterparts of the need for an international air authority and perhaps even of the value of some degree of international operation.

Although it was not imperative for the War Cabinet to create a definitive policy at this point, some action could be taken. At a meeting on 24 June, the War Cabinet gave Lord Cranborne the responsibility for future conversations with the United States on post-war civil aviation. A new ministerial committee – the Committee on Post-war Civil Air Transport – was created under Cranborne and it included Sinclair, Jowitt, Leathers, and Alan Barlow.[37]

By the first week of July, a statement of principles had been drafted and cabled to the dominions for their consideration. The British were hopeful that the principles would be acceptable to the other members of the Commonwealth and could be used as a basis for discussion with the United States. Briefly, the statement noted that the United Kingdom was willing to accept more freedom of the air, 'subject to satisfactory international settlement,' in conjunction with Commonwealth support for the creation of an international authority and international operating agencies to run specific routes. Inter-Common-

wealth services should be run on a 'co-operative basis,' and the possibility for a single operating authority for all of Europe was left open to debate. In addition, six freedoms were listed:
1 Right of innocent passage

2 Right to land for non-traffic purposes
3 Right to land passengers, etc., from country of origin
4 Right to pick up passengers, etc., for country of origin of aircraft
5 Right to convey passengers, etc., between two countries neither the country of origin
6 Right to convey between two points in one country, not country of origin[38]

These freedoms were not given as absolutes, and the last three, in particular, would have to be negotiated, but they could provide a frame of reference for future discussions.

As for the stubborn Canadians, Cranborne was anxious not to split the Commonwealth in two over the civil aviation issue, and he strongly felt that the Canadians should be encouraged to participate in a preliminary conference. In this he had the support of the Committee on Post-War Civil Air Transport, and, on 22 July, the War Cabinet agreed as well that a serious effort should be made to get the Canadians on side.[39] With or without the Canadians, however, Commonwealth discussions would be held.

Further action was postponed until Prime Minister Churchill had the opportunity to discuss the matter face to face with the Canadians when he visited Canada early in August for meetings with President Roosevelt at Quebec. The first of the two famous allied conferences at Quebec was not scheduled to begin until 17 August, but Churchill arrived in Canada more than a week early. On 11 August he and Sir John Anderson, lord president of the council, attended a meeting of the Cabinet War Committee in the Chateau Frontenac. Mackenzie King raised the question of the proposed preliminary conference and recorded Churchill's reaction later, in his diary: 'Churchill was quite outspoken on this, saying he had taken the whole matter in hand himself. They must have a preliminary conference in Britain with the other Dominions. If we could not see our way to attend, they would have to proceed without us. He was quite strong on his views there.' King tried to explain the Canadian position, noting that if there was projected an appearance that the empire was 'ganging up' on the United States, the Americans would react in kind, and 'it would become a test of strength.' Mackenzie King added

that we in Canada might wish to take a North American point of view on some things rather than the British Empire point of view. That with four thousand miles of boundary between us, planes going back and forth, Russia our nearest neighbour on the north, U.S. relations with Russia, etc., the whole problem here was a continental trans-oceanic problem in a very different way than it was in so far as Britain was concerned. I pointed out that naturally we would wish to co-operate as completely as possible with Britain. That we were at the mercy of the U.S. without being part of a larger combination, but what we were really thinking of was how question of co-operation could be best worked out.[40]

Churchill was impressed by the strength of the Canadian position, at least so Mackenzie King believed, and he asked Sir John Anderson to explain the situation to the British War Cabinet on his return to London. Anderson was back in England within a week and on 19 August he briefed the War Cabinet on his and Churchill's discussion with the Canadian ministers. Anderson then claimed that the Canadians had suggested to Churchill that he clarify the situation with Roosevelt to ensure that the American government would not misunderstand Canadian participation in any preliminary talks.[41] Mackenzie King's diary makes no reference to this suggestion, while the CWC minutes indicate that it came from Churchill himself. In any event, the proposal received support from Cranborne and other ministers who were becoming increasingly restive over the lack of action, particularly on the Canadian side, and felt that action by Churchill could force the issue.

There is no evidence that Churchill and Roosevelt discussed post-war civil aviation during the Quebec Conference (although they did a few weeks later in September). Nevertheless, Canadian resistance to preliminary Commonwealth discussions had begun to collapse. The Canadian position had always been to avoid the appearance of the formation of a Commonwealth bloc before talking with the Americans, not to be uncooperative with Britain and the other dominions. Nor was there any desire to be seen as the country that was holding up the beginning of international discussions on civil aviation.

Thus, when the United Kingdom exhibited its determination to hold the talks even without Canadian participation, it was not so easy to decide to withdraw; not to participate might damage Canada's prestige more than sending a representative to the talks would. Conversely, it might prove advantageous to have a Canadian representative at the talks, providing Canada's case could be well explained beforehand.

The decision was made on the evening of 30 August at Mackenzie King's home in Ottawa following a dinner with Howe, J.L. Ralston, T.A. Crerar, J.L. Ilsley, and Angus Macdonald. 'All favoured maintaining Canadian position – Canada to have her own policy,' King wrote in his diary later that evening. 'Agreeable to representation by Howe at any meeting in London,' he continued, 'but informing Americans in advance of our intention of participating in the conference in London and the position we intended to maintain which is one of control of aviation within our own country and the right to making our own policy.'[42]

Mackenzie King and his ministers left for Quebec City that night and informed Churchill of their decision during the meeting of the CWC the following day. At that point, Churchill, who was leaving soon for Washington, raised the possibility of his talking it over with Roosevelt before any talks were held. King reiterated that his government's concern was more with the reaction of the American press and Congress and their effect on public opinion than with reassuring the president, but he did not press the matter further. Churchill was good on his word, cabling Mackenzie King on 14 September that he had discussed the situation with Roosevelt, who 'did not see any objection to our talking things over amongst ourselves.'[43] Then, on 22 September, the Canadian government officially agreed to attend the preliminary Commonwealth discussions.

II

The Commonwealth civil aviation conversations were scheduled to begin in London on 11 October 1943, but before the delegation left for England, an important discussion of Canadian policy occurred. Near the end of June the interdepartmental committee was reconstituted under a new name: the Interdepartmental Committee on Air Transport Policy (ICATP). The membership remained the same, but it was felt that the new name more accurately reflected the purpose of the committee.[44]

There had always been two streams of thought in the interdepartmental committee; the larger group supported some form of internationalization in world aviation, the other argued for an independent TCA-based policy in which Canada would use its aviation power to ensure an important role for Canada in post-war aviation. Baldwin, Reid, and Robertson formed the core of the former group, while Herbert Symington and C.P. Edwards supported the latter. The ICATP report of 28 September reflected these differences by compromising on the internationalization issue and not going as far in that direction as some in the committee would have liked.[45]

Symington and Edwards may have been in the minority in the ICATP, but they found a much more important ally in C.D. Howe. Howe never believed in full internationalization; his idea of an international authority was one that would *regulate* not *operate* international aviation. In other areas, too, he and Symington held similar views. On 28 September he wrote Symington concerning the upcoming Commonwealth talks. 'Obviously, your thoughts and mine coincide almost exactly as to a reasonable Empire arrangement for post-war aviation,' he wrote, but 'I am afraid that we will not find much in common with the United Kingdom in any of our ideas.'[46] Thus, when the ICATP proposals for internationalization were discussed in the CWC on 6 October, Howe charged that 'Canada would have little to gain ... by initiating proposals for internationalization. On the basis of experience under the 1935 Agreement, operation by internationally owned corporations would not meet Canadian requirements nor afford us a measure of control consistent with our position. On the other hand, there would be certain regions where international operations would be desirable. A preferable solution was the proposal, contained in the Interdepartmental Committee's report, for the establishment of an international licensing authority, which would divide and allocate routes and services between the various nations.'[47]

Howe was more interested in air routes than he was in international schemes, and he went to England at the head of the Canadian delegation with specific ideas in his mind. First, he wanted an equal share of the transatlantic service with the United Kingdom; second, he wanted to participate in the development of the Pacific service to Australia, even to the point of excluding the British; and third, he wanted TCA to operate the 'all-red' service to the British West Indies. Howe had already been approached by West Indian officials to begin an air service there after the war, and he hoped that eventually it would be extended to Brazil. Howe would leave the planning for internationalization to others. 'Our plan must be to do much in the way of listening,' he wrote Symington, 'and to come back either with a satisfactory agreement or no agreement whatever.'[48]

Howe was accompanied to England by only Symington and Baldwin (Vincent Massey and Frederic Hudd, who also attended the meetings, were, of course, already in London). Symington was cool to any scheme of internationalization, especially if it was likely to interfere with the growth of his precious TCA, and this left Baldwin as the only internationalist. Baldwin was further handicapped – as secretary to the delegation rather than an adviser, he was restricted in his ability to participate in the discussions. Moreover, before leaving, Baldwin 'was instructed orally ... not to attempt to press any particular points of view on Mr. Howe, but rather to use Mr. Massey as intermediary.' This system proved cumbersome and unworkable, Baldwin later complained to A.D.P. Heeney. Eventually Baldwin 'disregarded the instructions to some extent.'[49]

If support for complete internationalization was on the wane in Canadian government circles, it had virtually disappeared in Britain. Internationalization had always had its detractors in Britain and the dominions, and, as it became apparent that such a scheme would be rejected by the Americans, other avenues of approach were investigated. Prime Minister Churchill, who was never convinced that internationalization was either desirable or workable, did, however, believe it was important to get along with the United States. Gradually, the focus of attention shifted from internationalization towards the American stance of preparing for the negotiation of bilateral or multilateral agreements, based on the exchange of reciprocal rights or freedoms.

The shifting emphasis of British policy was nowhere better symbolized than in the person of Lord Beaverbrook. Beaverbrook (whose personal 'finest hour' may have come during his work as minister for aircraft production in 1940) returned to government service as Lord Privy Seal on 24 September 1943, replacing Lord Cranborne, who moved back to the Dominions Office. As Lord Privy Seal, Beaverbrook was automatically appointed chair of the influential Committee on Post-War Civil Air Transport and was given the responsibility for all future aviation negotiations. One of his first tasks was to chair the Commonwealth talks.

Beaverbrook was a man of action, concerned more with the great sweep of things than in the more mundane, nitty-gritty world of details and fine print. In this respect he was an ideal match for C.D. Howe; both men preferred backroom face-to-face negotiations – to be sealed with a handshake, then worked out in detail by subordinates. Beaverbrook also shared with Howe a suspicion of internationalization; it was too hazy an idea to merit much consideration. He, too, was more concerned with specific air routes and protecting British interests. In a mid-October memo, Beaverbrook outlined his position for Churchill: Britain should control its own internal services and the routes to the colonial empire and should also maintain a significant share of the services with the dominions and India. Finally, for economic and strategic reasons, Britain must play a major and exclusive role in European civil aviation. 'Our geographical position and our vital commercial interests entitle us to expect that Britain can become and should become a dominating factor in the air transport system of the Continent.'[50] The most significant difference between Beaverbrook and Howe was one of perspective; Howe perceived Canadian interests in terms of independence from British policy, while Beaverbrook considered the participation of Canada as a necessary part of British policy.

Thus, when the Commonwealth discussions opened on the morning of 11 October, the leaders of the delegations representing the two largest air powers arrived with a clear understanding of what they wanted individually and what they were willing to give up in order to achieve it. Interestingly, other than the United Kingdom, Canada alone sent a representative of ministerial rank to lead its delegation; Australia, New Zealand, South Africa, and India were represented only by their high commissioners. Distance and the precarious nature of wartime travel undoubtedly prevented the attendance of more senior representatives from the dominions, but, nevertheless, it does give some indication of the importance the Canadians attached to the talks.

Beaverbrook opened the first meeting of the conference with warm words of welcome, noting: 'We are prepared to give attention to the views of each and every representative of all the Dominions and Colonies represented.' But, he continued, 'we must remember, of course, that we are here as a family party, that we are all one family about to carry on discussions that may bring differences, but these

The Shape of Things to Come 139

differences are confined to our own family party, the Empire party.'[51] An agenda had been distributed, and, with the niceties out of the way, the conference got down to work.

'It was at once evident,' Baldwin reported to Escott Reid, that Beaverbrook 'wished to get [the discussions] finished as rapidly as possible.' Beaverbrook introduced the first item on the agenda – internationalization – and asked for comments. S.M. Bruce, the Australian high commissioner, was taken by surprise when Beaverbrook called on him first and he recommended that a subcommittee be formed to study the security aspects of internationalization. Beaverbrook responded by saying that security and internationalization were 'linked together' and proposed that a subcommittee be set up to study the whole question of internationalization. Howe did not object and internationalization was relegated to a subcommittee over the embarrassed protests of Bruce. 'Internationalization came up at the very beginning of the discussions,' Baldwin ruefully reported, 'and it was obvious at once that as far as the majority of the United Kingdom people were concerned the prospect of internationalization had been discarded completely.'[52]

The abrupt banishment of internationalization set the tone for the whole talks. William Hildred introduced a proposal for the creation of an international operator's conference, arguing his case cogently and persuasively. But Howe would have nothing to do with any kind of arrangement in which Canada would be represented by a nongovernment agency. It was expensive to build airports and foster an aircraft industry; it was relatively cheap to start a small airline company: Should the Canadian government step aside and permit individual companies to negotiate on behalf of Canada? Would it not be easier to negotiate directly with the American government rather than the dozen or so private airlines that were competing for international routes? Beaverbrook agreed, and the whole idea was dropped.[53]

Next on the agenda were the first four freedoms mentioned in the Dominions Office cable of 3 July. There were few dissenters over granting freedoms 1 and 2 (the 'right of innocent passage' and the 'right to land for non-traffic purposes'), but Howe had difficulty with numbers 3 and 4 (the right to land or pick up passengers in another country). Canada's long boundary with the United States could produce special problems for Canada and transborder services had always been negotiated bilaterally rather than being based on 'rights'. By accepting freedoms 1 and 2, Canada was already giving up one of its strongest cards – its ability to use its geographical location to demand reciprocal privileges from others to fly over its territory. The granting of freedoms 3 and 4 as rights without restriction, moreover, could trigger a flood of American airlines into Canada. In Howe's mind such a development was unacceptable without tying freedoms 3 and 4 to an international convention and to an international regulating authority to set rates and frequencies. Again Howe got his way; acceptance of freedoms 3 and 4 was reserved until a regulatory authority was in place to prevent abuse.[54]

Several other issues were discussed during the open meetings and other subcommittees were formed, but the real negotiating took place behind closed doors, between Howe and Beaverbrook. No secretaries were present taking notes, but Baldwin made a point of breakfasting with Howe each day in order to pry out of the minister the talk of the night before.[55] Howe and Beaverbrook agreed to the creation of an all-red route encircling the globe – the goal of several earlier British administrations. For his part, Howe received Beaverbrook's agreement to leave the operation of those routes with which Canada was concerned – across the Atlantic and Pacific and to the West Indies – either in Canadian hands or, with respect to the Atlantic service, equally divided between Canada and the United Kingdom.

The Commonwealth discussions, which began on a Monday morning, ended 'in a blaze of glory' two days later.[56] No unanimous report was published, although three short memos were produced. The first was a brief declaration signed by Howe and Beaverbrook confirming their agreement on the all-British air route; the second was the subdued decisions of the subcommittee on internationalization, which noted how important security was and recommended that the future air authority be associated with the United Nations; the third was a draft outline of an international convention prepared by the Committee of Technical Experts. The latter document, which became known as the Balfour subcommittee report, contained a draft convention for the creation of an international body to settle disputes and regulate air routes and frequencies in the post-war world. The Balfour subcommittee report was received with interest by the members of the ICATP, who were working on a similar proposal.[57]

The whole conference, well orchestrated by Beaverbrook and Howe, went off almost without a hitch. Almost is the key word here: on the final day, Beaverbrook informed Howe that he and Lord Leathers were soon hoping to visit Washington to carry on the civil aviation discussions with the Americans, and he asked if the Canadian would care to participate. Howe's immediate response was affirmative – there was even some talk of Beaverbrook and Howe flying over in the same airplane – but he should have known how such an action would be received at home.

In a letter to Arnold Heeney on 19 October, Baldwin noted that the invitation to Howe 'was not intended, certainly as far as we were concerned, to imply that these three men were to go as a Commonwealth or Empire delegation.'[58] But this was exactly how it looked in Ottawa. 'The political implications of a Canadian Minister forming part of a joint delegation responsible to the Commonwealth Governments collectively, are pretty important,' Norman Robertson wrote the prime minister when he heard the news; 'you will, I imagine, wish to have them considered in the War Committee.' It did not matter what Howe's role in Washington was to be, Robertson added: 'It would I think be desirable to have him come back to Ottawa to talk things over with the War Committee before the discussions with the United States authorities begin.'[59] Mackenzie King couldn't agree more.

Howe quickly realized the bad impression that his acceptance of Beaverbrook's offer would create in Canada, so he changed his mind and returned to Ottawa, presenting his report to the CWC on 27 October. Beaverbrook, for his part, postponed his trip to Washington after receiving indications that the Americans were not ready to begin discussions.[60] There would be talks with the Americans, but the time was not yet right.

III

'Conclusion of the Civil Aviation Talks,' Charles Ritchie wrote in his diary on 13 October 1943. 'This is a test case for our post-war relations with the Empire. Unless Ottawa reacts strongly we shall have accepted in these talks the idea of a Commonwealth body presiding over an "all-red route." What functions and powers such a body would have is as yet by no means clear, but the precedent is interesting. It is the first post-war Empire body to be set up.'[61] Ritchie was not a participant at the Commonwealth conference and may be forgiven for reading a little too much into it. Yet there was much truth in what he wrote. The first round of discussions was over and a kind of Commonwealth unity had been preserved, largely symbolized by the announcement of the creation of the all-red route. The public impression of the talks was not helped by the concluding press conference: Beaverbrook did not show up as promised, leaving Howe on his own to speak on the outcome of the conference as a whole rather than specifically on Canadian aviation. This cast Howe in the role of Commonwealth spokesman, partly, J.R. Baldwin later wrote, 'because the newspapermen were looking for something on the All-Red Route to play up.'[62]

All in all, however, the outcome of the talks was satisfactory from a Canadian perspective. Howe travelled to London with specific goals in mind and, for the most part, achieved them without sacrificing too much in return. He had conceded on the all-red route but in return had received what he believed to be firm guarantees concerning Canadian operation of those services in and out of Canada. In addition, he had reasserted the primary role of the federal government in domestic and international civil aviation and had refused to accede to freedoms that might jeopardize Canada's ability to negotiate with the United States unless they were tied to an international regulatory body.

The question that remains is how much of Howe's success in London was essentially a personal victory. The Canadian government on both the ministerial and official levels had great success in designing an international civil aviation policy; it proved far more difficult implementing it. Early in 1943, the Canadian government was sending out conflicting signals through its representatives in London and Washington, especially over Canada's willingness to participate in Commonwealth discussions. The actions of Canadians such as Vincent Massey, for example, tended to leave an impression that was, in fact, contrary to the wishes of the government. The evidence, meanwhile, makes it difficult to put the blame on Massey's shoulders alone.

The Canadians were also outmanoeuvred by their more experienced British counterparts. The hastily proposed conference in Ottawa with American representatives was unwise, ill conceived, and badly fumbled, and it was cleverly sidestepped by the British government. Perhaps most illustrative was the Canadian decision to participate in the Commonwealth talks. Canadian policy was founded on the twin pillars of international co-operation and independence of action; thus, the Canadians were reluctant to participate in preliminary negotiations for fear that this independence of action would be compromised. When Churchill called their bluff and the Canadians were presented with the possibility of talks being held without them, their resistance crumbled.[63] Unfortunately, they failed to make their position clear respecting the talks, and in the end appeared to compromise when pressed by Churchill after he had talked over the situation with Roosevelt. There was irony, indeed, in having Canada's 'independent' policy sanctioned and preserved by Churchill and Roosevelt.

There would be other negotiations, other arrangements. There was also a clearer understanding of what Canadian policy makers were up against. The day after the Commonwealth discussions ended, Norman Robertson wrote in a memo for the prime minister: 'Recent developments in civil aviation and related fields are, I am afraid, going to force us to look pretty seriously at the implications for Canada of the prevailing trend towards Imperial centralization.' Robertson saw 'no good reason' to rock the boat at this time, but he was 'rather afraid that efforts in other quarters to strengthen and tighten the Imperial connection at the expense of our relations with other countries may not only have some bad effects on our relations with those other countries, but may reopen domestic political differences about our relationship to the Commonwealth and to the international community in general.' But what could be done? Robertson continued: 'It is very difficult to see clearly the shape of things to come after the war is over or to be dogmatic about the sort of orientation of international relationships in which Canada's true interest lies. At the same time we should I think be pretty careful about accepting any modification of our present relationships with the countries of this Commonwealth, the United States, or other foreign countries, until we are clear in our own minds as to just what these altering relationships may imply.'[64]

7 The Road to Chicago

The one thing Sir Peter Masefield disliked about working for Lord Beaverbrook was the late hours. Masefield, a graduate of Cambridge and part of the design staff at the Fairey Aviation Company before the war, had been the air correspondent for the *Sunday Times* since 1940. When Beaverbrook became Lord Privy Seal and chair of the Committee on Post-War Civil Air Transport in 1943 he asked his old friend to act as secretary. It was a tough assignment, and in taking on the job Masefield was forced to assume new work habits: Beaverbrook would often come in at noon, work until four, sleep for two hours, and then work through most of the night. To make matters worse, he expected his staff to do the same and would call any time during the night. On one Sunday morning at 4:00 AM Masefield was jolted from a deep sleep by his telephone, only to hear Beaverbrook's voice on the other end of the line say: 'Am I ringing you or are you ringing me?'[1]

Beaverbrook's biographer has written that Beaverbrook's years as Lord Privy Seal were dominated by two campaigns: the first was to prepare for the looming political conflict in Britain and the other was 'the defence of British independence against American encroachments.'[2] As Beaverbrook put it in a letter to Prime Minister Churchill, getting along with the Americans was 'an unchallengeable principle. But in seeking that friendship we should aim, with an equal consistency, at maintaining and strengthening our own position as a world power.'[3] International civil aviation became one of Beaverbrook's primary concerns in 1944, and its development over the following months provides a good case study of the enormous difficulties in maintaining this delicate balance between friendship and independent strength – a task not unknown to many of Beaverbrook's Canadian contemporaries.

Beaverbrook's efforts were further complicated by his suspicion of American intentions in civil aviation. He was convinced of the necessity of holding international discussions before the end of the war – before the United States moved in to dominate the whole field. Subsequent American wavering on the holding of international discussions was thus perceived not as evidence of the lack of a clear American policy but rather as a stalling tactic – an effort to gain time for American aviation interests while they moved to secure landing rights around the globe. From Tripoli to Benghazi to Cairo, from Uruguay to Barbados to the Azores, it appeared that the United States was less interested in achieving a multilateral agreement than it was in securing bilateral arrangements that would ensure for the United States a predominant position in post-war civil aviation.

Beaverbrook took his case to his colleagues. In the Committee on Post-war Civil Air Transport he criticized the actions of the United States, and 'stated that vigorous independent British action was essential in South America and elsewhere unless we were to surrender air transport throughout the World to the Americans.'[4] With respect to aircraft production, he was equally certain that Britain must meet the American challenge. 'The choice that must now be made should be understood,' he wrote in a December 1943 War Cabinet memo. 'It is between having or abandoning British Civil Aviation after the War. On this issue we must take our decision. If we cannot provide the machines, we cannot establish the services. The Americans, who will possess suitable machines, will capture the traffic. And once their aircraft, ground organisation, repair services and equipment are installed, we will find it impossible to oust them.' Beaverbrook's concern extended to the dominions as well. 'If we fail to provide British aircraft and British engines for the Dominions at the end of the War,' he concluded, 'then the leadership of air routes in the Empire must pass to the United States.'[5]

Some American observers had a different perspective. In the weeks following the Commonwealth civil aviation conversations, dominion affairs received a good deal of attention in the British press; to one official in the American Embassy this attention reflected 'more the growing fear of a serious decline in British prestige and power in world affairs than a sudden interest in the Empire for its own sake.' The apparent interest in empire solidarity, he continued, 'suddenly became more vocal just when current events had demonstrated that

Soviet Russia and the United States could work whole-heartedly together in major enterprises.'[6] But, as the civil aviation talks proved, Britain no longer could control the foreign policies of the dominions as it had in the past – additional evidence of the decline of British power. What Beaverbrook saw as the need to achieve a balanced and equal partnership with the United States was interpreted, by this observer at least, as a last desperate attempt to preserve an international position Great Britain no longer merited.

For Canadians, too, there were different perspectives. C.D. Howe shared many of Beaverbrook's concerns over growing American power in civil aviation, and he realized that the framework for a Canadian civil aviation policy could only be built on a solid Anglo-American partnership. Ironically, however, such a partnership could prove disastrous for Canada, for the danger existed that the two major air powers would carve up the international aviation pie between themselves, leaving only the scraps for smaller nations like Canada. The only way to prevent such an occurrence was to make Canada an important part of the process: if Canadians were participating at the decision-making level, then they would be better able to protect Canadian interests when the time came. This statement was as true now as it was in 1932, 1935, and 1937, but, as Canadian policy makers discovered in 1944, participation and responsibility were not freely given; they had to be earned.

I

In the weeks following the Commonwealth aviation talks, work began in earnest in Ottawa on drafting a provisional statement on civil aviation that would include an outline draft of an international convention.[7] As in the past, the focal point for discussion was the ICATP and the burden of the work fell to Escott Reid and J.R. Baldwin. Much work had already been done and Reid in particular was full of ideas dating back to his 'World Airways' scheme. Now it was necessary to integrate Canadian ideas and a Canadian point of view with the Balfour subcommittee document that had been accepted during the Commonwealth discussions.

Yet there were enormous difficulties surrounding the questions of international civil aviation. Just what were Canada's interests and how would they best be served? What freedoms would Canadians need over foreign territories, and, conversely, what freedoms could Canada give in return without harming domestic interests? Furthermore, what effect would a blanket commitment to two, three, or four freedoms have on the very close relationship with the United States that would inevitably emerge after the war? And Canadian interests were only one small piece in the jigsaw puzzle of international organization. What point was there in drawing up a narrowly 'Canadian' convention, if, from the start, it was unacceptable to the British or, more important, the Americans? To raise the whole affair above the level of futile intellectual exercise, a truly international perspective would have to be taken from the beginning – to preserve Canadian interests, of course, but also to make a Canadian convention suitable for use, at least as a starting-point, on the international level.

First there were the fundamentals. Canada was the world's fourth leading air power (behind the United States, Great Britain, and the Soviet Union) and its place in the international authority should reflect this fact. The functional principle was at work here, and for the ICATP it translated itself into membership and substantial voting power for Canada in the executive of the international authority. In addition, Canada had no wish to submerge its aviation interests in a British Commonwealth bloc; to preclude this possibility, the international authority should be given jurisdiction over connecting services between Commonwealth countries and should allocate routes to individual member states, not to the Commonwealth as a whole. With respect to services to the United States, however, the Canadians were less eager to give the international authority power to allocate routes, rates, or frequencies.

On a higher level, co-operation was to be the key word: co-operation with the United States, co-operation within the Commonwealth, and, above all, co-operation within the United Nations. Post-war civil aviation would have an important security component and it was imperative not to lose sight of the primary goal of international peace and security: 'Any proposed international agreement on air transport will have to help solve the political and security problems of the post-war world and be judged by its contribution to the establishment of a permanent system of general security.'[8]

On the more specific question of air freedoms, Reid drafted a lengthy memorandum examining what effect the granting of each freedom would have on Canada. With respect to the first two freedoms (the right of innocent transit and landing for emergency purposes), it immediately became clear how special and advantageous Canada's geographical location was, and, at the same time, how precarious that advantage was. Most countries, including the United States and the United Kingdom, were ready and willing to concede the first two freedoms, but for the Canadians it was far more difficult. By conceding freedoms 1 and 2, Reid wrote, 'only Canada would lose valuable bargaining rights without obtaining commensurate advantages in return. Canada is not a rich source of international air traffic, either in passengers or freight, and it is improbable that foreign states, once they are assured that their air services to and from the United States may travel over Canadian airways and use Canadian airports for refueling and repairs, will be eager to grant Canada rights of commercial outlet in return for a share of Canadian traffic.' The logical development of granting only the first two freedoms would be the exclusion of smaller countries (like Canada) from air services; conversely, it 'would make it easier for countries which are important originators of air traffic to monopolize international air routes at the expense of other countries even if those other countries could run airlines on those routes more efficiently and more cheaply.' It would be better to grant no freedoms at all than only 1 and 2; this policy would permit bilateral negotiations in which transit rights could be exchanged for 'right of commercial outlet.'

If Canadians were obliged to concede the two freedoms then they would be better off with an exchange of four or even five freedoms. Freedoms 3 and 4, which permitted the dropping off and picking up of passengers in a foreign territory, and number 5, which permitted the carrying of passengers between two foreign countries, would give the advantage to those countries most capable of handling the traffic. This arrangement would favour the United States, obviously, but it was argued that Canada would be able to more than hold its own in a fiercely competitive free-for-all. 'Provided that there is a reasonable expectation that Canadian airline companies engaged in international traffic will be at least as efficient as the airline companies of other nations,' Reid mused, 'Canada's interests would probably be served by the grant of five freedoms.'[9]

Reid, Baldwin, and Robertson were convinced of the enormous importance of bringing negotiations on international civil aviation to a successful conclusion – not only as a litmus test for independent

Canadian participation in future international organizations, but to help preserve world peace. As Baldwin put it in an ICATP report for the CWC on the eve of the submission of the draft convention: 'From its studies over the past year and a half the Committee has become convinced of the importance of the decision which the United Nations must make during the next year or so on the post-war organization of air transport. The decision may be a key one. An enlightened settlement will constitute a model for the settlement of other difficult international problems. It will mean that the United Nations have gone a long way to establish a lasting peace and a new world order of security.' At the same time, Baldwin warned, 'failure to reach an enlightened settlement would prejudice the establishment of an effective world security organization and would thereby greatly increase the chances of another world war in the foreseeable future.' Given Canada's role as an important air power 'in war and in peace,' Baldwin concluded, Canada should 'be prepared to play a leading role in efforts to achieve an enlightened settlement.'[10]

The long-awaited 'Tentative and Preliminary Draft of an International Air Transport Convention' was completed by the middle of January 1944 and presented to the CWC on the 20th. The full document ran to twenty-three pages and was accompanied by a three-page summary of the main points (see appendix 3). Briefly, the draft convention proposed the creation of an international air authority consisting of a general assembly of all member nations and a smaller permanent executive committee elected by the members of the assembly. In broad terms the role of the authority would be to foster the development of air transport services in such a way as '(a) to make the most effective contribution to the establishment and maintenance of a permanent system of general security, (b) to meet the needs of the peoples of the world for efficient and economical air transport, and (c) to ensure that, so far as possible, international air routes and services are divided fairly and equitably between the various member states.'

Under the Canadian convention the assembly would meet annually to elect board members and approve the board's annual report. Furthermore, it would be the responsibility of the assembly to 'draw up and maintain regulations governing such matters as air safety, rules of the air, competency of air crew, ground signals, meteorological procedure, navigational aids, communications, airworthiness, national registration and identification of aircraft, carriage of dangerous goods, salvage.' The board would consist of twelve members and an elected president, and would include at least one member from the eight most important air nations. Under the auspices of this board, several regional councils would be created (comprising the North Atlantic states, or the countries of Europe, for example) which would have the power to grant or withhold licences for the operation of international air services. Each member nation would maintain absolute sovereignty over its own airspace, but would agree to concede the first four freedoms to the authority and designate its own international airports. Applications for an operating licence would be made through member governments to the regional council, which in turn could peg the frequencies of the service, set passenger and cargo rates, and establish quotas for the services of other nations along that route. Clearly, under the Canadian scheme, the regional councils and board would have considerable and extensive powers.

The draft convention went on to enumerate the obligations of each member nation and to discuss in some detail such topics as the provision of airports and ground facilities, the financing of the authority, and the relationship of the authority to the world security organization. Issues such as these, however, were not likely to stir up much controversy; the real focus of attention would be on the powers of the authority to allocate routes and establish rates and frequencies.

There were two other points – included essentially for Canadian purposes – that bear mentioning. First, one article indicated that 'services between two contiguous states, such as Canada and the United States,' were to be exempted from the convention and 'left to be dealt with by agreements between the two states concerned.' By removing Canadian-American services from the realm of the international authority, the Canadians would circumvent the risks attached to granting the first two freedoms and by forcing bilateral negotiations of transborder routes would prevent the swamping of Canada by American services. Other nations, of course, would see it quite differently.

The second matter dealt with colonial possessions, which the Canadians believed should *not* be exempted from the authority if the route crossed another country's airspace. In such cases the services between a mother country and its possessions could not be considered internal and preserved as domestic routes, but rather would be allocated by the board and/or regional council like any other. Hence, while the Canadians were keen to make a special exemption for their services to the United States, they were not so willing in the case of far-flung empires. The British Empire was not named specifically, but clearly was meant. The Canadians hoped to prevent British services to Newfoundland via Ireland from being considered 'internal' (to the potential exclusion of Canada). British opposition would have been rightly anticipated, but the Americans were equally resistant to this proposal, for they had desires to consider their services to Alaska, Hawaii, and the Canal Zone as domestic ones.[11]

The ICATP draft convention was discussed by the CWC on 20 January 1944 and approved as a tentative provisional statement of Canadian policy. There were no dissenters – but then the government had neither committed itself to any specific action nor staked out a position from which it could not move. Moreover, other than King and Howe, few of the ministers had shown any sustained interest in the formation of an aviation policy for the post-war period. There were more immediate – and pressing – wartime problems to be dealt with.

The question that remained was what to do with the draft convention now that it was ready: keep it secret, publish it, or circulate it to a select group in advance of international discussions? In Robertson's mind it was best to strike while the iron was hot: 'The sooner our draft is circulated,' he argued, 'the greater the influence it is likely to have on the framing of the final convention.' In addition, he continued, by circulating the convention it 'would also tend to substantiate our claim to be one of the important air powers of the world and as such entitled to full representation at any international conferences on air transport and on any international air transport authority that may be set up as a result of these conferences.'[12]

The CWC agreed that it should be distributed to other countries at a suitable date – but when? As it turned out, the issue was forced by outside events. On 26 January the Canadian ambassador in Washington received an aide-memoire from the State Department suggesting the holding of tripartite preliminary talks between Canada, the United States, and the United Kingdom, and asking 'if an early indication could be received of the views of the Canadian government on this general subject.'[13]

American opinion on post-war civil aviation had not gelled to any considerable degree, but some progress had been made. During November 1943, Berle's committee had met with the president and discovered at least the direction in which Roosevelt was leaning. At the top of his list were Germany, Japan, and Italy, and in his view they were to have no aviation industry nor be permitted to 'fly anything larger than one of these toy planes that you wind up with an elastic.' Turning to domestic aviation, Roosevelt told Berle that in principle he opposed government subsidization or ownership of airlines and that he did not support Pan Am's virtual monopoly of international operations; in his view the air routes of the world should be opened to other American companies, providing they could compete.

With respect to international arrangements, Roosevelt favoured a basic free-air policy, up to the exchange of five freedoms, but not the sixth (although he did not use these terms). As Berle reported afterwards, Roosevelt 'wanted arrangements by which planes of one country could enter any other country for the purpose of discharging traffic of foreign origin, and accepting foreign bound traffic. Thus, if Canada wanted a line from Canada to Jamaica, with stops in the United States of Buffalo and Miami, they should be able to discharge traffic of Canadian origin at Buffalo, and take on traffic at Buffalo for Jamaica; but they should not be allowed to carry from Buffalo to Miami.'[14] Settling arrangements such as these, however, would have to wait for a future United Nations conference; in the meantime Roosevelt gave his consent to hold quiet preliminary discussions with Great Britain and other countries.

The Canadians and British had already made it known that they were willing to begin discussions, and now that the president had given his approval, Berle could move ahead and initiate talks. But who to ask? The British were the obvious and most important rival; the Atlantic service would be an essential route in post-war American aviation, and, in addition, Britain was both the gateway to Europe and the key to a vast global empire. The Canadians were of less significance, but important nevertheless, if only as that large stretch of land over which American airplanes would have to fly. Besides, Pearson and Howe had made it clear to Berle that the Canadians planned to play an independent role in the unfolding of international aviation. Berle believed he had a potential ally north of the border, even if the Canadians had been 'subjected to the smooth and expert type of pressure that many hundred years of experience have made the British masters of,' as one US official put it.[15]

The American invitation was received in Ottawa without undue alarm: it was appropriate that Canada should participate from the beginning. The proposal was discussed in the CWC on 4 February 1944, and two decisions were made: one, to accept the invitation and, two, to send Washington and London the three-page summary of the Canadian proposals. By the middle of the month Pearson had met with Berle and confirmed Canadian participation and had received from Berle a proposed agenda.[16]

What the Canadians were unaware of was the storm brewing in London, fanned, to a considerable extent, by the gales of disapproval emanating from Beaverbrook's office. By the end of the first week of February, the British had received from Vincent Massey the full text of the Canadian draft convention, and they were not amused.[17] A hastily arranged meeting of officials from the Foreign Office, Air Ministry, and Beaverbrook's office was held on 12 February to review the draft convention and all agreed that 'it departed in several major particulars from the conclusions of the Commonwealth Conference. It was incomplete, ambiguous and certain of its clauses could not be supported.'[18] Reaction was swift and negative on the articles that surrendered colonial lines to the authority and exempted services between contiguous countries. These two articles would have to be removed. Also, from a tactical vantage it appeared unwise to give away too much up front, especially regarding the four freedoms listed in the Canadian draft. As Peter Masefield put it: 'American interests lie in gaining the greatest possible freedom of air passage. Our interests lie in not budging beyond Freedom Four except by reciprocal bargaining ... The reservation of Freedoms Three and Four thus acts as a "shock absorber" against America's attempted inroads. These inroads would be brought to a halt *at* Freedom Four instead of starting afresh *from* Freedom Four.'[19]

On another level there was the sense that the Canadians had anticipated events with their convention, and concern that the inclusion of only the Canadians in talks with the Americans would cause resentment among the other dominions. Beaverbrook in particular argued for Anglo-American talks first, again believing that the dominions could be brought into line afterwards. John G. Winant, the American ambassador in London, reported the comment of a member of Beaverbrook's staff on the 'impertinent' actions of the Canadians.[20] Three days later Winant added that the 'British seem to hope that the preliminary discussions will lead to agreement between the United

States and them on general principles and that subsequently these principles will be agreed to by other nations.'[21]

Others shared Beaverbrook's concerns but were less intransigent in their opposition. Lord Cranborne agreed that the other dominions would be upset if only Canada were invited to the Anglo-American talks. 'It is clearly embarrassing,' he informed the Department of External Affairs, 'that the United States Government should have invited only Canada and not the other three Dominions who took part in the London discussions, though no doubt this can be accounted for by the special position of Canada in relation to civil aviation in North America and on the North Atlantic.'[22] Cranborne, however, also believed that if Canadian participation was what it would take to begin the process, then he was ready to go along.[23]

Another interesting perspective was offered by Malcolm MacDonald, the high commissioner in Ottawa. He was equally uneasy with the phrase dealing with colonial air services, but he was far more appreciative of the risks of bruising Canadian sensibilities if too much of a fuss was made over the affair. Canadian attitudes towards international responsibilities were changing, he wrote, and they now appeared willing to play a larger role on the world stage – especially in civil aviation. Granted, the other dominions might be upset if excluded, but now in the present circumstances, it would be the Canadians who would be hurt if the other dominions were included for the sole reason that Canada had been invited. 'I naturally do not agree with everything that Canada had done or proposed in this instance,' he concluded, but 'if we give a chilly reception to moves of this kind, she will be more inclined to grow impatient at her ties with the Commonwealth.'[24]

Beaverbrook was unmoved. He had genuine concerns over certain aspects of the Canadian draft, although these difficulties probably could be remedied through negotiation. Clearly, Beaverbrook's opposition ran far deeper; he opposed the mere presence of the Canadians at the bargaining table at this stage of the game. It would be unfair to exclude the other dominions, and, more important, there was a growing concern that the Canadians would side with the Americans on important issues. The Canadians could not be counted on to support or follow the British lead, and, this being the case, there would be no meetings with the Canadians present unless the other dominions were included.[25]

Word of the impending crisis reached Ottawa by the middle of February 1944. The Canadians had already agreed to participate in the talks; now it appeared that the British were going to muddy the waters. The automatic inclusion of the other dominions appeared ludicrous in Canadian eyes and had the air of a common imperial foreign policy about it. 'I think the British attitude in this matter has dangerous implications for the future,' an angry Lester Pearson wrote from Washington. 'It certainly makes our functional idea of representation look rather silly and emphasizes the "unit" idea of British Commonwealth representation.'[26] Indeed, what would happen the next time, on some other issue? Would the Americans then hesitate to invite Canada, knowing that the other dominions might be dragged along?

A no-win situation had been created. If the Canadians were included in Anglo-American talks, the British would be annoyed; if the other dominions were excluded, then they would be angry; yet if they were invited to attend, then the Canadians would complain of unfair treatment. Further, the Australians were watching with care. Earlier that year a joint Australia-New Zealand statement on civil aviation was issued, calling for a strong international authority with powers to control international trunk lines. Now the Australian government was shocked and surprised to learn of the proposed tripartite discussions, and sharp telegrams of complaint were sent to Ottawa and Washington.[27]

The whole affair was over-inflated, but once national pride and 'status' were introduced, it assumed important overtones. Observing from Washington, Berle must have derived some amusement from the antics of his Commonwealth cousins; but it was a situation largely of his own creation. What Berle originally had in mind was a small informal meeting with the Canadians and British leading up to an international conference to be held later that year, perhaps in Ottawa. As for the inclusion of the Canadians, Berle told Michael Wright, the first secretary in the British Embassy, that he 'hoped it was clear to the British Government that our suggestion in regard to the Canadians had been due to the plain functional necessity of having Canada in at the beginning, in view of the fact that she was the greatest single corridor through which American overseas aviation would have to fly. We had no other thought in mind in including her, than to deal on this common-sense basis.'[28] At that stage, Berle had no wish to organize a full international conference that would include the other dominions, but, by the same token, he was equally unwilling to withdraw his invitation to the Canadians. 'We have been proceeding on the assumption that the Canadians would be represented in these talks,' he wrote Winant on 16 February, 'and propose to continue in that course.'[29]

Berle countered the British suggestion to invite the other dominions with the same tactic used by the British on the Canadians the year before. If all the dominions were invited, he responded, then the Americans would feel obligated to invite some Latin American delegates. As well, the Soviets had expressed an interest in holding informal discussions, and, if they, too, were included, surely the Chinese would have to be present. And what about the European governments in exile? Maybe they also should be invited.[30]

Berle's suggestions, which seemed to run counter to all his previous proposals, can only be seen as a ploy to deflect the British request to expand the preliminary talks. Yet if Berle was sanguinely confident that the British would retreat, he was sorely mistaken. On 7 March, Wright came to Berle's office with a new British plan to stage an international conference as soon as possible in North Africa or Morocco. Fourteen nations would be invited, including the United States, the United Kingdom, Russia, China, Canada, the three other dominions and India, Mexico, Brazil, France, and the Netherlands.[31]

Berle would have nothing to do with this plan – not surprisingly. He had already been thinking of reverting to his original suggestion of low-level informal talks and he scrapped any mention of a larger international conference at this time. What he did do, however, was to propose a series of bilateral talks – with the British, with the Canadians, with the Soviets, and so on. In this way, the discussions would remain informal, and, presumably, everyone would be happy. Discussions with the Soviets and Chinese would begin with State Department officials in Washington, while Berle would travel to London and Montreal to meet with the British and Canadians.

The Canadian government found this arrangement acceptable, and, indeed, much preferable to a mini United Nations gathering in Africa. The only stipulation was that the Canadian-American leg of the talks be held first. Berle had no objections and agreed to stop at Montreal before flying on to London. The British, too, were well disposed to Berle's offer; Beaverbrook had already mentioned to Winant that what he wanted above all else was a tête-à-tête with Berle.[32] The irony of the situation, however, was that the British were agreeing to the Americans' undertaking a series of bilateral civil aviation discussions – precisely what they had feared and complained of the previous autumn. Nevertheless, the log-jam was broken and Berle began packing his bags for an early-spring overseas trip.

II

Before any international discussions began, outside events prompted the Canadian government to make a public declaration of its international civil aviation policy. Late in February, D.C. Coleman, the president of the CPR, arrived at Mackenzie King's office with a request for his company to begin transcontinental and international air operations. Beginning in 1939, the CPR acquired a controlling interest in almost a dozen private Canadian air companies, including Yukon Southern Air Transport, Ginger Coote Airways, and Starratt Airways & Transportation. James Richardson died suddenly in 1939 and his interest in Canadian Airways was acquired by the CPR in December 1941. The following year these several companies were merged into one new enterprise – Canadian Pacific Air Lines (CPAL). With almost fifty routes already in existence, the new airline commenced operations on 1 July 1942.[33]

There had always been an uneasy relationship between TCA and CPAL. Coleman's proposal to merge the two companies was rejected by the government in 1943, and now he wanted to know where the government stood on the question of the post-war development of private air services and the private ownership of airlines.[34] Neither King nor Howe had changed his opinion on government ownership; indeed, on 9 March 1944 the prime minister reiterated to the CWC his desire to maintain complete government control of international operations, pointing out 'the need of the Government having a perfectly free hand in the world organization of the air and in the decision upon routes, what was needed for defence, strategic reasons, etc. We should not link up with private interests where there were these vaster national considerations.'[35]

The Canadian government had a relatively free hand in the conduct of its post-war international civil aviation policy. Nevertheless, King had promised Coleman a reply and when it was learned that civil aviation was on the agenda for the upcoming Commonwealth prime ministers' conference scheduled for May, King decided that a public statement of Canadian principles was called for. There were also political reasons. If the government did not act soon, he wrote in his diary, then 'we would find that the c.c.f. would declare for out and out control. It would be supported by the Social Credit party and we would find that large numbers of our own men would join with them; that Hanson and some Tories would join with us, and we would have succeeded in completely handing over control of Government for the next five years to the c.c.f. That would be giving them exactly what they wanted: the two old parties standing for private interests against the people's rights to control natural monopolies, etc.'[36]

The scope of the proposed statement, however, was decided by foreign developments. Early in March it was learned that Wayne Parrish, the editor of *Aviation Daily*, had obtained a copy of the Canadian draft convention and was planning to publish some or even all of it. There was no doubt in Howe's mind that the document had been leaked from Beaverbrook's office. 'There seems to be little doubt,' he wrote Robertson on 11 March, 'that everything that has been sent to England on the subject of aviation either by Canada or by the United States has reached the hands of this publication.'[37] Berle thought likewise, but, not unexpectedly, Beaverbrook denied any involvement in the affair, claiming that a member of Mackenzie King's staff gave 'a detailed and accurate account' of the convention to Alfred Critchley, the director-general of BOAC, and that the leak spread from this source. Others suggested that Parrish received his information directly from the State Department.[38]

Whatever the source of the leak, the Canadian hand had been forced, and on 17 March 1944 C.D. Howe rose in the House of Commons to give a lengthy speech on civil aviation, at the conclusion of which he tabled the Canadian draft convention. Howe began with a brief history of the development of civil aviation in Canada leading to the creation of TCA in 1937. He went on to explain the background of the Canadian position on government monopoly and the use of a chosen instrument in international civil aviation. Then, after describing the more recent wartime developments, Howe presented the case for the creation of an international authority with real power to safeguard the smooth functioning of international air transport. In conclusion, Howe reassured the members of the House that the necessary steps had been taken to protect Canadian interests and that everything that needed to be done was being done. 'Our representatives in the international discussions,' he concluded, 'will be authorized to support or initiate such proposals as, in the government's opinion, will be likely to result in the establishment of an international air transport authority, with effective powers, supported by all governments concerned, which will further international cooperation and goodwill, ensure that international air routes and services are divided fairly and equitably among all member nations, meet the needs of the peoples of the world for efficient and economical air transport, and contribute to the establishment and maintenance of a permanent system of general security.'

Howe made two other announcements of some interest. First, he declared that the railways (including the CPR) would have to divest themselves of their airlines within one year of the end of the war. This proposal sent a few tremors through the CPR head office, but it never came into effect, and was, in fact, rescinded in 1946. The second announcement concerned the creation of an air transport board to take over the duties of the Board of Transport Commissioners (established in 1938) and to advise the government 'on ways and means and means of bringing about a rapid and well-planned expansion of transport by air.'[39] The Air Transport Board (ATB) came into being later that year and, apart from its advisory role, its primary function was to 'license, regulate and control commercial air services in and over Canada.'[40]

It was an important speech, however badly timed. The prime minister recorded that 'the policy outlined is as fine as anything the Government of Canada had done at any time.' Indeed, Mackenzie King continued, 'I cannot but regret that I did not make the statement regarding international aviation, leaving to Howe that statement regarding domestic aviation. I outlined both in relation to the Trans-Canada Airways in part last year, but should, as Minister for External Affairs, and Prime Minister, have outlined the international policy this time.'[41]

III

Berle, accompanied by Edward Warner, vice-chair of the CAB, arrived in Montreal on 29 March 1944 for the prearranged preliminary exchange of views with the Canadian authorities. He was met by what was becoming the standard Canadian negotiating team: Howe,

Symington, and Robertson, with Baldwin acting as secretary. The talks were brief, lasting only two days, with each side explaining its position and feeling the other out. No bargaining was undertaken, but, where possible, common ground was sought.

Both sides agreed that all nations of the world should be able to participate in international civil aviation, while at the same time preserving national sovereignty and control over domestic services. In addition, there was general agreement on the need for an international aviation organization which the major air powers would participate in and control. That was as far as agreement went. There were major differences over the scope and powers of the international authority; for example, the Americans were unwilling to hand over any regulatory powers unless it was absolutely necessary. Berle threw up the old bogey of congressional intransigence and reluctance to surrender any powers to foreign or international agencies. 'Accordingly,' Baldwin reported, the Americans suggested that 'the authority should in the initial stages be limited to the collection of information which might provide an effective basis for international control and regulation at a later stage if such control and regulation proved necessary.'[42]

Central to the American proposals was the desire to open up the world as much as possible to air commerce. An international organization should deal with technical matters in an effort to standardize air travel – but should have no power to control, allocate, or operate air services. Market forces would take care of rates and frequencies; universal acceptance of freedoms 1 and 2 was needed, followed by bilateral negotiations for freedoms 3 and 4. Furthermore, there should be an initial transition period in which operators could set their own rates and frequencies; an equilibrium would presumably emerge and then be confirmed at an international conference at some later date.

This proposed transitional period held certain attractions for Howe, at least so far as it would furnish TCA with the opportunity to establish itself on some key post-war routes, and he was quoted in an American memo as saying: 'What you have in mind is to let the international authority develop gradually, and I see nothing wrong with that.' Still, his endorsement was lukewarm at best. The 'American Statement of Principles' that was produced during these discussions received only the following recommendation: 'The Canadian representatives recognized that these proposals represented a possible method of attempting to achieve the objectives in question and as such should be the object of further study.'[43]

It was clear that there were fundamental differences between the two governments. The US proposals, Baldwin pointed out, 'leaving as they do to each government the right to increase of its own accord its initial allocation of frequencies, would be likely to lead to undesirable results. The United States would probably be one of the few countries in a position to increase frequencies extensively and might embark upon a heavy programme of expansion. Once initiated, services are not likely to be dropped.'[44]

A more critical problem arose over the role of the international organization. For the Americans, who would emerge from the war as the dominant air power, there was little need for the protection of a world organization and even less desire to be dictated by one. What they wanted was the freedom to fly anywhere (freedoms 1 and 2) and to negotiate independent agreements from a position of strength. For the Canadians it was a different matter. Giving away freedoms 1 and 2 without receiving something in return would be a serious tactical error; Canada's strategic location was a valuable bargaining chip to be negotiated in exchange for commercial rights in other countries. The Canadian position, remember, supported the exchange of four freedoms, but only after securing them to a strong international organization that would have sufficient power to ensure a 'fair' allocation of routes and frequencies to member nations. As Baldwin pointed out judiciously, the unconditional granting of freedoms 1 and 2 'would not be likely to be acceptable to a number of other nations unless linked with rights of commercial outlet and placed in a general framework of international cooperation and control.'[45]

Despite these serious differences, however, the conversations did help to clear the air. The Canadians had made their position clear and hoped they had removed, at least from Berle's mind, any hint of a united Commonwealth aviation policy. There was also a lesson learned, Baldwin later wrote in his report for the Cabinet War Committee: 'The discussions demonstrated fully the usefulness of preparing and circulating a Canadian draft convention. The discussions centered around the objectives of the convention and the methods suggested for obtaining them with the result that the Canadian delegates found themselves in a stronger position than had been expected.'⁴⁶ If nothing else, there was satisfaction in knowing that the Canadian convention (however 'impertinent' and ill timed) was being taken seriously by those who mattered.

IV

No Canadian was involved in the Berle-Beaverbrook talks held in London from 3 to 6 April 1944, but they were followed with great care in Ottawa. The discussions in Canada had revealed major differences between the Canadian and US positions, and it was expected that the same would be true of the Anglo-American talks. This, indeed, was the case.

On the first day, Berle and Beaverbrook agreed to disagree with the Canadian position on the definition of cabotage, or internal air traffic. Neither the British nor the Americans wished to open up to other nations the traffic to their colonies and possessions – and the British specifically included Newfoundland here. The two sides also agreed on the need for as much uniformity of air rules and regulations, and in technical and operational standards, as possible. To this end, arrangements were made for future Anglo-American conversations on questions such as communications, meteorological services, air-navigation aids, customs and immigration, air-traffic control procedures, and standards of airworthiness of aircraft.⁴⁷

Another area of broad but rather vague agreement concerned the use of US-built air-bases in British territories – an issue of some importance to the American negotiators. Despite Foreign Office insistence that Britain must never give away any rights in these bases without getting something in return, Beaverbrook assured his US counterparts that the United Kingdom would not attempt to exclude other nations from the use of these bases. What this meant exactly was, of course, still to be negotiated.

Subsequent agreement was not so easy to achieve. As in the earlier Canadian discussions, there was a wide gap between the United States and British positions on the role of the proposed air authority, with the British sharing the Canadian view that the new organization should have real executive power. Yet, the British position should not be seen as a mere reflection of the Canadian, or vice versa. Canadian international civil aviation policy had always been founded to some degree on the manipulation of Canada's geographical location in return for a piece of the traffic that crossed over it, and, conversely, was linked to the fear that Canada could be excluded from that traffic by an Anglo-American agreement. Hence the wish to remove the possibility of United Kingdom – Newfoundland services being considered internal, which would create the potential for a transatlantic service bypassing Canadian soil. Great Britain, in contrast, would be an originator of traffic (rather than a conduit), and British policy was geared to ensuring that British services carried their share (or an equivalent US share) of the traffic. Under the circumstances present at the time, the British believed themselves unable to compete effectively with the Americans under a system of open competition: only through a regulated system would British interests be protected. The British also believed that the years immediately following the war would be crucial; British weakness in transport aircraft, for example, would be most glaring at this time. As a result, the British put far more emphasis than did the Canadians on the division of frequencies during the critical transitional period between the resumption of commercial aviation and the eventual creation of an international regulatory body.

The latter issue concerning the division of frequencies was the major snag in the Berle-Beaverbrook discussions. The British proposed splitting the Anglo-American traffic equally during the transitional period – a proposition Berle dismissed as unacceptable. Knowing of the US dominance in long-range aircraft and that most transatlantic traffic would be American in origin, at least for the immediate post-war period, it was not surprising that Berle argued for the implementation of a more competitive system in which US carriers likely would secure the preponderance of traffic.[48] A wide gap was apparent. The civil air attaché in the American Embassy flippantly described it: 'Several times when Englishmen have asked me what I think the United States wants in the post-war air I reply, "to fly airplanes." That is what they are afraid of.'[49]

Attention turned to the proposed international authority on 6 April, when Beaverbrook introduced the Canadian draft convention and proclaimed that Great Britain stood behind it. Berle argued against the draft convention (as he had in Montreal), later telling Lester Pearson that 'the Canadian plan went further in an international direction than the Americans could possibly accept and that it should be regarded more as an objective ultimately to be attained than a starting point. He [Berle] felt that they would have to be satisfied with something less than this at present.'⁵⁰ Berle had found the Canadian draft 'too rigid,' Beaverbrook, with appropriate regret, wrote to Howe; and in response the British submitted the Balfour report from the 1943 Commonwealth conversations for consideration. This document, much to Beaverbrook's satisfaction, was looked on more favourably by the Americans. Indeed, Berle was quoted as saying that the Balfour report did 'present sufficient possibility of agreement' to be brought forward and used during a future full-scale international aviation conference.⁵¹

The Balfour report was much more general in content and limited in scope than the Canadian convention, and it was just vague enough to be open to wide interpretation. But even then the Americans were by no means committed to the document, and they repeatedly stressed how some parts would have to be amended. Nevertheless, when the discussions ended Beaverbrook was ecstatic. He wrote Howe immediately and brought together the high commissioners to tell them the good news; the following month he informed the country in a speech to the House of Lords. On 7 April, the day after the talks concluded, he reported triumphantly to the War Cabinet that the agreement with the Americans on the Balfour report was 'eminently satisfactory.' But, Beaverbrook cautioned his minsterial colleagues, 'given the degree of criticism under which Dr. Berle might find himself on return to the United States in view of the concession he had made to our point of view, ... no undue satisfaction with the outcome of these discussions should reflect itself in press comment in this country.'⁵²

Beaverbrook's comments suggest that he genuinely believed there had been a shift in American opinion, closer to the British position, but the evidence makes such a claim difficult to support. While Berle did agree that the Balfour report might be suitable for further discussion, there was no mention of this document in the State Department memorandum on the London conversations. On the question of an international authority, there appeared to be little change in the US position: 'It was agreed that international control in the technical field is desirable and in many cases is essential. However, in the economic field the view of the United States has been that since pre-war experience is not adequate as a guide and post-war conditions are still speculative, the facts of the case cannot yet be fully developed. Therefore the degree of international control which would be desirable cannot yet be determined.'⁵³ As for the Balfour report, Secretary of State Cordell Hull informed one ambassador that it was 'far from acceptable itself in its present form and does not set forth principles and practices on which there was agreement between the British and American spokesmen at the exploratory talks. Specific reservations were made on many points, notably the power of the international body.'[54] Clearly the three corners of the North Atlantic triangle were still far apart.

V

During the long spring and summer of 1944, the discussion of international civil aviation questions quite properly took a back seat to the immediate unfolding of events in Europe. The Normandy invasion and the march of Allied forces across the continent gave hope that the war might be over within a year, or, with luck, as early as the end of 1944. Inevitably, however, the developing war situation had a profound effect on international commercial aviation. First, with the liberation of southern and western Europe some attention was paid in American and British circles to the re-establishment of air services to the previously occupied European capitals – and such services were a potential source of conflict. Second, once it became clear that the end of the war was approaching it was no longer possible to avoid settling the difficult questions: all the decisions that had been evaded and postponed now had to be faced. This circumstance applied equally to the Canadian government, and over the following months work began on revising the draft convention in preparation for the international aviation conference that everyone knew would have to take place before too long.

Prime Minister King received a firsthand briefing on recent developments in Anglo-American aviation relations from Lord Beaverbrook during the Prime Ministers' Conference in London in May 1944. The prime minister did not relish the thought of once more having to defend Canadian independence of action against, as he saw it, the supporters of a more centralized empire and Commonwealth. King recorded in his diary his resentment at the 'unfair' position in which he and the other dominion prime ministers were placed in dealing with foreign policy issues that were 'carefully studied ... by a special Committee selected in advance in which none of the Dominions had been represented. That we should be there without any advisers. That there should be six British Ministers to the four other self-governing parts, all of them with their colleagues and officials close at hand. Also British Ministers were prepared to lead off on discussions, knowing what they were to say, but expecting Premiers to deal with matters in reply. Personally I felt the hopelessness of the situation.'[55]

Yet, however hopeless the situation, when the conversation turned to the future united nations organization, Mackenzie King stoutly defended the Canadian principle of functionalism: 'We would wish to have our own right of representation,' he told Prime Minister Churchill at one point, 'if not as one of the big three or four, at least as one of the medium powers that would be brought into the World Organization in some relation which would recognize that power and responsibility went together and recognize our individual position.'[56]

Mackenzie King took the same line with Beaverbrook on 10 May when the latter, along with Sir Archibald Sinclair and Richard Law, attended a conference session on civil aviation. 'Beaverbrook looks like a gnome,' Mackenzie King had written a few days earlier; but he was still capable of surprising everyone. Bolstered by his agreement with Berle over cabotage, Beaverbrook resurrected the old idea of a joint operating company to run a world-wide empire service. Gone was the commitment to the independent operation of the all-red route reached with Howe the previous October; Beaverbrook now called for a Commonwealth company to operate a single service. The proposal found some support in prime ministers John Curtin of Australia and Peter Fraser of New Zealand, but Mackenzie King found it unacceptable and he said so.[57]

Nevertheless, over the following weeks Beaverbrook continued to press the Canadians for support, but with little success. 'Canada has had an unfortunate experience in being a minority shareholder in Commonwealth company with U.K. the majority shareholder and responsible for operation,' Howe wrote to Beaverbrook with reference to the 1935 agreement. 'I am convinced that Canada will not again be placed in a similar position.'[58] Why not have the Canadians run that part of the route that concerned them, Howe added; they could do it just as well as any joint Commonwealth company. Unfortunately, for Beaverbrook and his staff, such a suggestion missed the point, and, in light of new developments in aircraft, Peter Masefield wrote, would be akin to 'enforcing a change of train at every county border on the journey from London to Scotland.'[59]

A more successful outcome of the Prime Ministers' Conference was the decision to hold further Commonwealth civil aviation discussions in the near future. Beaverbrook was convinced that the United States would not call an international conference until after the presidential elections in November 1944, and in the meantime, the United Kingdom and dominions could get together – on the official level – to work out the specifics on the services that would eventually connect the various Commonwealth nations. A conference along these lines was far more attractive to Howe than any discussions on fuzzy notions and joint operating companies, and he could count on Symington to ably defend TCA against any imperial centralizers.[60]

The Americans, meanwhile, were busily conducting several bilateral civil aviation conversations simultaneously, first with the Soviets and Chinese, then with French, Belgian, and Dutch representatives. Invitations for further discussions were also extended to, among others, Brazil, Mexico, and the Indian Agency General. Unfortunately these discussions proved largely unfruitful. The Soviets, for example, were overwhelmingly concerned with their security problems and were heading in the direction of a closed system – the antithesis of the American position. The Soviet proposal for the New York – Moscow service was to have the American carrier fly to Cairo where all the passengers would be taken the rest of the way to Moscow on a Soviet airplane. The discussions dragged on for weeks with little movement on either side. Lester Pearson described the situation this way: 'There are rumours, that the Russian delegation ... is spending most of its time outside Washington investigating, impartially, United States air lines and air fields and New York night life!'[61] As for the Chinese, the State Department was informed that China had no intentions of flying internationally but that the Chinese government was willing to give the United States transit rights in return for some American assistance to Chinese domestic aviation. What they had in mind at first were 300 DC-3s and 200 DC-4s.[62] The other conversations had similar results.

'It is quite obvious that the United States is engaged in arranging a series of bilateral agreements with countries involved in its post-war aviation plans,' C.D. Howe wrote early in July in a letter to Norman Robertson. 'Lord Beaverbrook recognizes this fact,' he continued, 'and has suggested that he will come to Canada shortly to discuss the situation with us. Perhaps we should examine the position and decide on Canadian procedure for the immediate future.'[63] Beaverbrook and Howe saw in American bilateralism a serious threat to the successful negotiation of a broad multilateral agreement. If the United States – the key nation in any post-war aviation system – were to negotiate a series of individual agreements and secure landing rights around the world, it would have little incentive at some future date to participate in any multilateral arrangement under an umbrella world aviation organization.

Beaverbrook flew to North America in July, primarily to deal with oil matters, but while in Washington he arranged to meet with Berle. There was increasing suspicion on both sides that the one was trying to get the jump on the other in the post-war scramble for landing rights: Beaverbrook was suspicious of the actions of Juan Trippe and Pan Am; Berle suspected Critchley of BOAC. There were also rumours that the British had begun negotiating services to Rome and Marseilles and were considering the purchase of a Caribbean-based company, while the Americans were seen to be moving into South America and eyeing the Middle East. Negotiations were in fact under way to acquire American landing rights in Spain, and within a few weeks the British government requested permission to institute a military service across North America to the South Pacific.[64]

Very little progress resulted from Beaverbrook's visit, except on the social level. On 29 July, Berle, Beaverbrook, Richard Law, and a few others flew to New Brunswick for a rendezvous with C.D. Howe. New Brunswick held sentimental attractions for Beaverbrook as well as Law, whose father – Bonar Law – was born there. As a result, the weekend was one long excursion into nostalgia, punctuated with the odd fishing expedition. Berle, who wrote a long diary entry describing it, noted that the 'whole thing from beginning to end was dominated by the abounding bounce, gaiety and endless vitality of Beaverbrook, who seems to have cooked all this up mostly for the fun of it.'[65] Aviation problems were discussed at odd moments, but without much success. 'Mr. Berle seemed quite discouraged about the result of the bilateral conversations which have taken place to date and which have been largely inconclusive,' Howe later wrote to Norman Robertson. 'The time we spent together was devoted largely to fishing which was about as productive as our talks on aviation.'[66]

By late August the situation had deteriorated further. The Foreign Office came out strongly against the United States negotiating landing rights, but the Americans would not back down. In a lengthy letter to Beaverbrook, Berle argued that the 'extension of civil aviation to regions now open for such communications appears to be dictated by the highest consideration of humanity and common sense, as well as by the inherent interest in reestablishing, so far as possible, normal commercial life.' While everyone hoped that an international authority ultimately would be established, it would take time. 'With this in mind,' he added, 'the United States feels that an *ad interim* arrangement should be immediately adopted under and by which, to the extent that equipment is released from strictly military use, airlines can be established serving the principal centers of population, including Latin America. This involves the securing of transit and landing rights by the United States and by Great Britain for the interim period to and in the centers to be served.'[67]

The Canadians were disappointed with this new American attitude, which, in the words of J.R. Baldwin, 'more or less wipes out the chances of a broader multilateral agreement at present.'[68] The British were equally distressed. Beaverbrook's aviation committee rejected Berle's telegram out of hand, and Beaverbrook responded to the Americans with a request 'for a postponement of your project for moving out on to civil air routes of the world.' An international aviation conference was needed in the immediate future to settle the outstanding issues. 'If for domestic reasons,' Beaverbrook concluded, 'you should find it difficult to hold a conference in Washington at the present time, we shall understand your position and stand ready to call a conference ourselves in London.'[69]

It is doubtful that Beaverbrook's offer to stage a conference received serious consideration in Washington. Nevertheless, the pressure of the British, the Canadians, and others did have some effect in the White House and State Department, as did domestic concerns over increasing criticism aimed at the administration for not seeming to have taken sufficient action with regard to civil aviation. In any event, on 8 September 1944, Roosevelt gave the go-ahead to hold an international conference, and three days later the invitations were sent out.

The announcement of the proposed international aviation conference to be held in Chicago beginning 1 November was widely welcomed in Canadian government circles and the Canadian reply was immediate and affirmative. Still, there was one small hitch – the Commonwealth discussions Canada had already agreed to attend. As one official minuted, these Commonwealth talks were mooted at a time when it seemed unlikely that an international conference would be held in the near future. It has been the Canadian view all along that nothing should be done which might in any way prejudice the success of an international conference, and it is quite possible that a Commonwealth conference at this stage would arouse suspicions and misgivings in Washington. This would, perhaps, have been less likely to happen if the Commonwealth talks had been announced before news of the United States Government's invitation appeared in the press, but I am afraid it would look unnecessarily provocative to follow our acceptance of the United States invitation with a statement that a preliminary meeting would be held by the Commonwealth.[70]

Robertson raised similar concerns at the CWC meeting on 13 September, but Howe was not convinced. He still believed that it would be profitable to discuss routes with other Commonwealth members because Canada would want to exchange services with some of them. Howe was backed by the committee and the decision was made to participate in both the international and Commonwealth negotiations.[71] At first it was hoped that the two sets could be held simultaneously (to minimize American suspicions), but ultimately it was agreed to hold the Commonwealth talks in Montreal one week before the convening of the Chicago conference.

On 8 September Lester Pearson met with Berle and learned of the developing (though still unofficial) plans for the international conference. The two men discussed who should or should not be invited – most of the neutral nations, yes, but not, for example, Argentina, which was dismissed as being 'merely "a dagger pointed at the heart of Antarctica."' Berle continued with a defence of the American position on negotiating bilateral agreements and a critique of recent British actions. 'There is no doubt,' Pearson reported, that Berle 'feels that the United Kingdom Government are aggressively and intelligently exploiting the situation. He feels that while legally they may always be on safe ground, practically they are taking advantage of the situation to the detriment of the United States. There was some indication that he felt that once again the wily Britishers were tricking them.' As for the Canadian memo protesting against the American negotiations for landing rights, Berle 'gave me the impression that he thought ... [it] was merely an extension of arguments already put to them by the United Kingdom and probably prompted by the United Kingdom.'[72]

Pearson protested this misunderstanding of Canadian motives and he emphasized the sincerity of his government's views, but these remonstrances could do little to ease the sting of Berle's insinuation. For many months the Canadian government had successfully trod the thin line between co-operation and independence in its dealings with Great Britain and the United States. Canadians had participated to a very full extent in the development of international civil aviation and had made important contributions through their draft convention and their efforts at negotiation and conciliation. Clearly, much had been accomplished, but, as Pearson discovered, on the eve of Chicago there was still much to be done.

8 'Everybody Is against Bad Weather'

The Chicago International Civil Aviation Conference was the single largest gathering of air-minded nations during the Second World War. It was exactly what the Interdepartmental Committee on Air Transport Policy had been working towards for more than a year: an opportunity for the allied nations to converse in a reasoned and intelligent manner on post-war civil aviation problems. The Canadians were well prepared: alone among the nations of the world, Canada had produced a sound and detailed draft convention and had, over the course of the summer, made an honest effort to revise this document to make its international acceptance more likely. Few states could boast of a cadre of men more talented or knowledgeable of civil aviation matters than Escott Reid, J.R. Baldwin, Herbert Symington, Norman Robertson, and the other members of the ICATP. It is doubtful whether there was any other international conference for which Canadians were more prepared and confident, and in which they were so willing to participate.

I

When the decision was made to accept the American invitation, the ICATP began work on a series of documents to be used as instructions and background information for the Canadian delegates to the conference. Work had already begun on similar documents for the Commonwealth discussions scheduled to take place in Montreal the week prior to the Chicago conference.[1] The two sets of instructions evidenced no significant change in Canadian policy, which was still predicated on the creation of a strong international authority with real power to regulate international aviation, including jurisdiction over questions of rates, capacity, routes, and frequencies. Within this context of a strong authority, all nations would maintain complete sovereignty over their airspace and cabotage, while at the same time grant the first four freedoms to the authority.

Yet there were a couple of additions to the Canadian proposals that, while made ostensibly to make the draft convention more palatable to the Americans, subsequently became the focus of considerable debate. The first dealt with the question of frequencies, or the number of actual flights over a specific route made over a given time by any nation. During the spring and summer 1944 a clear division had appeared on the frequencies question: the American position called for no limitations on the number of regular flights, while the British government sought a flat fifty-fifty division of frequencies. The Canadians responded with what was called an escalator clause: all nations were to be entitled to a fair share of the traffic originating in their own territory and would be guaranteed at least one round trip per week. If an airline could show that its service was running at a capacity of over 65 per cent (over an unspecified length of time) then it would automatically be permitted to increase its frequency. Conversely, if capacity fell below, say 40 per cent, then it would be forced to reduce frequencies. This escalator clause seemed to meet both sides – first by rewarding competition and efficiency, second by ensuring that concerned nations could not be permanently excluded from participating in a service that embarked from their own territories.

The second addition was a clause calling for a transitional period to cover that time between the end of hostilities and the coming into effect of the international convention. It had been part of American thinking that the establishment of an international authority and the negotiation of its powers inevitably would be a slow process and that some arrangement would be needed in the interim. Berle had discussed with Howe the possibility of a transitional period when he visited Montreal in March 1944; the new Canadian proposal called for a brief transitional period in which all nations would be permitted to negotiate arrangements freely, without being limited to a strict number of frequencies or routes. The transitional period would last only until the international convention came into effect.

The other key element in Canadian civil aviation policy was not included anywhere in the Canadian proposals. The essential ingredient for any broadly based multilateral agreement was an Anglo-

American understanding on the fundamental issues within which the Canadian government could participate. If either the Americans or British refused to embrace the outcome of the negotiations, then any agreement subsequently reached would not be worth the paper it was written on. Equally dangerous was the threat of a bilateral Anglo-American accord in which Canadian interests were ignored. For the Canadians the lesson was straightforward: Canadian negotiators should do their best to secure the Canadian proposals, but not to the point of alienating either the United Kingdom or the United States. A degree of flexibility was required at all times.

All things considered, the Canadian government was better prepared than the British to sit down at a large aviation conference. On the whole, there was remarkable unanimity between Howe and Mackenzie King and the officials who were appointed to carry out Canadian policy. Such agreement was not manifested in Whitehall. In Britain the making of aviation policy involved dozens of politicians and civil servants from the Foreign Office, Air Ministry, War Transport, and Dominions Office, not to mention Beaverbrook's Committee on Post-war Civil Air Transport (for which there was no Canadian counterpart). With more individuals taking an active interest in international civil aviation it should come as no surprise that a number of different viewpoints were expressed.

Beaverbrook, moreover, had clashed with the Foreign Office on several occasions over the previous year. Beaverbrook was far more pessimistic about the chances of success at Chicago and he had angered some segments of the Foreign Office through his apparent willingness to permit the United States access to British bases. While the Foreign Office strongly advocated at all costs reaching an agreement with the United States, Beaverbrook appeared more concerned with uniting the Commonwealth *before* dealing with the Americans.

There were also divisions over whether or not to attend Chicago at that time or trying to postpone the conference. Late in September, Beaverbrook recommended in a Cabinet memo that the Chicago conference be postponed until after an empire policy had been reached. He also expressed support for an Australian proposal to hold the advance Commonwealth talks in Canberra rather than Montreal or Ottawa. If he could get C.D. Howe to come, Beaverbrook argued, 'beyond the shadow of Mr. Mackenzie King, we might expect to develop concerted plans for Commonwealth air routes and exert a combined influence which would enable us to stand up before the United States and in front of the World.'² Beaverbrook was the lone voice supporting this scheme and he was quickly overruled by the War Cabinet.

Once the decision was made to attend the conference, the British issued a White Paper on international air transport. On the major points it was evident that the British position stood very much as it had at the time of Berle's visit in April. Like the Canadian draft, the British White Paper called for a strong international authority with regulatory powers that would include the four freedoms. The most salient difference remained the British determination to include a rigid formula for the setting of rates and the division of frequencies. Although the Canadians had introduced an escalator clause and proposed a transitional period, the British chose to stand firm. It was recognized within the British government that the Americans would be unlikely to accept the British proposals, but on 12 October the White Paper was approved by the War Cabinet, virtually without amendment.³

One other important development was the appointment of a minister of civil aviation on 8 October 1944. There were domestic roots for this action dating back to before the war, and there had always been pressure to separate civil aviation from the Air Ministry. This separation was largely accomplished during the course of the war as the planning and execution of Britain's civil aviation policy increasingly was left in the hands of men like Beaverbrook, who had little to do wth the Air Ministry. But the timing of the decision was significant: with the Chicago conference looming it was necessary to have someone on the job full time, something Beaverbrook could not do.⁴

The man chosen for the post was Lord Swinton, who had considerable experience in civil aviation matters from his years as air minister between 1935 and 1938. Swinton was a tough and intelligent negotiator, ideally suited to pursue British interests to the fullest as head of the British delegation to Chicago. He had been out of Britain since 1942 as resident minister for West Africa and had fallen out of touch with more recent developments. This circumstance was really only a minor concern, however, for policy decisions were still to be made in the ministerial committee in London: Swinton was charged only with the execution of these decisions.⁵

Lord Swinton returned to London immediately; although he would head the delegation to Chicago, it was left to Sir Arthur Street, the permanent under-secretary in the Air Ministry, to handle the Commonwealth discussions that began in Montreal on 22 October. Because these talks were to be on the official level only, Howe did not attend. In his place Herbert Symington chaired the discussions. In addition there were representatives from Australia, New Zealand, South Africa, Newfoundland, Southern Rhodesia, and India. On the insistence of the British government, Ireland was not invited (although it had been invited to Chicago) because of its wartime neutrality: it would be unacceptable as well as impossible to act 'as though nothing had happened,' the War Cabinet concluded.[6]

The Commonwealth civil aviation conversations were held in Montreal's Windsor Hotel and lasted until 27 October. Given the nature of the talks, the delegates had no authority to commit their respective governments to anything, only to make unanimous recommendations. Technical questions were included along with a general review of wartime air routes. Also on the agenda were plans to consider the Balfour report of the previous year, the UK White Paper, the Australia–New Zealand proposals, and the Canadian draft convention 'in the light of developments during 1944.' Specific Commonwealth routes were on the agenda, too, and five committees were established to examine a number of broad issues more closely, including routes (civilian and military), operations, and technical matters.[7]

If nothing else the Montreal talks furnished the opportunity for last-minute Anglo-Canadian negotiations on the Canadian draft convention. On the question of services between contiguous countries, for example, the British won a minor victory. Under the original draft proposal, services between contiguous countries could be reserved from the authority if only one of the two nations involved wanted it; during the Montreal talks the Canadians agreed to amend this article to state that both nations had to agree to reserve the services.[8] On the surface this change appears rather insignificant, but it is illustrative of the divergent Canadian and British perspectives. The Canadians were concerned primarily with services to the United States and they wanted to be able to ensure that they could reserve these services whether the Americans wanted to or not. The British, in contrast, were looking more to Europe, where, if the continental nations reserved all the services with their neighbours, Britain would be hard pressed to compete effectively. Hence the desire to make it more difficult to reserve services by stipulating the agreement of both parties.

No such agreement was achieved on either the transitional period or the escalator clause. Symington and Howe were sympathetic to the thinking behind the transitional period and the escalator clause, for they believed that Canada and TCA were ready and able to compete effectively as soon as the war ended. The major problem – lack of suitable aircraft – no longer seemed so ominous: 'The present indication,' Howe wrote to Beaverbrook a few weeks before the conference, 'is that Canada will have modern airplanes as soon as the U.S.A. We are building more than we need ourselves, and we can possibly share ours with the U.K. If so, we will both be as well off as our friends to the South.'[9] The British were not so sure. There were real fears in London that the American superiority in aircraft would be especially acute in the early post-war years, before the British aircraft industry had been converted to civilian production. The last thing the British government wanted was to allow the Americans to establish services all over the world – getting them out after the convention came into effect would be a next-to-impossible task. As Lord Swinton put it: 'Canadian proposals as I see it would give United States all they are asking for; a flying start, and an automatic increase in traffic because they will have the aircraft when other countries have not. It entirely abandons the principle agreed at Empire Conference that national quotas should be in proportion to passengers and mail embarked in country of origin.' If the Canadians got their way on this issue, he concluded, 'I think it would hopelessly prejudice our position for all time.'[10] On these issues of real substance the British would not budge. The report of the convention committee openly stated that the other delegations were free to disagree with the Canadians on these points. 'We do not think that we can afford to concede either of these two points since each is vital to us,' Sir Arthur Street argued, 'and we feel that in the last resort we must take our stand at Chicago even if it involves open disagreement with the Canadians there.'[11]

A good deal of attention was paid to Commonwealth services, and a committee was formed to discuss the issue. Maps were drawn and lists were prepared naming the specific routes each member wished to fly. As expected there was considerable overlapping and it was evident that the division of services would be an ongoing process, lasting long after the Montreal talks. For this reason there was general support for the creation of the Commonwealth Air Transport Council (CATC), to facilitate the evolution of the process through the provision of permanent machinery for consultation and the exchange of views within the Commonwealth. Only the Canadian delegation reserved its final decision on the CATC, but there was unanimity on the 'desirability' of such a board.[12]

There was some satisfaction in London over the proposed CATC – 'probably the outstanding result of the Montreal Conference,' wrote Sir Archibald Sinclair[13] – but there was also considerable disappointment in not being able to bring the Canadians into line. The question facing the British cabinet at this time was what to do if, as seemed likely, agreement on a wide multilateral convention could not be reached with the Americans. Should a convention be signed excluding the United States or should the convention itself be modified in such a way as to make it acceptable to the United States? On 26 October the War Cabinet agreed on the latter course: if a broad agreement did not emerge, the British delegation should push for a convention covering technical and non-commercial matters only, and should reserve rates, routes, and frequencies for future bilateral negotiations.[14]

Australia and New Zealand could be counted on to support this line of approach, but the Canadians, and Swinton was keen to 'avoid any open breach of the Empire front.'[15] Swinton received advice from a number of sources, including Beaverbrook, who suggested that if Swinton could meet privately with Howe 'and could offer to make some concessions to the Canadian point of view on relatively minor points, it would, he thought, be possible to obtain the support of the Canadian Government for our main thesis.'[16]

By the time Lord Swinton embarked on his long journey to Chicago, British policy had hardened considerably. While the Canadians continued to stress the importance of reaching a broad multilateral agreement, the British were setting up limits beyond which they would not go. The control of frquencies, quotas, and rates had become the focus of the British position, increasingly at the expense of a multilateral convention and international authority. The Canadian escalator clause and transitional period were regarded with suspicion, and as for the leased bases, no concessions were to be made unless a satisfactory convention was negotiated. As a final parting gift, the War Cabinet gave Lord Swinton the right to grant the first two freedoms unconditionally – something the Canadians would have difficulty with.[17]

II

A total of fifty-four nations were invited to Chicago, almost every country in the world with the exception of the enemy states. Only Saudi Arabia and the Soviet Union refused to participate, the latter ostensibly because of the invitations to Spain, Portugal, Switzerland, and other neutral states that had 'adopted during the course of many years a hostile position in regard to the Soviet Union.'[18] In addition to the fifty-two countries that sent full delegations, Denmark and Thailand sent observers. The result was a conference of very large proportions indeed, with approximately 185 delegates, 156 advisers, 45 secretaries, 105 clerks and stenographers, a conference secretariat of 306, and 158 press representatives.[19]

The brief conference agenda that was included with the inivtations referred to the 'approaching defeat of Germany,' which, in turn, 'sets up the urgent need for establishing an international civil air service pattern on a provisional basis at least, so that all important trade and population areas of the world may obtain the benefits of air transportation as soon as possible, and so that the restorative processes of prompt communication may be available to assist in returning great areas to processes of peace.' In an effort to meet this challenge, the Americans proposed, first, the 'establishment of provisional world route arrangements,' which would permit the inauguration of services as soon as possible. Second, the Americans called for the creation of an interim council 'to act as the clearing house and advisory agency during the transitional period.' Third, the conference should aim to agree on principles on which to found a permanent international authority and multilateral convention.[20] Based on what they had learned from their preliminary discussions, the Americans believed that there was wide support for these proposals. Chicago would provide the forum in which they would be realized.

For the almost 1000 participants who arrived at the beginning of November, the centre of activity for the next six weeks was the Stevens Hotel in downtown Chicago. A 'mammoth second-rate hotel,' Escott Reid described it, 'whose lobby was like the lobby of the Grand Central Station in New York, a hotel in which it was necessary to waste an hour a day waiting for elevators and probably half an hour a day waiting to complete telephone calls.'[21] It was crowded and clamorous inside and complaints against the hotel and accommodations were common. Inevitably the cramped quarters had a deleterious effect on the individuals involved; as J.R. Baldwin succinctly put it: 'Rooms were small and tempers easily became frayed.'[22]

Canada sent three delegates: C.D. Howe, Herbert Symington, and J.A. Wilson. In addition, there were four advisers: Reid, Baldwin, R.M. MacDonnell from external affairs, and Air Vice-Marshal W.A. Curtis. There were also more than a dozen technical advisers attached to the delegation from TCA and the departments of Transport and National Defence. On average, the delegation was large, except when compared to those of the Americans and the British. The United Kingdom delegation headed by Lord Swinton contained eight delegates (including Air Arthur Street, Sir William Hildred, and two representatives for Newfoundland) and almost thirty advisers. The American delegation was the largest of all, running to over forty delegates, consultants, advisers, and experts. Berle was in the chair, and other senior members included Senators Josiah Bailey and Owen Brewster, Welch Pogue and Edward Warner of the CAB, and Fiorello LaGuardia, the chair of the American section of the Permanent Joint Board on Defence.

The unfolding of the Chicago conference was dictated largely by the United States, the United Kingdom, and, to a lesser degree, Canada. Still, other nations made significant contributions. France and China both were represented by delegations over a dozen strong, while the Australians and New Zealanders came armed with a well-prepared joint statement of proposals. The Irish arrived with their own agenda: keep clear of the British and remnants of the 1935 agreement, and support anything that might 'favour the development of the Shannon Airport and the possibility of Irish operations on the transatlantic main service and connecting services.'[23] Finally, the Latin American delegations, though small individually, soon realized that collectively they had significant clout as a voting bloc.

The published proceedings of the Chicago conference include almost 500 documents and fill over 1400 pages in two volumes. Millions of words were written, spoken, and debated over the six-week period. Above all, an enormous amount of work was accomplished by the hundreds of participants who assumed thankless tasks for what they believed to be a good cause.

Adolf Berle was appointed president of the conference and spoke first. After reading a statement of welcome from President Roosevelt, he turned the floor over to a variety of speakers from the delegations. C.D. Howe spoke on 2 November and set the tone for subsequent Canadian actions. He began his speech by listing the virtues of open competition (which pleased the Americans) and continued with a demonstration of how competition could best be achieved under a strong international authority:

We are firm believers in healthy competition. We are convinced that it will develop most fruitfully under an international authority. We want to see free choice for the traveller between competing airlines; competition in service, but not in subsidies; a guaranteed minimum of routes and frequencies to the airline companies of all nations, large or small; the most frequencies, where need exists, whether a nation is large or small; the substitution of international regulation for national restrictions; and the complete absence of discriminations, preferences, exclusive rights, and arbitrary landing fees and charges. We also seek a control of subsidies, not through any impractical method of direct control, but rather through control of uneconomical consequences of subsidies, such as rate-cutting and the maintenance of services at levels greater than traffic warrants.[24]

Howe continued with an overview of the Canadian draft convention and made a strong defence for rate controls and some kind of mechanism to adjust frequencies. Turning to the issue of transit rights, Howe explained Canadian difficulties over the unlimited granting of freedoms 1 and 2 – how it would open up Canada to abuse from stronger air powers. Equally, however, he recognized that Canada had responsibilities in the international community – responsibilities from which Canada would not shirk. If no general agreement emerged from the conference, he noted, 'Canada has no intention of pursuing an obstructionist attitude in dealing with transit or landing rights. Our record has been good in the past. It will remain good in the future. But though Canada's immediate and direct national interests probably would not be endangered by a continuance of the pre-war system, we know that our long-run interest in the creation and maintenance of a peaceful and prosperous world would be gravely endangered.'[25] He finished with these words: 'The opportunity before this Conference is great. The responsibility it bears is grave. I am confident that this assembly will grasp the opportunity and accept the responsibility and thus guarantee one essential of lasting peace.'[26]

Howe's speech was widely praised, both by the other delegates and in the Amnerican press. Even Lord Swinton, who had exchanged draft speeches in advance with Howe, was impressed. The Englishman still had trouble with parts of the Canadian convention, but, he wrote to Sir Edward Bridges, the secretary of the Cabinet: 'I think they [the Canadians] would be quite prepared to be defeated on these in Committee in a friendly way.'[27]

After the official words of welcome and opening speeches, the conference got down to work. One of the first jobs was to establish committees to deal with special aspects of the agenda. C.D. Howe was on the Executive Committee, which consisted of all the delegation heads, and he was elected to the more influential Steering Committee of thirteen. There were also committees on credentials, nominations, and rules and regulations, but no Canadians were appointed. In addition, there were some twenty technical committees and subcommittees covering the gamut of technical and non-economic questions, from airworthiness to registration, from accident investigation to the organization of an interim council. A Canadian was a member of every one of these bodies.[28]

Four documents were officially tabled early in the conference: the Canadian draft convention, the United Kingdom White Paper, a detailed American plan for an international authority, and the joint Australia–New Zealand proposals, which were alone in calling for the internationalization of international trunk routes and received only lukewarm support. On 9 November, in the Committee on Multilateral Aviation Convention and International Aeronautical Body (better known as Committee 1), the Australia–New Zealand proposals were formally rejected on an American-backed motion by the Brazilian delegation.[29] This left the American, British, and Canadian proposals – and the differences between them remained at the centre of the debate for the rest of the conference.

Each morning the Canadian delegation met to plan the day's events before spreading out into the various committees. Meals were reserved for informal meetings with other delegates, and usually produced equal portions of arm-twisting and indigestion. In the evenings, the Commonwealth delegations usually gathered to compare notes and assess recent developments. Nicolas Cheetham, the joint secretary of the British delegation, recorded in his diary that these after-dinner meetings were 'long and verbose affairs, and all, except the Indians, have had a few drinks by then. Everyone helps himself liberally from the whiskey laid out (by myself) on a side table.' Cheetham took 'no active part' in the meetings but attended anyway because it was 'fascinating to watch the Commonwealth in action – agreement and disagreement. His Lordship [Swinton] is not always very tactful; he has usually dined fully and well, tête-à-tête, with a member of the delegation who is rewarded with an immense Havana.'[30]

As is so often the case when individuals with dynamic and intense personalities are thrown together in negotiation, friction arose between members of the Canadian and British delegations. Lord Swinton was a man who commanded the respect of those he dealt with, but he also had a ruthless and competitive streak and was easily irritated by those who opposed him. Swinton's aristocratic ways also caused some problems. While the Canadians and Americans frequented each other's room for information discussions, Swinton would remain in his room and insist that all come to him. Moreover, as J.R. Baldwin noted, he lacked 'that mastery of under-statement which is normally required of diplomatic negotiators.'[31]

Swinton may have felt that the divergent Canadian views ran contrary to his idea of imperial solidarity, and he found the Canadians obsessed with securing an international convention. Whenever the Canadians 'thought a convention might be jeopardized,' he wrote, 'they tried to influence us to the American point of view.'[32] Swinton claimed that this did not hinder his ability to work with the Canadians, but Malcolm MacDonald later found Swinton 'pretty angry' at them. MacDonald confessed that he liked Swinton, but noted that 'he is not everybody's cup of tea, and some of his conduct of relations with the Canadian delegation at Chicago seems to have been unfortunate in the extreme.'[33] MacDonald added that Howe and Symington were 'incensed' over Swinton's rude and arrogant behaviour. 'Howe,' MacDonald wrote, 'is usually a splendid friend and colleague to work with. But when he is rubbed up the wrong way he can become unreasonable and difficult.'[34]

Relations between the Canadian and British delegations were further strained when Commonwealth meetings were held to which the Canadians were not invited. The primary reason for excluding the Canadians, Malcolm MacDonald wrote, was that they were perceived as being too close to the American camp and would therefore 'promptly give away to the United States delegation any secrets which were discussed in the Commonwealth meetings,'[35] In a sense it was a self-fulfilling prophecy: the Canadians were occasionally excluded because they were not perceived as Commonwealth players, but being absent from Commonwealth meetings only gave credibility to such allegations, especially to the other Commonwealth delegations that believed that the Canadians had in fact been invited but had chosen not to attend.

Notwithstanding personality clashes and differences in perspective, the Canadian and British delegations worked very well together. Indeed, the Canadians were more successful in shifting British opinion to a compromise position than the Americans were. During the first ten days of the conference relatively little progress was made in the committees dealing with the economic powers of the international authority. In the meantime, however, the Commonwealth delegations worked on revising the Canadian convention. Progress was slow, but by 9 November Swinton was optimistic enough to report to London that, after a meeting of all the Commonwealth delegations, 'all present agreed that we could safely support a Canadian draft, which we slightly amended in the course of our discussion.'[36]

The British and Canadians were becoming increasingly anxious to get the Americans involved in private discussions on the main points of contention, but at first the Americans seemed reluctant. Berle explained to Escott Reid on 10 November that the American delegation had been holding 'prolonged meetings to try to arrive at conclusions on United States policy.' Berle was hampered by conservative elements within his delegation and by outside pressure orchestrated by Pan Am to do little more than open up the airways of the world to American airlines, and certainly not to give any real power to the international authority.[37] Berle was undoubtedly jockeying for position, but he gave Reid an indication of which way the American delegation was heading when he asked why the Canadians had not included the fifth freedom in their air convention. This was the freedom on which American aviation interests hinged – and a freedom that the British and Canadians were reluctant to give.

Berle's feelings for the British fluctuated between grudging respect, suspicion, and outright contempt. He saw the British proposals on frequencies as little more than an elaborate scheme to implement a quota system unfavourable to the United States. He was furious over the White Paper, which gave no indication of a change in British thinking prior to the conference, and things were not improved when he met face to face with Lord Swinton. After listening to Berle's explanation of American opposition to the White Paper, Swinton responded: 'Did you really think we were going to change our minds?' To this Berle acidly replied: 'as far as I could see the British Government was asking not merely for United States money and for United States planes, but likewise for United States traffic to put in her planes.'[38]

Berle and Swinton did not like each other, but eventually did agree on the need for private discussions – ones that would include the Canadians. It was here, in the so-called ABC discussions, that Canadian influence reached its zenith. The Canadians were invited because they had come to the conference with a well-thought-out and detailed plan that was widely respected. In addition the Canadians were seen to be flexible and sitting somewhere between the British and American positions, and the talents of the Canadian representatives were well appreciated. As J.R.K. Main, one of the Canadian advisers, put it: 'We Canadians are exerting an influence here altogether out of proportion to the size or political importance of our country. Our neutral position between the big boys is our ace card.'[39]

The first ABC meeting was held on the afternoon of 12 November. After a few formalities, Berle presented Howe and Swinton with copies of an American document that neither man had seen previously, and which promptly 'precipitated a first-class crisis.' The Americans now appeared less optimistic over the chances of reaching agreement on the establishment of an international authority, and instead were pressing for the signing of an international convention. At the heart of their new document were two proposals: (1) no frequency control, and (2) the unreserved granting of the fifth freedom by all nations that signed the convention. Swinton immediately balked at any such suggestion and tempers flared. 'Before the discussion had gone on for more than perhaps thirty minutes,' Reid reported, 'it became clear that we were heading in the direction of a full-dress debate between the United Kingdom and the United States on the general principle of whether there should be international control of frequencies. It also became clear that if this debate took place, Lord Swinton would have evinced remarkably little knowledge of what he was talking about.'[40]

On the pretext that Howe had not been sufficiently briefed before the meeting, the Canadians secured a short adjournment, but even after private discussions with Swinton and Berle it was evident that no progress would be made that night. Some effort was made to limit any permanent damage by shifting attention to the clause in the Canadian convention dealing with the division of frequencies, but only with limited success.

Swinton liked the Canadian proposal that frequencies would be divided on the 'traffic-embarked' principle: that national carriers should have an amount of traffic equivalent to that embarking from their territory (and because most people who fly in one direction will usually return home, this meant that traffic would be divided almost equally). But Swinton had difficulty with the suggestion that national quotas would not be given as a right at the beginning but only after an application had been made. In the meantime, foreign services could be begun based on the same system, and when an application was made by the national carrier the foreign services would not be cut back. The result would be more frequencies than the market could bear.[41]

The Canadians persisted over the next few days in an effort to prevent the breakdown of the ABC discussions. Neither the Americans nor the British, for example, liked the provision for the automatic reduction of frequencies if capacity fell below 40 per cent, and the Canadians removed it. On the larger questions, there were hopeful signs that the two great powers were coming closer together. At one point Berle offered to accept the Canadian 'traffic-embarked' principle in establishing frequencies if, in return, the British would accept the American fifth-freedom proposals.[42] Swinton received from the ministerial committee in London a cautious endorsement of the fifth freedom, provided a number of safeguards were included: (1) it would have to be accepted by most nations; (2) it would have to be tied to a strong international authority; (3) there would have to be a trial period after which the British could withdraw; and (4) there would have to be safeguards to prevent long-distance services (e.g., New York–London–Paris) from diverting traffic from local services (eg., London–Paris).[43] One safeguard suggested was to force the long-distance operator to charge a higher fare between two intermediate points than a local operator charged. Using the New York–London–Paris example, an American operator from New York would have to charge more to carry those passengers picked up in London bound for Paris than a local British operator would on the same route.

Human error had a role to play in determining Britain's stand on the escalator clause. When Lord Swinton first telegrammed London for instructions on this matter, he received word that the British government would agree to the escalator clause. By the time he was informed that a mistake had been made, that the British reply should have read 'would *not* agree,' Swinton had already committed his government to the escalator clause on traffic embarked. 'To his credit,' Baldwin wrote, Swinton 'stood by the escalator clause as far as he had gone up to that point, i.e. based on the third freedom, but, of course, insists now that he cannot go a step farther.'[44]

For one brief moment there was real optimism that an agreement could be reached, but in a matter of days all hopes had collapsed like a house of cards. The sticking-point concerned the application of the escalator clause to the fifth freedom; that is, should additional traffic picked up under the fifth freedom be included in the initial division and increase of frequencies? Swinton was clear in his own mind, and wrote to London:

I have reported in various telegrams all the main features of the provisional draft conventiion. It accepted that capacity on each route should be settled on a basis of equilibrium and divided into quotas on basis of traffic embarked. The traffic between each originating country and each other country being considered separately would be assessed separately. It included grant of fifth freedom. It contained Escalator clause to reward efficient operator which had figured from the start in the Canadian draft convention and had been inserted long before there was any question of introducing freedom five ... When freedom five was introduced it was clearly understood by all of us, and certainly by some at least of the Americans that application of Escalator clause was confined to traffic between one terminal point and another and was entirely unaffected by grant of fifth freedom.

Now the Americans wanted to change everything by altering 'the whole basis both of the assessment of capacity and of escalator clause.'[45]

Briefly, the British were willing to have the escalator clause apply only on the traffic embarked from the country of origin, that is based on the third freedom. Under this scheme the Americans would be restricted in expanding services between two foreign locations. Under the new American proposal the escalator would apply to fifth-freedom traffic as well, which would make it easier to increase frequencies, for example, between the European capitals or between Britain and the dominions. On this point the whole conference stalled.

'The conference is at the worst point as regards an air transport convention that it has yet reached,' a somber J.R. Baldwin wrote on 21 November.[46] A stalemate had emerged and both Berle and Swinton appeared to have given up hope of achieving any kind of settlement. In fact, at the Commonwealth meeting the following evening, Symington was hard-pressed to keep Swinton from lining up all the delegates behind his plan to bring the conference to a close.[47]

The stalemate between the British and Americans was fully aired at a joint meeting of three major committees on 22 November. Most of the work of the technical committees had been completed or suspended and there was increasingly less for the delegates to do while the ABC discussions dragged on. 'Small countries getting restive at being kept in the dark,' J.R.K. Main wrote in his diary. 'There is an air of gloom since it is known that U.K. & U.S. cannot agree on fundamentals.'[48] Now Berle and Swinton proposed that a convention consisting of those points of agreement be signed, leaving unanswered questions to future negotiations.[49]

Symington, who was by this time close to complete exhaustion, spoke for Canada in a last-ditch effort to prolong the discussions. 'While we are considering each clause of what has been agreed upon between the great powers,' he said to the gathered delegates, 'Let us go on with some hope that this Convention can be made a final and complete Convention. May I say, as one who sat between them, that I can see no reason why that cannot be done during the rest of this week, and, therefore, I will continue to press them to reach that position.'[50]

Symington was supported by Fiorello LaGuardia, who gave an impassioned and brilliant appeal to the conference not to lose sight of the larger goals. 'Great work has been done,' he noted with reference to technical matters and rules and regulations. This was not surprising, he added: 'Everybody is against bad weather. Everybody wants safe planes. Everybody wants to utilize all the miraculous progress of science in navigation, landing, structure of planes and motors. That is not our big job. Our big job, as I understand it, was to meet here and so utilize this new method of transportation, now being evoked as an instrument of destruction, for the safety and happiness of the people of the world, to forget everything that has happened in the past, and to start anew with this method of transportation.' LaGuardia urged the delegates to make one more try to reach an equitable solution. 'Gentlemen,' he declared,

the world will be disappointed if we dodge or duck or detour or evade the principles and the fundamentals upon which you are talking for an interim congress. Our distinguished Chairman [Berle], in the language of diplomacy, referred to the complete picture as an 'ambitious dream.' Let us make that a definite mandate. I cannot agree, Lord Swinton, that we may achieve more limited objectives and then call it a day. To fail in establishing fundamentals that will eliminate the irritations that have caused trouble in this world before would not be carrying out or reaching the objectives that the majority of us seek. Now, it was stated by every speaker, we propose that all shall be as fair to the smallest country as it is to the greatest. Let us translate that idea, that objective, and those beautiful words into actions.[51]

Thanks in part to Symington's and LaGuardia's speeches, collapse was averted and the Anglo-American differences were thrown back into committee for one last attempt at resolution. Symington, meanwhile, was whisked off to bed. 'We locked his doors,' Baldwin wrote, 'put "Do Not Disturb" signs out, and cancelled all his telephone calls.'[52] Although efforts to mediate between Berle and Swinton continued, the moment of Canadian effectiveness had begun to fade. Howe had already left Chicago, having been called back to Ottawa by a looming cabinet crisis over conscription. More important, the channel of commuication between the United States and Great Britain had been removed from Chicago and elevated to the highest level.

On 22 November, President Roosevelt intervened with a personal request to Prime Minister Churchill to accept the American proposals. 'We have met you on a number of points,' he argued,

notably an arrangement for regulation of rates and an arrangement by which the number of planes in the air shall be adjusted to the amount of traffic. This is as far as I can go. In addition, your people are now asking limitations on the number of planes between points regardless of traffic offering. This seems to me a form of strangulation. It has been a cardinal point in American policy throughout that the ultimate judge should be the passenger and the shipper. The limitations now proposed would, I fear, place a dead hand on the use of the great air trade routes. You don't want that any more than I do.

The issue will be debated tomorrow. I hope you can get into this yourself and give instructions, preferably by telephone, to your people in Chicago so that we can arrange, if possible, to agree. It would be unfortunate indeed if the Conference broke down on this.

When Churchill refused to budge from the British position, Roosevelt sent a second message. He repeated that the United States could make no more concessions and then added: 'We are doing our best to meet your Lend-Lease needs. We will face Congress on that subject in a few weeks and it will not be in a generous mood if it and the people feel that the United Kingdom has not agreed to a generally beneficial air agreement. They will wonder about the chances of our two countries, let alone any others, working together to keep the peace if we cannot even get together on an aviation agreement. I hope you will review the situation once more and see if we cannot get together.'[53]

Winant delivered the telegram to Churchill personally. 'It was pure blackmail, threatening that if we did not give way to certain unreasonable American demands, their attitude about Lease Lend supplies would change,' one colleague complained in his diary. 'Winant was shame-faced about presenting it and didn't want to stay to lunch, but the PM said that even a declaration of war should not prevent them having a good lunch. The rest of the weekend was largely devoted to concerting, by telephone with Beaverbrook, a long reply.'[54]

Outside the conference, meanwhile, an Anglo-American dispute that had been brewing for months nearly came to a boil. The problem concerned Clipperton Island, a French possession in the South Pacific. The British had begun to investigate the possibilities of utilizing this strategic island in a Pacific service. The Americans were not keen and heated telegrams were exchanged across the Atlantic. The dispute came to a head late in November and within a fortnight the United States sent an armed party to Clipperton with orders to defend the island against all foes.[55]

Even with the implied threat to lend-lease and deteriorating relations over Clipperton Island, however, Churchill remained firm. It would be unfortunate if British policy led to difficulties on lend-lease, Churchill informed Roosevelt, but 'even if I thought that we were to be so penalized, I would not feel myself able to agree to a decision contrary to merits, as we see them, on this matter.' Better to adjourn the conference based on agreements reached thus far, and continue the search for a solution behind the scenes.

The conference was deadlocked. Further attempts to bridge the gap were made, each with increasingly complex formulas to divide frequencies and set capacity, and each was as unsuccessful as its predecessor. Even the plenary sessions were becoming more polarized, with the Latin American delegations firmly behind the United States, and with Australia, New Zealand, and France (usually) behind the United Kingdom. Accusations of blame were hurled back and forth, fingers were pointed, charges of bad faith were laid. J.R. Baldwin described the situation in a letter to Howe: 'We have reached a sufficiently advanced stage of the conference to be able to label most of the articles we started with as "killed, wounded or missing." Unless something quite unforeseen happens, there remain only lesser points of drafting to be completed and the plenary sessions for approval of final documents.'[56]

By 30 November Swinton was freely admitting that all proposals were 'now entirely academic.'[57] This the Canadians discovered first hand. 'On Friday morning' (1 December), Baldwin wrote, 'Mr. Symington was busy with another last minute effort trying to find some means of reconciliation. Neither Mr. Berle nor Lord Swinton, however, was movable. Neither was willing to give the impression of making a move and neither would authorize Mr. Symington to follow up any proposal, leaving it entirely to him to do as he saw fit.'[58] To make matters worse, a reorganization of the State Department was announced on 27 November with the replacement of Secretary of State Cordell Hull by Edward Stettinius (who was Juan Trippe's brother-in-law), followed by the obligatory resignation of the other State Department officials, including Adolf Berle. Although Berle was asked to stay with the conference until the end, his effectiveness was over.

All that remained was to salvage what could be recovered from the ruins of the Anglo-American stalemate. On 29 November Berle proposed the addition of a protocol to the permanent convention under which all signatories would grant the five freedoms. Symington did not like this idea: if in signing the convention each nation was automatically obligated to accept the protocol too, then many states (including Canada) would have difficulty in agreeing. Symington worked long and hard, and as it turned out successfully, to remove the proposed protocol from the convention into what ultimately became a separate five-freedoms agreement[59] (see appendix 5).

A more serious problem arose on 1 December, when Berle invited a motion from the Netherlands delegation to include the first two freedoms in the permanent convention.[60] Symington was outraged at this unannounced motion and secured an adjournment to give the delegation time to think. Later that day he learned that Swinton also agreed with Berle on the granting of the two freedoms. It appeared that the unthinkable was happening: the inclusion of the first two freedoms in a permanent convention without the countervailing force of an international authority with regulatory powers. Symington moved swiftly to persuade Swinton that the wisest course of action would be to again have a separate agreement – this one for the two freedoms – to be signed at the same time but in no way part of the permanent convention. Last-minute negotiating paid off, largely because there was sympathy for Symington's argument that the inclusion of the two freedoms would make it impossible for many nations to sign the permanent convention.[61] To prevent this from happening, the two freedoms were removed from the convention and embodied in a separate agreement similar to that arranged for the five freedoms (see appendix 4). Symington had come to Chicago hoping to achieve one agreement; now it seemed that he would leave with several.

III

That there would be an international aviation authority was never in doubt: the only question concerned the size and shape this new body would take. Everyone *was* against bad weather and so agreement on many of the fundamentals was easy to reach. The failure to agree on the economic issues, however, made it impossible to have an authority with anything more than advisory powers.

The committee members were faced with a difficult situation: the proposed international organization would deal with very important and sensitive issues, and it would likely take some years to set all the machinery in motion. In the meantime, however, it was vital to have some organization in place as soon as possible in order to prevent a post-war free-for-all. The solution was to create two organizations: a provisional body to handle immediate issues and make preparations for the establishment of the second, permanent authority – what would eventually become the International Civil Aviation Organization (ICAO).

The two questions that most concerned the Canadian delegation (outside the vital economic issues) were the location of the new aviation organization and membership on its council. Berle made it known to the Canadians that he favoured locating the new organization in Canada.[62] Both the American and Latin American delegations supported choosing a site in the western hemisphere and Canada was a logical choice as an important aviation nation and one with strong links to Europe.

The British delegation, which arguably might have had good reasons for supporting Canada, was, in fact, decidedly lukewarm to the proposition. Shortly before the location of the interim council came up for discussion, Swinton reported his views to Whitehall. London and Washington cancelled each other out, he believed, and although he suspected that the committee might go for Canada, the British delegation felt 'that Paris might be best choice provided we could induce the French not to insist on running the organisation in the French language.'[63] Three days later Swinton received the advice of the British government: 'We have considered various possible alternatives. We strongly favour Bermuda as first choice, and Paris, despite language difficulties, as second choice.' Why did the British government not support Canada as home for the new organization? Because, the telegram continued, 'we are unwilling to press Canada in view of United States influence in Ottawa.'[64]

Swinton was put in a difficult position: how could he openly oppose the choice of Canada as headquarters for a new international organization without offending the Canadians and making a mockery of his cherished imperial solidarity? It was especially tricky when Berle raised the issue in the ABC discussions on 14 November. The Americans wanted Canada picked, so did the Canadians. How could he do anything else but agree? By that time it was becoming clear that the powers of the new organization would be limited in scope and this made the bitter pill easier to swallow. Because the interim council 'will have no executive authority but will make recommendations to the governments,' he concluded, 'I suggest that the political dangers of Canada to which I am very much alive, have less force.'[65]

Even with the support of the American and Latin American delegations however, the vote was very close. With only Luxembourg abstaining, the vote went 26–25 in favour of Canada over France as the seat for the interim organization. The second vote – for the permanent seat – was equally close in Canada's favour, but on 5 December Symington moved that the final decision be held off until the final meeting of the Interim Assembly. This was a magnanimous gesture and was widely praised, especially by the French delegation, which still held hopes for Paris, but, as Symington later wrote, 'Canada did not want its selection to be the result of an American bloc which it in principle was strongly opposing.'[66]

With respect to membership on the council of the new provisional organization, the Canadians based their actions on the functional principle: Canada deserved to be represented on the council because of its role and contribution as an important air power. Unfortunately, however, when it came time to vote, the other nations of the world appeared oblivious to the functional principle.

Originally the Canadians wanted to limit the size of the council to fourteen of the world's major air powers. The British and Americans concurred on this approximate size, but in committee the large powers were outnumbered by the Latin American bloc, which successfully enlarged the council to twenty-one. The make-up of the council was divided into three groups: (1) the seven most-important air nations, (2) the five most-important providers of facilities, and (3) eight representatives from different geographical areas to ensure representation for all regions. The twenty-first seat was reserved for the Soviets, if and when they decided to join.[67]

The election of the first Interim Council took place on 6 December 1944. Dispassionate reasoning and logic vanished, and back-room bargaining and political manoeuvring took over as votes were withheld and exchanged. In the first category, the Canadians were disappointed when Canada received fewer votes than the Netherlands, Brazil, France, Mexico, and Belgium as a major air power. The Canadians were more successful in the second category, winning a seat on the council as a provider of navigational facilities, along with Cuba, Peru, Norway, and Iraq.

When all the smoke cleared, the voting strength of Latin America was plain to see. Fully one-third of the Interim Council (seven of twenty-one) went to Latin American states, including Columbia, Chile, and El Salvador under the geographical category. 'It still seems a little ridiculous that Chile *and* Peru *and* Columbia should have been elected,' one Foreign Office official minuted. 'I should have thought that European countries had far more experience in running their own international services. Before the war there were plenty of lines running in South America, but very few not owned and operated by foreigners.'[68] Especially galling was the absence of India, which seemed far more deserving of a seat on the council than most of the Latin American states. This latter issue was settled on 7 December, the last day of the conference, when Cuba resigned its seat in India's favour.

With the creation of the Provisional International Civil Aviation Organization (PICAO) and the election of the Interim Council, the work of the Chicago conference was finished. The long-discussed international organization was a reality at last, although not in the form first envisaged by the Canadians. The provisional organization was created with a full and busy mandate: to find solutions for all the questions on which the Chicago conference had floundered.

IV

If the measure of success of an international conference is in the number of agreements produced, then the Chicago International Civil Aviation Conference was successful indeed. When the various delegations returned home, they carried with them five documents: a Final Act, an international convention, an interim agreement, and two agreements on transit rights. Yet few would have argued that the sum total of these documents produced any greater outcome for the conference as a whole. 'We have been in travail for a month,' J.R. Baldwin noted ruefully, 'and have brought forth a mouse.'[69] While there was value in each document, there was also the grim realization that on the fundamental economic issues the conference had failed.

The Final Act consisted of resolutions covering a wide spectrum of topics, such as the use of the metric system, technical personnel, and transferring the title of aircraft. It also laid out standard clauses to be used in subsequent bilateral air agreements – clauses to prevent discrimination and the exclusion of third parties and to make mandatory the filing of all agreements with PICAO to prevent secrecy. Last but not least, the Final Act recommended that 'the matters on which it has not been possible to reach agreement between the States represented at this Conference ... be referred to the Interim Council ... with instructons to give these matters continuing study and to submit a report thereon with recommendations to the Interim Assembly as soon as practical.'[70]

The Interim Agreement on International Civil Aviation established 'a provisional international organization of a technical and advisory nature of sovereign States.' It consisted of an assembly and council of twenty-one elected at Chicago and would function for up to three years or until the permanent convention came into effect. The council would in turn establish three committees: (1) the Committee on Air Transport, which would study, collect, and analyse information on the volume of air traffic, subsidies, and the operation of air services, and make recommendations to the council; (2) the Committee on Air Navigation, which would study and advise on all those issues pertaining to air navigation, such as communications and ground facilities, air-traffic control, airworthiness, customs, immigration, aeronautical maps, registration, the establishment of minimum standards, and procedures for the operation of air services; and (3) the Committee on International Convention on Civil Aviation, to continue the search for the elusive multilateral convention that could not be secured in Chicago.

The Convention on International Civil Aviation, or the Permanent Convention, was concerned with the creation and make-up of the International Civil Aviation Organization, which, like PICAO, would consist of an assembly and executive council that would elect a president and appoint the committees on air transport and air navigation. In general, the aims and objectives of ICAO were to encourage and foster growth of international civil aviation and the development of aircraft, airports, and other facilities, to ensure air safety and prevent waste, and to 'promote generally the development of all aspects of international civil aeronautics.'[71] The powers of ICAO were to be investigative, consultative, and advisory, and although the members would not be bound by any decisions, it was expected that all nations would voluntarily accept the recommendations and decisions of the council. The permanent seat of ICAO would be determined by the Interim Council and the Permanent Convention would come into effect when it had been ratified by twenty-six states.

The final two documents produced at Chicago were the International Air Transit Agreement (the Two Freedoms Agreement) and the International Air Transport Agreement (the Five Freedoms Agreement). These two agreements granted the signatories two and five freedoms respectively and, although they in effect symbolized the failure of the conference, they were hailed as 'landmarks' in aviation history by some American commentators. Edward Warner, for example, wrote in *Foreign Affairs* with respect to the Two Freedoms Agreement that 'for the first time, nations which wish to trade with one another through the air can plan to do so, feeling assured that they can reach each other's territories without needing to meet the terms imposed separately by every state along the way.'[72]

Fifty-three of a possible fifty-four states signed the Final Act (only Liberia abstained), while thirty-four and thirty-two states signed the Interim Agreement and Permanent Convention respectively. But the number dropped off dramatically for the transit agreements. Twenty-six nations agreed to the Two Freedoms Agreement and only sixteen signed the Five Freedoms Agreement, most of which were from Central and South America. As for the ABC delegations, the divisions of the conference remained: the Americans signed all five agreements, the British were still reluctant to grant the fifth freedom and consequently accepted the Two (but not the Five) Freedoms Agreement, while the Canadians, who had always been uneasy with the granting of any freedoms unless accompanied by the creation of an international authority with regulatory powers, signed the Final Act and the two conventions but declined on both the Two and Five Freedoms Agreements. There was some flexibility on granting the two freedoms, the Canadians announced, but only after bilateral arrangements had been negotiated with the British and the Americans.[73]

The end of the Chicago conference marked the beginning of a period of sober reflection and analysis. Why had the conference failed? Could disappointment have been averted with last-minute bargaining? In general there were ambivalent feelings – the sense that much had been accomplished and, yet, much had been left undone. 'The Chicago Conference worked a minor miracle,' Escott Reid reflected. 'It failed, however, by a hair's breadth to work a major miracle.'[74] Not surprisingly, the British placed the responsibility for the failure on the American desire to gobble up for themselves the world's air routes; the Americans pointed to British intransigence and unwillingness to compromise. The Canadians blamed them both.

The individuals involved also came under fire. Claims were made that Swinton and Berle – the 'supercilious peer and the cerebral Puritan'[75] – were badly suited for each other and could not rise above personal animosity to reach an accord. 'In temperament the heads of the U.K. and U.S. delegations were completely incompatible,' Baldwin wrote. 'Mutual lack of trust was increased by belief on each side in the lack of ability in negotiation and the uncooperativeness of the other. Tempers ran high and at times there was virtually a complete refusal to meet or even to authorize an intermediary to act.'[76] Baldwin was also critical of Berle's handling of some aspects of the conference in his role as president. Reid added to the list the American and British draughtsmen, and noted that Berle shared 'with Lord Swinton, Mr. Cribbett, Lord Beaverbrook, Mr. Roosevelt and Mr. Churchill responsibility for the failure of the United States and the United Kingdom to close the small gap which prevented a full agreement at Chicago.'[77]

In a later memo Reid added: 'We are here dealing with the frustrated ambitions of an influential United Kingdom politican [Swinton] who, having been unable himself to reach an accord with the United States, was jealous lest a colleague's efforts be crowned with success. We are here dealing with the sub-conscious motives of the leaders of two great nations who, because they have done so much for mankind, are in danger of believing that to them alone is reserved the right to cut Gordian knots, even if the knot is a small one and could easily be unravelled.'[78] To be fair, the Canadians were capable of throwing Lord Swinton into a rage at a moment's notice, and as for Reid, one British official later recorded that although he was 'fundamentally a friend,' at one point he 'had become excitable to the point of hysteria and the [UK] Delegation, in common with others, got a little tired of him.'[79]

Ray Atherton, the American ambassador in Ottawa, offered a somewhat different perspective. At a dinner with the governor general and C.D. Howe, the topic of conversation turned to the recent conference in Chicago and Atherton reported that Lord Athlone

added that everyone in London knew that when Beaverbrook passed up heading the British delegation that he would not let anyone who was chairman for the British in Chicago make a success of the conference. (He expressed surprise that the American Government did not know this and insist that Beaverbrook come personally to Chicago). However, since Beaverbrook did not come to Chicago, Lord Knollys' (head of the B.O.A.C.) friends refused to let him head the British delegation, which he was in every way qualified to do, because they knew there would be no glory in it and they looked around and found Lord Swinton who was, in reality, (and I quote) 'a SH-T.'[80]

As for the Canadians, one American official noted that overall 'when the chips were down Canada preferred our views to those of the British although neither was too well suited to Canadian requirements. At any rate, Canada has been of service to us during the conference.' Care must be taken not to lose the advantage of the moment, he added, and steps should be taken to 'gain a friend within the Empire who would have an interest in siding with us in negotiations with the United Kingdom and others.'[81]

Clearly the failure at Chicago was the result of more than personality conflicts or cramped quarters. The lines of division between the United States and the United Kingdom were well drawn out before the conference and although both countries were willing to bend towards compromise, when it came down to it neither was willing to break. Still, the two sides had come close, and one legacy of the conference was optimism that an acceptable agreement soon would be reached. Reid was confident: 'At Chicago we nearly won the war against international anarchy in the air. We failed to win the war but we won a campaign. A well-planned brief campaign in the spring of 1945 can deliver the knock-out blow.'[82] But for the time being that goal remained, as Adolf Berle described it, a 'splendid dream.'

Praise for Canada's role at the conference was universal. Howe and Symington demonstrated intelligence, shrewdness, and common sense while acting on Canada's behalf and had won the respect of the other delegates, not only as Canadian representatives but as businessmen who together ran one of the world's most-efficient airlines. The Canadian convention also had provided a basis for discussion and provided the Canadian negotiators with an entrée to the highest-level discussions. And, although on the economic issues the Canadian convention was defeated, many of the ideas and much of the wording of the Permanent Convention were Canadian.

The greatest praise was reserved for Canada's role as a mediator, or honest broker, between the superpowers. 'In a sense our greatness was thrust upon us,' Reid boasted, 'and once it was generally realized that the main struggle at the Conference was between the United States and the United Kingdom with Canada in between, our role as mediator became obvious.' The part of mediator cast Canada in a unique role, neither leader of the small powers nor the equal of the great powers, but rather 'in a peculiar position by itself, an important air power which, for certain well understood reasons, was one of the three leading powers at the Conference.'[83]

Canada as mediator is perhaps the most enduring legacy of the Chicago conference and subsequently has become, for good reason, the stuff of after-dinner speeches and luncheon-club addresses. It is nevertheless important not to lose sight of the fact that mediation was only one part of a larger Canadian international aviation policy. Canadians were pursuing their own interests at Chicago – the creation of a strong international authority with regulatory powers, the reservation of services between contiguous states, the escalator clause, and so on. Within that framework, Anglo-American co-operation was considered essential and it was as a mediator that Canada could best ensure that such co-operation developed. But only so far: when the United States and United Kingdom agreed on the inclusion of the two freedoms in the convention they found their stiffest opposition in the Canadian delegation – hardly the action of a mediator. In the end, Canada played more the role of a middle power than simply a power in the middle between the superpowers. It was a comfortable position to be in: big enough to play a constructive role and take some small credit for the successes, but not quite big enough to be blamed for the failures.

9 Swallowing the Pure Wine of Bermuda

The atmosphere during the Chicago conference, one British observer wrote early in 1945, 'was never more favourable for Commonwealth air co-operation on a grand scale. It is fervently to be hoped that our Commonwealth statesmen will not let the moment pass without action.' Seize the moment, he contended, and 'Chicago may go down in history as the event which established the British Commonwealth for longer than Hitler's boasted thousand years.'[1] Not everyone shared the enthusiasm of the *Round Table*, yet there was a sense that Chicago marked only the first step towards a more comprehensive international arrangement. It was not to be. The immediate consequence of Chicago was not a rush to multilateralism but rather a reversion to bilateralism, especially on the part of the United States.

The fourteen months following the Chicago conference were crowded with civil aviation negotiations and international conferences. The end of the war signalled the resumption of international air transport on a significant scale, while the absence of a comprehensive multilateral convention forced the formation of a patchwork series of bilateral agreements. Canadians were involved in four separate sets of aviation talks, as well as in numerous informal discussions, primarily with the two chief aviation nations – the United States and the United Kingdom. The Americans and British undertook negotiations of their own, which, although no Canadians participated in them, inevitably had an enormous influence on Canadian international aviation policy. Individually, the significance of each conference or new agreement was not always readily apparent; but taken collectively, they established the framework for the modern system of international air transport.

I

The presence in North America of the British Chicago delegation, as well as representatives from Australia, New Zealand, and the other Commonwealth nations, furnished an opportunity for consultation that Lord Swinton believed should not be missed. Late in the conference he raised the possibility of holding further Commonwealth discussions, in an effort to clear up the loose ends from the October talks. It would be relatively simple for all the Commonwealth delegations to reassemble in Montreal for a few days before returning home. The Canadians were willing, but Swinton was informed that they would want to discuss two important issues: turning TCA's transatlantic service into a commercial operation, and the creation of a TCA service to the Caribbean.[2]

The upshot of Lord Swinton's suggestion was a two-day Commonwealth conference in Montreal on 9–10 December. As in October, the meetings were held in the Windsor Hotel; the difference this time was that the chief delegates were on the ministerial rather than official level. Howe, Symington, and Baldwin represented Canada, while Swinton, Street, Cribbett, and Malcolm MacDonald headed the British team. Others included Arthur Drakeford, the Australian minister for civil aviation (and air minister); D.G. Sullivan, the New Zealand minister of industries, commerce, supply, and munitions; Sir Frederick Tymms, the director of civil aviation in the Indian government; and representatives from South Africa and Newfoundland.

The first item on the agenda was the new-born Commonwealth Air Transport Council. Basic agreement had been reached in October and only some minor fine-tuning was required at this time. The only problem evolved over the inclusion of Ireland in the council. Howe proposed that Ireland be permitted to join, and although there appeared to be no opposition from the other representatives, the British were decidedly cool. A compromise was accepted; the British agreed to keep an open mind on the subject but no final decision on Irish participation would be made until after the war.[3]

The CATC was created as an advisory agency to meet at regular (though unspecified) intervals at different Commonwealth locations. The rank of each representative was to be left to the individual countries and it was planned eventually to establish a permanent secretariat. In the interim, the functions of a secretariat would be

performed by the British Department of Civil Aviation, and it was anticipated that the first scheduled meeting would be held in London, with Commonwealth representatives from the various high commissions in attendance. The duties of the CATC were:
- 'To keep under review the progress and development of Commonwealth Civil Air communications.
- To serve as a medium for exchange of views and information between the Commonwealth countries on Civil Air Transport matters.
- To consider and advise on such civil aviation matters as any Commonwealth Government may desire to refer to the Council.'[4]

The second issue discussed was the transpacific service. In October 1943 Howe had made it clear to Beaverbrook that Canada had no interest in participating in a joint operating company for the operation of a Pacific service, preferring instead that Canada operate the North America–Hawaii leg, with either an Australian/New Zealand or joint company operating the Hawaii–Australia section. Now, in December 1944, Swinton again pressed for joint Commonwealth operation of empire trunk routes. Howe easily brushed this proposal aside, but his counter-proposal came under fire on a different flank. The Australians wanted some role to play in a through service over the whole route and consequently argued against the division of the service into segments. If there was to be no Canadian participation in a Commonwealth service, then the only alternative would be the creation of parallel services: one Canadian, one Commonwealth. 'The Canadians were sticky at first,' Swinton informed London, but ultimately this course of action was approved. There would be two services: Vancouver–Australia via San Francisco and Hawaii (once arrangements had been made with the United States, of course), with some agreement on the division of traffic and schedules to be reached if and when the services were put into effect.[5]

The most controversial moment of the December meetings followed the introduction by Swinton of a list of standard clauses that the British wanted included in subsequent bilateral agreements negotiated by Commonwealth nations. Baldwin later wrote that the Canadians had no prior warning that the British would table these clauses, but noted that they 'had obviously been discussed with the Commonwealth countries other than Canada and had received general support and approval.'[6] Included on the list were clauses that entrenched what the

British had failed to obtain at Chicago – that is, an equal and firm predetermined division of traffic.

Howe objected immediately. These particular clauses were precisely what the Canadians had opposed only a few days earlier at Chicago and Howe refused to accept them now. Lord Swinton tried to buffer the Canadian opposition by arguing that the standard clauses 'had been prepared in the hope that they might be of assistance in securing a measure of regulation until such time as an international convention on the subject could be concluded.' The Canadians counter-attacked: Howe told Swinton that he found the clauses 'inconsistent' with the decisions reached at Chicago; Symington noted that if accepted these standard clauses would automatically handicap Canadian negotiators in any future bilateral discussions; and Baldwin warned that other countries were likely to interpret the inclusion of standard Commonwealth clauses in bilateral agreements as proof of the existence of a Commonwealth bloc –something that must be avoided. In the end, the standard clauses were accepted, but only as 'a statement of United Kingdom intentions circulated for the information of the other Commonwealth countries.'[7]

Howe left it to private meetings with Lord Swinton to raise the two issues he considered of special interest to Canadians: the commercialization of the transatlantic air service and the proposed service to the West Indies. Neither would come into effect as long as the war continued, but Howe hoped at least to arrive at some understanding with the British on these matters. But Swinton was less than forthcoming, and he argued on both counts that he would have to consult with his government before any final decisions could be made. This was not entirely satisfactory to the Canadians, and although they agreed to maintain the status quo for the time being, there were suspicions that the British were merely stalling for time, until they were in a stronger and more competitive position.[8]

Shortly after the conference adjourned, Baldwin wrote that he sensed a shift in the other dominions towards increasing support for joint Commonwealth action – a changing attitude prompted, he believed, by the belief that only as part of a larger and more powerful group could they find protection. 'The outstanding feature of all the Commonwealth conversations,' he wrote, 'has been the readiness of the Commonwealth nations, other than Canada, to move in the direction of a united bloc. While Australia or South Africa might on a specific matter differ with a u.k. proposal, in general they all appeared ready to fall in with the idea of concerting policy in advance, agreeing upon a common front, participating in common schemes for operation or control, and seem to have no fear of presenting a common front in public.' All, of course, except for Canada.

Baldwin went on to suggest that 'in spite of the experience of the last twenty years,' the British did not truly understand either Canadian policy or motives. As a result, the British 'consider us in some respects obstructive and extreme nationalists, bent upon preventing the establishment of a united Commonwealth front in world affairs.' Because of this misunderstanding, Baldwin added, the Commonwealth talks were often 'lively with little recognition being given by the United Kingdom to the principles of Commonwealth relations which evolved during the 1920's and 1930's. Lip service is given to the right of any Dominion to freedom of action, but surprise and frequently a measure of annoyance is always evident when this right is exercised even in discussion.'[9] Baldwin did not elaborate further on how these circumstances might affect relations in the future, but if the trend continued, of the dominions moving closer in the direction of a 'Commonwealth bloc,' it could only strengthen the British hand and, in turn, exacerbate the tensions in Anglo-Canadian aviation relations.

Subsequent events seemed to bear out Baldwin's fears. A few weeks after the Montreal talks, more informal discussions took place in London. An official from the high commissioner's office represented Canada but played no significant part. Swinton reported progress on several of the empire routes – to Australia via India and to South Africa via Cairo, East Africa, and Rhodesia, in particular – and found considerable support for the British standard clauses discussed at Montreal. 'Canada takes it own line over this,' Swinton noted, 'but Canada's independent action does not compromise the Empire routes.'[10] Indeed, with the exception of Canada, the empire appeared more unified in its international civil aviation policy than ever before – a turn of events that prompted Sir Stafford Cripps to envision a CATC 'which will be not only advisory and consultative, as at present, but later may have more power of control and be more executive in its capacity.'[11] But in the meantime there were other problems to be solved.

II

The failure at Chicago did not radically alter American international civil aviation policy. If anything, the Chicago conference itself was the aberration in American policy; and with the failure of multilateralism, the Americans reverted to their previously held policy of bilateralism. In fact, as the walls of multilateralism collapsed around the ears of the delegates at Chicago, the Americans were busy laying the foundations for a series of bilateral arrangements.

From Spain the United States had recently secured fifth-freedom rights through Madrid and Barcelona to Marseilles and Algiers, and from North Africa to Paris. Shortly after Chicago, a deal was struck with the Swedish government exchanging fifth-freedom rights on through services and a similar agreement was signed with Denmark and Iceland. In gaining fifth-freedom rights in these countries, the United States naturally granted equal rights to Spanish, Danish, Swedish, and Icelandic services in American territory. Clearly, the United States gained the greatest advantage, because fifth-freedom rights in Spain, Sweden, etc., opened up the rest of Europe to American airlines and circumvented the need for an immediate agreement with the United Kingdom.

Canada, too, became a target for American bilateralism. On a number of occasions during 1944, American officials intimated to their Canadian counterparts that perhaps the time was right to renegotiate the agreement for transborder services between Canada and the United States. The arrangements made in 1939 and 1940 were still in effect, but circumstances had changed dramatically, making a re-examination of existing arrangements necessary. At first the Canadians demurred, arguing that the signing of a bilateral Canadian-American agreement would prejudice the eventual conclusion of a multilateral agreement.[12] The Americans persisted, raising the matter again during the Chicago conference, and by then the Canadian attitude had changed. Once there was little chance of negotiating a multilateral agreement before the end of the war, it made sense to settle important issues on a bilateral basis. Besides, if the Canadians were ever to sign the Two Freedoms Agreement, it was imperative to have the question of transborder services settled in advance.

The primary concern for the Canadians going into bilateral talks with the Americans was whether the United States would be willing to preserve the monopoly system of 1940, or, rather, would insist on some kind of competition, such as parallel operation on certain transborder services. The 1940 exchange of notes designated specific routes that each country could operate into the other's territory –

without fear of competition – and the Canadians wished to preserve this system. The alternative would open Canada to severe American competition and make some kind of frequency control essential. On monopoly services, frequency control was left to the individual operators, but on parallel services, there had to be a degree of regulation to prevent one side from overwhelming the other.[13]

The proposed bilateral discussions between Canadian and American representatives took place in New York City on 25-26 January 1945. Originally scheduled to last three or four days, the talks were wound up in a day and a half. The Canadian fears were unjustified; neither side wished to overturn present arrangements, so the discussions focused on confirming and extending the existing system of strict allocation of routes. The American government gave Canadian airlines the sole right to operate services on the following routes: Halifax–Boston, Toronto–New York, Toronto–Cleveland, Toronto–Chicago, Port Arthur–Duluth, Victoria–Seattle, Whitehorse–Fairbanks. In exchange, the Americans received permission to operate the following services: Boston–Moncton, Boston–Montreal, New York or Boston–Quebec, New York–Montreal or Ottawa, Washington–Montreal or Ottawa, Buffalo–Toronto, Fargo–Winnipeg, Great Falls–Lethbridge, Seattle–Vancouver, Seattle–Whitehorse, and Fairbanks–Whitehorse.[14]

Included in the new agreement were the 'Chicago standard clauses,' covering such items as customs, immigration, charges for fuel oil, and the prevention of discrimination in the use of airports. These services did not include fifth-freedom rights, but the two countries did agree to grant each other transit and non-traffic rights. Finally, the two countries could introduce the new services as they saw fit, and were under no obligation to commence operations immediately.

The new arrangements were satisfactory to the Canadian government. The ratio between American and Canadian services had been reduced from approximately eight to one in 1940 to not quite two to one. More important, the crucial Toronto–New York service was preserved and a new potentially lucrative Toronto–Chicago service was obtained. Howe was pleased. On 7 February 1945 the Cabinet War Committee gave its approval and the official exchange of notes was issued on 17 February.[15] Shortly thereafter, Canada formally signed the Two Freedoms Agreement.

While this round of Canadian-American conversations was under way, the Americans were also conducting negotiations with the Irish government. Like the Canadian and other delegations, the Irish delegation was approached at Chicago by American representatives, and formal discussions began in Washington early in 1945. The most interesting aspect of the Irish-American agreement was the stipulation that American services crossing Irish territory make mandatory stops at Shannon airport. The Irish government hoped to make Shannon the foremost American terminal on that side of the Atlantic and, although this arrangement did not develop, many Canadians feared that the Irish would wish to include a similar clause in agreements negotiated with other countries.[16]

The conclusion of agreements with Ireland, Sweden, Denmark, and Iceland could only antagonize the British. American actions seemed to have one goal in mind: the bypassing of Great Britain by American airlines on the North Atlantic and European services. There was also friction on other fronts. In Egypt, the United States gave the American-built Payne Field to the Egyptian government in return for rights at Cairo. Invitations were also extended to other Middle Eastern nations to begin discussions. When the American proposals were met with some resistance, the United States suspected that the British government had used its influence in the Middle East to prevent the negotiation of additional agreements in that area. The State Department complained to London about what it felt was unfair play on the part of Great Britain, and requested 'assurances that the British Government will not oppose the efforts of the United States Government to acquire landing rights at this time in the Near and Middle East for United States commercial air services.'[17]

The British, of course, did not see their actions as obstructionist. As one official wrote in a brief for the prime minister: 'Many European and Middle Eastern countries naturally turned to us for advice when asked to negotiate an Agreement with the Americans. The failure to agree at Chicago had left us with fundamentally different policies, but we could not be expected, in tendering advice to others, to advocate any policy other than our own. These countries were then left to judge the course of action they should take in relation to their Agreement with the United States.' This unnamed official added that only a few European countries had 'succumbed' to American pressure, and added: 'In view of the positive terms in which we have assured the European and Middle Eastern countries that we shall adhere to our Chicago policy and of our attempts to dissuade them from negotiating Agreements conferring unrestricted commercial rights on the Americans, any concession we make to the American viewpoint must be carefully considered in this context, as well as in the context of Commonwealth unity.'[18]

There were, however, increasing divisions within the British government over the best course of action to take with respect to the growing friction with the United States. Lord Swinton and those in his civil aviation committee were keen to maintain the policy established at Chicago in the face of mounting American pressure. For some ministers, however, it seemed ludicrous to continue a policy antagonistic to the United States at the greatest moment of Allied triumph as victory was achieved in Europe. For example, Lord Cherwell, who had followed Sir William Jowitt as paymaster-general at the end of 1942, suggested that adopting an aviation policy in opposition to the United States could have more serious repercussions in other fields. 'I think we should stop these pinpricks against the Americans,' he wrote to Prime Minter Churchill. 'We have already received lease-lend from the United States up to something like £5,000 million. We want about £1,000 million more during the Japanese war. We shall need further American assistance in some form or other amounting to between £1,500 million and 2,000 million after the Japanese war. With all these benefits in hand – and we hope in store – can we not modify the policy of obstructing the U.S. airlines' desire to carry passengers from one point of the Levant to another?'[19]

Prime Minister Churchill adopted a rather cautious attitude at this stage, not wanting to antagonize the United States any more than necessary. The death of Roosevelt in April removed one of his closest allies and friends, but Churchill still counted on his ability to resolve thorny Anglo-American problems through face-to-face meetings with the American president.[20] What he had not counted on was the mercurial temperament of the British electorate: by the end of July he found himself out of office and relegated to observer status.

III

A more positive note in international civil aviation relations was struck in April 1945 with the creation of the International Air Transport Association (IATA). During the Chicago conference, Herbert Symington chaired a meeting of airline representatives at which a drafting committee was established to look into the establishment of an operators' organization. A statement was prepared outlining the aims of the proposed association: '(1) To promote safe, regular and economical air transport for the benefit of the peoples of the world, to foster air commerce and to study the problems connected therewith. (2) To provide means for collaboration among the air transport enterprises engaged directly or indirectly in international air transport service. (3) To co-operate with the International Civil Aviation Organization and other national organization.'[21] In addition, the new operators' association would co-operate in the setting of rates for international air travel, thereby resolving one of the sticky economic issues left over from Chicago. IATA rates would still have to receive government approval, but the initial process would be removed from political pressures and most governments would likely accept the rates agreed upon by IATA.

IATA's articles of association were officially approved at an operators' conference in Havana in April 1945. The new organization officially replaced the earlier IATA, formed in The Hague in 1919, and opened its doors to virtually any operator of international air services whose nation was a member of ICAO. Non-international operators could join IATA, but only as associate members. All the expenses of the new body were covered by the members themselves, not by goverments.[22]

The first annual general meeting of IATA was held in Montreal's Windsor Hotel in October 1945, with forty-six airlines from twenty-four countries in attendance. Symington was elected IATA's first president, and, along with Pan Am's John Cooper, was appointed to the twelve-member policy-making Executive Committee. In addition, four standing committees were established: (1) financial, (2) legal, (3) technical, and (4) traffic. Finally, a permanent head-office secretariat was created with a director-general, secretary, and treasurer appointed by the Executive Committee. Sir William Hildred was appointed director-general and to him fell the responsibility for keeping everything going. Montreal was chosen as the permanent home of IATA, to facilitate liaison with ICAO, leading one commentator on the opening of the first general meeting to proclaim Montreal 'the air capital of the world.'[23]

IV

The election of a Labour government in Great Britain was not followed by an immediate shift in British international civil aviation policy. The Labour party supported the complete nationalization of domestic civil aviation, including state ownership of airports and control of all internal air services, but in the international arena there was no noticeable difference in approach between Labour and Conservative governments. A new minister for civil aviation was appointed – Lord Winster – and the Cabinet Civil Aviation Committee was reconstituted with new members. Winster was a charming individual with a keen intellect, but a 'much milder sort of man' than Swinton, and he lacked his predecessor's aggressive, competitive streak.[24] Yet, in terms of international policy, Winster and Swinton were similar: both believed it essential to negotiate an agreement with the Americans, both wanted Commonwealth co-operation on empire routes (although Winster wanted any Commonwealth corporation to be publicly owned), and both supported a 'policy of regulation, but not restriction.'[25]

International civil aviation was an important but obviously not a primary concern for the new Labour government. The British economy lay in ruins and British planners were counting on the continuation of American aid for some time after the cessation of hostilities. Thus, when the United States cut off lend-lease aid within a fortnight of the Japanese surrender, Attlee's government was confronted with a financial crisis of unprecedented proportions. Britain faced a number of equally unattractive options: cut imports, devalue the pound, reduce foreign spending, and/or negotiate large loans from those who had the money. The last alternative offered the most hope, and loan negotiations were initiated with the American and Canadian governments.[26]

Britain's precarious financial situation inevitably coloured all facets of British foreign policy, including international civil aviation. Late in August, informal discussions were held in London between Lord Winster and William Clayton, the American assistant secretary of state, and Stokeley Morgan, the chief of the aviation division in the State Department. Although nothing concrete emerged from the talks, there were hints that the Americans might link the signing of a satisfactory aviation agreement to the ongoing loan negotiations.[27] Winster was pressed to go to Washington to settle the aviation issue, but he, along with Ernest Bevin, the foreign secretary, and Lord Keynes agreed 'that negotiations on this topic should, in time and space, be kept as far apart as possible from the financial talks.'[28] Far easier said than done.

The need for agreements with both the Canadians and Americans was becoming more apparent. With the end of the war the United States put their wartime military transatlantic air services on a fare-paying basis until their commercial services could take over. The Canadians responded in kind; on 22 September the TCA transatlantic operation began taking on fare-paying customers as well. The number of TCA passengers had risen from 21,569 in 1939 to 183,121 in 1945 and the volume of mail carried more than quadrupled over the same period. With the introduction of the Atlantic service under TCA (Atlantic) Ltd, the numbers rose even more sharply. In the last eight months of 1945, for example, nearly 16,000 passengers were carried on the Atlantic service alone.[29]

The three major aviation issues facing Canada and the United Kingdom at the end of the war were the negotiation of agreements for the transatlantic service, for services to the West Indies, and for the civil use of the Newfoundland air-bases. Canada had little immediate use for fifth-freedom rights through the United Kingdom, and besides, Canadian air services would constitute only a tiny fraction of the total international air traffic in British airspace. On the question of the Newfoundland bases, all discussion of commercial use of the airports was postponed until after the war, when the two sides would be obliged to talk. None of these issues was critical or intractable, and the two countries moved towards negotiations in the latter stages of 1945.

The Americans were a different matter. In addition to US supremacy in transport aircraft, one estimate put the US share of world commercial air traffic in 1945 at over 70 per cent, compared to only 12 per cent for Great Britain.[30] Moreover, Pan Am, which still had rights to a transatlantic service from its pre-war agreement, threatened to reduce its transatlantic fare to $275, down from the IATA set rate of $375. This was really only Pan Am flexing its muscles, but it was taken very seriously in British government circles.[31]

The British solution to the immediate problems was to negotiate an agreement for transatlantic service only, leaving any discussion of fifth-freedom rights to later talks. In November the United Kingdom offered to sign a one-year interim agreement with the United States – an agreement that would split the traffic fifty-fifty and would not include the fifth freedom. This may have suited the authorities in

London, but for the Americans the fifth freedom was the key element of any agreement and had to be addressed. The British deal was rejected and a new Air Coordinating Committee was established in Washington from the skeletal remains of Berle's committee, to 'act as a clearing house for all aviation policy.'[32] In addition, efforts were stepped up to force Great Britain to the bargaining table.

A golden opportunity presented itself in November 1945, when prime ministers Attlee and Mackenzie King visited Washington for top-secret discussions with President Truman on the international control of atomic energy. During one private meeting with Truman and James Byrnes, the secretary of state, the Americans again linked the loan arrangements with the successful conclusion of an aviation agreement. Byrnes 'stressed the point that the Aviation Lobby was very strong,' Attlee recorded on 15 November. 'He was afraid that when finance matters came up the Aviation Lobby would induce a number of Senators and Representatives to vote against the proposals with a view to bringing pressure to bear on the Civil Aviation problem.'[33]

The Americans made it clear that they wanted negotiations to begin as soon as possible, and they continued to pressure the British government. In December, Lord Halifax was cornered by Dean Acheson, the under-secretary of state, who told him that 'the civil aviation question constitutes one of our greatest dangers in the forthcoming congressional discussions on the loan.' Halifax added that other members of the embassy staff had received similar warnings from 'other friendly officials in the State Department.' What Acheson and the others wanted to know was 'whether it would not be possible to get one or two fair minded people on both sides to come over to Bermuda or to the Azores and explore the ground.'[34]

The American ambassador to the USSR, meanwhile, was instructed to put pressure on Ernest Bevin who happened to be in Moscow on other business. 'Strongly urge you take this opportunity to emphasize to Bevin importance of negotiating at earliest possible moment US-UK long-term agreement on international commercial air transport,' the State Department advised. 'We are definitely on notice that unless bilateral negotiations are at least under way before loan terms are discussed in Congress powerful opposition to approval of loan will develop in House and Senate.'[35]

The pressure began to have an effect. Lord Winster wrote Hugh

Dalton, the chancellor of the exchequer, that recent developments in the United States seemed 'to suggest once again that a Congress lobbied by Pan American Airways might try to force complete freedom of action in the air as opposed to the regulated competition which we know to be right.'[36] He noted how he had tried to come to some agreement with the Americans but without success; but if the Americans were determined to hold further discussions he had no objections. Not that Dalton needed convincing. In December the British cabinet wrestled with the difficult and painful loan negotiations, and Dalton was clear in his own mind of the consequences of breakdown:

We would go deeper into the dark valley of austerity than ever during the war. Less food – except for bread and potatoes – in particular less meat and sugar; little cotton, and therefore, less clothes and less exports; and worst of all from the point of view of public morale, practically no smokes since 80% of our tobacco costs dollars. Very soon, after a tremendous patriotic upsurge, the tide of public feeling would turn. Everywhere the Tories would exploit the situation, attributing every shortage to the Government's incompetence. We should be on the downward slope, leading towards defeat at the next election.[37]

If it came to a decision between talking with the Americans on civil aviation matters or potentially damaging the crucial loan arrangements, the choice was obvious. The British government informed Washington that it was ready to meet the Americans in Bermuda whenever they saw fit.

In December, before the Anglo-American negotiations took place, Canada and the United Kingdom held their own discussions -- also in Bermuda. There was no connection between the two sets of talks, other than if conversations were to be held anywhere during the winter-time, Bermuda was an ideal place to hold them. The convening of a conference on telecommunications, which C.D. Howe planned to attend, seemed to offer the best opportunity to hold some concurrent Anglo-Canadian aviation conversations.

At first there was some discussion of broadening the talks to include the military use of the Newfoundland air-bases but this suggestion was dropped. What would receive attention, however, was the American request for third- and fourth-freedom rights in Newfoundland. The

Canadians were willing to agree, provided the Canadian government was granted the same rights as the United States. There were fears, nevertheless, particularly in American circles, that Newfoundland's peculiar constitutional situation would be used to Britain's advantage or that local pressure in Newfoundland might obligate the United States to make economic concessions to Newfoundland in return for transit rights.[38] Inevitably there was an overlapping of the American requests in Newfoundland and the general Anglo-American discussions over the post-war use of the American leased bases – no matter how much the Canadians wished to keep them separate.

In advance of the scheduled meetings the relevant issues were thoroughly studied and an interdepartmental committee was created with J.R. Baldwin and Herbert Symington, along with other officials from the departments of External Affairs and National Defence and the Air Transport Board. R.A. MacKay, a Dalhousie professor who had come to the Department of External Affairs during the war, was included as a specialist on Newfoundland. Memorandums were prepared concerning the North Atlantic and West Indies services, and on the post-war use of Newfoundland air-bases.[39]

The Bermuda civil aviation conversations began on 17 December in Bermuda's Belmont Hotel. Actually there were two sets of negotiations: the first included representatives from the Newfoundland Commission of Government and dealt with the North Atlantic service and the international use of Newfoundland's air-bases; the second set was attended by representatives of the Bermuda government and dealt with the proposed Canadian service to the West Indies. C.D. Howe led the Canadian delegation and chaired most of the sessions, and his negotiating team included, among others, Baldwin, Symington, and MacKay. The British delegation was officially headed by Lord Winster, but unfortunately he was trapped in the Azores by bad weather and arrived in Bermuda only in time to sign the final agreement.[40] George Cribbett, the deputy director-general of civil aviation, acted on Winster's behalf, and other British delegates included John Chadwick, a member of the Dominions Office who had considerable knowledge of Newfoundland affairs, and Maj. J.R. McCrindle, the deputy director-general of BOAC.

For four days the various delegations met in conference and although the negotiating was at times difficult, the minutes of the meetings reveal that there were no problems of a critical nature. As usual, the relations between the Canadian and British delegations were cordial and friendly, and as an indication of the benefits of Commonwealth co-operation, both sides came well briefed on what the other would or would not accept. In the end a substantial degree of consensus was reached.

On the North Atlantic route, Canada and the United Kingdom agreed essentially to split the service in two, between TCA and BOAC, with each providing the other with adequate airport facilities. Dorval airport in Montreal was designated the Canadian airport, and the Canadians agreed to continue using Prestwick airport in Scotland until the construction of Heathrow was completed. Originally the Canadians asked permission to operate a shuttle service between Prestwick and London, but the British believed such a service 'would create an embarrassing precedent vis-à-vis foreign operators.'[41] In the end the British promised to assume the responsibility. The exchange of the fifth freedom was discussed, but neither side was eager to grant it. The Canadians, for example, still wanted to hold off on the fifth freedom until a multilateral convention was signed.

Turning to Newfoundland, Gander was designated an international airport and the Canadians agreed to maintain the meteorological services while the British would continue to provide the air-traffic services. At Goose Bay the Canadians received the first four freedoms, but for everyone else the airport would be used only as a bad-weather alternative. Furthermore, at Torbay airport outside St John's, Canada retained its title and received rights for the civil use (to be shared with a Newfoundland airline should one be established). It should come as no surprise that Canada received virtually exclusive civil use of Goose Bay and Torbay, for both these sites were built and paid for by the Canadian government. As for the American request for rights in Newfoundland, it was agreed that Newfoundland would grant freedoms 3 and 4 provided that Newfoundland receive reciprocal rights to the United States – these rights to be assigned, in the short term, to BOAC.[42]

The arrangements for the West Indies proved to be a little more complicated. The Canadians wanted to operate a service to Bermuda for the obvious reason: to fly Canadians to and from there. But they also wanted fifth-freedom rights: to make feasible a through service to South America. On the Canada–Bermuda route the Canadian government believed that there would be insufficient traffic for parallel services, and, as a result, they requested monopoly rights. The request for a monopoly service stemmed from the 1943 Commonwealth conversations, when Howe believed he had secured an agreement with Beaverbrook on the matter. Beaverbrook was long gone now, however, and there were fears that the United Kingdom would wish to have British West Indian Airlines (BWIA) operate a parallel service. With respect to the through service, it was argued that to make a service to South America viable the Canadians would need fifth-freedom rights between a number of Caribbean islands (as well as at Rio de Janeiro for any service that continued on to Buenos Aires). The catch, of course, was that any service between Bermuda and other British islands would be considered British cabotage (an internal service) and, thus, what the Canadians were requesting were, in fact, sixth-freedom rights.[43]

The representative from Bermuda balked at any suggestion of permanently excluding a Bermudan service to Canada. Bermuda was willing to promise not to operate a service for at least four years after the agreement came into effect (or 1 January 1947). This suited both the Canadians and the Bermudans, for the latter had no plans to operate a service in any event. On the other issues a compromise was reached. Canada was given the right to operate a service to and from Bermuda, and fifth-freedom rights onwards – Bermuda–Nassau, Bermuda–Jamaica, and Bermuda–Trinidad. Canada was denied those rights between British colonies in the West Indies that were covered by the operations of BWIA.[44]

Howe, Symington, and Baldwin returned to Ottawa having considerably enhanced Canada's ability to participate in international civil aviation. The Atlantic service had been put on a solid footing and the lingering issue concerning the Newfoundland bases had been cleared up. Moreover, access to the Caribbean (and South America, eventually) had been secured.

Some preliminry work was undertaken in 1946, but the Bermuda service did not begin operations until 1 May 1948. When Howe pressed for its extension southward, he met resistance from TCA president Gordon McGregor, who argued that a Caribbean service would not be profitable. Howe's reply was interesting: 'I have been well aware that profitable business does not exist at the moment, and that the hope for the route is that tourist business from Canada can be built up to a profitable level, particularly during the winter months. Canada desires to offer an outlet for Canadian tourists in sterling areas, and, for that reason, I think that the route should be operated in the national interest.'[45] Once again Howe got his way: the Caribbean service to Trinidad, Jamaica, and the Bahamas opened 1 December 1948.

V

Negotiations between the United States and the United Kingdom began in Bermuda on 15 January 1946. The British delegation was led by Sir Henry Self, who had headed the British Purchasing Commission during the war, and William Hildred. George Baker, the director of the State Department's office of transport and communications policy, headed the American team, which included Garrison Norton (Baker's deputy), J.D. Hickerson of the office of European affairs, Welch Pogue, and Stokeley Morgan.[46] Self assumed the chair for the conference as a whole.

There were two thrusts to the discussions: first, the negotiation of a bilateral Anglo-American aviation agreement and, second, reaching an agreement with respect to the commercial use of the US leased bases. The major points of contention on the latter issue revolved around fifth-freedom rights to and from the bases and cabotage rights between them. Regarding the bilateral agreement, the main problems remained the three R's: routes, rights, and rates.

On the American side there appeared to be a willingness to compromise on the rates question through the acceptance of IATA as the rate-control body (though still requiring final government approval). On the fifth-freedom and frequency-control questions, however, the Americans remained firm. The most the United States would offer was an after-the-fact review of the initial frequencies set by the individual operators. Lord Winster argued that such proposals 'in effect commit us to free enterprise' in international aviation, rather than the more planned though unrestricted basis advocated by the United Kingdom.[47]

By the end of January two tentative agreements were on the table. 'Agreements involve British giving way completely from Chicago position on control of frequencies and capacity and on our giving way completely on rate control,' Baker informed Washington. 'On Fifth Freedom, the British have also given way. Since our delegation, including all the CAB members, all believe rate control desirable, anyway we believe this arrangement constitutes a real victory.'[48] The texts were approved by Washington and Baker was given the go-ahead to sign.

At that moment in Washington, Lord Halifax was called to a meeting with Dean Acheson and William Clayton in which the two Americans 'expressed the very strong hope' that the British government would see its way to signing the agreements. After the meeting Halifax urged London to accept the American terms; Acheson and Clayton 'emphasized the powerful effect which a successful outcome to the Conference would have on Congress in connexion with consideration of loan agreements,' he noted. Given this scenario, he had 'no hesitation in urging you to accept settlement of this inflammatory question.'[49]

The American pressure to sign, together with Britain's severe economic crisis, began to colour the debate over the Bermuda negotiations within the British government. On 4 February 1946, for example, Bermuda was on the cabinet agenda, but the focus of discussion was less on the agreement itself than on the effect that not agreeing to the American demands would have on the loan agreement. Lord Winster argued that, from 'the point of view of civil aviation,' the Bermuda agreement was unacceptable; it 'represented a fundamental departure from the policy which had hitherto been common ground among Commonwealth countries; it was likely to place B.O.A.C. in an unfavourable position, and the principles laid down in it to meet the point of view of His Majesty's Government would not be enforceable in practice.' Winster had little faith in ex post facto review of frequencies and capacity, especially because the American government appeared to exercise only minimum control over the private American airlines. But, he concluded, 'if the Cabinet felt that the signing of the agreement was of vital importance from the point of view of our general relations with the United States and the consideration of the loan agreement by Congress, he was willing that our Delegation should be authorised to sign.'

Others expressed similar opinions. Lord Addison, the dominions secretary, said he would have a hard time selling Bermuda to the dominions; Bevin agreed, but noted that 'there seemed to be no alternative but to accept this draft.' Hugh Dalton did not bother to argue the merits of the proposed agreement; in his view there was little chance of negotiating any better deal with the Americans, while refusing to sign could have serious repercussions elsewhere. Dalton was 'satisfied that the immediate signature of the Agreement would have a powerful effect on the consideration of the loan agreement by Congress ' – a sufficient inducement for action. Prime Minister Attlee spoke last and agreed with the others, noting that 'from the point of view of the loan debate in Congress, it was desirable that we should meet the desires of the American Government.'[50]

Larger issues had intervened in Anglo-American aviation relations, making it next to impossible for the British government to withdraw. All that could be done was to amend the proposed agreements, hoping to make them more palatable to British tastes. With respect to the leased bases, the British asked the United States to remove the clauses that (1) obliged all civil aircraft using the bases to obtain their supplies from the American authorities, and (2) obligated the United Kingdom to persuade Canada and Newfoundland to accept a similar agreement for the American bases in Newfoundland (which were exempted from these discussions). The Americans accepted these amendments, but made the conclusion of a final bases agreement conditional on a subsequent satisfactory agreement with the Canadians.[51]

As for the bilateral agreement, the British government suggested the inclusion of a clause preventing the change of gauge for fifth-freedom traffic: that is, downgrading to smaller aircraft on successive stopovers. 'If we agree to change of gauge,' Lord Addison warned, 'a United States operator running a service, say from New York to Paris, would be able to bring a load of passengers to this country in a trans-oceanic aircraft and thereafter carry on those who wished to proceed to Paris or elsewhere in one or more smaller aircraft.' The fear was that 'this would enable the American operator to run an unlimited number of smaller aircraft from this country to Paris or elsewhere in competition with our air lines, and thus virtually establish an advanced base here.' The British solution was to insert the following clause: 'All Fifth Freedom traffic shall be carried in aircraft which started from the country of origin and in no other aircraft, except where for convenience or economy permission is given to transfer the passengers on such aircraft to a smaller aircraft, which permission will not be unreasonably withheld.'[52]

All efforts by the British delegation to insert the above clause failed. Further discussion ensued, but, finally, the most that the Americans would do was to include a vague commitment to maintain capacity within a general level of potential traffic, and promise to bear in mind local services when establishing frequencies. A change of gauge would still be permitted, but an effort would be made to ensure that changes would be made only as a connecting service with a larger aircraft. The United States would go no further. The Civil Aviation Committee studied the final proposals, a few minor last-minute changes were endorsed, and on 11 February, the British cabinet accepted the deal.[53] On the same day, across the Atlantic, the Bermuda Agreement was signed and the Heads of Agreement on the leased bases was initialled.

The agreement on the leased bases was fairly straightforward. Kindley Field in Bermuda and the bases in Antigua, St Lucia, and British Guiana were designated for regular civil use and the bases in Trinidad and Jamaica were designated as bad-weather alternatives. The United States received fifth-freedom rights at the above bases and cabotage rights between them for American government personnel and cargo. Other countries that signed the Two Freedoms Agreement were to be permitted transit rights, but no state was to be granted any privileges not granted to the United States (with the obvious exception of British cabotage between its colonies).[54]

The signature of a final bases agreement was postponed until the Newfoundland bases could be included. To this end, negotiations with the Canadians and Newfoundlanders were undertaken over the following months. The Canadians were anxious not to permit the Americans more rights in Newfoundland than they were allowed themselves, so negotiations were slow. For their part, the Americans had their own cards to play; they could prohibit the Canadians from using Kindley Field in Bermuda, on the premise that the Canadians had been granted more freedoms between Bermuda and other British colonies than the United States, which was in conflict with the Heads of Agreement. Eventually the problems were solved: Canada was permitted to utilize Kindley Field, and the United States was granted fifth-freedom rights at Gander, 'pending the execution of a formal agreement.' After Newfoundland entered Confederation in 1949, the new province fell under the existing Canadian-American arrangements and in June 1949 the civil use of the bases was finally settled through an exchange of notes permitting the international use of Gander and the relegation of the American bases to bad-weather alternatives.[55]

The Bermuda Agreement itself consisted of a Final Act, a bilateral agreement (which followed the Chicago standard form), and an attached annex. Briefly, the United States and the United Kingdom exchanged transit rights and granted each other freedoms 3, 4, and 5 over specific routes and at specific airports listed in the annex. Neither side was obligated to commence operations immediately but could begin services if and when they were ready. Changes in routes could be made only after mutual consultation.[56] More important, the key fifth-freedom rights could not be withheld or separated from the agreement as a whole. Furthermore, IATA's rate-control machinery was accepted in principle, subject to government review and approval. As for the crucial questions of capacity and frequencies, there were to be no controls. The relevant clause read:

That it is the understanding of both Governments that services provided by a designated air carrier under the Agreement and its Annex shall retain as their primary objective the provision of capacity adequate to the traffic demands between the country of which such air carrier is a national and the country of ultimate destination of the traffic. The right to embark or disembark on such services international traffic destined for and coming from third countries at a point or points on the routes specified in the Annex to the agreement shall be applied in accordance with the general principles of orderly development to which both Governments subscribe and shall be subject to the general principle that capacity should be related: a) to traffic requirements between the country of origin and the countries of destination; b) to the requirements of through airline operation, and c) to the traffic requirements of the area through which the airline passes after taking account of local and regional services.[57]

If one or the other felt it had a grievance, an appeal could be made to PICAO. This appeal, of course, could be made only after operations had commenced and neither government was obligated to accept the decision or recommendation of PICAO. Hence, there would be a review process – something the British had long called for – but it would have no teeth.

On the surface, it appeared as if the Americans had triumphed. On the crucial questions, the British had succumbed to American pressure and clearly had given in on some issues in an effort to enhance other, more-important areas of Anglo-American relations. Yet it was also the first time that the United States granted to a major foreign competitor rights to operate services across the United States, and no one could foresee in 1946 where this right would lead. After all, there were no guarantees that the American dominance of international civil aviation would continue forever.

A few weeks after the Bermuda Agreement was signed, Lord Halifax wrote to his old friend Lord Swinton, who was now in opposition. 'All things considered,' he opined, 'the Agreement as concluded seems to me not too bad a reconciliation of American and British views, and may be really valuable in the developing of International Air Transport along sound and economic lines.' Halifax then put his finger on the crux of the matter: 'I suppose in the last resort most of it comes back to whether our airlines can achieve real efficiency. Whether the policy of my present Masters will conduce to this end is not for an Ambassador to argue, and no doubt must remain to be seen.'[58]

VI

'The Bermuda Agreement represents a compromise between the American doctrine of unrestricted competition in the air and the British theory of controlled competition,' a Foreign Office official wrote in July 1946. 'It satisfies the Americans by imposing no limitation on frequencies but reassures the British by allowing *ex post facto* review and remedy if it can be shewn that the airlines of one of the parties is resorting to uneconomic practices which violate certain principles of the orderly development of international civil aviation as laid down in the Final Act of the Bermuda Conference.' The agreement was good for all concerned; indeed, he argued, it was up to the British government to show the world that 'Bermuda can serve as a practical and sensible basis of a multinational arrangement.'[59]

In the months following the signature of the Bermuda Agreement both the United States and the United Kingdom undertook further negotiations with other states – this time following 'Bermuda principles.' The Americans, for example, approached the Mexican and Indian governments to initiate talks, while for their part, the British struck deals with the Irish, French, and Swedes. Even though the Bermuda Agreement committed neither side to negotiate similar agreements with other countries, there were suspicions on the American side that the British government was taking a more restrictive attitude with respect to the bilateral arrangements it was making with other nations.[60] For example, the agreement with France divided the London–Paris traffic on a fifty-fifty basis. Meanwhile,

Livingston Satterthwaite, the civil air attaché in the American Embassy, reported to Washington a speech given by Ivor Bulmer-Thomas, the parliamentary secretary for civil aviation, in which the latter went through a list of agreements reached by the United Kingdom without reference to Bermuda. After the speech Satterthwaite cornered Bulmer-Thomas and confronted him over the omission. 'Thomas colored and said it [the Bermuda Agreement] was so important he forgot it,' Satterthwaite recorded. 'He would not say it was a good aviation agreement, but thought it was good for Anglo-American relations.'[61]

The British protested their innocence of course. In the case of Sweden, one official wrote, the British were trying 'to ram Bermuda down the Swedes' reluctant throats,' and as for Argentina: 'We tried our best, but in vain, to induce the Argentines to swallow the pure wine of Bermuda. They insisted, however, on something more restrictive and we had to defer to their view. Otherwise we would not have been able to operate to South America at all.'[62]

Canadians were forced to consider the effect that Bermuda would have on them. Would they, too, be forced to swallow the pure wine of Bermuda? The contrast with Chicago was painfully obvious. At Chicago the Canadians had played an influential role from start to finish and at all times were, if not masters of their own fate, at least in a small way able to control their own destiny. There were no Canadians at Bermuda. There were no avenues through which Canadians could contribute; there was no role for a mediator. The exclusion of Canada was neither unfair international treatment nor a violation of functionalism, but it is important that at the moment that the commercial questions in international civil aviation were finally settled, the Canadians were nothing more than observers. Still, the Bermuda Agreement would have 'a direct bearing on Canadian aviation policy,' J.R. Baldwin wrote in February 1946.[63] Canada had always been reluctant to grant the fifth freedom over its territory, and the fifth freedom was the corner-stone of the Bermuda Agreement. If, as seemed likely, Bermuda became the standard in international agreements, how would this affect Canada?

Bermuda would have an equally profound effect in the international arena. In July, the United States, after ratifying the Chicago Convention, announced its decision to withdraw from the Five Freedoms Agreement, which would become superfluous if the principles and approach contained in the Bermuda Agreement would form the basis of most other bilateral agreements. More significant, over the next year the Bermuda Agreement presented the most serious challenge to PICAO, the fledgling international organization, in its efforts to find that elusive multilateral aviation agreement and to deal successfully with the legacy of Chicago.

10 ICAO and the Failure of Multilateralism

Herbert Symington returned to Ottawa after the Chicago conference convinced of the need to solve the remaining economic questions. Symington wrote to Sir Arthur Street, the permanent under-secretary in the Air Minstry, that he was 'apprehensive that the international authority is not going to amount to much unless we can get a regulatory convention fairly soon.' Subsequent events seemed to bear out his fears: the Americans proceeded to negotiate a series of bilateral agreements and endeavoured to sign up as many nations as possible to the Two and Five Freedoms agreements. Hence, in Symington's mind, the need for international unity and co-operation was greater than ever before. 'Our task,' he continued, 'is to make the best instrument that we can make. All great historic documents are a bundle of compromises and we must think not in terms of details but in terms of larger issues. Time will correct defects, but defects can only be corrected if there is a convention basically sound to correct. A regulatory authority seems to me to be fundamental; with this, other things will come round.' For Symington it was essential not to lose the momentum of Chicago; to postpone action was tantamount to acknowledgment of failure. 'Now, my dear Sir Arthur,' he concluded, 'you will probably think that I am a hog for punishment, but I feel that a permanent convention with control should be set up soon or it may not be set up at all, and that we ought to be big enough to do it and that if we don't, we may seriously regret it.'[1]

More so than most countries, Canada held an advantageous position in international civil aviation that enabled it to contribute to and participate in the debate over any proposed multilateral convention. Canada was recognized as an important air power and the actions of the Canadian delegates at Chicago earned universal respect and admiration. Also, the Canadians were uniquely situated with respect to the British and the Americans, the two major air powers, and had, in the past, proved that they could act as mediator between them. Finally, and perhaps most important, as host of PICAO (and as members of the Interim Council and the key Air Transport Committee), the responsibility fell to the Canadians to set the machinery of the new international organization in motion.

The first annual meeting of the Interim Assembly was scheduled for May 1946; it was believed that by then the Chicago Convention would have been ratified by a sufficient number of states. In the meantime, the Interim Council would have to look after dozens of unspectacular but necessary decisions and details. The role of the president of the council and the secretary-general, for example, had to be clarified. The size and shape of the secretariat had to be determined, suitable personnel had to be found, and salaries needed to be pegged at proper rates. Adequate quarters would need to be reserved to house the hundreds of delegates and their staffs.[2] To this end the Canadian government established a small Preparatory Committee, chaired by Wing Cmdr P.A. Cumyn (RCAF), who was at that time attached to the Privy Council Office. This committee, one American official noted, was 'made up of energetic young officers who are thoroughly familiar not only with the city of Montreal and who have business and social connections there, but men who are also well versed in the workings of the Canadian Government and who have had previous organizational experience.'[3]

The Preparatory Committee included representatives from the Department of External Affairs, the Air Transport Board, and the military, and it held eighteen meetings between 27 June and 15 August 1945 in an effort to make all the arrangements for the first session of PICAO. A number of rooms in the Windsor Hotel were set aside for offices and press and secretarial staff, and additional office space was acquired in the Dominion Square Building in downtown Montreal. The committee received outside help from Albert Roper, the secretary-general of ICAN, and Edward Warner, vice-chair of the CAB, both of whom came to Montreal to help get things going.[4]

The first session of the Interim Council opened on 15 August 1945 and lasted until 30 August. C.D. Howe welcomed the delegates to Canada and to the task that lay ahead: 'Your work will not be light,' he cautioned, 'above all there rests with you the responsibility of carrying out the directives of the Chicago Conference and seeking a satisfactory method for the adjustment of rates and services on international routes, the attainment of a working pattern for realization.' He went on to explain briefly Canadian views on multilateralism, and he emphasized the importance of these meetings. 'You are in a position to exercise a larger measure of influence on the future course of civil aviation,' he said, 'an influence that must be based upon realization of the importance of the task that lies ahead of you. In all your efforts you may rest assured of the assistance and co-operation of the Canadian Government in every respect. We are prepared to do all in our power to help you, and to make your work here fruitful in order that all nations may look forward with hope and confidence to a new era in the development of international aviation.'[5]

During the first days of the session the proposed rules of procedure were discussed and the first meetings of several committees (on organization, personnel, finance, for example) were held. The work of Edward Warner and Albert Roper was recognized as they were elected president of the council and secretary-general respectively. Roper was to remain secretary-general of ICAN until it formally merged with ICAO. Additional ad hoc committees were formed to prepare the constitutions for the all important Air Navigation Commission and the Air Transport Committee.

The work of the Air Transport Committee was especially important, for it assumed the task of drafting a multilateral convention. F.H. Copes van Hasselt of the Netherlands was appointed chair of the committee and it held its first meeting on 3 October 1945. Canada's representative was Anson McKim. McKim was a Montreal native and a Harvard MBA who had worked in Howe's Department of Munitions and Supply during the war and had become a vice-president of TCA in 1945. In 1946 he was appointed Canadian representative on the Interim Council. The other members included Sir Frederick Bowhill (United Kingdom), Henri Bouche (France), Gerald Brophy (United States), and Ali Fuad Bey (Iraq).[6]

Over the course of 1945 and early 1946 the Air Transport Committee and its various ad hoc committees met over twenty times and considered over fifty working papers. The Canadian government's views were incorporated in a memorandum presented to the committee by McKim. There were primary reasons for achieving an international convention, the Canadian document argued: first, for the 'healthy development of international civil aviation throughout the world' and, second, for 'the fostering of international peace and security.' The Canadian government refused to accept the premise that these goals would be achieved through a system of bilateral agreements; multilateralism was 'the only solution.'[7]

By February 1946 a draft multilateral agreement was prepared and circulated to the Interim Council and through it to the PICAO member governments. Comments and opinions were requested, to be digested before the opening of the PICAO session in April. In its report the Air Transport Committee described the objectives of the agreement with these words:

It is the belief of this Committee that international air transportation, properly developed, can be an extremely important influence for peace, but that, if developed in a spirit of international jealousy and selfishness, its contribution to peace may be negative. The general motivating purpose of the draft Multilateral Agreement is to foster and encourage the widest possible distribution of the benefits of air transport for the general good of mankind at the cheapest rates consistent with sound economic principles, and to stimulate international air travel as a means of promoting friendly understanding and good will among peoples, insuring as well the many indirect benefits of international air transport to the common welfare of all nations of the world. In this way, we think international air transport can best realize its potentialities as an influence for peace.

To attain these lofty goals, the committee concluded, it would be necessary for all members to grant each other the five freedoms – to 'facilitate the international circulation of aircraft.' There would also be certain economic principles within which each member would operate, including 'fairness of competitive relationships, reasonable equilibrium between capacity operated and traffic offering, establishment of reasonable rates, and elimination of unfair competitive practices.'

Briefly, each member country would be free to establish routes to and from its territory without seeking the permission of ICAO, and the right to pick up some fifth-freedom traffic on longer services was recognized. Airline capacity would not be predetermined, but would be tied to:

a 'traffic requirements between the country of origin; and the countries of destination
b the requirements of through airline operation; and
c the traffic requirements of the area through which the airline passes, insofar as these requirements are not being cared for by local and regional airlines.'

One further twist to the proposed agreement was the inclusion of the rights of third- and fourth-freedom operators to force fifth-freedom traffic over the same route to charge a higher fare than the local service. For example, on an American New York–Paris service, the rate charged passengers picked up in London for Paris (i.e., fifth-freedom traffic) would be higher than that charged by the French and British operators over the same London–Paris service (i.e., third- and fourth-freedom traffic). It was hoped that a rate differential (10 per cent was the recommended amount) would offer enough economic protection to soothe the fears of smaller nations who were concerned that larger through services would steal their traffic.

To ensure that the economic principles were followed by all members, the Air Transport Committee recommended the creation of an International Civil Air Transport Board within ICAO. The proposed board would be 'composed of men of outstanding integrity and ability in their particular field,' who would be responsible to the board and not to their native countries. The board would hear grievances and have the authority to settle disputes between members and to see that its decisions were carried out.[8]

The Air Transport Committee's proposed multilateral agreement was accepted by the Interim Council as a discussion paper to be examined at the first PICAO assembly in May 1946. Nevertheless, support for the document was not unanimous. Not unexpectedly, the main source of opposition came from the American government, which submitted a brief statement to the Air Transport Committee outlining its objections. Although the Americans were full of praise for the good work of the committee members, it was pointed out that the draft agreement 'was prepared without reference to the viewpoints of particular States and it should not be expected that it would find universal acceptance.'

More specifically, the Americans warned that they would not accept the proposed rate differential on fifth-freedom traffic. The idea was a 'novel' one to be sure, the American representatives noted, but 'it is nevertheless administratively cumbersome, economically unsound and inherently invites international controversies which would tend to defeat the purposes of the Convention on International Civil Aviation as embodied in its Preamble.' A second point of objection was raised over the proposed International Civil Air Transport Board, which was given far too much regulatory power for American tastes. 'It is felt that the settlement of disputes between member States,' the Americans argued, 'should be accomplished in a manner that is more consistent with the arbitral provisions of the Interim Agreement and the Convention on International Civil Aviation and in order to foster cooperation and understanding among nations engaged in international air transportation the actions of the Council on such matters should tend towards advisory opinions, which would involve effective moral sanctions.'[9] Given the strength of these objections, it was difficult for the Canadians to be optimistic of success on the eve of the first gathering of PICAO.

The first meeting of the Interim Assembly opened in Montreal on 21 May 1946 and lasted until 7 June. The meetings were held in the Windsor Hotel, which had a long history of acting as host for aviation conferences. There were delegates from forty-four nations in attendance, along with numerous other organizations and states, which participated as observers. One of the first acts of the new assembly was the election of Louis deBrouckere, the Belgian minister of state, as its president.

C.D. Howe occupied his familiar position as leader of the Canadian delegation to the first assembly, and the rest of the delegation included his close associates, Herbert Symington, Anson McKim, R.A.C. Henry (of the Air Transport Board), and Lionel Chevrier, the minister of transport. Sir Donald Banks headed the British team, along with Sir Frederick Bowhill, the United Kingdom representative on the Interim Assembly. Of Banks, the Canadians noted that he 'was determined to be as unlike Swinton at Chicago as was possible and in this respect he was successful. He was not equally successful in his few attempts to bring the happy Commonwealth family together, since some members persisted in squirming in their chairs.'[10] Other Commonwealth representatives included Sir Frederick Tymms for the Indian government, A.S. Drakeford, the Australian minister of civil aviation, and T. O'Driscoll, an official in the Irish Department of Industry and Commerce.

As usual, the American delegation was the largest. Led by William Burden, the assistant secretary of commerce, and including Stokeley Morgan and Welch Pogue, the American delegation consisted of sixty-five delegates, alternates, and advisers – almost 25 per cent of the total number of participants in the assembly according to one estimate.[11] The American delegation also included, according to the Canadian report, a 'party whip' who did all he could to elicit support for the American position from the Latin American countries, the Chinese, the Irish, and others.

'The [American] delegation knew its strength and made the most of it,' the Canadian report noted,[12] and this position was made clear during the opening session, when Burden revealed the American reservations on the important economic issues dealt with in the Air Transport Committee's draft agreement. 'Our great concern,' he explained, 'is over the possibility that the universal desire of all of us to develop a multilateral agreement will lead us to move too quickly on matters of tremendous importance, without sufficient international background for the subjects included or without the ability, at this time, adequately, to foresee the consequences and complications that may result from an agreement arrived at in a spirit of enthusiasm rather than experience.'[13] Some delegates questioned the propriety of staking out a position before any discussion had taken place but few could doubt the effect. 'Some others spoke in the same vein,' McKim later wrote in the *International Journal*, 'and from then on the Assembly discussed the draft in a spirit of hopelessness, having resolved that the best course was to conduct a frank discussion for the guidance of the P.I.C.A.O. Council during the ensuing year with the object of reaching the goal then.'[14] All the delegates were well aware of the bilateral Bermuda Agreement signed earlier in the year and of the challenge of 'Bermuda principles' to any attempt to achieve a comprehensive multilateral agreement. Now, with the failure to win American support for the Air Transport Committee document, the best the supporters of multilateralism could do was secure one more year for further discussion and study.

The Canadians protested strongly against postponement, arguing 'that the longer the member states followed the course of concluding bilateral agreements the less chance there was for securing the adoption of a multilateral agreement. Unsaid but implied in the Canadian argument was the fear that in the present state of aviation the United States, politically powerful and further advanced than any other in its civil aviation development, would have a clear field to apply their power and utilize their development to capture the major airways of the world.'[15] The Canadian delegation could not withstand the American determination to shelve the draft agreement, and in the end reluctantly accepted the inevitable. 'Everyone agreed that multilateralism was a beautiful and desirable thing,' McKim concluded, 'but – not yet!'[16]

Despite the failure of the draft multilateral agreement however, a good deal was accomplished during the first meeting of the PICAO assembly. Several committees and commissions were established to oversee the transition from provisional to permanent organization and to carry on the enormous administrative, technical, and legal work that fell under the jurisdiction of the new organization – work that was neither spectacular nor controversial, but work central to the smooth operation of international aviation. The Interim Council was authorized to act in co-operation with the United Nations to enhance relations between the two international organizations. Invitations were extended to former enemy nations to participate as observers in future meetings.

A more thorny problem emerged over the allocation of the final seat on the Interim Council. At Chicago it was decided that the twenty-first council seat would be reserved for the Soviet Union – the hope being that the Soviets would see the wisdom of PICAO membership and join the organization. By spring 1946 the Soviets had made no move in the direction of membership and the question before the assembly was whether to preserve the empty seat or fill it with a participating member. The United States (with the support of the Latin American countries and Ireland) claimed that the Soviets had had their chance and now it was time to give the seat to a deserving member. Most of the European states and the Commonwealth members (other than the Irish) took the opposite point of view, and supported the continued preservation of a seat for the Soviets. The Canadians suggested that the council was already large enough and that there was no pressing need for an additional member. The vote was close – 20 to 18 in favour of opening the seat up.

The debate over which country would be elected to the twenty-first seat was much less acrimonious. Ireland had recently staged a regional meeting of PICAO states interested in navigational problems in the

North Atlantic area and had earned the praise of all those who attended. In addition, the Irish delegates were well respected as able and talented negotiators. Most important, however, the Irish had the committed support of the United States and Latin American bloc. There were no serious challengers (South Africa received one vote, Argentina six), and Ireland easily was elected to the council.[17]

The other key issue, at least for the Canadians, was the choice of a permanent home for ICAO. There were problems for any host country of a major international organization – finding sufficient office space and housing for the personnel, headaches over questions involving diplomatic immunity for foreign representatives, and so on – but there were also distinct advantages. In addition to the savings in Canadian dollars from not having to send delegates to a foreign country, it was estimated that PICAO would bring Canada $2,500,000 in foreign currency in 1946 and a further $3,500,000 in 1947 and in subsequent years. In addition, the presence of ICAO in Montreal would ensure that IATA would be there, too, which would produce a further inflow of foreign currency. There were other, less tangible, benefits as well. The presence of ICAO and IATA would make Montreal a first-class international air centre, and the city's culture would greatly benefit from the influx of hundreds of foreign visitors. Finally, the country as a whole would benefit from the great prestige and advertising that Canada would receive around the world.[18] It was not hard to understand why the government wished to keep ICAO in Montreal.

A final decision on the choice of headquarters was postponed during the Chicago conference and left over for the Interim Assembly to settle, but when it came to a vote the original division remained. The western hemisphere stood united in favour of Montreal, while most of Europe supported a European site, and the French were lobbying hard for Paris. Early on, it looked like the vote would be very close, with the decision resting with the uncommitted delegations – the United Kingdom and Commonwealth members. Howe believed that Sir Donald Banks personally favoured Montreal, but he had not forgotten how, at Chicago, the United Kingdom had favoured Paris. A telegram was sent off to Great Britain asking Prime Minister King, who was attending a Commonwealth Conference, to use his influence to ensure a vote favourable to Montreal. Mackenzie King discussed the matter with Lord Addison and received assurances of United Kingdom support, but there is little evidence that any pressure was put on the

British government.[19] In any event, the final vote was not even close: Montreal received twenty-seven votes, Paris got nine, Geneva four, and the Chinese voted for a site in China.[20]

The report of the Canadian delegation following the conclusion of the first and only full meeting of the Interim Assembly reflects the rather ambivalent feelings of those who participated in the session. 'The First Assembly was a successful shareholders' meeting,' one section of the report began. 'The Assembly expressed unqualified approval of the work of the Council and adopted an extensive programme of Council activities. There was a general recognition of the importance of the organization, a keen interest in its problems and a determination to establish a permanent organization as early as possible. An acknowledgement of the common objective and a cooperative spirit were evident in even the most controversial issues.' Indeed, there had been valuable discussion of the Air Transport Committee's draft agreement, and the need for multilateralism was widely recognized. The process of transition to a permanent organization with a permanent headquarters was well under way, and there had been 'no clashes of personality and no aftermath of bitterness such as marred the Chicago Conference and detracted from its substantial achievements.'[21] Yet the very real successes of PICAO were once again tainted by the failure to settle on a multilateral agreement. Worse, that which had looked so very close at the end of 1944 now seemed farther away than ever before.

I

The transition from provisional to permanent organization went through its final stages through 1946 and early 1947. At the same time, the Air Transport Committee continued to wrestle with the intractable problems of multilateralism. A smaller, more workable subcommittee was formed within the Air Transport Committee, with Anson McKim acting as chair, and including, among others, Paul David (United States) and Sir James Cotton (United Kingdom). To this subcommittee of seven men fell the responsibility for drafting a revised multilateral agreement.

The difficulties facing this small subcommittee were compounded by the fact that the United States had rejected the two significant proposals of the earlier draft: the creation of an international board within ICAO and the implementation of a rate differential between fifth-freedom and third- and fourth-freedom traffic. Deadlock on these issues meant that the new committee had to find wholly different ways to reach agreement. More ominously, in September 1946, Anglo-American aviation discussions were held in London, the upshot of which was a pronouncement that 'the Bermuda Agreement has demonstrated that the principles enunciated in that Agreement are sound and provide ... a reliable basis for the orderly development and expansion of international air transport.'[22] Bermuda principles were founded on the three pillars of: (1) bilateral negotiation of rates and services, (2) no predetermination of capacity and frequencies, and (3) the granting of fifth-freedom rights based on general guidelines, with only ex post facto review.

The long shadow of the Bermuda Agreement threatened to engulf the work of the Air Transport Committee and the hopes for a multilateral solution to the economic problems of international civil aviation. In 1946, for example, the United States concluded eleven Bermuda-style bilateral agreements, and sixteen more were negotiated in 1947.[23] In circumstances such as these, it was not surprising that the optimism of Howe and McKim began to fade. In November 1946 McKim was writing Howe that the chance of reaching a multilateral agreement was slim; by February 1947 he had concluded that it was next to impossible. And the Canadians were not alone; the Irish representatives had concluded likewise.[24]

Despite the growing pessimism, however, the Air Transport Committee subcommittee held over twenty meetings between October 1946 and January 1947 in an attempt to conclude some kind of workable agreement. Unanimity was never achieved and two draft agreements were submitted to the Air Transport Committee. The major points of contention focused on the old questions of frequency, capacity, and the allocation of routes. The majority report (which was supported by Canada and opposed by the United States and the United Kingdom) made no provision for the bilateral exchange of routes, and offered up a new, albeit hazy, clause to regulate capacity. Article Ten read:

The amount of capacity which a contracting State shall be entitled to permit any of its airlines to provide from time to time over various stages of each route shall be that required for the carriage, at a reasonable load factor of both:

i) passengers, mail and cargo taken on or to be put down by such airline in the territory of such State; and

ii) passengers, mail and cargo moving by such airline between points in the territories of other States which the route touches, insofar as capacity for such traffic is not being provided by airlines of the States in which such traffic is taken on or put down.[25]

To suggest that this clause was confusing would be an understatement. Just what did it mean? The minority report argued that, as written, it would lead to significant duplication of services on many routes. In its stead, the minority report recommended the full exchange of traffic rights with rates and services to be determined through bilateral negotiations. John Cooper, an aviation specialist and a member of IATA's Executive Board, tried vainly to 'clarify' the above clause in *The Journal of Air Law and Commerce*:

On all routes from country A to countries B, C, and D, airlines of Country A can put on all the traffic desired to carry available traffic at a reasonable load factor. If any substantial amount of the traffic is disembarked at B, then B is a point at which capacity must be recalculated. No aircraft of A can be operated beyond B except at a load factor based on the through traffic from A to C and beyond if local services of countries B or C provide capacity for traffic beyond B. In such a case, the only fifth freedom traffic which an airline of A could pick up at B would be the amount which would fill up the seats still available after the new capacity is determined.[26]

The root of the problem was perhaps best characterized by Anson McKim, when he wrote in the *International Journal* in 1947 that 'everybody's 5th Freedom traffic is someone else's 3rd or 4th.' At the heart of the debate was the fear that by granting the fifth freedom to another nation, some local traffic inevitably would be sacrificed. Conversely, McKim noted, 'if every nation insists on carrying its own traffic there can be no right to carry between other nations.'[27] In an effort to find some middle ground, the Air Transport Committee had accepted the premise that frequencies and capacity on through services should be gradually reduced as passengers disembarked along the way. Such reasoning had always been rejected by the United States government and by 1947 was also opposed by the United Kingdom. In the end, the majority report was accepted by the Air

Transport Committee, but with American and British opposition the draft agreement stood little chance of gaining acceptance during the opening session of ICAO.

The first assembly of ICAO opened in Montreal on 6 May 1947 and lasted until 27 May. The Canadian delegation was again led by C.D. Howe, and although there was some initial optimism, it was 'immediately apparent,' McKim wrote, that 'the desire for a multilateral agreement was as much torn by national interests as ever.'[28] To McKim the year-long wait had not made the prospects for success any brighter. Nor had the views of the other nations changed significantly: 'The general policy of the United Kingdom delegation in all these Commissions,' Lord Winster later reported, 'was to press for the limitation of the activities of I.C.A.O. to essential functions and to check a manifest tendency to inflate the organization and to assume added responsibilities.'[29]

The majority draft agreement of the Air Transport Committee was put forward during the session, as was, on the instigation of the American and British delegates, the minority report. Debate on the relevant issues was wide ranging and thorough, but no agreement was reached. To comfort those who still believed a multilateral agreement was a possibility, however remote, a commission was established to undertake further study – much the same as had been done the previous year. The difference this time was that the commission was open to all nations, and the plan was to hold an international conference later that year, at which time a multilateral agreement would be effected.[30]

On a more positive note, the permanent organization was a reality at last, and the good work in which it was involved was well under way. Discussions between a committee of the Interim Council and the Negotiating Committee of the United Nations Economic and Social Council had been held at Lake Success in New York State on 27–28 September 1946, and a draft agreement to bring ICAO under the auspices of the United Nations as a specialized agency (under Article 57 of the UN Charter) was produced.[31] This agreement was confirmed by the ICAO first assembly in May 1947.

For all intents and purposes, the debate over multilateralism was finished, but efforts continued for another six months. At first an international conference was scheduled for Rio de Janeiro in the autumn, but when the Brazilian government withdrew its invitation, the location was switched to Geneva. The interesting feature of this proposed conference was that the advance work would be the responsibility of those states wishing to participate – not that of any ICAO body.

It did not make sense to enter a further round of negotiations with the same proposals that were rejected in the ICAO assembly; this procedure was a sure recipe for disaster. Thus, over the summer of 1947, Baldwin and McKim, in conjunction with Howe, worked on devising a new set of articles that just might surprise everyone and be universally accepted as the basis for a multilateral agreement. The problem was to close the wide gap that was apparent first at PICAO and then during the ICAO session.

It was the same old story. The United States traditionally wanted as much freedom of the air as possible, within certain rather general guide-lines. This led American negotiators to consistently argue for the unfettered granting of the fifth freedom. The only drawback with such unconditional granting was that it opened up American traffic to outside competition. Fair enough. But a problem could arise with a country that had a small traffic output and also a large and efficient airline – such as the Netherlands – because an airline like KLM would be able to carry far more American traffic to different places than could an American service from the Netherlands. The Bermuda principles obviated this possibility by stipulating the grant of fifth-freedom rights up front – leaving the decision on routes to bilateral negotiations.

For the Canadians there were concerns over granting the fifth freedom if they would then be forced to negotiate routes on a one-to-one basis with a far more powerful nation like the United States. Canadian policy had always been to grant the fifth freedom only within the context of a multilateral agreement (or under a strong international authority), which would have some impartial say in the division of routes. So when the Canadians looked at the problem, they argued that if the United States insisted on maintaining bilateral negotiations to decide routes, then the Canadians should also insist on bilateral negotiations for the fifth freedom. 'Otherwise Canada,' one memorandum warned, 'as an intermediary country on the main routes from the United States to Europe and Asia would lose a great proportion of the traffic originating in Canada to foreign airlines without getting anything in return since Canadian airlines would not be operating to or across the majority of the countries whose lines cross Canada.'[32]

By early September Baldwin had prepared a draft cabinet document for Howe's approval. The Canadian delegation to Geneva could offer a 'compromise proposal' for an agreement that would 'provide for a multilateral exchange of rights limited to carriage of traffic to and from the country of origin of a service (3rd and 4th freedoms only). Fifth freedom fill-up traffic rights would then be left to bilateral negotiations. This approach would simplify the preparation of a multilateral agreement and make much easier establishment of agreed principles for the operation of services under it.'[33] Howe agreed with the thrust of the draft agreement, as did the rest of the cabinet, and he wrote Baldwin that this new proposal 'is as far as Canada should go in the direction of a multilateral agreement at this time. We should not be a party to any so-called multilateral agreement which involves individual bargaining on fundamental matters.'[34]

Before the Geneva conference opened, the Canadians discussed their proposals informally with other delegations, with less-than-positive results. American, British, and French representatives had discussed the upcoming conference a few weeks earlier and concluded that a comprehensive multilateral agreement was 'not attainable at this stage.'[35] As for the Canadian plan, the British had serious reservations. George Cribbett, who headed the British delegation to Geneva, told Baldwin and McKim, the Canadian delegates, the day before the conference opened that his government believed that giving away freedoms 3 and 4 but not 5 would only make it more difficult for his country to negotiate for the fifth freedom later.[36] Great Britain was a traffic-producing country and in relative strength and efficiency of its national airline it was second (albeit a distant second) only to the United States. In its aviation relations with the rest of the world, Britain wanted fifth-freedom rights in order for BOAC to successfully operate routes to all corners of the globe, but like the United States, it did not want to open up the United Kingdom to serious competition from dozens of foreign airlines. Thus, once the British were forced to accept Bermuda principles with their major competitor – the United States – it made sense to support similar arrangements in the negotiations it undertook with other nations. For this reason, the Canadians could not count on British support during the Geneva conference.

The ICAO conference in Geneva ran from 4 to 27 November 1947. There were thirty nations participating and an additional three attending as observers. The meetings were held in the historic Palais des Nations, and Edward Amstutz, the head of the Swiss delegation, was nominated chair. A working committee of four nations (United Kingdom, United States, France, and Canada) and a drafting committee (also with a Canadian representative) were established to undertake the burden of the work. The majority draft agreement of the Air Transport Committee was introduced as a 'guide' for the discussion, and, in time, so were the Canadian and other proposals.

Everything went according to plan, except for reaching an agreement. Barely forty-eight hours into the conference, Baldwin reported to Howe that 'both the United States and the United Kingdom will flatly refuse to accept any multilateral agreement which would automatically commit [sic] them to any exchange of routes or traffic rights in advance.' This being the case, he added, it was evident 'that they cannot accept the Canadian proposals even in modified form.'[37] Even though the Canadian proposals were favourably received by several smaller nations, Baldwin knew that they did not stand a chance.

On the crucial questions a prominent division emerged between the delegations. On one side ranged the small countries, which believed that granting the fifth freedom would seriously damage their local services; on the other were the United States and the United Kingdom (and a few other countries), calling for the inclusion of the fifth freedom in the multilateral agreement, but with the preservation of route allocation to bilateral negotiations. The latter group had enormous power and influence; the former found safety in numbers. Neither side could be made to accept any proposal, and, by the same token, neither could force its will on the other side. Stalemate again.

The Canadian proposals were introduced, only to be flatly rejected by the United States and Great Britain. In turn, the Americans and British insisted on keeping the division of routes out of any multilateral agreement. The other delegations followed suit and began watering down what they would accept in a multilateral agreement. The crucial vote came on a Mexican motion on the Canadian proposal to permit nations to opt out on negotiating the fifth freedom. The vote went thirteen for, nine against, five abstaining, and three absent.[38] Canada and the smaller nations voted for the motion; the United States and United Kingdom voted against.

The conference had gone as far as it could go. Within a few days the proceedings were brought to a close. No final document for signature was prepared. A meaningless final report was drawn up containing only suggestions for use in future agreements.[39] The 'hard fact,' one American observer wrote, 'was that on the root economic issue there was a clear cleavage between the nations who feel the need for protecting local and regional air services and those who do not.' Why had the conference failed? 'In general,' he continued, 'the countries which are now the major operators of long-range international services have not yet succeeded in convincing the other nations of the world that local operators stand to gain more than they lose through providing in a multilateral agreement for a reasonable balance between the two kinds of operation – or else they have failed to convince the local operators that the kind of agreement which they have been advocating will provide an equitable balance.'[40]

One interesting aspect of the conference not noted by this American observer was the absence of any semblance of Commonwealth unity. 'So far there has been no attempt to develop any regular series of Commonwealth meetings,' Baldwin wrote Howe on the second day of the conference, 'a situation which we do not regret.'[41] The reasons were not hard to discern. Lord Nathan (the minister of civil aviation) and George Cribbett were not Lord Swinton and Lord Beaverbrook – their concept of empire differed from that of wartime leaders. More important, on the key issues at stake in Geneva most Commonwealth nations sided with Canada and were opposed to the United Kingdom. On the Mexican motion, for example, Canada, Australia, New Zealand, and India voted for it, and South Africa abstained. Only Ireland voted with Great Britain, and the Irish had their own peculiar reasons for doing so. In international aviation circles at least, the Commonwealth had come a long way from the heyday of imperial solidarity in 1943–4.

Multilateralism had failed before: first in Chicago, then at the 1946 PICAO session, and again at the ICAO assembly in 1947. The difference this time was that the conference broke up with no plans for future negotiations. The divisions ran as deeply as ever, but the collective will was gone. Bilateralism had triumphed: there would be no multilateral agreement.

II

The failure to achieve a comprehensive multilateral solution to the economic problems in international aviation should not be allowed to overshadow the numerous successes and good work of the International Civil Aviation Organization. From its creation in 1947, ICAO has continued to collect and publish statistical information and has set the standards and procedures for operational practices – rules of the air, personnel licensing, air-traffic control, etc. In the post-war era, a vast and complex network of international air transport has evolved, producing equally vast problems of linking the flight of aircraft with ground stations over enormous distances, in addition to man-made obstacles such as customs, public-health concerns, and immigration procedures. The burden of these problems, and others dealing with air safety and regulations, has fallen to ICAO, which through its adoption of International Standards and Recommended Practices attached as annexes to the Chicago Convention has done everything that it could to facilitate international co-operation in air transport.[42]

By 1980 ICAO consisted of over 150 members, including the Soviet Union and the nations of Eastern Europe. In 1962 in Rome, during the fourteenth session of ICAO, it was decided that the assembly would meet at least once every three years. The council was enlarged in 1973 to include thirty-three states; but the division of seats (between important aviation nations, providers of air-navigational facilities, and regional representatives) remained unchanged. The Air Navigation Commission, Air Transport Committee, and Legal Committee established in 1947 continue to function, along with the Finance Committee and the Committee on Joint Support of Air Navigation Services. In addition, regional ICAO offices have been opened in Paris, Bangkok, Cairo, Lima, Mexico City, Dakar, and Nairobi. ICAO continues to publish technical manuals and air-transport studies, and in recent years has had to adapt to new conditions in order to provide safeguards against terrorism and to deal adequately with environmental issues such as engine emissions and aircraft noise. Clearly, of all the international organizations to emerge from the ashes of war, ICAO has been, and still is, one of the outstanding successes.

11　Across the Pacific and Beyond

'Geneva failed because of the inability to close a gap as wide as it was at Chicago,' Anson McKim mused on his return to Ottawa from the Geneva conference. In a long letter to C.D. Howe he described the problems of multilateralism, from which he concluded that it was 'clear that the U.S.A. want to sell air transport all over the world and do not, to the same extent, want to buy it. Small countries are genuinely afraid of overpowering competition from these big air states. Canada, as a middle air power depending so far entirely on the Third and Fourth Freedoms, has not aroused any fear and our stand, having been consistent for four years, commands respect.'

Regardless of how Canadians viewed the actions of their neighbour to the south, the lesson of Geneva was plain to see: 'We are in bilaterals for some years to come.'[1] By default, the failure of multilateralism forced air-minded nations to accept bilateralism, or 'straight horse-trading' as McKim described it. Canadians could either complain and refuse to play the game, or get on with it the best they could. Fortunately, they chose the latter.

Early in 1948 a new Interdepartmental Committee on Civil Aviation was created to deal with questions concerning Canadian policy and participation in ICAO, other issues such as the granting of fifth-freedom rights for non-scheduled services, and the use of American-operated bases by Canadian aircraft. The new committee included R.A.C. Henry of the Air Transport Board, C.P. Edwards from the Department of Transport, H.O. Moran from the Department of External Affairs, and, of course, J.R. Baldwin. One other member was Gordon McGregor, the new president of TCA. McGregor was a Montreal native who jointed TCA's traffic department in 1945 after serving in the RCAF.

Across the Pacific and Beyond 245

A man of strong opinions and forceful personality, McGregor rose quickly in the organization, heading the Canadian delegation to the IATA conference in Brazil in 1947. A few months later he followed Herbert Symington as TCA's president.[2]

Even before the first ICAO assembly and the Geneva conference, Canadian officials had initiated or were involved in bilateral negotiations with several countries – the United Kingdom and the United States in 1945 being the obvious examples. By the end of 1947 informal talks had been held with Argentina, Brazil, and Cuba, and a Canadian draft bilateral agreement was under consideration. Likewise, discussions were under way with the governments of Norway, Denmark, Iceland, and the Netherlands, and the fifth freedom was on the negotiating table in all of them. Other deals were being negotiated with Portugal for transit rights through the Azores, and in August 1947 a bilateral agreement was signed with the Irish government in which Canada made promises to utilize Shannon airport on some of its transatlantic services.[3]

The last frontier, so to speak, of Canadian international civil aviation was the Pacific service to Australia and New Zealand. From a geographical perspective the Pacific route was the most challenging; from a diplomatic perspective it was equally complex, involving, as it did, one last thrashing out of the Commonwealth relationship. The Pacific service also deserves special attention because its negotiation signalled a shift in Canadian international civil aviation, away from the policy of a single chosen instrument.

I

Canadian policy with respect to the Pacific service was clearly enunciated during the Commonwealth discussions held in Montreal just before and after the Chicago conference in 1944. Efforts to initiate a Commonwealth-operated service were vetoed by Ottawa; and although they were willing to co-operate with any parallel Commonwealth service, the Canadians stressed that they would want to operate their own independent service. It was assumed that the Pacific service would be operated by TCA.

Transpacific services next received serious consideration during the first meeting of the Commonwealth Air Transport Council, which did not take place until 9 July 1945, in London. Lord Swinton was elected to the chair of the CATC and committees were set up to deal with research and development, the provision of ground facilities, and Commonwealth routes. No permanent secretariat had as yet been established, and as a result the work was still being handled by the Ministry of Civil Aviation in London. Some preliminary discussion of a Pacific service was undertaken during these meetings; estimates of passenger loads in both directions were tabled, specific routes and landing sites were discussed, and some attention was given to the division of frequencies in any future operations. The Australians and New Zealanders were the prime movers at this point; the Canadians seemed more determined to protect their interests against Commonwealth encroachments than to actually establish a service – perhaps reflecting the sense that the establishment of a service was still a few years in the future.[4]

The Australians and New Zealanders continued to press the issue over the following months. Negotiations were undertaken with the United States to permit the Americans to operate additional Pacific services in return for landing rights at Hawaii and San Francisco for the Commonwealth/Canadian services. In February 1946 a civil aviation conference was convened in Wellington with representatives from Australia, New Zealand, the United Kingdom, Fiji, and the Western Pacific High Commission. Walter Riddell, the Canadian high commissioner in New Zealand, represented Canada but as an observer only. The main purpose of the conference was to organize the joint Commonwealth operating company to run the Sydney–Vancouver service parallel to the anticipated TCA service. To this end, the governments of the United Kingdom, Australia, and New Zealand recommended the creation of British Commonwealth Pacific Airlines (BCPA), to begin operations as soon as possible. A second outcome of the conference was the creation of a South Pacific Air Transport Council (SPATC) to 'provide machinery for consultation and to advise Commonwealth Governments concerned in all matters connected with the coordination and development of civil air transport services in the Pacific.'[5] The new body would have a permanent secretariat of its own and would be located in Australia. An invitation was extended to the Canadian government to participate.

Decision on Canadian participation in the SPATC was deferred for later consideration, but action was taken with respect to bilateral negotiations with Australia. There were no serious problems between the two nations and an agreement was signed on 11 June 1946. Under the terms of the agreement, Australia and Canada exchanged the right to operate a return service from Sydney to Vancouver via a number of intermediate stops. Fifth-freedom rights were not exchanged and capacity was to be divided fairly equally, 'in proportions corresponding to the proportions in which traffic to be carried between Australia and Canada in both directions is embarked in Australia and Canada respectively. Unless otherwise agreed this capacity shall be shared equally between the airlines of the two contracting parties.'[6]

Although not specifically mentioned in the agreement, it was assumed that the airline designated by Australia would be BCPA, the joint Commonwealth venture, while C.D. Howe announced in the House of Commons that TCA would operate the Canadian service. By the end of the summer BCPA had launched a Pacific service, and it was in full operation by May 1947. TCA, however, did not begin operations at that time. When approached by C.D. Howe, TCA president Gordon McGregor was pessimistic about the route and he expressed doubts about the suitability of the North Star (the Canadian version of the Douglas DC-4) to fly the route. He also noted that BCPA's service was not overly successful, and he could not foresee the operation of a Pacific service without incurring large deficits.[7]

In the meantime, the government was approached by Canadian Pacific Air Lines with a request for permission to operate two Pacific services: one to Australia, the second to Hong Kong via Tokyo and Shanghai. CPAL's request found support in the government. In a lengthy cabinet memorandum dated 11 May 1948, Lionel Chevrier put CPAL's case forward. He began with a review of the American services in the Pacific and argued that 'consideration of the early inauguration of a trans-Pacific air service would appear appropriate at this time.' The establishment of a Pacific service, Chevrier continued, 'would tend to protect Canada's trade position in the Pacific to some extent before American air lines operating in this area have become too strongly entrenched.'

Having explained the need for a Pacific service, Chevrier went on to suggest that serious consideration be given to CPAL's request. CPAL would put the services into operation as soon as possible, he claimed, and, more important, the company was not asking for one cent of government subsidy. Chevrier concluded with a list of reasons why CPAL believed 'it would be in Canada's national interest' to have CPAL operate on two Pacific routes. The CPR had the experience and a Pacific organization already in place ready to handle Pacific travellers, which would enable CPAL 'to commence operations with a minimum of delay, which is felt to be essential if Canada's position in the field of Oriental trade as well as international air transport is to be developed and maintained.' A CPAL Pacific service, moreover, would feed passengers into TCA's transcontinental route, and, finally: 'In the event of a third world war, Canada would have two air lines operating internationally, with personnel trained in international and overseas operations. This would be a distinct advantage in aiding and augmenting the armed forces for purposes of national defence.'[8]

Chevrier's memorandum was prepared in close consultation with Howe and was discussed by the cabinet on 20 May 1948. The crucial issue was whether or not the government would overturn a policy established the previous decade and reconfirmed during the war, namely, that Canadian international civil aviation be developed by one government-owned-and-operated 'chosen instrument' – TCA. By 1948 much of the fervour with which Howe and Mackenzie King had supported the chosen-instrument policy had dissipated and the two men now seemed more concerned with avoiding the need to subsidize either TCA or CPAL on the Pacific service.

The staunchest support for retaining the existing chosen-instrument policy came from the Department of External Affairs. In a memo signed by Lester Pearson (but probably written by Escott Reid) the genesis of the policy was reviewed. The September 1943 report of the ICICA and Mackenzie King's April 1943 speech to the House of Commons were quoted in the memo, and it was argued that only through government monopoly would the government be free from outside pressures and able to conduct its aviation policy based 'on the overriding political and security factors.' At Chicago, for example, the Canadian government was not, like the United States, 'subjected to heavy pressure from privately-owned air lines. This meant that the Canadian Government had less difficulty than did other governments in pursuing consistently that policy which it considered to be in the long-run national interest of Canada, even though it might not be in our short-run commercial interest.' Indeed, Pearson concluded: 'Once the Government permits the Canadian Pacific Air Lines to run international air transport services from Canada to the Far East and to Australia, a private Canadian interest will be created in the maintenance of those services. This may mean that at some time in the future it will be more difficult for the Canadian Government to pursue in respect of Pacific services that policy which at that time is in the long-run general national interest of Canada, taking into account the over-riding political and security considerations, as well as the purely commercial considerations.'[9]

The decision to permit CPAL to operate the Pacific services was made by the cabinet on 13 July.[10] The reasons for the government's apparent about-face were primarily economic ones; as C.D. Howe pointed out, TCA was already stretching to its limits and would have to be subsidized heavily to get a Pacific operation off the ground. CPAL, for its part, promised that it would need no subsidy, which was a crucial factor for the prime minister. It has also been suggested that Howe, at least, was concerned that if a Canadian company did not begin operations in the Pacific, then the initiative and potential might be lost permanently to British or American companies. Furthermore, Howe had already announced publicly that Canada would inaugurate a Pacific service and some negotiations had taken place with the Americans for third and fourth freedoms in Hawaii. A few months earlier Howe had told Ambassador Atherton 'that the Canadian Government has not only committed itself to the citizens of the Dominion to operate a trans-Pacific air service, but that the Government has made similar commitments of an Empire nature, and with other members of the Commonwealth.'[11] Having made this commitment, J.D. Hickerson pointed out in a memo to the State Department, 'it would seriously embarrass [Howe's] political position if he cannot carry out the plan.'[12]

It is also clear, however, that the raison d'être for a chosen-instrument policy was no longer present. So long as the pattern of international commercial air transport was uncertain, it was considered essential to have a free hand to implement Canadian policy and pursue Canadian interests to the greatest extent. By 1948 all this had changed. With the creation of ICAO, international collaboration in aviation was set on a permanent footing, while the international conferences at Chicago, Bermuda, and, indirectly, Geneva removed virtually all the pressing aviation issues that confronted the Canadian government before and after the Second World War. In 1948 there did not seem to be any more need for a government monopoly over international services, especially for a government that was not ideologically committed to it. As Louis St Laurent put it to Escott Reid:

'It all depends on where you draw the line between liberalism and socialism.'[13] That the decision to overturn the previously held position was not accompanied by fierce debate should not come as a surprise – because the philosophical underpinnings of that policy had evaporated. Nevertheless, the absence of debate should not be permitted to obscure the very real significance and symbolic nature of that change.

The government's decision regarding the Pacific service was met with mixed feelings in the ranks of TCA.[14] There were some misgivings outside the country as well, but for different reasons. The Australian government expressed some surprise that a private company had been given the route and doubted whether it could be operated without substantial government subsidies. The New Zealanders went even further and argued that the Canadians were committed to run a parallel service to BCPA that would include the pooling of revenue and passengers. There were even rumours that Australia, New Zealand, and the United Kingdom would again raise the possibility of creating a Commonwealth company to operate the service jointly.[15]

Soon after the announcement that CPAL had been given the Pacific service, the Canadian government received an invitation to a meeting of the SPATC to discuss the whole question of Commonwealth services across the Pacific. Canada had never officially joined the SPATC and at first the government was inclined to send only an observer to the talks. However, following pleas from the high commissioners in Australia and New Zealand, and with the support of Brooke Claxton and Lionel Chevrier, the cabinet decided to send a delegation to the meetings and to accept full membership in the SPATC.[16]

The third meeting of the SPATC opened in Wellington on 29 November and lasted until 7 December. The New Zealand minister of civil aviation, F. Jones, acted as chair. A.S. Drakeford, the Australian civil aviation minister, a veteran of many Commonwealth gatherings, was once again at the head of his delegation. The United Kingdom and Canadian delegations were led by their high commissioners, Sir Patrick Duff and Alfred Rive, respectively. In addition to the political representatives, the conference was also attended by advisers from seven Commonwealth airlines, including BOAC, BCPA, Qantas, and CPAL. The last was represented by Grant McConachie, the president.

The Australians and New Zealanders were clearly concerned about the possible ramifications of the allocation of the Pacific route to CPAL, and when the meetings began they 'expressed disappointment that the Canadian Government had chosen to designate a private company, especially as it would involve a competitive rather than a co-ordinated effort.' McConachie tried to allay the fears of the Australians and New Zealanders, Rive reported to Ottawa, as he, 'with the full consent of the Canadian delegation, answered questions relating to the proposed frequency and capacity of operation and the possibility of exchange of servicing facilities.'[17]

In the end, there was nothing that the Australians or New Zealanders could do about CPAL's rather than TCA's operating the Pacific service. The British government soon thereafter made it clear that it had no objections to the planned service.[18] The conference adjourned without producing significant documents or resulting in major policy changes – but with a better understanding of Canada's position in international civil aviation. Within six months CPAL inaugurated its service to Australia, followed, before the end of 1949, by a second route to Japan. What C.D. Howe had dismissed only five years earlier in 1943 – a private company negotiating on Canada's behalf – had become a reality. Strangely enough, nobody seemed to mind.

II

At the end of 1948 the framework of the modern system of international civil aviation was in place. The product of years of negotiation, the rules of modern international civil aviation sprang from wartime experience and were shaped by the Chicago and Bermuda conferences and the subsequent work of organizations like ICAO and IATA. The post-war system was never static; it evolved continuously and was changed, for example, with the introduction of the jet engine and the rise in popularity of charter-class air flight. Still, the basic foundations have remained, and only in recent years have they come under serious challenge.[19]

For Canada the symbolic moment came in 1948 when Canadian Pacific Air Lines was granted permission to operate the Pacific services. The decision was made primarily for sound economic reasons, but it also indicated a shift in government thinking towards a more flexible international policy in which private operators had a role to play. Indeed, the need for government monopoly had disappeared. By the end of the decade, services to the United Kingdom and the

Caribbean were well established, and other routes, to Europe and South America, were on the horizon. Transborder services to the United States were entrenched through a series of bilateral agreements and, although Canadian-American arrangements were adjusted periodically (in 1949, for example), the pattern was set.[20] In subsequent years, international air transport retained its vital importance in Canadian society and politics, but it no longer was viewed as an expression abroad of the Canadian national interest in the same way that it was in the years during and just after the Second World War. Nor has it been as near the heart of Canadian foreign policy as it was for a short period of time in the 1940s.

Beginning in the early 1930s it was recognized, at least on the official level, that Canadians needed to participate in the development of international civil aviation if the country was not to be left behind in a new and promising field. Unable to act independently, the Canadian government was a willing participant in a Commonwealth scheme for the transatlantic service. The birth and growth of TCA from 1937 to 1941, the emergence of strong leadership, and the tremendous expansion of Canadian aviation power during the war, however, led directly to the pronouncement of an independent Canadian policy in 1943 and resulted in the breakdown of the 1935 agreement and the inauguration of an independent transatlantic air service. From that moment, Canadians pursued an independent policy in the Commonwealth meetings; at Chicago, Bermuda, Geneva, and Montreal; and in their dealings with the United States. Only with the easing of international uncertainty did the government consider surrendering its solitary role in the conduct of Canadian international civil aviation.

For a brief moment of time many Canadians believed that the air was Canada's. Aviation offered the potential to overcome the domestic transportation problems that had plagued the country for all its history. Not only did the potential of aviation strike a responsive chord in the Canadian psyche, but for some it also provided a vehicle for making a practical contribution on the world stage. A grasp of the great possibilities of aviation, a strong sense of international responsibility, and the determination not to repeat the mistakes of the 1930s combined to produce a faith and dedication to internationalism in aviation that would last for the better part of a decade.[21]

Only two members of the Cabinet/Cabinet War Committee exhibited a strong and continuing interest in the development of international civil aviation during the period covered in this study: Mackenzie King and C.D. Howe. King was his usual cautious self; but behind the veil of circumspection and the fudging of the issues there lurked a man who was clear, in his own mind at least, what direction Canadian policy should take. Howe was more forthright in his views and deeds, but he shared with King that goal of a strong Canadian airline playing an independent and co-operative role on the international scene.

To achieve the goal it was necessary to stand firm on some occasions and to compromise on others. Especially in dealing with the United States and the United Kingdom, Canadians were obliged to perform a balancing act between international co-operation and Canadian autonomy. The Commonwealth tie was used to advantage – in 1935 for example. During the war, efforts were made to play the one off against the other: Canada's unique relationship with the United States was used to diminish the pull of traditional ties to empire, while, at the same time, security from possible American encroachments was found within the Commonwealth and through international co-operation.

On the other side of the same coin, however, was the desire to participate within an international framework. The potentially harmful consequences of either being ignored by the United States and the United Kingdom or possibly descending into international anarchy in the air were too great to permit Canadians to remain idle. Indeed, the direction of Canadian international civil aviation policy had always been towards the greatest amount of international collaboration to establish effective and acceptable ground rules within which Canadian aircraft could operate. There was irony, perhaps, but no contradiction in the fact that only through international co-operation and compromise could Canadians achieve that goal of independence.

King and Howe found support for their views in the Department of External Affairs and in a few other individuals like John Baldwin and Herbert Symington. It was a heady time, when dozens of working groups and committees labouring in a creative atmosphere attacked a whole range of problems dealing with reconstruction, the reconversion of industry, the introduction of social welfare measures, and, on the international scene, the birth of the United Nations. Part of that creative energy was devoted to international civil aviation: schemes were produced that would revolutionize air transport – and they were given serious consideration. Other more modest plans wound their way along the long road in the policy-making process: from original idea to memorandum, through the interdepartmental committee to the minister, and, ultimately, to the cabinet. By the time most proposals made it that far the radical fringes were smoothed over and the original bureaucratic zeal tempered by political reality.

Canada was well served by the individuals who guided Canadian international civil aviation policy in those years. Howe stayed on in government (although he did flirt with the idea of leaving politics to become the president of TCA), but by the end of 1949 most of the others either were gone or had moved on to do other things. Mackenzie King gave up his position as secretary of state for external affairs in 1946 and retired as prime minister in 1948. Herbert Symington left TCA in 1947 and was replaced by Gordon McGregor; Norman Robertson had already removed himself from the centre of things, becoming high commissioner in the United Kingdom in 1946; Lester Pearson entered politics and in 1948 he and Escott Reid turned the focus of their energies towards the creation of the North Atlantic alliance.

The one exception was John Baldwin, who went on to chair the Air Transport Board in 1949 and to become deputy minister of transport in 1954 and president of Air Canada in 1968. Baldwin and Howe continued their long association until the latter's defeat at the polls in the election of 1957. The last time the two men met, Howe, out of office for the first time in twenty-two years, was sitting on the steps of the East Block pondering his future. The two exchanged greetings adnd Howe told his old friend that he was thinking of moving to Montreal. Looking up, he said: 'One thing I want you to promise me ... you'll always keep an eye on TCA.'[22]

Appendix 1

Committee on Civil Air Communications Resolution 10 June 1937

(i) Appreciating the many benefits, direct and indirect, immediate and potential, to be secured by nations possessing substantial and extensive civil aviation enterprises, the Conference is unanimous in its approval of the Members of the British Commonwealth of Nations pursuing a vigorous policy in regard to their air services, embracing expansion within each of their territories and inter-connection between Members.

(ii) In order to promote arrangements whereby air lines of the Members of the British Commonwealth of Nations will link them together, the Conference affirms the willingness of the Members to co-operate with each other to the greatest possible extent.

(iii) In emphasising the importance of continued co-operation in the development of air services connecting the territories of the various Members, the Conference recognises that the most effective method of co-operation and efficient organisation can best be settled by the Governments concerned in each particular case as it arises, but any method should recognise, where desired by a Government, local control not only over services operating within its own territory, but also, by agreement with the other Governments concerned, in adjacent areas in which it is particularly interested.

(iv) It is agreed that, whenever an application received by one Member for facilities for foreign air services is likely to affect another Member, there should be consultation between the respective Governments concerned before facilities are granted; and if an agreement has been reached between the Commonwealth Governments concerned as to the service to be required in return for such facilities, the Commonwealth Government to whom the foreign application has been made will use its best endeavours to secure the reciprocal facilities agreed upon.

(v) The conference notes with approval the practice followed by Nations of the Commonwealth whereby, when operational rights are granted to a foreign air line the concession expressly provides for reciprocal rights as and when desired; and suggests for consideration the desirability of including in such concessions a general safeguard of the right of the Government, at its option, to take over the ground organisation within its territory on suitable terms.

SOURCE: Report of the CCAC, NA King Papers, J4, vol. 177, file: F1637

Appendix 2   The Six Freedoms

1 Right of innocent passage
2 Right to land for non-traffic purposes
3 Right to land passengers, etc., from country of origin
4 Right to pick up passengers, etc., for country of origin of the aircraft
5 Right to convey passengers, etc., between two countries neither the country of origin
6 Right to convey between two points in one country, not country of origin

SOURCE: SSDA to SSEA, 3 July 1943, NA RG2, series 18, vol. 52, file: A-15-1(W) pt. 1

Appendix 3

A Tentative and Preliminary Draft of an International Air Transport Convention 8 January 1944

1 The convention establishes an International Air Transport Authority, gives it a constitution and endows it with powers. The Authority has the normal structure of an international organization: an Assembly representing all the member states and a small executive committee which is called a Board of Directors. In each region a Regional Council is set up to deal with matters of regional concern.

2 The Authority is charged with the duty of planning and fostering the organization of international air services so as
   (a) to make the most effective contribution to the establishment and maintenance of a permanent system of general security,
   (b) to meet the needs of the peoples of the world for efficient and economical air transport, and
   (c) to ensure that, so far as possible, international air routes and services are divided fairly and equitably between the various member states.

3 The convention is an agreement between states and is not concerned with such domestic questions as whether the international air services of the various member states should be government-owned or privately-owned or whether a state should have more than one government-owned or privately-owned airline company engaged in international air transport. These are matters of domestic policy which each individual member state decides for itself. They are, therefore, outside the scope of the international convention.

4 The number of votes which each member state can cast in the International Air Transport Assembly varies from one to six depending on its importance in international air transport. The Board of twelve members, which is elected by the Assembly, must include at least one national of each of the eight member states of chief importance in international air transport.

5 A company wishing to operate an international air service makes application first to its own government. The government, if it approves of the application,

forwards it to the appropriate Regional Council. The Regional Council holds formal hearings on the application before deciding whether the applicant should receive a license and, if so, under what conditions.

6 The Regional Council has power to issue a license entitling a company not only to
  (a) freedom of air transit over the airways of all the member states of the region but also to
  (b) the right to land at airports in the region for refueling, repairs and in emergency,
  (c) the right to carry passengers, mails and cargo from the home state to any other member state and
  (d) the right to bring back passengers, mails and cargo to the home state from any other member state.

7 A state which considers that a decision by a Regional Council is unfair has the right to appeal to the Board of Directors and the Board can set aside or modify the decision.

8 The application for a license from an airline which wishes to operate a service passing over territory under the jurisdiction of two or more Regional Councils does not go to all the Regional Councils concerned but goes to the Board.

9 The Authority, acting through either the Board or a Regional Council is given power to determine frequencies of service on each route, to allocate quotas between the various member states and to determine rates of carriage for passengers and cargo.

10 On questions affecting world security the International Air Transport Authority is made subject to the international security organization which is to be set up by the United Nations. That organization may, in the interests of world security, order the International Air Transport Board to withdraw, suspend or modify a license, take certain measures concerning technical services, operating facilities and bases or set up one or more operating organizations to operate the air services on certain routes or in certain regions.

11 Two or more member states may decide that the best way of operating all or some of the air services between them is not by rival companies each carrying a national flag but by a joint organization. The member states are not prevented from establishing such joint operating organizations. Indeed the Board or a Regional Council may recommend to the member states concerned that they pool the air services on certain routes or in certain regions or constitute joint operating organizations to perform certain air services. A state has the right to participate in a joint operating organization either through its government or through an airline company or companies designated by its government. The

companies may, at the sole discretion of the state concerned, be state-owned or partly state-owned or privately-owned.

12 Services between two contiguous states, such as Canada and the United States, are excepted from the provisions of the convention and are left to be dealt with by agreements between the two states concerned. Contiguous states may, however, by mutual consent, give the International Air Transport Authority jurisdiction over the services between them.

13 Airlines between a state and its colonies, possessions, protectorates, mandates or territory abroad or between different colonies etcetera of the same state are subject to the provisions of the convention if the route passes through the air space of another state. This means that a state cannot reserve all its colonial services to its own airline companies.

14 In order that the air regulations throughout the world should be as uniform as possible, an agreed set of regulations will be drawn up by the International Air Transport Assembly and brought into force by each member state. These regulations will cover such matters as air safety, rules of the air, competency of air crew, ground signals, meteorological procedure, navigational aids, communications, airworthiness, national registration and identification of aircraft, carriage of dangerous goods and salvage.

15 The aircraft licensed by the Board or the Regional Councils will be assured wherever they go in the world of being able to use adequate airports and other ground facilities on payment of reasonable fees and charges. Member states may elect to bear all or a portion of the costs of constructing and maintaining the necessary facilities. If a member state does not so elect, the costs are advanced by the Board and borne by the Board or apportioned among states using the facilities. The Board may require, in return for advancement of costs, a reasonable share in the supervision of the construction work and in the control of the airports and other facilities. If a member state so requests the Board may itself provide, man and maintain any or all the airports and other facilities which it requires on the territory of that state and may impose reasonable fees and charges for their use.

16 The expenses of the International Air Transport Authority will be borne by the member states in proportion to the number of votes at their disposal in the Assembly, provided that those expenses of a Regional Air Transport Council which are properly chargeable to the states participating in the Council, will be borne by those states.

17 Some time will be required after the coming into force of the convention before the International Air Transport Authority is in full working order. The Assembly must meet, the Board must be elected, the Regional Councils constituted, their rules of procedure agreed upon. Certain temporary arrange-

ments are therefore contemplated to cover the initial period of existence of the Authority. The convention does not terminate the rights of companies now engaged in international air transport. These companies are given two years to secure licenses from the Authority. Furthermore, airline companies designated in a schedule to the convention are deemed to possess licenses issued by the Authority to operate routes designated in the schedule and these licenses remain valid until modified or withdrawn by the Board or the competent Regional Council.

SOURCE: NA, Cabinet document 693, PCO reel 4576

Appendix 4 The Two Freedoms Agreement

International Air Services Transit Agreement

The States which sign and accept this International Air Services Transit Agreement, being members of the Internatinal Civil Aviation Organization, declare as follows:

ARTICLE I

Section 1
Each contracting State grants to the other contracting States the following freedoms of the air in respect of scheduled international air services:
(1) The privilege to fly across its territory without landing;
(2) The privilege to land for non-traffic purposes.
The privileges of this section shall not be applicable with respect to airports utilized for military purposes to the exclusion of any scheduled international air services. In areas of active hostilities or of military occupation, and in time of war along the supply routes leading to such areas, the exercise of such privileges shall be subject to the approval of the competent military authorities.

Section 2
The exercise of the foregoing privileges shall be in accordance with the provisions of the Interim Agreement on International Civil Aviation and, when it comes into force, with the provisions of the Convention on International Civil Aviation, both drawn up at Chicago on December 7, 1944.

Section 3
A contracting State granting to the airlines of another contracting State the privilege to stop for non-traffic purposes may require such airlines to offer reasonable commercial service at the points at which such stops are made.
Such requirement shall not involve any discrimination between airlines operating on the same route, shall take into account the capacity of the aircraft, and shall be exercised in such a manner as not to prejudice the normal

operations of the international air services concerned or the rights and obligations of a contracting State.

Section 4

Each contracting State may, subject to the provisions of this Agreement,

(1) Designate the route to be followed within its territory by any international air service and the airports which any such service may use;

(2) Impose or permit to be imposed on any such service just and reasonable charges for the use of such airports and other facilities; these charges shall not be higher than would be paid for the use of such airports and facilities by its national aircraft engaged in similar international services: provided that, upon representation by an interested contracting State, the charges imposed for the use of airports and other facilities shall be subject to review by the Council of the International Civil Aviation Organization established under the above-mentioned Convention, which shall report and make recommendations thereon for the consideration of the State or States concerned.

Section 5

Each contracting State reserves the right to withhold or revoke a certificate or permit to an air transport enterprise of another State in any case where it is not satisfied that substantial ownership and effective control are vested in nationals of a contracting State, or in case of failure of such air transport enterprise to comply with the laws of the State over which it operates, or to perform its obligations under this Agreement.

ARTICLE II

Section 1

A contracting State which deems that action by another contracting State under this Agreement is causing injustice or hardship to it, may request the Council to examine the situation. The Council shall thereupon inquire into the matter, and shall call the States concerned into consultation. Should such consultation fail to resolve the difficulty, the Council may make appropriate findings and recommendations to the contracting States concerned. If thereafter a contracting State concerned shall in the opinion of the Council unreasonably fail to take suitable corrective action, the Council may recommend to the Assembly of the above-mentioned Organization that such contracting State be suspended from its rights and privileges under this Agreement until such action has been taken. The Assembly by a two-thirds vote may so suspend such contracting State for such period of time as it may deem proper or until the Council shall find that corrective action has been taken by such State.

Section 2

If any disagreement between two or more contracting States relating to the interpretation or application of this Agreement cannot be settled by negotiation, the provisions of Chapter XVIII of the above-mentioned Convention shall be applicable in the same manner as provided therein with reference to any disagreement relating to the interpretation or application of the above-mentioned Convention.

ARTICLE III

This Agreement shall remain in force as long as the above-mentioned Convention; provided, however, that any contracting State, a party to the present Agreement, may denounce it on one year's notice given by it to the Government of the United States of America, which shall at once inform all other contracting States of such notice and withdrawal.

ARTICLE IV

Pending the coming into force of the above-mentioned Convention, all references to it herein, other than those contained in Article II, Section 2, and Article V, shall be deemed to be references to the Interim Agreement on International Civil Aviation drawn up at Chicago on December 7, 1944; and references to the International Civil Aviation Organization, the Assembly, and the Council shall be deemed to be references to the Provisional International Civil Aviation Organization, the Interim Assembly, and Interim Council, respectively.

ARTICLE V

For the purposes of this Agreement, "territory" shall be defined as in Article 2 of the above-mentioned Convention.

ARTICLE VI

SIGNATURES AND ACCEPTANCES OF AGREEMENT

The undersigned delegates to the International Civil Aviation Conference, convened in Chicago on November 1, 1944, have affixed their signatures to this Agreement with the understanding that the Government of the United States of America shall be informed at the earliest possible date by each of the governments on whose behalf the Agreement has been signed whether signature on its behalf shall constitute an acceptance of the Agreement by that government and an obligation binding upon it.

Any State a member of the International Civil Aviation Organization may accept the present Agreement as an obligation binding upon it by notification of its acceptance to the Government of the United States, and such acceptance shall become effective upon the date of the receipt of such notification by that Government.

This Agreement shall come into force as between contracting States upon its acceptance by each of them. Thereafter it shall become binding as to each other State indicating its acceptance to the Government of the United States on the date of the receipt of the acceptance by that Government. The Government of the United States shall inform all signatory and accepting States of the date of all acceptances of the Agreement, and of the date on which it comes into force for each accepting State.

In WITNESS WHEREOF, the undersigned, having been duly authorized, sign this Agreement on behalf of their respective governments on the dates appearing opposite their respective signatures.

DONE at Chicago the seventh day of December, 1944, in the English language. A text drawn up in the English, French, and Spanish languages, each of which shall be of equal authenticity, shall be opened for signature at Washington, D.C. Both texts shall be deposited in the archives of the Government of the United States of America, and certified copies shall be transmitted by that Government to the governments of all the States which may sign or accept this Agreement.

SOURCE: Department of State, *Proceedings of the International Civil Aviation Conference*

Agreement

International Air Transport Agreement

The States which sign and accept this International Air Transport Agreement being members of the International Civil Aviation Organization declare as follows:

ARTICLE 1

Section 1

Each contracting State grants to the other contracting States the following freedoms of the air in respect of scheduled international air services:
  (1) The privilege to fly across its territory without landing;
  (2) The privilege to land for non-traffic purposes;
  (3) The privilege to put down passengers, mail and cargo taken on in the territory of the State whose nationality the aircraft possesses;
  (4) The privilege to take on passengers, mail and cargo destined for the territory of the State whose nationality the aircraft possesses;
  (5) The privilege to take on passengers, mail and cargo destined for the territory of any other contracting State and the privilege to put down passengers, mail and cargo coming from any such territory.

With respect to the privileges specified under paragraphs (3), (4) and (5) of this section, the undertaking of each contracting State relates only to through services on a route constituting a reasonably direct line out from and back to the homeland of the State whose nationality the aircraft possesses.

The privileges of this section shall not be applicable with respect to airports utilized for military purposes to the exclusion of any scheduled international air services. In areas of active hostilities or of military occupation, and in time of war along the supply routes leading to such areas, the exercise of such privileges shall be subject to the approval of the competent military authorities.

Section 2

The exercise of the foregoing privileges shall be in accordance with the provisions of the Interim Agreement on International Civil Aviation and, when it comes into force, with the provisions of the Convention on International Civil Aviation, both drawn up at Chicago on December 7, 1944.

Section 3

A contracting State granting to the airlines of another contracting State the privilege to stop for nontraffic purposes may require such airlines to offer reasonable commercial service at the points at which such stops are made.

Such requirement shall not involve any discrimination between airlines operating on the same route, shall take into account the capacity of the aircraft, and shall be exercised in such a manner as not to prejudice the normal operations of the international air services concerned or the rights and obligations of any contracting State.

Section 4

Each contracting State shall have the right to refuse permission to the aircraft of other contracting States to take on in its territory passengers, mail and cargo carried for remuneration or hire and destined for another point within its territory. Each contracting State undertakes not to enter into any arrangements which specifically grant any such privilege on an exclusive privilege from any other State.

Section 5

Each contracting State may, subject to the provisions of this Agreement,

(1) Designate the route to be followed within its territory by any international air service and the airports which any such service may use;

(2) Impose or permit to be imposed on any such service just and reasonable charges for the use of such airports and other facilities; these charges shall not be higher than would be paid for the use of such airports and facilities by its national aircraft engaged in similar international services: provided that, upon presentation by an interested contracting State, the charges imposed for the use of airports and other facilities shall be subject to review by the Council of the International Civil Aviation Organization established under the abovementioned Convention, which shall report and make recommendations thereon for the consideration of the State or States concerned.

Section 6

Each contracting State reserves the right to withhold or revoke a certificate or permit to an air transport enterprise of another State in any case where it is not satisfied that substantial ownership and effective control are vested in nationals of a contracting State, or in case of failure of such air transport enterprise to comply with the laws of the State over which it operates, or to perform its obligations under this Agreement.

ARTICLE II

Section 1

The contracting States accept this Agreement as abrogating all obligations and understandings between them which are inconsistent with its terms, and undertake not to enter into any such obligations and understandings. A contracting State which has undertaken any other obligations inconsistent with the Agreement shall take immediate steps to procure its release from the obligations. If an airline of any contracting State has entered into any such inconsistent obligations, the State of which it is a national shall use its best efforts to secure their termination forthwith and shall in any event cause them to be terminated as soon as such action can lawfully be taken after the coming into force of this Agreement.

Section 2
Subject to the provisions of the preceding section, any contracting State may make arrangements concerning international air services not inconsistent with this Agreement. Any such arrangement shall be forthwith registered with the Council, which shall make it public as soon as possible.

ARTICLE III
Each contracting State undertakes that in the establishment and operation of through services due consideration shall be given to the interests of other contracting States so as not to interfere unduly with their regional services or to hamper the development of their through services.

ARTICLE IV

Section 1
Any contracting State may by reservation attached to this Agreement at the time of signature or acceptance elect not to grant and receive the rights and obligations of Article I, Section 1, paragraph (5), and may at any time after acceptance, on six months' notice, given by it to the Council, withdraw itself from such rights and obligations. Such contracting State may on six months' notice to the Council assume or resume, as the case may be, such rights and obligations. No contracting State shall be obliged to grant any rights under the said paragraph to any contracting State not bound thereby.

Section 2
A contracting State which deems that action by another contracting State under this Agreement is causing injustice or hardship to it, may request the Council to examine the situation. The Council shall thereupon inquire into the matter, and shall call the States concerned into consultation. Should such consultation fail to resolve the difficulty, the Council may make appropriate findings and recommendations to the contracting States concerned. If thereafter a contracting State concerned shall in the opinion of the Council unreasonably fail to take suitable corrective action, the Council may recommend to the Assembly of the above-mentioned Organization that such contracting State be suspended from its rights and privileges under this Agreement until such action has been taken. The Assembly by a two-thirds vote may so suspend such contracting State for such period of time as it may

deem proper or until the Council shall find that corrective action has been taken by such State.

Section 3
If any disagreement between two or more contracting States relating to the interpretation or application of this Agreement cannot be settled by negotiation, the provisions of Chapter xviii of the above-mentioned Convention shall be applicable in the same manner as provided therein with reference to any disagreement relating to the interpretation or application of the above-mentioned Convention.

ARTICLE V

This agreement shall remain in force as long as the above-mentioned Convention; provided, however, that any contracting State, a party to the present Agreement, may denounce it on one year's notice given by it to the Government of the United States of America, which shall at once inform all other contracting States of such notice and withdrawal.

ARTICLE VI

Pending the coming into force of the above-mentioned Convention, all references to it herein other than those contained in Article iv, Section 3, and Article vii shall be deemed to be references to the Interim Agreement on International Civil Aviation drawn up at Chicago on December 7, 1944; and references to the International Civil Aviation Organization, the Assembly, and the Council shall be deemed to be references to the Provisional International Civil Aviation Organization, the Interim Assembly, and the Interim Council, respectively.

ARTICLE VII

For the purposes of this Agreement, "territory" shall be defined as in Article 2 of the above-mentioned Convention.

ARTICLE VIII
SIGNATURES AND ACCEPTANCES OF AGREEMENT

The undersigned delegates to the International Civil Aviation Conference, convened in Chicago on November 1, 1944, have affixed their signatures to this Agreement with the understanding that the Government of the United States of America shall be informed at the earliest possible date by each of the governments on whose behalf the Agreement has been signed whether signature on its behalf shall constitute an acceptance of the Agreement by that government and an obligation binding upon it.

Any State a member of the International Civil Aviation Organization may accept the present Agreement as an obligation binding upon it by notification of its acceptance to the Government of the United States, and such acceptance shall become effective upon the date of the receipt of such notification by that Government.

The Five Freedoms Agreement

This Agreement shall come into force as between contracting States upon its acceptance by each of them. Thereafter it shall become binding as to each other State indicating its acceptance to the Government of the United States on the date of the receipt of the acceptance by that Government. The Government of the United States shall inform all signatory and accepting States of the date of all acceptances of the Agreement, and of the date on which it comes into force for each accepting State.

In WITNESS WHEREOF, the undersigned, having been duly authorized, sign this Agreement on behalf of their respective governments on the date appearing opposite their respective signatures.

DONE at Chicago the seventh day of December 1944 in the English language. A text drawn up in the English, French, and Spanish languages, each of which shall be of equal authenticity, shall be opened for signature at Washington, D.C. Both texts shall be deposited in the archives of the Government of the United States of America, and certified copies shall be transmitted by that Government to the governments of all the States which may sign or accept this Agreement.

SOURCE: Department of State, *Proceedings of the International Civil Aviation Conference*

Abbreviations

ATB	Air Transport Board
Atfero	Atlantic Ferry Organization
BCPA	British Commonwealth Pacific Airlines
BED	British Empire Delegation
BLEPS	British Library of Economics and Political Science, London
BOAC	British Overseas Airways Corporation
BWIA	British West Indian Airlines
CAB	Civil Aeronautics Board
CATC	Commonwealth Air Transport Council
CCAC	Committee on Civil Air Communications
CIIA	Canadian Institute of International Affairs
CPAL	Canadian Pacific Air Lines
CWC	Cabinet War Committee
DCER	*Documents on Canadian External Relations*
DEA	Department of External Affairs
Dhist	Directorate of History, Department of National Defence
DND	Department of National Defence
DRCN	*Documents on Relations between Canada and Newfoundland*
EAMS	Empire Air Mail Scheme
FRUS	*Foreign Relations of the United States*
HCUK	High Commissioner in the United Kingdom
HLRO	House of Lords Record Office
IATA	International Air Transport Association
ICAN	International Commission on Air Navigation
ICAO	International Civil Aviation Organization
ICATP	Interdepartmental Committee on Air Transport Policy
ICICA	Interdepartmental Committee on International Civil Aviation
JOC	Joint Operating Company
NA	National Archives of Canada
NAW	National Archives, Washington
PICAO	Provisional International Civil Aviation Organization
PRO	Public Record Office, Kew
SPATC	South Pacific Air Transport Council

SPO   State Paper Office, Dublin Castle
SSDA   Secretary of State for Dominion Affairs
SSEA   Secretary of State for External Affairs
TCA   Trans-Canada Airlines
USATC United States Air Transport Command

Notes

Chapter 1 'Them Things That Buzzed'

1 Rudyard Kipling, *Actions and Reactions*, 136
2 Ibid., 140
3 J.A. Wilson, 'The World's Airway System,' 2
4 Quoted in Oliver Lissitzyn, *International Air Transport and National Policy*, 57
5 Ibid., 15
6 Ibid., 56
7 Frank Ellis, *Canada's Flying Heritage*, 60
8 F. Handley Page, 'The Future of the Skyways,' 404. See also Alfred Gollin, *No Longer an Island*, chapter 14.
9 John Cooper, 'Some Historic Phases of British International Civil Aviation Policy,' 190–1
10 Peter Fearon, 'The Growth of Aviation in Britain,' 23
11 Ibid., 24
12 Civil Aerial Transport Committee Interim Report, 7 February 1918, NA, Borden Papers, vol 429, file: 14. See also Cooper, 'Some Historic Phases,' 192
13 Margaret Mattson, 'The Growth and Protection of Canadian Civil and Commercial Aviation, 1918–1930,' 8–10; Colonial Secretary to Governor General, 28 November 1918, DCER, vol. 2, document 3
14 S.F. Wise, *Canadian Airmen and the First World*, 21. See also his 'The Borden Government and the Formation of a Canadian Flying Corps, 1911–1916,' 121–44.
15 Wise, *Canadian Airmen*, 5
16 Ibid., 115–16. See also Fred Gaffen, 'Canada's Military Aircraft Industry: Its Birth, Growth and Fortunes,' 48–53, and William McAndrew, 'The Early Days of Aircraft Acquisition in Canadian Military Aviation,' 35–43.
17 Robert Borden, *Robert Laird Borden: His Memoirs*, vol. 2, 865
18 See R. Craig Brown and Robert Bothwell, 'The "Canadian Resolution,"' 121–44.

19 Mattson, 'Growth and Protection,' 40
20 Arthur Sifton memo, 29 April 1919, NA Borden Papers, vol. 444, file: 141
21 Arthur Sifton memo, 3 May 1919, NA Sifton Papers, vol. 1, file: March 1919; Mattson 'Growth and Protection,' 51
22 'Conversation re Draft Convention on International Air Navigation,' 14 April 1919, NA Sifton Papers, vol. 7, file: Air Navigation, International 1919
23 P.R.C. Groves to Borden, 8 May 1919, ibid.
24 For a general review see Edward Warner, 'International Air Transport,' 278–93; Wilson, 'The World's Airway System,' 2–3; Cooper, 'Some Historic Phases,' 193–5.
25 Brancker speech to Empire Club of Canada, 22 March 1926, Dhist Wilson Papers, folder A, file: A10
26 J.A. Wilson memo, 17 November 1931, ibid., folder B, file: B19
27 See James Eayrs, *In Defence of Canada: From the Great War to the Great Depression*, 187–96; David Corbett, *Politics and the Airlines*, 31–2; W.A.B. Douglas, *The Creation of a National Air Force*, 56–7.
28 Wilson to Shelmerdine, 11 May 1932, Dhist Wilson Papers, folder A, file: A3
29 Wilson, 'The World's Airway System,' 15–16
30 Robin Higham, *Britain's Imperial Air Routes, 1918 to 1939*, 44; Brancker to Wilson, 12 May 1926, Dhist Wilson Papers, folder A, file: A10. On Scadta, see Wesley Newton, 'International Aviation Rivalry in Latin America, 1919–1927,' 345–56; and Stephen Randall, 'Colombia, the United States, and Interamerican Aviation Rivalry, 1927–1940,' 297–324.
31 Higham, *Britain's Imperial Air Routes*, 48, 70–5; Corbett, *Politics and the Airlines*, 26–8
32 Corbett, *Politics and the Airlines*, 29; Brancker to Wilson, 12 May 1926, Dhist Wilson Papers, folder A, file: A10
33 Mattson, 'Growth and Protection,' 312–19; Norman Hillmer, 'Mackenzie King, Canadian Air Policy, and the Imperial Conference of 1923,' 189–96
34 Mattson, 'Growth and Protection,' 325–6; 'Air Navigation in Canadian-American Diplomacy,' *Round Table*, 599–601
35 Wilson, 'The World's Airway System,' 9–11; Betsy Gidwitz, *The Politics of International Air Transport*, 39
36 Corbett, *Politics and the Airlines*, 286–7. See also Marylin Bender and Selig Altschul, *The Chosen Instrument*.
37 Nawal Taneja, *U.S. International Aviation Policy*, 1–2; Donald Whitnah, *Safer Skyways: Federal Control of Aviation, 1926–1966*, 81; David Haglund, '"De-lousing" Scadta: The Role of Pan American Airways in U.S. Aviation Diplomacy in Colombia, 1939–1940,' 177–90
38 Douglas, *Creation of a National Air Force*, 82–3; Mattson, 'Growth and Protection,' 297
39 Douglas, *National Air Force*, 83
40 Ibid., 80; Wilson memo 'Air Mail Services – Historical,' 30 March 1932, Dhist Wilson Papers, folder BB, file: BB1

Notes to pages 19-29   275

41 Douglas, *National Air Force*, 85. See also J.A. Wilson, 'The Expansion of Aviation into Arctic and Sub-Arctic Canada,' 130-41.
42 Quoted in Peter Russell, ed., *Leading Constitutional Decisions*, 142-3. See also Corbett, *Politics and the Airlines*, 33-5.

Chapter 2 An Effort in Commonwealth Collaboration

1 J.A. Wilson, 'The World's Airway System,' 2
2 Unsigned memo, 'Existing Combined Steamer and Air Trans-Atlantic Services,' 9 August 1932, NA McNaughton Papers, vol. 11, file: Canadian Airways Limited
3 See Wilson, 'The World's Airway System'; Roger Beaumont, 'A New Lease on Empire: Air Policing, 1919-1939,' 84-90.
4 Taneja, *U.S. International Aviation Policy*, 2-3
5 Riddell to O.D. Skelton, 22 June 1932, NA Bennett Papers, reel 1091, pp. 267900. For more on the conference, see the file on ICAN in NA RG25 G-1, vol. 1616
6 J.A. Wilson, 'Internationalization of Civil Aviation,' 18 May 1932, Dhist Wilson Papers, folder BB, file: BB1
7 Bender and Altschul, *The Chosen Instrument*, 196. See also Edward Warner, 'Atlantic Airways,' 467-83
8 Wilson to P.D. Ackland, 25 April 1932, Dhist Wilson Papers, folder A, file: A8
9 For background on Wilson see Douglas, *Creation of a National Air Force*, 41-2.
10 Wilson to Ackland, 25 April 1932, Dhist Wilson Papers, folder A, file: A8
11 John Swettenham, *McNaughton*, vol. 1: *1887-1939*, 249-50
12 Ibid., chapter 6; Douglas, *National Air Force*, 87
13 Douglas, *National Air Force*, 89
14 Carl Solberg, *Conquest of the Skies: A History of Commercial Aviation in America*, 288
15 Wilson, 'Trans-Atlantic Air Routes,' 9 July 1932, Dhist Wilson Papers, folder BB, file: BB1
16 Memo of conversation, 11 March 1932, NA McNaughton Papers, vol. 102, file: Civil Aviation Committee
17 Wilson, 'Trans-Atlantic Air Routes,' 9 July 1932, Dhist Wilson Papers, folder BB, file: BB1
18 Ibid
19 Wilson, 'Pan-American Airways,' 20 July 1931, Dhist Wilson Papers, folder A, file: A8
20 Desbarats to Skelton, 15 July 1932, Dhist Wilson Papers, folder B, file: B15
21 Keith Feiling, *The Life of Neville Chamberlain*, 211-12. On the conference, see Ian Drummond, *British Economic Policy and the Empire, 1919-1939*, chapter 3.
22 Wilson, 'Air Mail Connection with Trans-Atlantic Mail Steamers in the Straits of Belle Isle,' 9 May 1932, Dhist Wilson Papers, folder BB, file: BB1

23 Quoted in Swettenham, *McNaughton*, 258
24 A copy can be found in Dhist Wilson Papers, folder C, file: C8
25 Committee on Trans-Atlantic Air Service minutes, 15 August 1932, ibid., folder BB, file: BB1
26 Order in Council, 30 August 1932, NA RG25 G1, vol. 1616, file: 72-R pt. 1
27 Shelmerdine report of visit to Ottawa, 4–18 August 1932, PRO AVIA2 1899
28 Desbarats to Skelton, 27 October 1932; L.R. LaFlèche to Skelton, 22 April 1933, NA RG25 G1, vol. 1616, file: 72-R pt. 1
29 Wilson memo, 10 January 1933, NA McNaughton Papers, vol. 11, file: Air Mail Routes
30 Skelton to Wilson, 28 April 1933, Dhist Wilson Papers, folder BB, file: BB2
31 Wilson to Skelton, 10 May 1933, NA RG25 G1, vol. 1616, file: 72-R pt. 1
32 D.M. Bain, *Canadian Pacific Air Lines: Its History and Aircraft*, 9–10; Philip Smith, *It Seems Like Only Yesterday: Air Canada, the First 50 Years*, 18
33 Bain, *Canadian Pacific*, 10; McNaughton to Skelton, 5 June 1933, NA RG25 G1, vol. 1616, file: 72-R pt. 1; 'Memorandum of Communications between Imperial Airways Limited and Canadian Aviation Interests,' April 1933, Dhist Wilson Papers, folder BB, file: BB2
34 McNaughton to Bennett, 30 May 1933, NA RG25 G1, vol. 1616, file: 72-R pt. 1
35 'Civil Aviation Policy,' 24 May 1933, ibid.
36 Minutes, 9 June 1933, ibid.
37 Vanier to Skelton, 16 June 1933, ibid.
38 Wilson, 'Trans-Atlantic Air Services Negotiations –Government of Newfoundland,' 26 June 1933, Dhist Wilson Papers, folder BB, file: BB2
39 Perley to Wilson, 30 June 1933, NA RG25 G1, vol. 1616, file: 72-R pt. 1
40 Wilson to Perley, 18 July 1933, NA McNaughton Papers, vol. 11, file: Canadian Airways Ltd
41 Mulock, 'Imperial Airways,' ibid., file: Civil Aviation, Interdepartmental Committee on Trans-Canada Airways, July–Dec. 1933, vol. 2
42 Skelton to McNaughton, 12 July 1933, NA RG25 G1, vol. 1616, file: 72-R pt. 1
43 This paragraph was drawn from R.K. Smith, 'The Intercontinental Airliner and the Essence of Airplane Performance, 1929–1939,' 436.
44 Ibid., 429–33
45 Quoted in ibid., 437. See also 'D,' 'Pacific Airways,' 60–9.
46 House of Commons *Debates*, 22 March 1937, vol. 2, 2043
47 A.T. Cowley, 'Memo of Meeting with the Prime Minister,' 19 May 1934, NA McNaughton Papers, vol. 101, file: Civil Aviation, Interdepartmental Committee on Trans-Canada Airways Jan.–Dec. 1935, vol. 3
48 Wilson memo, 5 March 1935, Dhist Wilson Papers, folder E, file: E4
49 Ibid.
50 See Peter Fearon, 'Aircraft Manufacturing,' 216–40; John Myerscough, 'Airport Provision in the Inter-War Years,' 41–70; Higham, *Britain's Imperial Air Routes*, 187.
51 Higham, *Britain's Imperial Air Routes*, 260
52 Vanier to Skelton, 21 June 1935, NA RG25 G2, vol. 1616, file: 72-R pt. 3
53 Ibid.; Skelton to Vanier, 8 July 1935, ibid.

54 J.H. Thomas to SSEA, t. 320, 9 August 1935, NA King Papers, J4, vol. 419, file: 1242
55 Wilson, 'Trans-Atlantic Air Services,' 24 August 1935, NA McNaughton Papers, vol. 102, file: C.A.I.C.T.C.A. Jan.–Nov. 1935, vol. 4
56 Acting SSEA to SSDA, t. 74, 7 October 1935, NA King Papers, J4, vol. 419, file: 1242
57 Vanier to McNaughton, 30 August 1935, NA RG25 G1, vol. 1616, file: 72-R pt. 3
58 Woods Humphrey to Wilson, 25 September 1935, Dhist Wilson Papers, folder A, file: A4
59 'Report of Inter-Departmental Committee on Transatlantic Air Services,' 18 November 1935, NA King Papers, J4, vol. 419, file: 1242
60 Higham, *Britain's Imperial Air Routes*, 85–7; United Kingdom, 'Empire Air Mail Scheme,' October 1935, NA RG25 G1, vol. 1685, file: 72-U
61 'Instructions to Saorstat Representatives in Discussions at Ottawa and Washington,' 7 November 1935, Dublin Castle, SPO S8238
62 Ibid. See Bernard Share, *The Flight of the Iolar: The Aer Lingus Experience, 1936–1986*.
63 Discussions on Transatlantic Air Services minutes, 22 November 1935, NA King Papers, J4, vol. 419, file: 1242
64 Sub-Committee, General, Finance and Co-ordinating minutes, 23 November 1935, ibid.
65 Ibid., 26 November 1935
66 Report, 'Trans-Atlantic Air Service,' 2 December 1935, NA RG25 G1, vol. 1646, file: 72-M pt. 2
67 Bender and Altschul, *The Chosen Instrument*, 261
68 Unsigned memo from Department of External Affairs, 20 January 1936, Dublin Castle, SPO S8238
69 'Report of the Canadian Representatives upon the Washington Conference on Transatlantic Air Services, 1935,' 10 February 1936, NA RG25 G1, vol. 1766, file: 72-M pt. 1; Bender and Altschul, *The Chosen Instrument*, 261
70 'Report of the Canadian Representatives,' 1936
71 Department of State press communiqué, 12 December 1935, ibid.
72 King diary, 25 March 1936; De Valera to SSDA, t. 24, 23 March 1936, Dublin Castle, SPO S8238; Higham, *Britain's Imperial Air Routes*, 189
73 Wilson, 'Trans-Atlantic Air Services: Pan American Airways Application for Flying Rights in Canada,' 8 January, NA RG25 G1, vol. 1766, file: 72-M pt. 1
74 Skelton to SSDA, t. 250, 10 September 1936, ibid., file: 72-M pt. 1
75 Wrong to Laurent Beaudry, 7 October 1936, ibid., file: 72-M pt. 3
76 See HCUK to SSEA, t. 412, 25 November 1936, ibid.; 'Notes of Meeting,' 23 November 1936, NA RG25 A-7, vol. 545, file: 247
77 HCUK to SSEA, t. 96, 27 November 1936, NA RG25 G1, vol. 1766, file: 72-M pt. 3
78 Bender and Altschul, *The Chosen Instrument*, 261
79 New York *Times*, 11 March 1937

80 Marler to SSEA, t. 237, 12 March 1937, NA RG25 G1, vol. 1766, file: 72-M pt. 4
81 See Order in Council, 10 February 1937 in DCER, vol. 6, document 231; Wilson memo, 15 March 1937, NA RG25 G1, vol. 1766, file: 72-M pt. 4
82 Department of Commerce press release, 20 April 1937; and Moore to Marler, 20 April 1937, NA RG25 G1, vol. 1766, file: 72-M pt. 4
83 Unsigned memo from Department of External Affairs, 20 January 1936, Dublin Castle, SPO S8238

Chapter 3 Atlantic Crossing

1 LaFlèche to Skelton, 4 February 1935, NA RG25 G1, vol. 1685, file: 72-M. Invitation to join the EAMS can be found in PRO AVIA2 1917.
2 See J.A. Wilson memo, 2 November 1937, Dhist Wilson Papers, folder D, file: D8.
3 Robert Bothwell and William Kilbourn, *C.D. Howe: A Biography*, 105
4 Interdepartmental committee minutes, 9 March 1936, Dhist Wilson Papers, folder E, file: E4
5 Bothwell and Kilbourn, *C.D. Howe*, 106
6 Ibid., 104–10; Smith, *It Seems Like Only Yesterday*, chapters 3 and 4; J.R.K. Main, *Voyageurs of the Air: A History of Civil Aviation in Canada, 1858–1967*, 143–8
7 Smith, *Only Yesterday*, 34
8 Ibid., 48
9 House of Commons *Debates*, 22 March 1937, vol. 2, 2041
10 Main, *Voyageurs of the Air*, 149–50; Bothwell and Kilbourn, *C.D. Howe*, 110
11 Bothwell and Kilbourn, *C.D. Howe*, 110–11
12 Main, *Voyageurs of the Air*, 150–1; C.A. Ashley, *The First Twenty-five Years: A Study of Trans-Canada Air Lines*, 16–20
13 See Rainer Tamchina, 'In Search of Common Causes: The Imperial Conference of 1937,' 79–105.
14 'The Commonwealth Air Route round the World,' E (37) 4, February 1937, NA King Papers, J4, vol. 177, file: F1637
15 Ibid.
16 Ibid.
17 'Competition from Foreign Air Lines,' E (37) 5, February 1937, NA King Papers, J4, vol. 177, file: F1637
18 'Policy for the Production of Civil Aircraft within the Commonwealth,' E (37) 16, 11 May 1937, ibid. See draft memo of Interdepartmental Committee on International Air Communications, May 1937, in PRO AVIA2 2121.
19 CCAC minutes, 28 May 1937, NA King Papers, J4, vol. 177, file: F1637
20 King diary, 7 June 1937
21 Crerar to J.W. Dafoe, 17 April 1937, quoted in James Eayrs, *In Defence of Canada: Appeasement and Rearmament*, 55
22 See Loring Christie, 'Draft Memorandum,' 23 March 1937, in DCER, vol. 6, document 235.

23 See Keith Middlemas and John Barnes, *Baldwin: A Biography*, 1027–9.
24 CCAC minutes, 28 May 1937, NA King Papers, J4, vol. 177, file: F1637
25 Meeting of Principal Delegates minutes, 9 June 1937, ibid.
26 CCAC, 'Draft Resolution 1,' 1 June 1937, ibid.
27 CCAC minutes, 31 May 1937, ibid.
28 Cabinet minutes, 2 June 1937, quoted in 'Civil Air Communications,' 23 July 1937, NA RG25 G1, vol. 1767, file: 72-M pt. 5
29 CCAC Sub-committee on the Trans-Tasman and Trans-Pacific Services minutes, 3 June 1937, NA King Papers, J4, vol. 177, file: F1637
30 CCAC, 'Revised Draft of Resolution No. 1,' 5 June 1937, ibid.
31 CCAC minutes, 4 June 1937
32 CCAC, 'Second Revised Draft of Resolution No. 1,' 5 June 1937, ibid.
33 Meeting of Principal Delegates minutes, 9 June 1937, ibid.
34 Ibid.
35 King diary, 9 June 1937; Tamchina, 'In Search of Common Causes,' 100
36 CCAC minutes, 10 June 1937, NA King Papers, J4, vol. 177, file: F1637
37 Ibid.
38 Mackenzie King wrongly believed that Swinton was, in fact, chair of the committee; see King diary, 9 June 1937.
39 See Department of Industry and Commerce memo, 3 December 1938, Dublin Castle, SPO S11030A.
40 The minutes for the committee can be found in NA RG25 G1, vol. 1766, file: 72-M pt. 3.
41 See the documents in NA RG25 A-7, vol. 546, file: 255; J.E. Stephenson to Lester Pearson, 3 February 1939, PRO FO371 23895 w888/168/27.
42 On the development of the service, see the memos in NA RG25 A-7, vol. 545, file: 250. On the Dublin conference, see the record of proceedings in BG25 G1, vol. 1856, vile: 72-F.
43 Bender and Altschul, *The Chosen Instrument*, 292. See also R.K. Smith, 'The Intercontinental Airliner,' 446.
44 Note by P.J. Stirling, 9 January 1939, PRO FO371 23895 w479/168/27
45 R.K. Smith, 'The Intercontinental Airliner,' 447
46 Lester Pearson, *Mike: The Memoirs of the Right Honourable Lester B. Pearson*, vol. 1, *1897–1948*, 135. For another description of an early transatlantic flight, see Malcolm MacDonald to Sir Eric Machtig, 17 October 1941, University of Durham, MacDonald Papers, file: 14/2/1-23.
47 Higham, *Britain's Imperial Air Routes*, 197. See also Gerald Campbell to Skelton, 27 July 1940, NA RG25 G1, vol. 1767, file: 72-M pt. 9.
48 ICICA, doc. 2, 8 May 1942, ibid., vol. 1768, file: 72-M pt. 10
49 Solberg, *Conquest of the Skies*, 244–5, 297.

Chapter 4 Connecting the Capitals

1 Gidwitz, *The Politics of International Air Transport*, 44–5. Sabena's fleet of aircraft in the Congo remained in service during the war.
2 Higham, *Britain's Imperial Air Routes*, 278–83; Derek Aldcroft, 'Britain's

Internal Airways: The Pioneer Stage of the 1930's' 113–23. On British Airways, see Robin Higham, 'British Airways Ltd, 1935–40,' 113–23.
3 Whitnah, *Safer Skyways*, chapter 6; Corbett, *Politics and the Airlines*, 289
4 Taneja, *u.s. International Aviation Policy*, 5–6; Solberg, *Conquest of the Skies*, 239–40
5 Bender and Altschul, *The Chosen Instrument*, 333–51; Solberg, *Conquest of the Skies*, 260. For a list of us air rights, see 'Military and Civil Foreign Air Rights Held by the United States,' NAW RG59, FW 711.0027/1-349.
6 Bender and Altschul, *The Chosen Instrument*, 365. See also Deborah Ray, 'The Takoradi Route,' 340–58.
7 Solberg, *Conquest of the Skies*, 262–6, 274
8 Ibid., 284
9 On Atfero and the growth of the RCAF, see Douglas, *The Creation of a National Air Force*; F.J. Hatch, *Aerodrome of Democracy: Canada and the British Commonwealth Air Training Plan 1939–1945*; Don McVicar, *Ferry Command*; Jeffery Davis, 'ATFERO: The Atlantic Ferry Organization,' 71–97.
10 Gaffen, 'Canada's Military Aircraft Industry,' 50–1
11 J.A. Wilson, 'Civil Aviation Agreement between Canada and the United States,' 29 December 1937, Dhist Wilson Papers, folder D, file: D8; Main, *Voyageurs of the Air*, 169
12 Main, *Voyageurs of the Air*, 169
13 Ibid.; CWC minutes, 18 February 1943. See also 'Proposed Civil Arrangements with U.S.' 17 June 1938, NA King Papers, J4, vol. 419, file: 1242.
14 Escott Reid, 'Present United States Air Services in Canada,' 14 January 1943, NA RG25 G2, vol. 2711, file: 72-FX-40 pt. 1. For a list, see 'Operation in Canada of United States Aircraft other than Licensed Commercial Carriers,' 28 January 1943, in the same file.
15 Pearson to J.R.K. Main, 30 December 1941, NA RG25 G2, vol. 2711, file: 72-FE-40
16 Reid to Pearson, 6 October 1943, ibid.
17 For differing opinions, see Norman Robertson to C.P. Edwards, 23 October 1943; Edwards to Robertson, 16 November 1943, ibid.
18 See McCarthy to Robertson, 14 December 1943; Reid to Heeney, 6 January 1944; 'Proposal for Direct Air Service between Ottawa and Washington,' February 1944, ibid.
19 CWC minutes, 7 June 1944
20 Bothwell and Kilbourn, *C.D. Howe*, chapter 1
21 HCUK to SSEA, 6 December 1941, DRCN, document 1041
22 ICICA, doc. 2, 8 May 1942, NA RG25 G1, vol. 1768, file: 72-M pt. 10
23 Power to Robertson, 9 February 1942, DRCN, document 1042
24 HCUK to SSEA, 14 April 1942, ibid., document 1047
25 Vincent Massey, *What's Past Is Prologue*, 371
26 CWC minutes, 22 May 1942
27 'Canadian Trans-Atlantic Air Services,' summary of Committee Meeting, 1 June 1942, NA RG25 G1, vol. 1768, file: 72-M pt. 10

28 See ICICA doc. n. 10, 16 June 1942, NA RG2, series 18, vol. 18, file: A-15-1-A (vol. 1).
29 Robertson to Edwards, 6 June 1942, NA RG25 G1, vol. 1768, file: 72-M pt. 10
30 Baldwin memo, 4 June 1942, NA RG2, series 18, vol. 18, file: A-15-1-A (vol. 1)
31 Edwards to Robertson, 11 June 1942, and attached 'Heads of Agreement,' no date, ibid.
32 'Heads of Agreement,' ibid.
33 HCUK to SSEA, 23 June 1942, DRCN, document 1049
34 Smith, *It Seems Like Only Yesterday*, 54
35 Ibid., 86
36 J.L. Granatstein, *The Ottawa Men: The Civil Service Mandarins, 1935–1957*, 94–5. See also his *A Man of Influence: Norman A. Robertson and Canadian Statecraft, 1929–68*.
37 Granatstein, *Ottawa Men*, 237–43; J.R. Baldwin interview, Kingston, 21 August 1987
38 Baldwin interview
39 Baldwin memo for Robertson, 7 July 1942, NA RG2, series 18, vol. 18, file: A-15-1-A (vol. 1)
40 SSEA to HCUK, t. 1307, 9 July 1942, ibid.
41 Heeney memo for CWC, 7 July 1942, DRCN, document 1050
42 Copies of these telegrams can be found in NA RG25 G1, vol. 1768, file: 72-M pt. 10.
43 SSEA to HCUK, t. 1804, 3 October 1942, ibid.
44 Minutes of meeting, 10 October 1942, NA RG2, series 18, vol. 18, file: A-15-1-A (vol. 1)
45 CWC minutes, 21 October 1942
46 SSEA to HCUK, 22 October 1942, NA RG25 G1, vol. 1768, file: 72-M pt. 10
47 SSEA to HCUK. t. 636, 26 September 1942, ibid.
48 Attlee to Massey, 9 December 1942, ibid.
49 High commissioner in Ireland to SSEA, t. 12, 26 January 1943, ibid. For the response from Newfoundland, see W. Woods to high commissioner in Newfoundland, 29 December 1942, ibid.
50 Read memo for Robertson, 9 March 1943, and attached K.B. Bingay memo, ibid.
51 Robertson to high commissioner in Newfoundland, t. 125, 5 May 1943, NA RG25 G1, vol. 1768, file: 72-M pt. 11
52 SSEA to HCUK, t. 160, 30 January 1943, NA RG2, series 18, vol. 51, file: A-15-1-A (vol. 1)
53 Ibid. See also Main, *Voyageurs of the Air*, 154.
54 Woods to high commissioner in Newfoundland, 30 July 1943; J.P. Walshe to high commissioner in Ireland, 4 August 1943, ibid.
55 SSEA to HCUK, t. 1029, 16 June 1943, ibid.
56 House of Commons *Debates*, 16 June 1943, vol. 4, 3697
57 Main, *Voyageurs of the Air*, 154; Ashley, *The First Twenty-five Years*, chapter 4; Massey to Robertson, 21 May 1943, NA RG2, series 18, vol. 51, file: A-15-a-A (vol. 1)

58 Howe to Beaverbrook, 4 March 1944, HLRO Beaverbrook Papers, D/161

Chapter 5 Globaloney

1 F.M.G. Willson, *The Organization of British Central Government*, 106–7
2 Lord Gladwyn, *The Memoirs of Lord Gladwyn*, 73
3 Arthur Greenwood to Eden, 9 July 1941, PRO FO371 28728 W7829/7829/802
4 Shelmerdine report, War Cabinet, RP (42) 5, 5 January 1942, NA Reid Papers, vol. 10, file: 38. The Atlantic Charter is attached to the report as an appendix. The minutes of the committee can be found in PRO CAB87 85. For another look at some of these issues, see Christopher Brewin, 'British Plans for International Operating Agencies for Civil Aviation,' 91–110.
5 Jowitt's draft statement attached to Finlay Report, War Cabinet RP (42) 48, 18 December 1942, NA Reid Papers, vol. 10, file: 38
6 Wood to Jowitt, 28 April 1942, attached to ibid.
7 Finlay Report, ibid. Many of these questions are asked by Jowitt in his draft statement in ibid.
8 Finlay report, ibid.
9 Finlay to Jowitt, 17 December 1942, attached to ibid.
10 Foreign Office memo , 15 December 1942, attached to ibid.
11 See RIIA, 'International Air Transport,' written by Sir Osborne Mance, January 1943, PRO FO371 36431 W2909/2/802.
12 Quoted in *The Economist*, 'Air and Sea Transport,' 6 March 1943, 309; see HCUK to SSEA t. 49, 1 March 1943, NA RG25 A12, vol. 2107, file: AR 405/2 pt. 1.
13 One author, in calling for government action, labelled civil aviation as 'the key to world intercourse in the future and the parent of military aviation, which has cast so sinister a shadow across the world in recent years' (*The Economist*, 'Air Transport,' 6 March 1943, 286–8). See also *New Statesman and Nation*, 'Freedom of the Air,' 13 February 1943, 103; Peter Masefield, 'Fundamentals of Air Power'; The Society of British Aircraft Constructors, *The Future of British Air Transport* (June 1943), HLRO Beaverbrook Papers, D/228.
14 London *Times*, 9 February 1943
15 Sir Robert Perkins interview, Downton, UK, 8 November 1986
16 UK House of Commons *Debates*, 17 December 1942, vol. 385, 2118–54
17 See, for example, the three files PRO FO371 36430/31/33.
18 UK House of Commons *Debates*, 11 March 1943 vol. 387, 995–7. On the Brabazon committee, see its 9 February 1943 report in PRO FO371 36432 W3438/2/802. See also Peter Fearon, 'The Growth of Aviation in Britain,' 35.
19 Sargent note, 29 December 1942, PRO FO371 36430 W218/2/802
20 Stanley memo, attached to Barlow report, War Cabinet RP (A) (43) 10, 22 March 1943, NA Reid Papers, vol. 10, file: 38
21 Amery to Eden, 27 January 1943, PRO FO371 36430 W1877/2/802
22 Noel Baker to Jowitt, 3 February 1943, ibid., W2112/2/802
23 Barlow Report, NA Reid Papers, vol. 10, file: 38. The minutes of the Barlow

committee can be found in PRO FO371 36432 W3653/2/802; for the Jowitt committee minutes, see PRO FO371 W1505/2/802.
24 Sargent note, 26 March 1943, PRO FO371 36433 W5251/2/802. See also Sargent to Law, 4 February 1943, ibid., 36430 W1505/2/802; Le Rougetel to Sargent, 17 March 1943, ibid., 36433 W5250/2/802.
25 Barlow report
26 Sargent note, 26 March 1943, PRO FO371 36433 W5251/2/802
27 UK House of Commons *Debates*, 11 March 1943, vol. 387, 996–7
28 Halifax to Eden, t. 61, 3 February 1943, NA RG25 A12, vol. 2107, file: AR 405/2 pt. 2
29 Ibid.
30 *Fortune*, 'The Logic of the Air,' April 1943, 72
31 Ernest Lindley, 'Air Routes of the Future,' 231
32 *Fortune*, 'The Logic of the Air.' See also Edward Warner, 'Airways for Peace,' 11–27; Oliver Lissitzyn, 'The Diplomacy of Air Transport,' 156–70; Grayson Kirk, 'Wings over the Pacific,' 293–302; Chamber of Commerce of the USA, 'Statement of Policy on International Transport,' October 1943, NAW RG59 800.70/154.
33 Quoted in 'Public Statements in the United States Regarding Post-War International Civil Aviation,' May–June 1943, NA RG25, vol. 2715, file: 72-MK-40, vol. 3
34 Solberg, *Conquest of the Skies*, 278
35 Wallace article reprinted in 'The Future of International Air Transport,' 8 April 1943, NA Reid Papers, vol. 10, file: 37. See also 'Wallace Proposes World Air Force,' *New York Times*, 1 January 1943.
36 A.M. Buden memo, 5 June 1943, NAW RG59, Records of the Office of European Affairs, box 11, file: Aviation, Civil. See Berle to Welles, 3 March 1943, NAW RG59 800.796/258.
37 Quoted in John Wilson, 'The Shape of Things to Come: The Military Impact of World War II on Civil Aviation,' 264
38 Welch Pogue, quoted in 'The Future of International Air Transport,' 8 April 1943, NA Reid Papers, vol. 10, file: 37. See also Taneja, *U.S. International Aviation Policy*, 6.
39 Harold Balfour, *Wings over Westminster*, 202
40 John Holmes, *The Shaping of Peace: Canada and the Search for World Order, 1943–1957*, vol. 1, 67
41 Berle's statement, 15 February 1943, reprinted in 'The Future of Air Transport,' NA Reid Papers, vol. 10, file: 37
42 Adolf Berle, *Navigating the Rapids*, 483. For the minutes for Berle's committee, see 'Interdepartmental Committee on International Aviation: Minutes,' NAW RG59, Records of Harley A. Notter, 1939–45, box 43.
43 Berle, *Navigating the Rapids*, 483. See 'Proposals for Consideration by the Principal Committee,' 19 June 1943, NAW RG59, Records of the Office of European Affairs, box 11.
44 Quoted in F.I. Cox memo, 27 July 1943, attached to Halifax to Eden, t. 640, 11 August 1943, NA Reid Papers, vol. 10, file: 38. See also W.A. Patterson,

'International Trans-Ocean Air Transport and the Domestic Airlines,' 30 September 1943, NAW RG59 FW 800.796/458; Taneja, U.S. International Aviation Policy, 6–7.
45 D.C. Blackford memo, 27 July 1943, attached to Halifax to Eden, 11 August 1943, NA Reid Papers, vol. 10, file: 38

Chapter 6 1943: The Shape of Things to Come

1 Harold Balfour, *Wings over Westminster*, 210–11
2 *Fortune*, 'Canada's Postwar Air Policy,' May 1943, 90
3 Quoted in J.L. Granatstein, *Canada's War: The Politics of the Mackenzie King Government, 1939–1945*, 296
4 Ibid., 295–302; John Holmes *The Shaping of Peace*, vol. 1, 33–44
5 Quoted in Robert Bothwell and J.L. Granatstein, 'Canada and the Wartime Negotiations over Civil Aviation: The Functional Principle in Operation,' 585
6 Ibid. See also Peter Boehm, 'Towards Principled Influence; An Overview of Canadian Foreign Policy, 1943–1948'; Douglas Anglin, 'Canadian Policy towards International Institutions, 1939–1950.'
7 Leslie Roberts, 'Assets for an Air Age,' 8–9, 38, 40
8 Trevor Lloyd, 'Canada: Mainstreet of the Air,' 31. See also Grant Dexter, 'Whose Air?' 13, 51–2, 54; Dexter, *Canada and the Building of Peace*, 112–36. See the collection of Dexter's clippings on aviation in Queen's University Archives, Dexter Papers, series IV T.C. 10, folder 17.
9 Roberts, 'Assets for an Air Age,' 40
10 *Public Opinion Quarterly* 7 (Fall 1943): 504
11 George Drew, 'Where We Fit in the Global Air Map,' 19
12 Baldwin 'International Control of Aviation,' 20 December 1943, NA Reid Papers, vol. 10, file: 37
13 Reid, 'The Internationalization of Civil Aviation,' 24 December 1942, ibid.
14 Robertson to Massey, t. 70, 28 January 1943, NA RG25 A12, vol. 2107, file: AR 405/2 pt. 1. The CIIA paper, 'Canada and Post-War Civil Aviation' (November 1942), can be found in NA Reid Papers, vol. 10, file: 37.
15 Howe to Robertson, 8 February 1943, NA RG2, series 18, vol. 18, file: A-15-1-A (vol. 1)
16 House of Commons *Debates*, 2 April 1943, vol. 2, 1777–8
17 Pearson, 'Memorandum of Conversation with A.A. Berle,' 16 February 1943, NA RG25 A12, vol. 2107, file: AR 405/2 pt. 1. See also Pearson to Berle, 3 March 1943, NAW RG59 842.796/294.
18 Pogue to Berle, 28 April 1943, NAW RG59 Records of Harley A. Notter, 1939–45, box 43, file: Aviation Reports 1–8
19 Attlee to Sinclair, 18 February 1943, PRO FO371 36432 W3435/2/802
20 Sinclair to Attlee, 20 February 1943, ibid., W3436/2/802
21 Draft minutes, 25 February 1943, NA Reid Papers, vol. 10, file: 38
22 Vincent Massey, *What's Past Is Prologue*, 423

23 For Australian views on civil aviation, see Australian government to Dominions Office, t. 116, 13 May 1943, PRO FO371 36435 W7531/2/802.
24 SSDA to SSEA, t. 316, 27 May 1943, NA Howe Papers, vol. 101, file: 61–6(25)
25 HCUK to SSEA, t. 1182, 31 May 1943, NA RG2, series 18, vol. 19, file: A-15-1(W)
26 Memo of informal discussion, 1 June 1943, NA RG25 A12, vol. 2107, file: AR 405/2 pt. 2
27 SSEA to SSDA, t. 96, 6 June 1943, NA Howe Papers, vol. 101, file: 61–6(25)
28 Draft minutes of meeting, 15 June 1943, NA RG25, vol. 2107, file: AR 405/2 pt. 2
29 Massey to Attlee, 24 June 1943, NA Howe Papers, vol. 101, file: 61–6(25)
30 ICICA report, 17 June 1943, NA Reid Papers, vol. 10, file: 38
31 Reid memo for the CWC, 1 July 1943, NA RG25, vol. 2715, file: 72-MK-40, vol. 3
32 CWC minutes, 2 July 1943
33 Massey to Attlee, 12 July 1943, NA Howe Papers, vol. 101, file: 61–6(25). See also MacDonald to SSDA, t. 1698, 15 July 1943, HLRO Beaverbrook Papers, D/235.
34 Le Rougetel to Sargent, 25 May 1943, PRO FO371 36436 W8182/2/802
35 Churchill memo, 22 June 1943, NA Reid Papers, vol. 10, file: 38. The other memos can be found in PRO CAB 66: WP (43) 259, 22 June 1943 (Balfour); WP (43) 262, 23 June 1943 (Amery); and WP (43) 251, 18 June 1943 (Jowitt).
36 Le Rougetel memo, 11 June 1943, PRO FO371 35437 W9792/2/802
37 War Cabinet conclusions, 24 June 1943, PRO CAB 65
38 Cable to Dominions, 3 July 1943, attached to 'British Commonwealth Conversations,' A.T.L. (43) 1, 9 October 1943, NA RG2, series 18, vol. 52, file: A-15-1(W) pt. 1. The Six Freedoms are reprinted as Appendix II.
39 War Cabinet conclusions, 22 July 1943, PRO CAB 65. See also Cranborne's memo, WP (43) 325, 21 July 1943, PRO CAB 66.
40 J.W. Pickersgill, ed., *The Mackenzie King Record*, vol. 1, 539
41 War Cabinet conclusions, 19 August 1943, PRO CAB 65
42 King diary, 30 August 1943
43 SSDA to SSEA, t. 141, 14 September 1943, NA Howe Papers, vol. 101, file: 61–6(25)
44 CWC minutes, 23 June 1943
45 See unsigned memo, 28 September 1943, NA RG25 A12, vol. 2107, file: AR 405/2 pt. 3.
46 Howe to Symington, 28 September 1943, NA RG70, vol. 23, file: TCA 3-2
47 CWC minutes, 6 October 1943
48 Howe to Symington, 28 September 1943, NA RG70, vol. 23, file: TCA 302. See CWC minutes, 8 September 1943.
49 Baldwin memo for Heeney, 25 October 1943, NA Reid Papers, vol. 10, file: 38
50 Beaverbrook memo for Churchill, 14 October 1943, PRO FO371 36444 W14948/2/802
51 Minutes of meeting, British Commonwealth Conversations, 11 October

286 Notes to pages 139–51

1943, NA RG2, series 18, vol. 52, file: A-15-1(W) pt. 1. The draft agenda is in the same file. The minutes can also be found in PRO CAB 87/86.
52 Baldwin to Reid, 13 October 1943, NA Reid Papers, vol. 10, file: 38. See also minutes to the first meeting.
53 Minutes of meeting, 11 October 1943
54 See 'Report of Canadian delegation to the Commonwealth Air Conversations,' 26 October 1943, NA Howe Papers, vol. 99, file: 61-6(20).
55 Baldwin to Reid, 13 October 1943, NA Reid Papers, vol. 10, file: 38
56 Ibid.
57 A copy of the Balfour subcommittee report is attached to the minutes.
58 Baldwin to Heeney, 19 October 1943, NA Reid Papers, vol. 10, file: 38
59 Robertson memo for the prime minister, 14 October 1943, ibid.
60 Beaverbrook to Howe, 18 November 1943, HLRO Beaverbrook Papers, D/262; James Dunn to State Department, 29 December 1943, NAW RG59 800.796/505-1/2
61 Charles Ritchie, *The Siren Years: A Canadian Diplomat Abroad, 1937–1945*, 158
62 Baldwin memo for Heeney, 25 October 1943, NA Reid Papers, vol. 10, file: 38
63 Escott Reid interview, Ste Cecile de Masham, 4 November 1987
64 Robertson memo for the prime minister, 14 October 1943, NA Reid Papers, vol. 10, file: 38

Chapter 7 The Road to Chicago

1 Sir Peter Masefield interview, London, 16 April 1987
2 A.J.P. Taylor, *Beaverbrook*, 552
3 Quoted in ibid., 555
4 Minutes of Committee on Post-War Civil Air Transport, 21 December 1943, PRO DO35, vol. 1111, file: A.341/1125
5 Beaverbrook War Cabinet memo, WP (43) 537, 3 December 1943, PRO CAB 66
6 W.J. Callman to State Department, t. 12860, 21 December 1943, NAW RG84, St John's Consulate files, vol. 10
7 CWC minutes, 10 November 1943
8 ICATP document no. 11, 5 November 1943. This document discusses many of the previous points, and it was approved by the CWC on 10 November.
9 Reid, 'The Six Freedoms,' 2 December 1943, NA RG25, vol. 2715, file: 72-MK-40, vol. 7. The sixth freedom – the right to make two or more stops in a foreign country to pick up or drop off passengers – was given only scant attention. Although an interesting concept on paper, it found little support in the international community: few nations were willing to open their domestic routes to foreign airlines.
10 Baldwin, revised ICATP document no. 22, 14 January 1944, NA RG25 A12, vol. 2108, file: AR 405/2 pt. 4
11 'A Tentative and Preliminary Draft of an International Air Transport Convention,' 8 January 1944, Cabinet document 693, PCO reel 4576

12 Robertson memo for the prime minister, 31 December 1943, NA Reid Papers, vol. 10, file: 38
13 Robertson to Howe, 31 January 1944, NA RG25 G2, vol. 2716, file: 72-MK-40C pt. 8
14 Memo of conversation, 11 November 1943, FRUS, 1944 vol. 2, 360–2. See also Berle's 'Aviation Policy: Reciprocity of Landing Rights,' 20 December 1943, NAW RG59, Records of the Office of European Affairs, box 11.
15 L. Satterthwaite to Joe Walstrom, 18 January 1944, NAW RG59, ibid.
16 CWC minutes, 4 February 1944; Pearson to Robertson, t. 899, 15 February 1944, NA Howe Papers, vol. 100, file: 61-6(22)
17 HCUK to SSDA, 8 February 1944, PRO DO35 1111
18 Memo of meeting, 12 February 1944, HLRO Beaverbrook Papers, D/237
19 Masefield memo, 14 February 1944, ibid.
20 Winant to State Department, 11 February 1944, FRUS 1944, vol. 2, 375
21 Winant to State Department, 14 February 1944, ibid., 379
22 SSDA to SSEA, t. 245, 18 February 1944, NA RG2, series 18, vol. 18, file: A-15-1(W)
23 Cranborne to Beaverbrook, 9 February 1944, PRO FO371 42554 W2245/10/802
24 MacDonald to SSDA, t. 594, 24 February 1944, PRO DO35 111
25 Winant to State Department, 19 February 1944, NAW RG59 800.796/549; unsigned memo, 17 February 1944, HLRO Beaverbrook Papers, D/237
26 Pearson to Robertson, 24 February 1944, NA RG25 G2, vol. 2716, file: 72-MK-40C pt. 8
27 High commission for Canada in Australia to SSEA, t. 23, 25 January 1944, ibid.; Australian prime minister to King, t. 4, 10 March 1944, NA Howe Papers, vol. 100, file: 61-6(21)
28 Berle memo of conversation, 3 March 1944, FRUS 1944, vol. 2, 399–400
29 Berle to Winant, 16 February 1944, ibid., 381
30 See Canadian ambassador in Washington to SSEA, t. 1186, 28 February 1944, NA RG25 G2, vol. 2716, file: 72-MK-40C pt. 8.
31 Berle memo of conversation, 7 March 1944, FRUS 1944, vol. 2, 404
32 Winant to State Department, 9 March 1944, ibid., 408; CWC minutes, 1 March 1944
33 Bain, *Canadian Pacific Air Lines*, 15–20; K.M. Molson, *Pioneering in Canadian Air Transport*, 234ff.
34 CWC minutes, 28 April 1943
35 Pickersgill, ed., *Mackenzie King Record*, vol. 1, 647
36 Ibid. See also S.G. Cameron, 'International Air Transport,' 155.
37 Howe to Robertson, 6 March 1944, NA Howe Papers, vol. 100, file: 61-6(21)
38 Beaverbrook to MacDonald, 15 March 1944, PRO DO35 1111; Masefield memo, 10 March 1944, HLRO Beaverbrook Papers, D/237
39 House of Commons *Debates*, 17 March 1944, vol. 2, 1580
40 ATB Report, 31 March 1947, NA Howe Papers, vol. 103, file: 34 61-6(34)
41 Pickersgill, ed., *Mackenzie King Record*, vol. 1, 648
42 Baldwin memo, 4 April 1944, NA RG2, series 18, vol. 18, file: A-15-1(W)

43 Walstrom memo, 1 April 1944, and 'American Statement of Principles,' 30 March 1944, FRUS 1944, vol. 2, 431-7
44 Baldwin memo, 4 April 1944, NA RG2, series 18, vol. 18, file: A-15-1(W)
45 Ibid.
46 Ibid.
47 War Cabinet conclusions, 7 April 1944 PRO CAB 65; Report of US-UK talks, 19 April 1944, FRUS 1944, vol. 2, 444-59; minutes of the meetings, PRO CAB 87/88
48 Report of US-UK talks, ibid.
49 Satterthwaite memo, 2 March 1944, NAW RG59, Records of European Affairs, box 11
50 Pearson to Robertson, t. 2279, 14 April 1944, NA RG25 G2, vol. 2716, file: 72-MK-40C pt. 10
51 Beaverbrook to Howe, 7 April 1944, NA RG25 G2, vol. 2716, file: 72-MK-40C pt. 10
52 War Cabinet conclusions, 7 April 1944, PRO CAB 65 (can also be found in PRO PREM 4 5/1). See also HCUK to SSEA, t. 828, 12 April 1944, NA RG25 A12, vol. 2108, file: AR 405/2 pt. 5.
53 Memo attached to Pearson to SSEA, t. 1196, 11 May 1944, NA RG25 G2, vol. 2716, file: 72-MK-40C pt. 10
54 Secretary of state to ambassador in Moscow, 22 June 1944, FRUS 1944, vol. 2, 496
55 Pickersgill, ed., *Mackenzie King Record*, vol. 1, 668. For more on the conference, see James Eayrs, *In Defence of Canada: Peacemaking and Deterrence*, 205-7.
56 Pickersgill, *Mackenzie King Record*, 668
57 Minutes of meeting, 10 May 1944, PRO AVIA2 2482 (minutes can also be found in HLRO Beaverbrook Papers, D/254).
58 Beaverbrook to Howe, 23 May 1944, PRO AVIA2, 2482
59 Masefield memo, 22 May 1944, HLRO Beaverbrook Papers, D/262
60 CWC minutes, 3 August 1944. Howe could easily have carried the CWC with him on the issue of participation when it was discussed on 3 August, for there appeared to be no opposition. But the government postponed any action, deciding instead to link Canadian participation to a successful conclusion to the negotiation of the Goose Bay agreement (which had been dragging on since 1941). With Goose Bay out of the way, the CWC agreed to participate on 31 August.
61 Pearson to Robertson, 4 July 1944, NA RG25 G2, vol. 2716, file: 72-40C pt. 11
62 Memo of conversation, 20 June 1944, FRUS, 1944, vol. 2, 492-3
63 Howe to Robertson, 8 July 1944, NA Howe Papers, vol. 101, file: 61-6(26)
64 See memo for Baldwin, 30 August 1944, NA RG70, vol. 23, file: TCA 3-2; CWC minutes, 31 August 1944; secretary of state to French committee, 3 August 1944, FRUS 1944, vol. 2, 523-4
65 Berle, *Navigating the Rapids*, 492-3
66 Howe to Robertson, 24 August 1944, NA Howe Papers, vol. 100, file: 61-6(21)
67 Secretary of state to Winant, 21 August 1944, FRUS 1944, vol. 2, 531-2

68 Baldwin memo for Heeney, 29 August 1944, NA RG2, series 18, vol. 18, file: A-15-1(W)
69 Beaverbrook to Berle, 29 August 1944, FRUS 1944, vol. 2, 533
70 'Memorandum for the Prime Minister,' 12 September 1944, NA RG25 G2, vol. 2716, file: 72-MK-4-40 pt. 1
71 CWC minutes, 13 September 1944
72 Pearson to SSEA, t. 5271, 8 September 1944, NA RG2, series 18, vol. 18, file: A-15-1(W)

Chapter 8 'Everybody Is against Bad Weather'

1 See Baldwin to Howe, 18 September 1944, NA Howe Papers, vol. 97, file: 61-6(11), and the several memos 20–22 September in NA RG2, series 18, vol. 18, file: A-15-1(W).
2 Cabinet memo, WP (44) 540, 23 September 1944, PRO CAB 66; War Cabinet conclusions, 25 September 1944, CAB 65
3 War Cabinet conclusions, 12 November 1944, PRO CAB 65. A copy of the White Paper can be found in Department of State, *Proceedings of the International Civil Aviation Conference*, 566.
4 Willson, *The Organization of British Central Government*, 107. Only a minister was appointed however; the department was not created until early in 1945.
5 Sir Nicholas Cheetham to author, 26 February 1987
6 War Cabinet conclusions, 29 September 1944, PRO CAB 65
7 An agenda and complete set of conference documents and minutes can be found in NA RG2, series 18, vol. 52, file: A-15-1(W) pt. 1.
8 Reid to Robertson, 9 November 1944, NA Reid Papers, vol. 5, file: 6
9 Howe to Beaverbrook, 4 October 1944, NA Howe Papers, vol. 100, file: 61-6(24)
10 Swinton to Street, 25 October 1944, PRO FO371 42576 W15415/10/802
11 Street to Swinton, 26 October 1944, ibid., 42577 W15445/10/802
12 Minutes of 3rd plenary session, 24 October 1944
13 War Cabinet memo, WP (44) 628, 8 November 1944, PRO CAB 66
14 War Cabinet conclusions, 26 October 1944, PRO CAB 65
15 Swinton to Street, 27 October 1944, HLRO Beaverbrook Papers, D/234
16 War Cabinet conclusions, 26 October 1944, PRO CAB 65
17 War Cabinet memo (Swinton) WP (44) 592, 25 October 1944, PRO CAB 66; Foreign Office to Washington, t. 9403, 28 October 1944, PRO FO371 42577 W15530/10/802
18 Soviet ambassador to secretary of state, 26 October 1944, FRUS 1944, vol. 2, 571
19 UN Information Organization, *Report of the Chicago Conference*, 2
20 Ibid., 1
21 Reid memo, part 2, 14 December 1944, NA Reid Papers, vol. 5, file: 6
22 Baldwin memo, 13 December 1944, NA Howe Papers, vol. 97, file: 61-6(11)
23 Memo by minister for industry and commerce, 4 October 1944, SPO S13562A

24 Dept of State, *Proceedings of the International Civil Aviation Conference*, 67
25 Ibid., 73
26 Ibid., 74
27 Swinton to Bridges, 1 November 1944, PRO FO371 42579 W15794/10/802. See also Canadian Embassy, press analysis section memo, 3 November 1944, NA Howe Papers, vol. 99, file: 61-6(19).
28 For a list, see UN, *Report of the Chicago Conference*, 3.
29 Ibid., 9. See also 'Backstage at Ottawa,' *Maclean's*, 1 November 1944, 13-14.
30 Cheetham diary
31 Baldwin to Robertson, 12 November 1944, NA Reid Papers, vol. 5, file: 6; J.R. Baldwin interview, Kingston, 21 August 1987; Sir Nicolas Cheetham interview, London, 14 April 1987
32 Swinton to Foreign Office, 15 November 1944, PRO FO371 42586 W16516/10/802
33 MacDonald to Cranborne, 12 December 1944, University of Durham, MacDonald Papers, file: 14/6/10-12
34 MacDonald to Cranborne, 25 January 1945, ibid., file: 14/6/13
35 Ibid.
36 Swinton to Bridges, 9 November 1944, PRO FO371 42581 W16157/10/802
37 Reid memo, 11 November 1944, NA Reid Papers, vol. 5, file: 6. See also Berle, *Navigating the Rapids*, 500-1.
38 Berle's report to FDR, 7 December 1944, FRUS 1944, vol. 2, 601
39 J.R.K. Main, diary, 14 November 1944, NA Main Papers, vol. 3, file: Diaries, 1942, 1943, 1944
40 Reid to Robertson, 12 November 1944, NA Reid Papers, vol. 5, file: 6
41 Swinton to Bridges, 12 November 1944, PRO FO371 42582 W16327/10/802
42 W.G. Hayter memo, 15 November 1944, ibid., 42585 W16412/10/802. See also Reid to Robertson, 12 November 1944.
43 Ministerial committee to Swinton, 16 November 1944, ibid.
44 Baldwin to Howe, 25 November 1944, NA Howe Papers, vol. 99, file: 61-6(19); Sir Nicolas Cheetham interview, London, 14 April 1987
45 Swinton to Bridges, 19 November 1944, PRO FO371 42586 W16675/10/802
46 Baldwin to Howe, 21 November 1944, NA Howe Papers, vol. 99, file: 61-6(19)
47 Baldwin to Howe, 23 November 1944, ibid.
48 J.R.K. Main diary, 21 November 1944, NA Main Papers, file: Diaries, 1942, 1943, 1944
49 Dept of State, *Proceedings of the International Civil Aviation Conference*, 447
50 Ibid., 453
51 Ibid., 464-5
52 Baldwin to Howe, 23 November 1944, NA Howe Papers, vol. 99, file: 61-6(19)
53 The Churchill-Roosevelt correspondence can be found in PRO FO371 42588 W16868/10/802.
54 Quoted in Martin Gilbert, *Winston S. Churchill*, vol. VI *Road to Victory, 1941-1949*, 1074

55 See David Day, 'P.G. Taylor and the Alternative Pacific Air Route, 1939–45,' 6–19.
56 Baldwin to Howe, 3 December 1944, NA Reid Papers, vol. 12, file: 49
57 Swinton to Bridges, 30 November 1944, PRO FO371 42591 W17313/10/802
58 Baldwin to Howe, 3 December 1944, NA Reid Papers, vol. 12, file: 49
59 UN, *Report of the Chicago Conference*, 37
60 Ibid., 39
61 Baldwin to Howe, 3 December 1943, NA Reid Papers, vol. 12, file: 49, and Reid memo part 2, 14 December 1944, NA Reid Papers, vol. 5, file: 6; Swinton to Foreign Office, 3 December 1944, PRO FO371 42593 W17414/10/802
62 Reid memo, 11 November 1944, NA Reid Papers, vol. 5, file: 6
63 Swinton to Foreign Office, 11 November 1944, PRO FO371 42582 W16285/10/802
64 Ministerial committee to Swinton, 14 November 1944, ibid.
65 Swinton to Bridges, 15 November 1944, ibid., 42585 W16448/10/802. One Foreign Office official noted that Swinton had no choice but to agree, adding that 'Bermuda was in any case a somewhat fantastic suggestion' (W.G. Hayter, 16 November 1944, ibid.).
66 Symington memo on Chicago conference, 29 December 1944, NA RG70, vol. 70, file: TCA 3-3-4 (vol. 2)
67 Reid memo on election of Interim Council, 11 December 1944, NA RG25 A12, vol. 2108, file: AR 405/2 pt. 6
68 Cheetham note, 14 December 1944, PRO FO371 42594 W17618/10/802
69 Baldwin to Howe, 30 November 1944, NA Howe Papers, vol. 99, file: 61-6(19)
70 UN, *Report of the Chicago Conference*, 50. The conference agreements can all be found here.
71 Ibid., 57
72 Edward Warner, 'The Chicago Air Conference: Accomplishments and Unfinished Business,' 406. See also Stokeley Morgan, 'The International Civil Aviation Conference at Chicago and What It Means to the Americas,' 33–8.
73 CWC minutes, 22 December 1944
74 Reid memo, part 1, 12 December 1944, NA Reid Papers, vol. 5, file: 6
75 Bender and Altschul, *The Chosen Instrument*, 389
76 Baldwin memo, 13 December 1944, NA Howe Papers, vol. 97, file: 61-6(11)
77 Reid memo, part 1, 12 December 1944, NA Reid Papers, vol. 5, file: 6
78 Reid memo, part 3, 14 December 1944, ibid.
79 P.H. Gore-Booth to Hayter, 15 January 1945, PRO FO371 50231 W1090/24/802
80 Atherton to Hickerson, 20 January 1945, NAW RG59 800.796 /1-2045
81 Graham Parsons memo, 30 November 1944, ibid., /11-3044
82 Reid memo, part 1, 12 December 1944, NA Reid Papers, vol. 5, file: 6
83 Reid memo, part 2, 14 December 1944, ibid. See also S.G. Cameron, 'The Chicago Air Conference,' 227–9.

Chapter 9 Swallowing the Pure Wine of Bermuda

1 *Round Table*, 'After Chicago,' 136
2 Swinton to Foreign Office, 3 December 1944, PRO FO371 W17427/10/802
3 Baldwin memo, 13 December 1944, NA Howe Papers, vol. 97, file: 61-6(11). The Irish had been excluded from both the October and December Commonwealth discussions (ostensibly because of their neutrality), but subsequently agreed that, if invited, they would participate in the CATC.
4 'Commonwealth Air Transport Council,' Doc. CAC (Dec) 5, 9 December 1944, NA RG2, series 18, vol. 18, file: A-15-1(w). See also War Cabinet memo, WP (44) 752, 19 December 1944, CAB 66.
5 Swinton to Bridges, 11 December 1944, PRO FO371 42596 W17596/10/802. A set of minutes can be found in NA RG2, series 18, vol. 52, file: A-15-1(w) pt. 1.
6 Baldwin memo. 13 December 1944, NA Howe Papers, vol. 97, file: 61-6(11)
7 Minutes of meeting, 10 December 1944
8 Swinton to Bridges, pt. 2, 11 December 1944, PRO FO371 42596 W17596/10/802; Baldwin memo, 13 December 1944, NA Howe Papers, vol. 97, file: 61-6(11)
9 Baldwin memo, 13 December 1944
10 War Cabinet memo, WP (45) 6, 3 January 1945, PRO CAB 66
11 Quoted in *Round Table*, 'After Chicago,' 135. See also D. Hall, 'The British Commonwealth as a Great Power,' 594–608.
12 See ICATP document no. 37, 22 July 1944, NA RG70, vol. 24, file: TCA 3-2-1; Baldwin to Howe, 27 February 1945, NA Howe Papers, vol. 99, file: 61-6(17).
13 Baldwin to Howe, 30 December 1944, 4 January 1944, NA Howe Papers, vol. 97, file: 61-6(12)
14 Exchange of notes, Baldwin to Howe, 17 February 1945, ibid.; Morgan to Kelchner, 17 January 1945, NAW RG59 800.796 /1-1745
15 CWC minutes, 7 February 1945
16 Department of Industry and Commerce memo, 25 January 1945, SPO S10325B; high commissioner in Ireland to SSEA, t. 17, 6 February 1945 and excerpts from Irish press, 5 February 1945, NA Howe Papers, vol. 98, file: 61-6(13)
17 Cheetham memo, 2 February 1945, PRO FO371 50233 W1504/24/802; Cabinet memo, CP (45) 19, 7 June 1945, PRO PREM 4 5/13; Taneja, *U.S. International Aviation Policy*, 12
18 Brief for the prime minister, no date, PRO PREM 8 /16
19 Cherwell to Churchill, 31 May 1945, PRO PREM 4 5/13; Swinton to Churchill, 4 May 1945, ibid.
20 Cabinet conclusions, 8 June 1945, PRO CAB 128
21 *Canadian Aviation* 'Men of 46 Airlines Meet in Montreal,' 18 (November 1945), 103; Winant to State Department, t. 943, 26 January 1945, NAW RG59 800.796 /1-2645
22 Arnold Raestad, 'International Air Transport Association: Notes on

Havana Conference,' attached to Satterthwaite to State Department, t. 21917, 24 March 1945, NAW RG59 800.796 /3-2445; Sir William Hildred, 'What Is IATA?' 54
23 Canadian Aviation, 103. Hildred was seen as somewhat pro-American and a strong supporter of Anglo-American understanding (see Gallman to State Department, t. 10908, 18 October 1945, NAW RG59 800.796/10-1845).
24 Sir Nicolas Cheetham interview, London, 14 April 1987
25 Cabinet memo, CP (45) 222, 12 October 1945, CAB 129. See also Cabinet memo, C.A.C. (45) 3, 3 September 1945, ibid.
26 See Roger Eatwell, *The 1945–1951 Labour Governments*, 70–1.
27 Cabinet memo, C.A.C. (45) 4, 12 September 1945, PRO CAB 134 57; Satterthwaite to State Department, t. 25188, 4 September 1945, NAW RG59 841.796 /9-445
28 Brief for the prime minister, no date, PRO PREM 8 /16
29 Smith, *It Seems Like Only Yesterday*, 83, 114–17
30 Taneja, *U.S. International Aviation Policy*, 12
31 Satterthwaite to State Department, t. 27472, 18 December 1945, NAW RG59 800.796 /12-1845; Cheetham note, 21 November 1945, PRO FO371 50268 W15380/24/802
32 Taneja, *U.S. International Aviation Policy*, 12; SSDA to SSEA, t. 156, 24 November 1945, NA Howe Papers, vol. 98, file: 61-6(13); Halifax to secretary of state, 13 November 1945, FRUS 1945, vol. 6, 228–9
33 Attlee note, 15 November 1945, PRO PREM 8 16
34 Halifax to Foreign Office, t. 8551, 24 December 1945, PRO FO371 50272 W16612/24/802
35 State Department to ambassador in Moscow, 14 December 1945, NAW RG59 740.00119 Council /12-1245. See also Allan Bullock, *Ernest Bevin: Foreign Secretary, 1945–1951*, 200–2.
36 Winster to Dalton, 1 January 1946, PRO FO371 50272 W16612/24/802
37 Dalton diary, 7 December 1945, BLEPS, Dalton Diaries, vol. 33. See also Keith Middlemas, *Power, Competition and the State*, vol 1: *Britain in Search of Balance, 1940–61*, 122–6
38 Cavanagh to State Department, t. 1108, 13 December 1945, NAW RG59 811.79600 /12-1345; Baldwin to Howe, 10 October 1945, NA Howe Papers, vol. 99, file: 61-6(17)
39 See, for example, MacKay memo, 6 December 1945, NA RG25 G2, vol. 2395, file: 72-NL-40C.
40 Winster to Addison, 27 December 1945, PRO DO35 1110
41 The minutes and conclusions of the conference can be found in NA RG25, vol. 2395, file: 72-NL-40C.
42 Ibid.; Donald to State Department, t. 5 16 January 1946, NAW RG59 811.79600 /1-1646
43 Minutes, NA RG25, vol. 2395, file: 72-NL-40C
44 Ibid.; Cabinet memo, C.A.C. (46) 1, 8 January 1946, CAB 134 57
45 Quoted in Smith, *It Seems Like Only Yesterday*, 140

46 For a complete list see Acheson memo for the president, 10 January 1946, NAW RG59 841.796 /1-746.
47 Cabinet memo, CP (46) 37, 1 February 1946, PRO CAB 129; Baker to Clayton, t. 8365, 23 January 1946, NAW RG59 841.798 /1-2346
48 Baker to Clayton, 27 January 1946, NAW RG59 841.796 /1-2746
49 Halifax to Foreign Office, t. 663, 30 January 1946, PRO PREM 8 138
50 Cabinet conclusions, 4 February 1946, PRO CAB 128
51 Ibid., 7 February 1946; Donald to State Department, n. 35, 7 February 1946, NAW RG59 841.796 /2-746
52 Cabinet memo, CP (46) 44, 6 February 1946, PRO CAB 129
53 Cabinet conclusions, 11 February 1946, PRO CAB 128; John Cooper, 'The Bermuda Plan: World Pattern for Air Transport,' 67
54 See Heads of Agreement, 11 February 1946, NA RG25 G2, vol. 2394, file: 72-AHF-40C
55 Donald report to State Department, t. 218, 3 September 1946, NAW RG59 843.00 /9-346. See Heads of Agreement, 4 June 1949, NA RG25 A12, vol. 2092, file: AR 26/9.
56 Joint press release, NA Howe Papers, vol. 98, file: 61-6(15)
57 Quoted in Cooper, 'The Bermuda Plan,' 66–7. See also John Cooper, 'Air Power and the Coming Peace Treaties,' 441–52.
58 Halifax to Swinton, 18 February 1946, Churchill College, Cambridge, Swinton Papers, SWIN II 6/1
59 Cheetham note, 30 July 1946, PRO FO 371 54513 W7615/8/802
60 SSDA to SSEA, t. 46, 17 September 1946, NA Howe Papers, vol. 98, file: 61-6(14)
61 Satterthwaite to State Department, t. 28775, 13 March 1946, NAW RG59 841.796 /3-1346
62 Cheetham note, 30 July 1946, PRO FO371 54513 W7615/8/802
63 Baldwin to Howe, 13 February 1946, NA Howe Papers, vol. 97, file: 61-6)11

Chapter 10 ICAO and the Failure of Multilateralism

1 Symington to Street, 19 February 1945, NA RG70, vol. 24, file: TCA 3-7
2 See, for example, Reid memo on the president and secretary-general, 28 February 1945, NA Reid Papers, vol. 12, file: 50.
3 Robert English to State Department, 5 July 1945, NAW RG59 800.796 /7-545
4 PICAO Journal 1, no. 1 (August–September 1945), 12–4. See the one-volume set of documents on the Preparatory Committee in ICAO Library, Montreal.
5 ICAO Library, Montreal, PICAO Documents, vol. 1, document 1. For a review of the first session, see PICAO Journal, ibid.
6 Minutes of 1st meeting, 3 October 1945, PICAO Documents, vol. 2, document 169. See also PICAO, Air Transport Documents 1946–1947 (2 volumes).
7 ICAO Library, PICAO Documents, vol. 5, document 24
8 Report of the Air Transport Committee, 17 April 1946, NA Reid Papers, vol. 12, file: 50

9 Ibid., Annex B
10 Report of 1st meeting of Interim Assembly, May-June 1946, NA RG25 A12, vol. 2114, file: AR 412/11
11 Ibid.
12 Ibid.
13 PICAO *Journal* 1, no. 6 (June 1946), 35
14 Anson McKim, 'World Order in Air Transport,' 231
15 Report of 1st meeting of the Interim Assembly, May-June 1946, NA RG25 A12, vol. 2114, file: AR 412/11
16 McKim, 'World Order in Air Transport,' 231
17 Report of 1st meeting of the Interim Assembly, May-June 1946, NA RG25 A12, vol. 2114, file: 412/11; Report of Irish delegation to 1st Assembly, May-June 1946, SPO S13851A
18 McKim to Pearson, 16 April 1947, NA Howe Papers, vol. 96, file: 61-6(8)
19 HCUK to SSEA, t. 1305, 4 June 1946, ibid.
20 Report of the 1st Interim Assembly, May-June 1946, NA RG25 A12, vol. 2114, file: 412/11
21 Ibid.
22 SSDA to SSEA, t. 47, 17 September 1946, NA Howe Papers, vol. 98, file: 61-6(14); 'Record of Discussion,' 12-14 September 1946, NAW RG59 711.4127 /10-1746
23 A.W. Stoffel, 'American Bilateral Air Transport Agreements on the Threshold of the Jet Age,' 122
24 McKim to Howe, 15 November 1946, NA Howe Papers, vol. 96, file: 61-6(7); 'Report of Irish Delegation to 1st Ass. ICAO,' May 1947, Dublin, Department of Foreign Affairs, file: 408/58
25 PICAO 'Multilateral Agreement on Commercial Rights in International Civil Air Transport' (doc 2866), 26 February 1947, NA Howe Papers, vol. 96, file: 61-6(7)
26 John Cooper, 'The Proposed Multilateral Agreement on Commercial Rights in International Civil Air Transport,' 141-2
27 McKim, 'World Order in Air Transport,' 238
28 Ibid., 234
29 Lord Winster memo, 23 June 1947, PRO CAB 134 58
30 R.J.G. McClurkin, 'The Geneva Commission on a Multilateral Air Transport Agreement,' 39
31 PICAO *Monthly Bulletin* (1 November 1946), 1-2
32 'Draft Cabinet document,' 2 September 1947, NA Howe Papers, vol. 96, file: 61-6(7)
33 Ibid.
34 Howe to Baldwin, 4 September 1947, ibid.
35 Cribbett to Baldwin, 10 September 1947, ibid. For the minutes/notes of the Anglo-French delegates, see Satterthwaite to State Department, t. 2281, 10 October 1947, NAW RG59 800.796 /10-1047.
36 Baldwin to SSEA, t. 1, 3 November 1947, NA Howe Papers, vol. 95, file: 61-6(6)
37 Baldwin to Howe, 5 November 1947, ibid.

38 ICAO *Monthly Bulletin* (January 1948), 7
39 Report on ICAO conference, December 1947, NA Howe Papers, vol. 96, file: 61-6(7)
40 McClurkin, 'The Geneva Commission,' 46
41 Baldwin to Howe, 4 November 1947, NA Howe Papers, vol. 95, file: 61-6(6)
42 See ICAO, *Memorandum on ICAO* (Montreal 1984)

Chapter 11 Across the Pacific and Beyond

1 McKim to Howe, 6 December 1947, NA Howe Papers, vol. 95, file: 61-6(6)
2 Smith, *It Seems Like Only Yesterday*, 120–3
3 'Memorandum for the Interdepartmental Committee on Civil Aviation,' 5 March 1948, NA RG2, series 18, vol. 55, file: A-15-1(D); Department of Industry and Commerce memo, 31 July 1947, SPO S14118A
4 HCUK to SSEA, t. 1959, 13 July 1945, NA Howe Papers, vol. 98, file: 61-6(6)
5 Minister for External Affairs, Wellington to SSEA, t. 4, 6 March 1946, ibid., file: 61-6(15)
6 'Agreement between Canada and Australia,' 11 June 1946, NA RG2, series 18, vol. 55, file: A-15-1-J 1944–7
7 Corbett, *Politics and the Airlines*, 97; Smith, *It Seems Like Only Yesterday*, 138–41
8 'Memorandum to the Cabinet,' 11 May 1948, NA RG2, series 18, vol. 55, file: A-15-1-J 1948
9 Memo for the SSEA, 17 May 1948, ibid.
10 Cabinet conclusions, 13 July 1948
11 Atherton to State Department, t. 4855, 12 February 1947, NAW RG 59 842.796 12-1247
12 Hickerson to Acheson, 12 March 1947, NAW RG59 FW 842.796/2-1247; Smith, *It Seems Like Only Yesterday*, 142
13 Escott Reid, 'Memories of Louis St. Laurent, 1946–9,' 77; Escott Reid interview, Ste Cecile de Masham, 4 November 1987
14 See Smith, *It Seems Like Only Yesterday*, 143–4; Gordon McGregor, *The Adolescence of an Airline*, 29–30.
15 High commissioner in Australia to SSEA, t. 71, 4 August 1948, NA RG2, series 18, vol. 55, file: A-15-1-J 1948. See also Baldwin to Howe, 13 August 1948, in the same file.
16 Memorandum for Cabinet, 2 November 1948, ibid.
17 High commissioner in New Zealand to SSEA, t. 231, 29 November 1948, ibid.
18 HCUK to SSEA, t. 2247, 17 December 1948, ibid.
19 See, for example, Andreas Lowenfeld, 'A New Takeoff for International Air Transport,' 36–50.
20 See Main, *Voyageurs of the Air*, 195–201; O.J. Lissitzyn, 'Bilateral Agreements on Air Transport,' 248–63; R.R. Hackford, 'The Colonial Airlines Challenge to U.S.-Canadian Transport Agreement,' 1–10.
21 John Holmes interview, Toronto, 22 October 1987
22 John Baldwin interview, Kingston, 21 August 1987

Selected Bibliography

Canada

National Archives of Canada

Francis Russell Baker Papers MG30 A84
R.B. Bennett Papers MG26 K (microfilm)
Sir Robert Borden Papers MG26 H
Robert Henry (Lord) Brand Papers MG27 II G 6 (microfilm)
Loring Christie Papers MG30 E44
Brooke Claxton Papers MG32 B5
John Dafoe Papers MG30 D45
George Desbarats Papers MG30 E 89
Sir George Foster Papers MG27 II D7
C.D. Howe Papers MG27 III B20
Sir Albert Edward Kemp Papers MG27 II D9
William Lyon Mackenzie King Papers MG26 J
R.A. MacKay Papers MG30 E 159
Ian Mackenzie Papers MG27 III B5
J.R.K. Main Papers MG30 E 336
Alexander Daniel McLean Papers MG30 A64
General A.G.L. McNaughton Papers MG30 E 133
Lester B. Pearson Papers MG26 N
J.L. Ralston Papers MG27 III B11
Escott Reid Papers MG31 E46
Norman Robertson Papers MG30 E 163
Louis St Laurent Papers MG26 L
Arthur Sifton Papers MG27 II D19

Air Canada Records RG70
Department of External Affairs Records RG25
Department of Finance RG19
Department of National Defence RG24

298   Selected Bibliography

Department of Transport RG12
Dominions Office MG42, DO35
Privy Council Office RG2

ICAO *Library, Montreal*

PICACO and ICAO records

Directorate of History, DND

J.A. Wilson Papers

Queen's University Archives

Grant Dexter Papers

McGill University Archives

Cyril James Papers

United Kingdom

Public Record Office, Kew
Air Ministry Civil Aviation Files AVIA2
Cabinet
– Civil Aviation Committees (1945–51) CAB 134
– Memoranda (from 1945) CAB 129
– Minutes (from 1945) CAB 128
Dominions Office, Original Correspondence DO35
Ferry and Transport Commands AIR 38
Foreign Office, Political Correspondence FO371
Prime Minister's Office
– Confidential Papers PREM 4
– Correspondence and Papers to 1940 PREM 1
– Correspndence and Papers 1935–51 PREM 8
– Operational Papers PREM 3
War Cabinet
– Committees on Reconstruction CAB 87
– Committees: (Misc) and (Gen) Series CAB 78
– Commonwealth and International Conferences CAB 99
– War Cabinet Minutes CAB 65
– War Cabinet Memoranda CAB 66

University of Durham Archives

Malcolm MacDonald Papers

Selected Bibliography

House of Lords Record Office, London

Lord Beaverbrook Papers
David Lloyd George Papers

British Library of Economics and Political Science, London

Hugh Dalton Papers

Churchill College Archives, Cambridge

Sir Francis Floud Papers
Lord Swinton Papers

Cambridge University Library

Stanley Baldwin Papers
Templewood Papers (Sir Sam Hoare)

Ireland

State Paper Office, Dublin Castle

Cabinet Memoranda and Papers

Department for Foreign Affairs, Dublin

File: 408/58

United States

National Archives, Washington
Central Files of the Department of State RG59
General Records of the Office of the Executive Secretariat
Records of the Office of European Affairs
Records of Harley A. Notter
Records of the Foreign Service Posts, St John's Consulate Files RG84

Interviews

J.R. Baldwin
Lord Balfour of Inchrye
Ivor Bulmer-Thomas
Sir Nicolas Cheetham
John Holmes
Hugh Keenleyside

Sir Peter Masefield
Sir Robert Perkins
J.W. Pickersgill
Escott Reid

Books, Articles, and Unpublished Manuscripts

Aldcroft, Derek H. 'Britain's Internal Airways: The Pioneer Stage of the 1930s.' *Business History* 6, no. 2 (June 1984), 113-23
Anglin, Douglas. 'Canadian Policy towards International Institutions, 1939-1950.' PhD thesis, Oxford 1956
Ashley, C.A. *The First Twenty-Five Years: A Study of Trans-Canada Air Lines.* Toronto 1963
Bain, D.M. *Canadian Pacific Air Lines: Its History and Aircraft.* Calgary 1987
Balfour, Harold. *Wings over Westminster.* London 1973
Beaumont, Roger A. 'A New Lease on Empire: Air Policing, 1919-1939.' *Aerospace Historian* 26, no. 2 (June 1979), 84-90
Bender, Marylin, and Selig Altschul. *The Chosen Instrument.* New York 1982
Berle, Adolf, *Navigating the Rapids, 1918-1971: From the Papers of Adolf A. Berle*, edited by Beatrice Bishop Berle and Travis Beal Jacobs. New York 1973
Boehm, Peter Michael. 'Towards Principled Influence: An Overview of Canadian Foreign Policy, 1943-1948.' PhD thesis, Edinburgh 1983
Borden, Henry, ed. *Robert Laird Borden: His Memoirs*, vol. 2. Toronto 1938
Bothwell, Robert, and J.L. Granatstein. 'Canada and the Wartime Negotiations over Civil Aviation: the Functional Principle in Operation.' *International History Review* 2, no. 4 (October 1980), 585-601
Bothwell, Robert, and William Kilbourn. *C.D. Howe: A Biography.* Toronto 1979
Brewin, Christopher. 'British Plans for International Operating Agencies for Civil Aviation.' *International History Review* 4, no. 1 (February 1982), 91-110
Brown, R. Craig, and Robert Bothwell. 'The Canadian Resolution.' In *Policy by Other Means, Essays in Honour of C.P. Stacey*, edited by Michael Cross and Robert Bothwell 165-78. Toronto 1972
Bullock, Allan. *Ernest Bevin: Foreign Secretary, 1945-1951.* London 1983
Cameron, S.G. 'The Chicago Air Conference.' *Canadian Forum* 24, no. 288 (January 1945), 227-9
– 'International Air Transport.' *Canadian Forum* 24, no. 285 (October 1944), 155
Canada. Department of External Affairs. *Documents on Relations between Canada and Newfoundland*, vol. 1, *1935-1949*, edited by Paul Bridle. Ottawa 1974
Canadian Aviation. 'Men of 46 Airlines Meet in Montreal.' Vol. 18 (November 1946), 103, 106
Christie, Carl, and Fred Hatch. 'The Directorate of Air Transport Command and the Growth of RCAF Transport Operations during the Second World War.' *Canadian Defence Quarterly* 16, no. 1 (Summer 1986), 50-7

Cooper, John C. 'Air Power and the Coming Peace Treaties.' *Foreign Affairs* 24, no. 3 (April 1946), 441–52
- 'The Bermuda Plan: World Pattern for Air Transport.' *Foreign Affairs* 25, no. 1 (October 1946), 59–71
- 'The Proposed Multilateral Agreement on Commercial Rights in International Civil Air Transport.' *Journal of Air Law and Commerce* 14, no. 2 (Spring 1947), 125–49
- 'Some Historic Phases of British International Civil Aviation Policy. *International Affairs* 23, no. 2 (April 1947), 189–201
Corbett, David. *Politics and the Airlines.* Toronto 1965
Currie, A.W. *Canadian Transportation Economics.* Toronto 1967
'D'. 'Pacific Airways.' *Foreign Affairs* 18, no. 1 (October 1939), 60–9
Dafoe, J.W. 'The Imperial Conference of 1937.' *University of Toronto Quarterly* 7, no. 1 (October 1937), 1–17
Davis, Jeffrey. 'ATFERO: The Atlantic Ferry Organization.' *Journal of Contemporary History* 20, no. 1 (January 1985), 71–97
Dawe, Louise M. 'The Air Board, the Air Ministry and the Handley Page Proposals for Transatlantic Flight, 1917–1919.' Paper presented to the Canadian Historical Association, University of Montreal 1985
Day, David, 'P.G. Taylor and the Alternative Pacific Air Route, 1939–45.' *The Australian Journal of Politics and History* 32, no. 1 (1986), 6–19
Department of State. *Foreign Relations of the United States.* 1942–48
- *Proceedings of the International Civil Aviation Conference, Chicago, Illinois: November 1–December 7, 1944,* 2 vols. Washington 1948
Dexter, Grant. *Canada and the Building of Peace.* Toronto 1944
- 'Whose Air?' *Maclean's* magazine, 1 July 1943, 13, 51–2, 54
Douglas, W.A.B. *The Creation of a National Air Force: The Official History of the Royal Canadian Air Force,* volume II. Toronto 1986
Drew, George. 'Where We Fit in the Global Air Map.' *Financial Post,* 3 April 1943, 11, 19
Drummond, Ian M. *British Economic Policy and the Empire, 1919–39.* London 1972
Eatwell, Roger. *The 1945–1951 Labour Governments.* London 1979
Eayrs, James. *In Defence of Canada: Appeasement and Rearmament.* Toronto 1965
- *In Defence of Canada: From the Great War to the Great Depression.* Toronto 1964
- *In Defence of Canada: Peacemaking and Deterrence.* Toronto 1972
Economist. 'Air and Sea Transport.' Vol. 144, no. 5193 (6 March 1943), 309
- 'Air Transport.' Vol. 144, no. 5193 (6 March 1943), 286–8
Ellis, Frank. *Canada's Flying Heritage.* Toronto 1954
Fearon, Peter. 'Aircraft Manufacturing.' In *British Industry between the Wars: Instability and Industrial Development 1919–1939,* edited by N.K. Buxton and D.H. Aldcroft, 216–40. London 1979
- 'The Growth of Aviation in Britain.' *Journal of Contemporary History* 20, no. 1 (January 1985), 21–40
Feiling, Keith. *The Life of Neville Chamberlain.* London 1946
Fortune. 'Canada's Postwar Air Policy.' Vol. 27, no. 5 (May 1943), 90–2

- 'The Logic of the Air.' Vol. 27, no. 4 (April 1943), 72–4, 188–94
Gaffen, Fred. 'Canada's Military Aircraft Industry: Its Birth, Growth and Fortunes.' *Canadian Defence Quarterly* 15, no. 2 (Autumn 1985), 48–53
Gidwitz, Betty. *The Politics of International Air Transport*. Lexington, MA, 1980
Gilbert, Martin. *Winston S. Churchill*, vol. III, *Road to Victory, 1941–1949*. Boston 1986
Gladwyn, Lord. *The Memoirs of Lord Gladwyn*. New York 1972
Glazebrook, G.P. de T. *A History of Transportation in Canada*, 2 vols. Toronto 1938, 1964
Gollin, Alfred. *No Longer an Island: Britain and the Wright Brothers, 1902–1909*. London 1984
Granatstein, J.L. *Canada's War: The Politics of the Mackenzie King Government, 1939–1945*. Toronto 1975
- *A Man of Influence: Norman A. Robertson and Canadian Statecraft, 1929–68*. Toronto 1981
- *The Ottawa Men: The Civil Service Mandarins, 1935–1957*. Toronto 1982
Hackford, R.R. 'The Colonial Airlines Challenge to U.S.-Canadian Transport Agreement.' *Journal of Air Law and Commerce* 19, no. 1 (Winter 1952), 1–10
Hagland, David. ' "De-lousing" Scadta: The Role of Pan-American Airways in U.S. Aviation Diplomacy in Colombia, 1939–1940.' *Aerospace Historian* 30, no. 3 (September 1983), 177–90
Hall, D. 'The British Commonwealth as a Great Power.' *Foreign Affairs* 23 (1944–5), 594–608
Handley Page, F. 'The Future of the Skyways.' *Foreign Affairs* 22, no. 3 (April 1944), 404–12
Hatch, F.J. *Aerodrome of Democracy: Canada and the British Commonwealth Air Training Plan, 1939–1945*. Ottawa 1983
Higham, Robin. *Britain's Imperial Air Routes, 1918 to 1939: The Story of Britain's Overseas Airlines*. Hamden, CT, 1960, 1961
- 'British Airways Ltd, 1935–40.' *The Journal of Transport History* 4, no. 2 (November 1959), 113–23
Hildred, Sir William. 'What Is IATA?' *Canadian Aviation* 19 (September 1946), 54, 58
Hillmer, Norman. 'Mackenzie King, Canadian Air Policy, and the Imperial Conference 1923.' *High Flight* 1, no. 5 (1981), 184–96
- 'The Pursuit Peace: Mackenzie King and the 1937 Imperial Conference.' In *Mackenzie King: Widening the Debate*, edited by John English and J.O. Stubbs, 149–72. Toronto 1978
Hodson, H.V. 'The Imperial Conference.' *International Affairs* 16, no. 5 (September–October 1937), 659–75
Holmes, John W. *The Shaping of Peace: Canada and the Search for World Order, 1943–1957*, vol. 1. Toronto 1979
Kaeckenbeeck, Georges. 'The Function of Great and Small Powers in the International Organization.' *International Affairs* 21 (1945), 306–12
Kipling, Rudyard. *Actions and Reactions*. Toronto 1909

Kirk, Grayson. 'Wings over the Pacific.' *Foreign Affairs* 20, no. 2 (January 1942), 293–302
Lindley, Ernest K. 'Air Routes of the Future.' *The Listener* 29, no. 737 (25 February 1943), 231
Lissitzyn, O.J. 'Bilateral Agreements on Air Transport.' *Journal of Air Law and Commerce* 30 (1964), 248–63
- 'The Diplomacy of Air Transport.' *Foreign Affairs* 19, no. 1 (October 1940), 156–70
- *International Air Transport and National Policy*. New York 1942
Lloyd, Trevor. 'Canada: Mainstreet of the Air.' *Maclean's* magazine 1 July 1943, 31–4, 45–8
Lowenfeld, Andreas F. 'A New Takeoff for International Air Transport.' *Foreign Affairs* 54, no. 1 (October 1975), 36–50
McAndrew, William. 'The Early Days of Aircraft Acquisition in Canadian Military Aviation.' *Canadian Defence Quarterly* 12, no. 2 (Autumn 1982), 35–43
- 'The Evolution of Canadian Aviation Policy following the First World War.' *Journal of Canadian Studies* 16, nos 3 & 4 (Fall–Winter 1981), 86–99
McClurkin, R.J.G. 'The Geneva Commission on a Multilateral Air Transport Agreement.' *Journal of Air Law and Commerce* 15, no. 1 (Winter 1948), 39–46
McEvoy, Fred. 'Canadian-Irish Relations during the Second World War.' *Journal of Imperial and Commonwealth History* 5, no. 2 (January 1977), 206–26
McGregor, Gordon. *The Adolescence of an Airline*. Montreal 1970
MacKenzie, David. 'Canada and the Civil Aviation Discussions during the 1937 Imperial Conference.' *British Journal of Canadian Studies* 2, no. 1 (June 1987), 97–109
- *Inside the Atlantic Triangle: Canada and the Entrance of Newfoundland into Confederation, 1939–1949*. Toronto 1986
- '"Sitting Pretty," The Creation of the First Canadian Transatlantic Air Service, 1935–1943.' *Aerospace Historian* 34, no. 1 (December 1987), 253–61
McKim, Anson. 'World Order in Air Transport.' *International Journal* (Summer 1947), 226–36
Maclean's magazine. 'Backstage at Ottawa.' 15 June 1944, 33
McVicar, Don. *Ferry Command*. Shrewsbury, UK, 1981
Main, J.R.K. *Voyageurs of the Air: A History of Civil Aviation in Canada, 1858–1967*. Ottawa 1967
Masefield, Peter. 'Fundamentals of Air Power.' *The Listener* 23, no. 735 (11 February 1943), 171–2
Massey, Vincent. *What's Past Is Prologue: The Memoirs of the Right Honourable Vincent Massey, C.H.* Toronto 1963
Mattson, Margaret. 'The Growth and Protection of Canadian Civil and Commercial Aviation, 1918–1930.' PhD thesis, Western Ontario 1978
Middlemas, Keith. *Power, Competition and the State*, vol. 1: *Britain in Search of Balance, 1940–61*. London 1986
Middlemas, Keith, and John Barnes. *Baldwin: A Biography*. London 1969

Miller, A.J. 'The Functional Principle in Canada's External Relations.' *International Journal* 35, no. 2 (Spring 1980), 309–28
Milner, S. 'Establishing the Bolero Ferry Route.' *Military Affairs* 11 (Winter 1947), 213–22
Molson, K.M. *Pioneering in Canadian Air Transport*. Winnipeg 1974
Morgan, Stokeley. 'The International Civil Aviation Conference at Chicago and What It Means to the Americas.' Department of State *Bulletin* 12 (7 January 1945), 33–8
Munson, Kenneth. *Airliners from 1919 to the Present Day*. New York 1983
Myserscough, John. 'Airport Provisiion in the Inter-War Years.' *Journal of Contemporary History* 20, no. 1 (January 1985), 41–70
Neatby, H. Blair. *William Lyon Mackenzie King*, vol. 3, *1932–39: The Prism of Unity*. Toronto 1976
New Statesman and Nation. 'Freedom of the Air.' Vol. 25, no. 625 (13 February 1943), 103
New York Times, 'Wallace Proposes World Air Force,' 1 January 1943
Newton, Wesley. 'International Aviation Rivalry in Latin America, 1919–1927.' *Journal of Inter-American Studies* 7, no. 3 (July 1965), 345–56
O'Brien, John. 'Empire v. National Interests in Australian-British Relations during the 1930s.' *Historical Studies* 22, no. 89 (October 1987), 569–86
Pearson, Lester B. *Mike: The Memoirs of the Right Honourable Lester B. Pearson*, vol. 1, *1897–1948*. Toronto 1972
Pickersgill, J.W., ed. *The Mackenzie King Record*, vol. 1, *1939–1944*. Toronto 1960
Pickersgill, J.W., and D.F. Forster, eds. *The Mackenzie King Record*, vols 2–4. Toronto 1968–70
Pimlott, Ben. *Hugh Dalton*. London 1985
Public Opinion Quarterly 7 (Fall 1943), 504, chart
Randall, Stephen. 'Colombia, the United States, and Interamerican Aviation Rivalry, 1927–1940.' *Journal of Interamerican Studies and World Affairs* 14, no. 3 (August 1972), 297–324
Ray, Deborah Wing. 'The Takoradi Route: Roosevelt's Prewar Venture beyond the Western Hemisphere.' *Journal of American History* 62, no. 2 (September 1975), 340–58
Reid, Escott. 'Memories of Louis St. Laurent, 1946–9.' In *On Canada: Essays in Honour of Frank H. Underhill*, edited by Norman Penlington, 71–82. Toronto 1971
Ritchie, Charles. *The Siren Years: A Canadian Diplomat Abroad, 1937–45*. Toronto 1974
Roberts, Leslie. 'Assets for an Air Age.' *Maclean's* magazine, 1 July 1943, 8–9, 38, 40
Round Table, 'After Chicago: Imperial Interests in Civil Aviation.' Vol. 35 (March 1945), 130–6
- 'Air Navigation in Canadian-American Diplomacy.' Vol. 28 (1937–8), 595–603
- 'The Imperial Conference.' Vol. 27 (1936–7), 695–708

Russell, Peter, ed. *Leading Constitutional Decisions.* Toronto 1968, 1973
Share, Bernard. *The Flight of the Iolar: The Aer Lingus Experience, 1936–1986.* Dublin 1986
Smallwood, J.R. 'Civil Aviation's Primitive Beginning.' In *The Book of Newfoundland,* vol. 6, edited by J.R. Smallwood, 377–8. St John's 1975
Smith, Philip. *It Seems Like Only Yesterday: Air Canada, the First 50 Years.* Toronto 1986
Smith, R.K. 'The Intercontinental Airliner and the Essence of Airplane Performance, 1929–1939.' *Technology and Culture* 24 (July 1983), 428–49
Society of British Aircraft Constructors. *The Future of British Air Transport.* London 1943
Solberg, Carl. *Conquest of the Skies: A History of Commercial Aviation in America.* Boston 1979
Stacey, C.P. *Arms, Men and Governments: The War Policies of Canada, 1939–1945.* Ottawa 1970
Stoffel, A.W. 'American Bilateral Air Transport Agreements on the Threshold of the Jet Transport Age.' *Journal of Air Law and Commerce* 26, no. 2 (Spring 1959), 119–36
Swettenham, John. *McNaughton,* vol. 1: *1887–1939.* Toronto 1968
Tamchina, Rainer. 'In Search of Common Causes: The Imperial Conference of 1937.' *Journal of Imperial and Commonwealth History* 1, no. 1 (October 1972), 79–105
Taneja, Nawal K. *U.S. International Aviation Policy.* Lexington, MA, 1980
Taylor, A.J.P. *Beaverbrook.* New York 1972
United Nations (UN). Information Organization. *Report of the Chicago Conference on International Civil Aviation, November 1–December 7, 1944.* London n.d.
Vincenti, Walter. 'Technological Knowledge without Science: The Innovation of Flush Riveting in American Airplanes, ca. 1930–ca. 1950.' *Technology and Culture* 25, no. 3 (July 1984), 540–76
Warner, Edward. 'Airways for Peace.' *Foreign Affairs* 22, no. 1 (October 1943), 11–27
- 'Atlantic Airways.' *Foreign Affairs* 16, no. 3 (April 1938), 467–83
- 'The Chicago Air Conference: Accomplishments and Unfinished Business.' *Foreign Affairs* 23, no. 3 (April 1945), 406–21
- 'International Air Transport.' *Foreign Affairs* 4, no. 2 (January 1926), 278–93
- 'What Airplanes Can Do.' *Foreign Affairs* 20, no. 2 (January 1942), 339–57
Whitnah, Donald. *Safer Skyways: Federal Control of Aviation, 1926–1966.* Ames, IA, 1966
Willson, F.M.G. *The Organization of British Central Government.* London 1957
Wilson, J.A. 'The Expansion of Aviation into Arctic and Sub-Arctic Canada.' *Canadian Geographical Journal* 41 (September 1950), 130–41
- 'The World's Airway System.' *The Engineering Journal* (December 1936), 2–18
Wilson, John M. 'The Shape of Things to Come: The Military Impact of World War II on Civil Aviation.' *Aerospace Historian* 28, no. 4 (December 1981), 262–7

Wise, S.F. 'The Borden Government and the Formation of a Canadian Flying Corps, 1911–1916.' In *Policy by Other Means: Essays in Honour of C.P. Stacey*, edited by Michael Cross and Robert Bothwell, 121–44. Toronto 1972
– *Canadian Airmen and the First World War: The Official History of the Royal Canadian Air Force*, vol. 1. Toronto 1980

Index

Acheson, Dean, 213, 219
Addison, Lord, 219–20, 234
Advisory Committee on Aviation, 114–16
Aer Lingus Teoranta, 46
Aerial Board of Control, 3
Aeroflot, 20; *see also* Soviet Union
Aeronautical Commission (1919), 10–12
Air Board, 14, 23
Air Coordinating Committee (USA), 213
Air France, 20–1, 74; *see also* France
Air Ministry, 40, 94, 104–5, 153; separation of civil aviation from, 175
Air Navigation Committee, 228
Air Navigation Convention (1919), 12–13
Air Transport Board, 159
Air Transport Committee (ICAO), 227, 228–30, 232, 235–8, 241, 243; *see also* International Civil Aviation Organization
aircraft: Boeing C-204, 34; Boeing 247D, 37; Boeing 314, 71–2; Curtiss JN-, 9; DeHavilland DH.88 Comet, 37; Douglas DC-2, 37; Felixstowe F5, 9; Glenn Martin M-130, 37–8, 40; Lockheed 14H, 60; Lockheed Constellation, 73; Lockheed Electra, 60; Short S.30, 72; Sikorsky S-42, 37–8, 40; North Star, 247

Alcock and Brown, 22
American Airlines, 17, 76, 79
American Export Airlines, 75, 76, 117
Amery, L.S., 107, 127, 131
Amstutz, Edward, 241
Anderson, Sir John, 133–4
Anglo-American agreement (1935), 50–1
Association of British Chambers of Commerce, 103
Atherton, Ray, 198, 249
Athlone, Lord, 198
Atlantic, 5
Atlantic Ferry Organization (Atfero), 76–7, 120
Attlee, Clement, 88–9, 95–6, 126–7, 131, 211, 213, 220
Australia, 21, 37, 46, 61, 63, 67–8, 127, 128, 138, 155, 174, 176, 178, 191, 202–3, 204, 242; and trans-pacific service, 245–51
Australia–New Zealand proposals (1944), 176, 180, 182
Aviation Corporation of Canada, 33
Azores, 71–2, 73, 75; *see also* France

Bailey, Josiah, 180
Baker, George, 218–19
Baldwin, John R., 84–6, 87, 121–4, 136, 137, 160–2, 169, 204, 205; and 1943 Commonwealth talks, 137–42; and draft international

convention, 146–51; and Chicago conference, 172, 180, 183, 187–8, 189, 191, 195, 197–8; and Bermuda conference, 215, 217; and Geneva conference, 239–42
Baldwin, Stanley, 64
Balfour, Harold, 83–4, 86, 87, 92, 94–5, 105–6, 118–19, 131
Balfour subcommittee report, 140, 146, 164–5; see also White Paper on International Air Transport
Banks, Sir Donald, 47, 48, 231, 234
Barlow, Sir Alan, 64, 108, 132; see also Barlow committee
Barlow committee, 108–10; report, 127, 128
Batterbee, Sir Harry, 35, 40
Beatty, Edward, 33–4
Beaverbrook, Lord, 77, 96, 153, 177, 178, 202, 217, 242; and commonwealth talks (1943), 137–42; and relations with USA, 144–6; and reaction to Canadian draft convention, 153–4, 156, 158; and talks with Berle, 162–4; and Prime Ministers' Conference (1944), 166–7; and visit to Canada, 167–9; and Chicago conference, 174, 190, 198
Belgium, 15, 20; see also Sabena
Bennett, R.B., 24, 28, 34, 39, 43, 44, 45
Berle, Adolf, 114–16, 151–3, 155–7, 170; early talks with Canadians, 126; 1944 Montreal discussions, 159–62; Berle-Beaverbrook discussions, 162–4, 166, 168–9; visit to Canada, 167–9; and Chicago conference, 173, 180, 181, 184–6, 188, 189, 191–2, 193, 197–8
Bermuda: Anglo-Canadian discussions (1945), 212, 214–18; Anglo-American discussions (1946), 213–14, 218–23. See also Bermuda Agreement
Bermuda Agreement, 232, 236; see also Bermuda

Bermuda Clipper, 73
Bevin, Ernest, 211, 213, 219
Bey, Ali Fuad, 228
Bingay, K.B., 89
Blackford, Air Commodore D.C., 117
Blériot, Louis, 5
Borden, Sir Robert, 8, 9–13
Bouche, Henri, 228
Bowhill, Sir Frederick, 228, 231
Bowring, Sir Edgar, 35
Brabazon committee, 106
Brancker, Sir Sefton, 13–14, 24
Brewster, Owen, 180
Bridges, Sir Edward, 182
British Airways, 74
British Commonwealth Air Training Plan, 77, 95, 120
British Commonwealth Pacific Airlines (BCPA), 246–7, 250
British Empire Delegation (1919), 10–12
British Overseas Airways Corporation (BOAC), 74–5, 76, 81, 82, 103, 104, 206, 250; see also Imperial Airways
British West Indian Airlines (BWIA), 217
British West Indies, 136–7, 204; see also Bermuda
Brophy, Gerald, 228
Brown, H.P., 67
Bruce, S.M., 129, 139
Bulmer-Thomas, Ivor, 224
Burchall, Col. H., 36
Burden, William, 232
Byrnes, James, 213

Cabinet Civil Aviation Committee, 211, 221; see also Committee on Post-War Civil Air Transport
Cabinet War Committee (CWC), 78, 80, 83, 88, 89, 92, 124–5, 170, 207; discusses holding Commonwealth discussions (1943), 129, 131, 133–4, 136, 141; and draft international convention, 151–2, 153

Index

Cabot, 72–3
Cadman committee, 74
Cadogan, Sir Alexander, 95
Canadian Aeroplanes Ltd., 9
Canadian Air Force, 8
Canadian Airways, 33–4; and TCA, 58, 60
Canadian-American relations: Aeronautical Commission, 11–13; in 1920s, 18–19; Second World War and Washington service, 78–80; and 1945 discussions, 206–7
Canadian National Railways (CNR), 33, 58–9
Canadian Pacific Air Lines (CPAL), 157; and transpacific service, 247–51
Canadian Pacific Air Services, 77
Canadian Pacific Railway (CPR), 33, 58, 157, 159; *see also* Canadian Pacific Air Lines
Canadian Vickers Limited, 77
Caribou, 72–3
Chadwick, John, 215
Chamberlain, Neville, 29, 60–1, 68–9
Cheetham, Sir Nicolas, 182–3
Cherwell, Lord, 209
Chevrier, Lionel, 231, 247–8, 250
Chicago International Civil Aviation Conference, 92, 169, 172, 179–200, 201, 224; ABC discussions, 185–8, 193; conference documents, 195–7
China Clipper, 38
Christie, Loring, 10, 13, 45, 47, 48, 64
Churchill, Winston, 15, 76, 94, 96, 97, 131–2, 137, 143, 166, 209; at Quebec, 133–5; and Chicago conference, 189–90, 198
Civil Aerial Transport Committee (1917), 7–8
Civil Aeronautics Administration, 75
Civil Aeronautics Board (CAB), 75, 109; and post-war policy, 113–14, 116–17
Clark, Champ, 116
Clark, Clifford, 45, 47, 48
Clark, Sir William, 30–1

Claxton, Brooke, 250
Clayton, William, 211, 219
Clipperton Island, 190
Coleman, D.C., 157
Colonial Air Transport Co., 17
Committee on Civil Air Communications, 61, 64–70
Committee on Post-War Civil Air Transport, 132–3, 137, 144–5, 174; *see also* Cabinet Civil Aviation Committee
Committee on Reconstruction Problems, 98–9, 107
Committee on Trans-Atlantic Air Services, 30–1
Commonwealth Air Transport Council (CATC), 178, 202, 245–6
Commonwealth aviation conference (1943), 135–41
Commonwealth civil aviation conversations (1944), 176–8, 202–5
Coolican, P.T., 30, 34, 45, 47–8
Cooper, John, 53, 210, 237
Cotton, Sir James, 235
Cranborne, Lord, 96, 118–19, 132–3, 134, 137, 154
Crerar, T.A., 63, 64, 66–7, 69, 135
Cribbett, George, 198, 202, 215, 240, 242
Cripps, Sir Stafford, 108, 127, 130, 205
Critchley, Alfred, 158, 168
Cumyn, Wing Cmdr P.A., 227
Curtin, John, 166
Curtis, Air Vice-Marshal W.A., 180

Dafoe, J.W., 63
Dalton, Hugh, 213–14, 219–20
David, Paul, 235
deBrouckere, Louis, 231
DeHavilland Aircraft of Canada, 77
Denmark, 15
Desbarats, G.J., 28
Deutsche Lufthansa, 20, 71
dominion/provincial conference (1927), 19

310 Index

Drakeford, A.S., 202, 231, 250
Drew, Col. George, 118, 121
Duff, Sir Patrick, 250
Dunning, C.A., 63, 64, 67

Eastern Airlines, 76
Eden, Anthony, 95–6, 107, 127, 130
Edwards, C.P., 30, 45, 47, 71, 79, 81, 84–5, 89, 136, 244
Elliott, J.C., 47
Emerson, L.E., 30, 35–6
Empire Air Mail Scheme (EAMS), 21, 46, 47, 56
escalator clause, 173, 178, 187, 200
Evatt, H.V., 129–30
Everard, Sir Lindsay, 105

Federation of British Industries, 103
Ferry Command, 77
Finlay, Lord, 99
Finlay report, 99–101, 103, 128
Fisher, Sir Warren, 40
Five Freedoms Agreement (International Air Transport Agreement), 191, 196–7, 224–5, 226
Foreign Office, 95, 106, 153; and internationalization, 101–2, 108; and use of bases, 162, 168, 174
Fortune, 111–12
Foster, Sir George, 10
France, 6–7, 15, 20, 22, 180, 191, 240–1; and Aeronautical Commission, 10–12; and transatlantic service, 27, 38, 41; and Anglo-American agreement (1946), 223. *See also* Azores; Clipperton Island
Fraser, Peter, 166

Gates, Artemus, 114
Geddes, Sir Eric, 23, 32–3, 34
General Council of British Shipping, 103
Germany, 15, 17, 20, 71, 73; *see also* Scadta
Ginger Coote Airways, 157
Guthrie, Hugh, 30, 35

Halifax, Lord, 111, 213, 219, 223
Handley Page, Sir Frederick, 5
Havana Convention (Pan American Convention on Commercial Aviation), 17
Heeney, A.D.P., 80, 137, 141
Henry, R.A.C., 231, 244
Herring, George, 36
Hickerson, J.D., 218, 249
Hildred, Sir William, 95, 108, 139, 180, 210, 218
Holland, 15
Holmes, John, 114
Howe, C.D., 64, 73, 151, 152, 157–9, 164, 166–7, 168, 170, 176–7, 178, 202–4, 207, 236, 238, 239, 240, 247, 248–9, 251, 253–4; and creation of TCA, 57–60; and transatlantic service, 79–81, 83, 85, 86–93; and post-war policy, 125, 127, 135, 136; and Commonwealth talks, 138–42; and discussions with Berle, 159–61; and Chicago conference, 173–4, 180–5, 189, 198–9; and Bermuda conference, 214–18; and first Interim Council, 227–8; and first Interim Assembly, 231–2, 234; and Geneva conference, 239–42
Hudd, Frederic, 127, 137
Hull, Cordell, 115, 191
Hungerford, J.S., 59
Hutchings, H.V., 30

Ilsley, J.L., 135
Imperial Airways, 16, 21, 23, 25, 27, 30, 32–3, 35, 40; and aviation conference in Newfoundland, 36–7; and Atlantic service, 40–1, 42, 48–9, 50–1, 54, 71–3. *See also* British Overseas Airways Corporation; Empire Air Mail Scheme
Imperial Conference: 1923, 16; 1926, 16; 1930, 24; 1937, 60–70
Imperial Economic Conference, 28–32

India, 46, 138, 176, 242; and seat on Interim Council, 195
Interdepartmental Committee on Air Transport Policy (ICATP), 135-6, 140; and draft international convention, 146-51; and Chicago conference, 172. *See also* Interdepartmental Committee on International Civil Aviation
Interdepartmental Committee on International Air Communications (Fisher committee), 40
Interdepartmental Committee on International Civil Aviation (ICICA), 84; and end of 1935 agreement, 86-7, 89, 92; and postwar policy, 121-3, 129; and interim report, 130-1. *See also* Interdepartmental Committee on Air Transport Policy
International Air Transport Association (IATA), 209-10, 212, 218, 222, 234, 251
International Civil Aviation Organization (ICAO), 6, 210, 228, 243, 244, 249, 251; creation and location of, 192-6, 234-5; and first assembly, 238-9; and Geneva conference, 238-42. *See also* Provisional International Civil Aviation Organization
International Commission for Air Navigation (ICAN), 13, 14, 18, 21, 228
Ireland, 27, 28, 30, 54-5, 62, 68, 71, 88-9, 91, 176, 242; and 1935 agreement, 46-50; and Dublin conference, 71; and Chicago conference, 180; and membership on CATC, 202; and negotiations with USA, 207-8; and seat on Interim Council, 233-4, 236; and 1947 agreement with Canada, 245

Johnson, Monroe, 50, 52
Johnson, Philip G., 59
Joint Operating Company, 49-50, 55, 71, 73, 80, 84, 88-9, 92

Jones, F., 250
Jordan, W.J., 129
Jowitt, Sir William, 96, 98, 101, 131, 132, 209
Jowitt committee, 107-8, 127, 129
Judicial Committee of the Privy Council, 19

Kearney, John, 89
Keynes, Lord, 211
King, William Lyon Mackenzie, 16, 43-4, 57, 59, 73, 76, 80, 83, 92-3, 118, 120, 174, 213, 234-5, 248, 253-4; and 1937 Imperial Conference, 60-70; and post-war policy, 125-6, 127, 131, 133-5, 151, 157-9; and Prime Ministers' Conference (1944), 165-6
Kipling, Rudyard, 3
KLM, 20, 74, 239
Knollys, Lord, 198

LaFlèche, Col. L.R., 56
LaGuardia, Fiorello, 180, 188-9
Lapointe, Ernest, 63
Law, Bonar, 95, 168
Law, Richard, 95, 108, 166, 168
League of Nations, 43, 44
League of Nations Disarmament Conference, 21-2
Leathers, Lord, 108, 132, 141
Lemass, Sean, 30
LeRougetel, Sir John, 95, 108-9, 131
Leydon, John, 47, 48
Lindbergh, Charles, 22
Lissitzyn, Oliver, 4
Lodge, Thomas, 47, 48
London Chamber of Commerce, 103
London *Times*, 104
Lovett, Robert, 114
Luce, Clare Booth, 112

McCarthy, Leighton, 79
McConachie, Grant, 250-1
McCrindle, Maj. J.R., 215
Macdonald, Angus, 135

MacDonald, Malcolm, 154, 183-4, 202
MacDonnell, R.M., 180
McGregor, Gordon, 217, 244-5, 247, 254
MacKay, R.A., 215
Mackenzie, Ian, 63
McKim, Anson, 228, 231, 232, 235, 236, 237, 238, 244; and Geneva conference, 239-42
McNaughton, Maj.-Gen. A.G.L., 24-5, 45, 55; and transatlantic service, 25-7, 29-30, 31, 33, 34-5, 38-40, 41-2
MacRobertson Race, 37
Main, J.R.K., 185, 188
Marler, Herbert, 53-4
Masefield, Sir Peter, 144, 153, 166
Massey, Vincent, 103, 123-4, 153; and transatlantic service, 81-4, 87, 88, 92; and Commonwealth discussions (1943), 127-30, 131, 137, 142
Mayo, Robert, 38
Montague, Frederick, 105
Montreal, 27, 29, 31, 45, 47, 48, 59, 60, 156, 202-5; and use in transatlantic service, 51-4, 72; as headquarters for IATA, 210; as headquarters for ICAO, 234-5
Montreal *Gazette*, 91
Moore, Walton, 50
Moore-Brabazon, Lt-Colonel, 4
Moran, H.O., 244
Morgan, Stokeley, 211, 218, 232
Munitions Priority Board, 82

Nash, Walter, 67
Nathan, Lord, 242
New York Times, 53-4
New Zealand, 62, 63, 64, 127, 128, 138, 155, 176, 178, 191, 202-3, 242; and transpacific service, 245-51
Newfoundland, 27, 28, 30, 32, 35, 38, 41, 49, 54, 62, 68, 71, 88-9, 91, 162-3; and 1933 aviation conference 36-7; and Second World War, 77-8; and post-war use of bases, 212, 214-16, 217, 220-1
Noel Baker, Philip, 107
Noorduyn Aviation Limited, 77
Northeast Airlines, 76
Northwest Airlines, 76
Northwest Staging Route, 78, 120
Norton, Garrison, 218

O'Driscoll, T., 231
Ottawa conference (1935), 44-50

Pacific Airways, 33
Pan American Airways, 17, 21, 23, 25, 27, 28, 30, 32-3, 35, 61, 81, 102, 104, 106-7, 113, 115-17, 184, 212, 214; and aviation conference in Newfoundland, 36-7; and Atlantic service, 37-8, 40-1, 50-1, 52-4, 71-3; and construction of aircraft bases, 75-6
Paris air conference (1910), 6
Paris Peace Conference, 10-13
Parkhill, Sir Archdale, 64, 67, 68, 69
Parrish, Wayne, 158
Patterson, John, 45, 47
Pearson, Lester, 72-3, 126, 152-3, 155, 163, 167, 248, 254; and meeting with Berle, 170-1; and service to Washington, 79
Perkins, Robert, 104-5
Perley, George, 36
Pogue, Welch, 114, 116, 126, 180, 218, 232
Power, C.G., 81-2
Provisional International Civil Aviation Organization (PICAO), 222, 225, 227, 229; and first Interim Assembly, 231-5. *See also* International Civil Aviation Organization; Air Transport Committee

Qantas, 46, 250

R101, 24
Ralston, J.L., 81, 86, 135
Read, J.E., 89-90

Reid, Escott, 84–5, 86, 91, 121–4, 129, 130–1, 136, 139, 248–9, 254; and draft international convention, 146–51; and Chicago conference, 172, 179–80, 184, 185, 197–9
Reith, Sir John, 74
Reitz, Colonel, 129
Richardson, James, 33, 58, 157
Rickenbacker, Eddie, 58
Riddell, Walter, 22, 44, 246
Ritchie, Charles, 141
Rive, Alfred, 250–1
Roberts, Leslie, 120
Robertson, Norman, 84–5, 87, 89, 121, 123–4, 136, 141, 143, 148, 160, 170, 172, 254
Roosevelt, Franklin, 44, 75, 76, 97, 114, 133, 134, 135, 143, 152, 169, 209; and Chicago conference, 181, 189–90, 198
Roper, Albert, 227–8
Round Table, 201
Royal Air Force, 77
Royal Canadian Air Force, 14, 18, 24, 32, 82; growth in Second World War, 77; military service to Washington, 79–80
Royal Canadian Naval Air Service, 8
Royal Flying Corps, 7, 8
Royal Flying Corps Canada, 8, 9
Royal Institute of International Affairs, 103

Sabena, 20, 74
St Laurent, Louis, 249–50
Samuel, Sir Herbert, 94
Sargent, Sir Orme, 95, 99, 107; and support for internationalization, 108–9
Satterthwaite, Livingston, 224
Scadta (Sociedad Colombo-Alemana de Transportes Aéreos), 15
Self, Sir Henry, 218
Shelmerdine, Col. F.C., 30–1, 35, 36, 47, 48, 53, 64, 65, 95, 99, 100, 108
Shelmerdine committee, 96–8, 103; report, 128

Sherwood, Lord, 94
Sifton, Arthur, 10–11, 13
Silver Dart, 5
Sinclair, Sir Archibald, 87, 94, 108, 110, 126–7, 132, 166, 178
Skelton, O.D., 28, 32–3, 37, 56, 85
Smart, V.I., 45, 47, 48, 64, 65
South Africa, 63, 64, 65, 127, 138, 176, 242
South Pacific Air Transport Council (SPATC), 246, 250
Soviet Union, 20; and Chicago conference, 179, 194; and membership in ICAO, 233, 243
Stanley, Oliver, 107
Starratt Airways, 157
Stassen, Harold, 112–13
Stephenson, Sir John, 64, 108
Stettinius, Edward, 191
Street, Sir Arthur, 176, 177, 180, 202, 226
Sullivan, D.G., 202
Sweden, 15
Swinton, Lord, 177, 202–5, 209, 211, 223, 242, 245; 1937 Imperial Conference, 64–70; appointed minister of civil aviation, 175–6; and Chicago conference, 178, 180, 182–3, 185–8, 189, 191–2, 193, 197–8
Syers, C.G.L., 47
Sykes, Maj.-Gen. Sir Frederick, 11
Symington, H.J., 83–5, 86, 136, 137, 160, 167, 226, 231, 245, 253–4; and Chicago conference, 172, 180, 183, 188–9, 191–4, 199; and Commonwealth discussions (1944), 176–7, 202, 204; and IATA, 209–10; and Bermuda conference, 215, 217

Taylor, Wayne, 114
Thomas, J.H., 41
Thomson, Lord, 24
Thornton, Sir Henry, 33–4
Trans-Canada Airlines (TCA), 73, 79, 124–5, 136–7, 167, 177, 216, 252, 254; creation of, 58–60; and war-

314   Index

time expansion, 77–8; and transatlantic service, 80–92, 212; relations with CPAL, 157; and transpacific service, 245–51
Trans World Airlines, 17
Trippe, Juan, 17, 23, 35, 50, 58, 75, 168, 191; and transatlantic service, 53–4
Truman, Harry, 116, 213
Two Freedoms Agreement (International Air Transit Agreement), 191–2, 196–7, 221, 226; Canada signs, 206–7
Tymms, Sir Frederick, 202, 231

United Airlines, 17, 117
United Kingdom, 6, 7–8, 10–12, 27; 1920s policy, 15–16; 1930s policy, 54–5; 1937 Imperial Conference, 61–2; civil aviation and war effort, 75; wartime aviation policy, 94–110; preparations for Chicago, 174–5; Anglo-American relations (1945–6), 208–9, 210–11, 212–14. *See also* Bermuda conference; Imperial Airways; British Overseas Airway Corporation
United Nations Relief and Rehabilitation Administration (UNRRA), 119
United States, 10, 12, 17, 21; civil aviation and Second World War, 75–6, 111–17; and post-war aviation, 151–3; policy after Chicago, 205–6; Anglo-American relations (1945–6), 208–9, 210–11, 212–14.

See also Bermuda conference; Civil Aeronautics Board
United States Air Transport Command (USATC), 76, 102, 112

Van Hasselt, F.H. Copes, 228
Vanier, Lt-Col. Georges, 35, 40–1, 42
Victory Aircraft Plant, 90

Wallace, Henry, 113
Walshe, J.P., 47, 48, 89
Warner, Edward, 159, 180, 196–7, 227–8
Wellington conference, 65
Western Canada Airways, 33
White Paper on International Air Transport, 175, 176, 182, 185; *see also* Balfour subcommittee report
Wilson, J.A., 23–4, 79, 84–5, 91, 180; and transatlantic service, 25–7, 29, 30, 32, 34, 39, 41, 42, 43; talks in Newfoundland (1933), 36–7; and Ottawa conference, 45–50, 51, 55
Winant, John G., 153–4, 156, 190
Winster, Lord, 211–12, 213–14, 215, 218–19, 238
Wise, S.F., 8
Wiseman, R.A., 35
Wood, Sir Kingsley, 98–9, 108, 127
Woods Humphrey, George, 42, 47, 50, 74
Wright, Michael, 155–6
Wrong, Hume, 30, 52, 119

Yankee Clipper, 72
Yukon Southern Air Transport, 157

www.ingramcontent.com/pod-product-compliance
Lightning Source LLC
Chambersburg PA
CBHW071149070526
44584CB00019B/2716